How the Color Line Bends

How the Color Line Bends

The Geography of White Prejudice in Modern America

Nina M. Yancy

OXFORD
UNIVERSITY PRESS

OXFORD
UNIVERSITY PRESS

Oxford University Press is a department of the University of Oxford. It furthers the University's objective of excellence in research, scholarship, and education by publishing worldwide. Oxford is a registered trade mark of Oxford University Press in the UK and certain other countries.

Published in the United States of America by Oxford University Press
198 Madison Avenue, New York, NY 10016, United States of America.

Library of Congress Cataloging-in-Publication Data
Names: Yancy, Nina, 1991- author.
Title: How the color line bends : the geography of white prejudice in
modern America / Nina M. Yancy.
Description: New York, NY : Oxford University Press, [2022] | Includes
bibliographical references and index.
Identifiers: LCCN 2021056053 | ISBN 9780197599426 (hardback) |
ISBN 9780197599433 (paperback) | ISBN 9780197599457 (epub)
Subjects: LCSH: Whites–Louisiana–East Baton Rouge Parish–Attitudes–Case
studies. | Whites–Race identity–Louisiana–East Baton Rouge
Parish–Case studies. | Racism–Louisiana–East Baton Rouge Parish–Case
studies. | Municipal incorporation–Louisiana–East Baton Rouge
Parish–Case studies. | East Baton Rouge Parish (La.)–Race
relations–Case studies. | East Baton Rouge Parish (La.)–Politics and
government. | Baton Rouge (La.)–Race relations–History–21st century.
Classification: LCC F379.B33 Y36 2022 | DDC
305.8009763/18–dc23/eng/20220103
LC record available at https://lccn.loc.gov/2021056053

1 3 5 7 9 8 6 4 2

Hardback printed by Marquis, Canada
Paperback printed by Marquis, Canada

For Clyde Yancy and Annelle Ahmed,
both children of Louisiana
who started with little and gave me so much

Acknowledgments

I owe my deepest gratitude to my academic mentors and professors. At Oxford, Desmond King taught me to see my own country in a new light, to understand and critique the workings of power, and to be a bolder thinker and writer. Ben Ansell guided me from the very start with rigor and endless optimism, and never failed to motivate me by believing things were possible before I did so myself. Nigel Bowles, Jane Gingrich, Ursula Hackett, Kimberley Johnson, Lisa Miller, and Sidney Milkis are others whose insight I was lucky to benefit from at Oxford. I similarly am indebted to my professors at Harvard, particularly Terry Aladjem, Anya Bernstein Bassett, Ryan Enos, James Kloppenberg, and Thomas Ponniah, in whose classrooms the seeds of this project were planted long before I would have imagined its existence.

With humility, I must thank the individuals I interviewed in Baton Rouge for sharing their perspectives with me; this book would not exist without them. This book also would not exist without generous financial support provided by the Rhodes Trust, University College, the Department of Politics and International Relations (DPIR), and the Rothermere American Institute (RAI). I further must thank the RAI and its staff for the space they provided me, metaphorically and literally, to develop many of the ideas in these pages.

I am grateful to have benefited from the expertise and guidance of Angela Chnapko and Alexcee Bechthold at Oxford University Press. I also extend my thanks to the anonymous readers who provided excellent feedback on my manuscript, which not only improved this book but also deepened my awareness of how language can either defer to the racial order or help break it down.

I found a deeply thoughtful and supportive community in graduate school. I thank the friends who helped me learn many of the truths this book tries to illuminate, particularly in reading groups that offered a sanctuary from the White world of Oxford: Joshua Aiken, Field Brown, Sarah Bufkin, Tim McGinnis, and Sarah Yerima. I thank the friends who helped me shape this project day by day, over lunch on the front steps of the RAI or the DPIR: Brett Rosenberg, Michaela Collord, Roosmarijn de Geus, Sam Rowan, and Alexa Zeitz. I thank the friends who read my drafts, shared their expertise, organized talks and seminars, and shaped my thinking: David Adler, Charlotte Baarda, Pepita Barlow, Helen Baxendale, David Carel, Josh Carpenter,

Louis Chambers, Arran Davis, Natalya Din-Kariuki, Alex Dyzenhaus, Julian Gewirtz, Rhiana Gunn-Wright, Max Harris, Margot Leger, Graeme MacGilchrist, Moizza Sarwar, Mubeen Shakir, Freya Shearer, Jake Thorold, Robbie Tilleard, and Ben Wilcox. And I thank the friends who, along with those named so far, made Oxford home for a while: Meredith Baker, Alex Baron, Ben Barron, Hugo Batten, Isabel Beshar, Jenny Bright, Lilly Corning, Margaret Hayden, Kiley Hunkler, Ben Hunn, Rachel Kolb, Cody McCoy, Wande McCunn, Yale Michaels, Merritt Moore, Kiron Neale, Rachel Riley, Amanda Rojek, Emma Sagor, Katie Stone, Evan Szablowski, Arturo Villanueva, and Caroline Whidden.

For sticking with me from afar, and for keeping both my politics and spirit in the right place, I thank Danny Bicknell, EJ Blair, and Griffin Gaffney. For welcoming me back to Chicago and New York, and for their friendship through the acute challenges of that time, I thank, among others throughout these acknowledgments, Julie Barzilay, Kathleen Goodwin, Andrea Henricks, and Gresa Matoshi. And for their company and advice as fellow writers/creators while I was in the home stretch of this project, I thank Julia Brown, Tatiana Schlossberg, and Grace Sun.

Part of the time I spent writing this book was outside of the academy. Much like studying the United States from afar, it helped me see the topics of both prejudice and place in new lights. To all my teammates, and particularly to Tati Brezina, Wan-Lae Cheng, Zoe Jacobs, Mike Kerlin, Erik Roberts, Ben Safran, and Saurabh Sanghvi: thanks for the opportunity to invest, alongside all of you, in American cities and states emblematic of many of the challenges this book recognizes. To David Baboolall, Aria Florant, JP Julien, Ng'ethe Maina, Nick Noel, Fiyin Oladiran, Duwain Pinder, Shelley Stewart III, Kelemwork Cook, and Jason Wright: thanks for practicing and preaching the truth that Black lives and livelihoods represent such immense potential for this country. To Natasha Korgaonkar: thank you for walking alongside. And to Stephanie Bell, Allison Cook, Sarah Kleinman, and Shayan Salam: thanks for providing guidance and friendship at critical times that (whether you knew it or not) enabled my attempt to finish a manuscript while working full-time.

I must extend particular thanks to several friends who made outsize contributions to this project. I am deeply indebted to Rachel Benoit, for always getting it and helping me say it better, particularly when it comes to the ways of White folks; to Julia Konrad, for the example she sets of using knowledge to empower others; to Ben Naddaff-Hafrey, for his thoughtful comments and the confidence he inspired along the way; and to Nora Wilkinson, an editor in her own right who has traveled with me in writing this book from start to end.

My final acknowledgments must go to my family. The lagniappe of my fieldwork was getting to spend time with Paula Fabre and Saundra McGuire, each a first cousin to one of my parents, and getting to see Baton Rouge through their eyes. My Louisiana roots are kept alive no matter where I am thanks to the love and recipes of my aunts Helene Metoyer and Marissa Monette. I am grateful for the faithful encouragement of Julia Atkin and Robin Bostic, both of whom I also owe thanks for, at times, kindly lending their desks to this project. To my cousins, Andrew and Claire Metoyer, my brother-in-law, Eric Chaves, and my sister, Kristin Yancy: thank you for keeping my cup full. To my partner, Jacob Taylor: thank you for drawing my first map and charting a course with me ever since. And to my father, Clyde Yancy: thank you for forging such an inspiring path to follow.

Contents

List of Figures

List of Tables

1
Prejudice and Place

> "White" is a metaphor for power.
> — **James Baldwin (2017)**

The heat was oppressive, even under the shade of one of the towering oak trees that cover the grounds of Louisiana State University (LSU). A blanket of humidity weighed down the campus, as did a tense silence. It had been a bloody start to summer in Baton Rouge.

The vigil I was attending was being held to commemorate two tragic events that took place in July 2016. The first was the killing of Alton Sterling, a 37-year-old Black[1] man who was shot six times at point-blank range by a Baton Rouge police officer on July 5th.[2] The second event was the killing of three local law enforcement officers—Montrell Jackson, Matthew Gerald, and Brad Garafola—who were shot by a Black Marine Corps veteran from Kansas City, MO, in an act of vengeance for Sterling's death only a week and a half later.[3]

The theme of the vigil was clear: it called for "unity" and "healing." What was unclear was how much Sterling was meant to be included in the service. The White student body representative who spoke framed his remarks as a tribute to the "ultimate sacrifice of the officers" and a condemnation of "the plague of violence that has found its way into our community." He mentioned Sterling's killing only as an event that tested the community's "bonds of friendship."

The Black student representative who spoke next appeared uneasy. "Just to reiterate," he said, "we are here to recognize *all* the lives. You may feel he (*referencing the previous speaker*) didn't say certain names, but we're here to 'vigilize' all the lives."

Technically, the Black student reaffirmed what the organizers had told us were the "ground rules" of the vigil: that "no side would be taken." Most of the other speakers, however, deferred to the true spirit of those rules: much was said about the importance of loving one another and condemning hate and violence. But Sterling, and the realities of life in the impoverished, Black community where he had lived, were all but invisible.

How the Color Line Bends: The Geography of White Prejudice in Modern America. Nina M. Yancy,
Oxford University Press. © Oxford University Press 2022. DOI: 10.1093/oso/9780197599426.003.0001

At the end of the service, I said a few hellos before seeking shelter in the air-conditioning of my rental car. Although I was a visitor to Baton Rouge, I knew from my family's roots (my great-grandparents were sharecroppers there) that Baton Rouge's Black–White color line had been both painfully obvious and easily ignored long before July 2016. I was nonetheless surprised to have found myself in Baton Rouge at a time when White residents' attentiveness to the color line was so acutely sharpened—and the dominance of their viewpoint so palpable. Hence the artificial silence around race when we all knew that what needed to be "healed" was a racial divide. And hence the invisibility of the part of town where Sterling lived and died: a severely segregated enclave in the north of Baton Rouge, a world away from the leafy university campus I had just left.

Ralph Ellison (1952, 3) perhaps best describes the kind of invisibility I encountered that day. As he writes, "I am invisible, understand, simply because people refuse to see me." To refuse to see implies that someone is in fact noticed, but then is rendered invisible. Unlike Sterling, some Black individuals were noticed and then remained visible at the vigil—most notably Montrell Jackson, one of the slain officers.

The question of how such decisions are made about Black visibility prompts another one, which Toni Morrison (qtd. in Als 2003) once posed in response to Ellison. "Invisible to whom?" she asked. "Not to me."

Tracing the Color Line

When either scholars or laypeople talk about the (in)visibility of Black Americans, they are usually talking about whether and how *White* Americans see Black people. Though obvious, this point often goes unstated in debates about how anti-Black prejudice influences racial politics in modern America. The failure to recognize White viewership is particularly apparent in debates that ask the sort of questions motivating this book—questions recognizing that Sterling's invisibility at his own vigil was a function of people and politics, but also of place.

Consider that the Baton Rouge area, according to 2019 census estimates, is 48% White and 47% Black, with a poverty rate around 18% and an unemployment rate that hovered between 4–6% from 2015 to 2020. Within Baton Rouge: How do White residents interpret their surroundings? How are these interpretations informed by White individuals' disparate opinions about race, as well as by their shared White racial identity? Beyond Baton Rouge: How would White individuals who see a different demographic landscape think differently about issues related to race? What if that other landscape had fewer Black residents, or richer or poorer ones? A higher unemployment rate, or a lower poverty rate? In other words: What is the relationship between where White Americans live and what they think on issues related to race?

Scholars have been asking this question for a long time. A relationship between prejudice and place is implicit in one of the oldest and most fundamental articulations of the "problem" of race in America—the problem of the color line. Frederick Douglass first used the term "color line" in writing in 1881, although W. E. B. Du Bois popularized it in 1903. Both authors' references to Black Americans' inferior political, economic, and social position as evidence of a dividing "line" between the races make intuitive sense. To use the color line analytically, however, it is important to define it explicitly as a divide that is as material as it is metaphorical. Sociologist Mary Pattillo (2015, xvi) captures this duality in her definition: "The color-line is a metaphor for the *mechanisms and practices* that maintain racial inequality as well as a more literal description of the many *places and systems* in which blacks are on one side and whites are on another side of a visible or invisible line" (emphasis added).

Whether conceptualizing the color line as metaphorical or material, there is a dizzying amount of complexity in contemporary America. When it comes to the metaphorical line—and White racial attitudes in particular—racial animus today might present itself as old-fashioned prejudice, subtle resentment clothed in egalitarian rhetoric, or the even subtler valorization of Whiteness by racially tolerant White people. At the same time, White antiracism and allyship have spread, such as in increased, if potentially tenuous, White support for the Black Lives Matter movement following the police killings of George Floyd and Breonna Taylor, among others, in the spring of 2020.[4] When it comes to the material color line, deep disparity persists between Black and White Americans in the political, economic, and social spheres. At the same time, a Black middle class that has grown, against the odds, should challenge the underlying assumption in too many debates that all Black people are poor. Throughout this book, I seek to recognize today's complexity in both attitudinal and material terms. I also seek to recognize the variety of ways the two dimensions of the color line intersect, and reinforce one another, in local environments across the United States. My primary focus, however, is on how the material line informs the attitudinal one, specifically as White individuals view their material surroundings and draw on what they see to inform their political behavior.

In asking how place shapes the expression of prejudice, I follow a long line of scholarship that offers an idea of what is likely to happen to the attitudinal color line in places where White attention to the material line is sharpened. In short, White residents will feel threatened. This prediction comprises the classic "racial threat" hypothesis, holding that as the relative size of a Black population grows—and, some would add, as general economic circumstances worsen—White residents are likely to respond with more racially hostile actions and attitudes (Key 1949; Blalock 1967). The rhetoric of threat is intuitive to many because the assumptions it carries are pervasive. To plenty of scholars and laypeople alike, it is logical both for White people to feel threatened where race is salient (i.e., psychologically/politically relevant), and for Black people to be interpreted as threatening. What researchers typically ignore is a question that logically follows from Morrison's response to Ellison: *From whose perspective does a nearby Black population constitute a threat?* Or, put differently: A threat to whom?

Failing to answer this question has two consequences. First, it leads many scholars to reproduce the very perspective they aim to study, tacitly stigmatizing Blackness and ignoring matters of power and positionality (or the idea that someone's structural position relative to others, reflected in aspects of identity such as race, gender, and sexuality, influences that person's understanding of the world). Second, it limits the ability of racial politics scholarship to explain deviation from the trope of unidimensionally racist White people reacting negatively to uniformly poor, "threatening" Black people.

The first of these two problems stems from scholars' tendency to normalize White racial prejudices when uncritically equating a Black population with a threat. Although I focus on this tendency in scholarship on racial geography, the assumption that what White people see is the objective truth, or at least the most important one, pervades political science. Consider the common failure to specify when White Americans (often normalized as simply "Americans") are being studied, or the failure to ask how a theory applies to non-White (and often, disenfranchised, disempowered, and disproportionately poor) individuals.[5]

The second problem, that we are limited in what we are able to explain, follows from the first. Failing to explicitly conceptualize White viewership not only reproduces a White perspective but also limits the imagination of research on prejudice and place. In particular, applications of the threat hypothesis do not often operationalize the variety of attitudes White Americans hold along with the variety of class positions that Black Americans occupy (i.e., asking who is looking, and whom they see). We therefore underappreciate the diversity of ways White viewers might respond when race is salient, as well as the diversity of ways Black people might be construed as threatening in the White gaze.

The Argument of This Book

This book responds to these two problems with a new approach to studying prejudice and place. Although the logic of the threat hypothesis is useful, it typically positions White people as passive recipients of a threat, and Black people as inherently threatening. I flip this logic by conceptualizing White Americans as viewers who interpret their surroundings through a racial lens. This is more than a rhetorical shift. Casting White people as viewers recognizes that Whiteness is not uniform—White individuals differ in the opinions they hold and the local contexts they see—but that White people nonetheless view the world from a common structural position. As a result, White people share a vantage point, viewpoint, or perspective from which they express opinions on matters of race.

The same could be said for many groups; moreover, based on the concept of positionality, any group's perspective will be subjective in some way. Yet, because White Americans' perspective is rooted in their dominant position in our racial hierarchy, their vantage point is one that is both subjective *and* racially privileged. Extending this logic to the study of racial threat, as this book will do, means appreciating that White people view not just the world in general but also their local worlds from a subjective, privileged position. Even more, it means assigning White viewers responsibility for the construal of Black people as threatening (while also recognizing White individuals' capacity to respond differently, if they choose).

Accordingly, this book brings a new emphasis on positionality to the tradition of studying White Americans' "sense of group position" (Blumer 1958). I use both interpretive and positivist approaches to trace the contours of White Americans' privileged perspective on racial politics, and I do so by investigating geographic variation in White preferences on three racial policy issues. The book first looks at school desegregation in an analysis that richly illuminates the White vantage point in Baton Rouge using interpretive methods, which focus on people's interpretations of the world in order to understand social realities. I illustrate in qualitative detail how, even when polarized over a racial issue, White people have a common vantage point on racial politics from the top of the racial order. I then show the empirical utility of accounting for this vantage point through two quantitative applications of the threat hypothesis, concerning White opinion on poverty assistance known as "welfare" and on affirmative action.

We'll begin where this chapter opened, in Baton Rouge, LA. My experience at the LSU vigil introduces not just the theme of Black visibility relevant throughout this book, but also Baton Rouge as the setting of Chapters 2 and 3 during a critical moment in the city's history related to racism and spatial inequality. This moment was acutely defined by Sterling's murder. However, I found myself at the vigil only because it coincided with my arrival in Baton Rouge to study a different (though not unrelated) issue, which also defined the moment. This was an ongoing effort by part of East Baton Rouge Parish[6] to incorporate as a new city, to be called St. George. The leaders of the effort made clear that their primary goal was to establish a new school district, independent of Baton Rogue's existing one—where the majority of students happen to be Black and poor.

Chapters 2 and 3 draw on interviews with forty-eight residents of the Baton Rouge area, coincidentally conducted while the parish was reeling from the racialized violence of July 2016. While much existing scholarship would suggest that Baton Rouge's demographics might lead White residents to feel threatened, I qualitatively illustrate the wide variety of White attitudes that are activated when race is salient. In the process, I show how White Baton Rougeans offer a vivid example of a shared White perspective: a view of the world conditioned by their racial privilege, influencing not only what they see but also how they see it. This shared perspective emerges in the form of several common discursive practices that engage White respondents in the maintenance of the color line, even as they express varied and at times contradictory points of view. Just as Blumer identified the sense of group position as made up of feelings directed toward an outgroup (such as fear) as well as toward one's ingroup (such as a sense of superiority), we will see that White residents' shared perspective in Baton Rouge stretches across both kinds of prejudicial feelings—showing the robustness of the White vantage point as it colors my respondents' views of their local world.

My analysis in Baton Rouge motivates my turn to quantitative methods in the second half of the book, revisiting the more conventional, positivist application of the racial threat hypothesis. With an appreciation of the White vantage point in hand, there is a clear epistemological imperative to reject common assumptions of White passivity or objectivity in quantitative analyses. This point then begs another question: How does our understanding of prejudice and place change if we are explicit about the White perspective from which Black people typically are perceived as threatening?

Chapters 4 and 5 demonstrate how conceptualizing White Americans' shared vantage point along with their diverse individual views can inform the quantitative study of racial threat. I choose two issues that allow me to further probe the outgroup- and ingroup-oriented dimensions of prejudice, respectively. The first issue is welfare, the archetypically racialized policy that White Americans have long associated with undeserving Black beneficiaries (e.g., the infamous "welfare queen"). The second is affirmative action, a quintessential case that requires White Americans to consider what they believe their ingroup deserves. By combining nationally representative survey data with census data, I examine White opinion on each issue in metropolitan areas across the United States.

As we will see, a focus on the White vantage point in these analyses unlocks new empirical insights. In Chapter 4, theorizing White viewership highlights how settings interpreted as threatening by racially hostile White viewers could simultaneously amplify *sympathetic* attitudes in racially tolerant White viewers—much like the issue of St. George led to amplified, polarized attitudes among White Baton Rougeans. In Chapter 5, remembering that White viewership is subjective highlights how even middle-class, "respectable" Black people may be construed as threatening by racially hostile and tolerant White people alike. In both chapters, a focus on White viewership also provokes new insights on how segregation shapes the landscapes White residents see in different metro areas. And throughout the latter half of the book, my observations from Baton Rouge continue to bring to life the dynamics of White racism we'll encounter, reminding us of both the subjectivity of White people's perspective and their agency in construing their surroundings as threatening (or not).

In short, this book examines the diversity of White Americans' racialized preferences in various geographic settings and shows that this diversity is nonetheless rooted in White Americans' shared, subjective vantage point. The book does so by illuminating the White perspective in detail within one geographic context and then showing how this perspective operates across contexts—in regard to White people's feelings toward their ingroup as well as toward Black people as an outgroup.

To be clear, this book is not a study of White opinion on education, or on welfare or affirmative action, per se. Rather, it is a study of White Americans' racialized preferences across contexts that are typically characterized as threatening. Each chapter offers its own specific findings on the policy area at hand, but together they show the value of incorporating interpretivist and critical approaches into the qualitative and quantitative study of prejudice and place. The second half of the book does not seek to quantitatively replicate my qualitative findings in Baton Rouge, but instead brings these qualitative lessons to bear on the quantitative study of racial threat. By making visible the White vantage point from which Black people are typically seen as threats, this book opens up new empirical insights on the diversity of White responses when race is salient, as well as the diversity of ways Black people might be construed as threatening.

I do not take my focus on White attitudes lightly. Focusing on the White perspective risks essentializing or even fetishizing Whiteness as an object of study with only vague implications for Black people. By explicitly conceptualizing rather than reproducing the White perspective, I hope to interrogate the epistemological foundations of racial politics scholarship and challenge its pernicious denigration of Blackness. By emphasizing the consequences of White racism for Black lives and livelihoods, I also hope to avoid centering White people for their own sake or letting Black people's experiences fade into the background. And ultimately, I hope my critical study of those who benefit from an oppressive system contributes more to the system's dismantling than to the reification of their position atop it. Nonetheless, my approach does leave White Americans in the spotlight—mirroring, in a sense, the tragedy of Sterling being invisible at his own vigil, and denying Black individuals their (our) subjectivity much as the racial threat hypothesis commonly does. Black histories and experiences still will play important roles in Chapters 2 and 3. Yet, my analysis uses Black residents' reflections primarily to illuminate Baton Rouge's racialized history, to offer contrast to White residents' views, and to highlight the Black respondents' insight into the "ways of White folks" (borrowing Langston Hughes's 1934 words)—rather than to paint a true picture of Black residents' experiences of race, class, and geography in Baton Rouge.

Different choices could have further centered Black subjectivity; I appreciate this particularly with the wisdom of hindsight. This book is about contemporary issues in fast-moving times—faster, at least it seems, than when I began to conceive of this project in 2014. Few could have anticipated how, on the one hand, the racial resentment that began to resurge after Barack Obama's election (Tesler 2012) would flourish and be fueled by Donald Trump (Abramowitz and McCoy 2019), or, on the other hand, how increased awareness of police brutality would provoke shifts in long-stagnant White views on whether anti-Black discrimination remains a problem in America (Tesler 2020). Arguably, fewer could have anticipated how a global pandemic and associated economic recession would wrench further open the racial fissures in American society.[7] The ultimate impact and permanence of the waves of both racial animosity and affinity that swelled in the Trump era and in the wake of George Floyd's murder remain to be seen.

But the title of composer Tyshawn Sorey's 2018 quartet says it all: "Everything Changes, Nothing Changes." At the very core of American political development has always been a war between competing "racial institutional orders," or evolving coalitions that are united by their stances on the pressing racial issues of the day (King and Smith 2005). We will see one dimension of that war in action throughout this book in the diversity of White reactions to context, even as these are constrained by a common White vantage point. Thus, the findings presented in this book should long remain relevant, thanks to their illustration of the remarkable flexibility of the color line to adapt to changing circumstances. The color line is both responsive to geographies of race and class, and resilient even as White prejudices soften and Black class positions rise. These workings will become apparent when bringing White viewership into focus in my analysis of racialized preferences across geographic contexts.

To call political preferences "racialized" as I have done is not simply to say that they are influenced by racial animus. Racialization more expansively refers to the "extension of racial meaning" (Omi and Winant 1986, 64) to something not inherently associated with race. This process explains why "welfare" calls to mind poor Black people and "inner city" calls to mind poor Black neighborhoods, and why race could so easily be talked *around* at a vigil commemorating some of the most racially contentious deaths Baton Rouge has experienced in decades. Only by appreciating the range of racial meanings White Americans draw from their varied experiences of race, class, and geography—while also appreciating that these meanings are conditioned by a common, privileged location in the American racial hierarchy—can we appreciate the endurance of the color line.

In other words, the color line endures not because it is rigid, but because it is flexible. We will be limited in our understanding of its persistence, let alone its capacity to harden in some places or to be dismantled in others, if we do not take seriously its capacity to bend.

Positionality and Threat: Putting White Viewers in Context

The rest of this introduction aims to do two things. First is to lay the theoretical foundation required to bring White Americans' positionality into the study of racial threat. Second is to explain the methodological approach I take, building on that foundation, to both qualitatively and quantitatively analyze White attitudes in contexts across the United States. This section takes on the former.

Bringing White positionality into the study of racial threat requires moving beyond *what* White people think about Black people, to further consider *why*, *where*, and *how* White people are likely to respond in defense of their racial group interests. To answer "why," I draw on structural theories of prejudice explaining White racism as a product of their position atop the racial hierarchy, which they are inclined to defend. To answer "where," I bring structural theories to bear on the racial threat hypothesis, explaining its insight into the relationship between prejudice and place while also arguing for a more explicit engagement with White people's agency in construing Black people as threatening. And to explain "how," I discuss how political psychology supports my conceptualization of White people as viewers, rather than victims, of a threat, before discussing how this conceptualization illuminates White political behavior in new ways.

Why: On Race and Power

Let's start with a simple premise: White Americans have an interest in racial politics. Granted, it can sometimes seem like they do not. The tradition of identifying, in neutral terms, America's racial "dilemma" has long minimized the violently ascriptive capacity of American liberalism to exclude Black people, along with many other groups.[8] This minimization takes on physical form in the residential segregation of Black households, which not only facilitates harsh inequalities but also gives most White people little personal investment in the well-being of isolated Black communities. As Black writer Zack Linly (2016) says of White people who seem either oblivious to or undisturbed by the unequal treatment and opportunities Black people receive: "[White people], both figuratively and literally, have no skin in the game."

From a different perspective, however, it is clear that White people *do* have skin in the game of racial politics—specifically, an interest in legitimating their historic place at the top of the American racial hierarchy. Far from a dilemma that came from nowhere, Black scholars have long pointed out that it is from White people's perspective that Black bodies represent the "Negro problem"—a problem that, as James Baldwin (2017, 82) once put it, "a guilty and constricted white imagination [has] assigned to the blacks," rather than to those who structurally benefit.[9] In other words, responsibility for addressing a problem resulting from White dominance is all too easily deferred to Black people, in lay and scholarly accounts alike.

In contrast, this book rests on the principle that White Americans benefit from their racially privileged position and thus have a political interest in defending it.[10] By recognizing this principle, I situate this book within socio-structural research that emphasizes White people's protectiveness of their racial group interests. Examples of this approach include the group position model (Blumer 1958), the realistic group conflict model (Bobo 1983), social dominance theory (Sidanius and Pratto 2001), and earlier hegemony models (Gramsci 1995), all of which share the same basic tenets. Societies are stratified into groups; politics puts these groups into competition for scare resources, opportunities, and symbolic capital; and ideological arguments serve as weapons in this competition. These group-level dynamics are meaningful for my analysis of White Americans' individual-level opinions on the grounds that individuals draw a meaningful "social identity" from group membership and thus will seek to enhance or maintain their group's status (Tajfel and Turner 1979). What social dominance and other theorists would add, however, is that the maintenance of the racial order is not just a question of identity. It is also a question of power.

The longstanding power imbalance between Black and White Americans has become harder to deny in recent years, as greater attention has been drawn to one of its most visceral consequences: the staggering amount of violence to which Black Americans are exposed. This goes beyond the deaths of Alton Sterling and countless other men, women, and children at the hands of state actors such as police. If a basic function of the state is to protect its citizens from danger, then the high rates of *civilian* violence to which Black Americans are exposed, and not just the high number of Black killings by the state, are an instance of racialized state failure (Miller 2015; for a historical perspective, see also Francis 2014).[11] These deaths reflect gendered state failure, too, in light of the extreme violence that Black women experience (Threadcraft 2016). Beyond direct physical violence: inferior schools, neighborhoods, health care, employment conditions, and other services unduly impact the lives of Black Americans, helping to explain Black mortality rates that are 40% higher than White rates.[12] These are among the many outcomes ignored by analyses that discuss White political behavior without also discussing power and positionality.

In response, this book seeks to keep the material consequences of the color line from fading into the background, primarily by emphasizing the empowered vantage point from which White attitudes are expressed (and often, analyzed). Such an emphasis is not standard in the empirical study of White attitudes, but it has firm theoretical grounding. Feminist standpoint theorists reject the idea that dominant viewpoints are ever value-neutral, as opposed to reflecting the dominant group's own interests (Collins 1986; Haraway 1988; D. E. Smith 1990; Harding 2004). Similarly, when philosopher Charles Mills (1997) points out that at the core of White dominance is an "epistemology of ignorance"—an agreement to *mis*perceive the world—he reminds us that, much like the Negro problem has been constructed through the eyes of White people, power brings the luxury of deciding what is seen and how. This critical perspective further informs my study of White racial attitudes as a group-level, socio-structural phenomenon.

The Ingroup- and Outgroup-Oriented Dimensions of Prejudice

Note that I do not set myself *against* scholarship on the individual-level psychology of racism, as some scholars taking a socio-structural approach do (e.g., Bobo 1983; Bonilla-Silva 2006). I instead integrate individual-level theories into my analysis to recognize the dimensions along which White attitudes vary. Thus, throughout this book I operationalize multiple measures of racial orientations, which can be positive or negative, normative or descriptive, but still emanate from White Americans' structural location in the racial hierarchy.

When operationalizing racial prejudice as a multidimensional phenomenon, I draw upon Herbert Blumer's (1958) classic work on prejudice as "a sense of group position." Blumer identifies four component "feelings" that tend to be present in a dominant group, emanating from its position in relation to a subordinate group. I organize these feelings into two categories (Table 1.1). First are feelings primarily concerned with an *outgroup*—a belief that the subordinate race is inherently different or alien, and fear or suspicion directed toward the subordinate race. Second are feelings primarily concerned with the *ingroup*—a sense of superiority, and a feeling of entitlement to certain privileges.

I am far from the first to emphasize this duality of prejudice. In particular, studies of Whiteness as a racial identity have shown that anti-Black animus is not necessary for the reproduction of White privilege or racial inequality (Frankenberg 1993; Bonilla-Silva 2006; Gallagher 2008; DiTomaso 2013; Feagin 2013). Neither is anti-Black animus necessary to produce pro-White sentiments in the first place (Brewer 1999; Jardina 2019; see also Allport 1954). The point is that White people can express racialized preferences in either the absence or presence of animus toward Black people.

Table 1.1 Feelings of Prejudice Comprising the Sense of Group Position

Ingroup-oriented	Outgroup-oriented
"a feeling of superiority"	"a feeling that the subordinate race is intrinsically different"
"a feeling of proprietary claim to certain areas of privilege and advantage"	"a fear and suspicion that the subordinate race harbors designs on the prerogatives of the dominant race"

As articulated in Blumer (1958).

Accordingly, Blumer's four feelings of prejudice, and the ingroup/outgroup dimension within them, serve as a key organizing principle throughout this book. We will see each feeling qualitatively come to life among White individuals both for and against the incorporation of St. George. I then quantitatively investigate each dimension of prejudice, in turn. Through pairing national survey data on White Americans' attitudes with census data about the places where White survey respondents live, I highlight how either outgroup- or ingroup-oriented feelings of prejudice can be activated when race is salient— and show the relevance of White Americans' racial vantage point in both cases.

It follows that, if White people's vantage point is relevant, so too is their context. Put differently, if White people's positionality is important, so too is their literal position—where they live.

Where: Connecting Prejudice to Place

The general concept of threat is of obvious relevance to socio-structural theories of prejudice: we anticipate White people to feel threatened by potential challenges to their dominant position. The specific rhetoric of threat is more closely linked, however, to a paradigmatic approach to studying the relevance of geography to racial politics.

The racial threat hypothesis, introduced earlier in this chapter, has its origins in V. O. Key's landmark study finding that White political participation in the South, almost exclusively in support of the segregationist Southern Democrats, was highest in counties with the largest Black populations. Key (1949, 646) identified an "intense political consciousness" among these White residents of the Black Belt as a result of their fear of Black empowerment. He theorized that the "symbolic potency" of a Black population motivated White people to vote, rather than any realistic electoral threat Black voters posed. Black people were broadly disenfranchised at the time. As Key noted, "[I]n no state would Negro voting produce 'black supremacy.'"

A long line of research has followed. The dominant approach, formalized by Blalock (1967), is to use the relative size of a minority population as an indicator of the magnitude of threat. Literature taking this approach has identified a threat response in the form of White electoral support for anti-Black (Allport 1954; Giles and Buckner 1993; but see also Voss 1996; Wright 1977) or anti-redistributive (Hersh and Nall 2015) candidates, as well as in the form of amplified anti-Black animus among White people (Giles 1977;

Fossett and Kiecolt 1989; M. C. Taylor 1998). Other scholars have specified the economic dimensions of threat, arguing that where resources are scarcer, race relations are more likely to seem like a zero-sum game (Quillian 1995). Recent research has placed even more emphasis on economic context—whether as a more significant factor than racial context (Oliver and Mendelberg 2000), or a key moderator of the relationship between racial context and White attitudes (Branton and Jones 2005). As noted in the opening of this chapter, these insights supply a ready answer to where we should look for the activation of White people's racialized policy preferences: in settings where either a relatively large Black population is present or where economic resources are scarce.[13]

Several complications remain. For one, the relationship between local geography and political behavior has always posed challenges for drawing causal inferences. A perennial concern is whether living in a certain place leads people to think or act a certain way, or if self-selection or local culture and history explain why people in certain places think and act similarly. Acharya, Blackwell, and Sen (2018) offer a compelling argument for the latter, showing how an area's historical reliance on slavery explains variation in White attitudes across the South, even when accounting for contemporary Black population share. This emphasis on the oppressive history of Black enslavement illustrates one way to bring questions of power into the study of prejudice and place: the authors offer an astute critique of much racial threat scholarship for assuming Black populations to be the source of a threat, rather than considering the political and economic incentives to which White people have historically responded when living near large Black populations (e.g., opportunities to exploit Black labor).[14] At the same time, there is strong evidence that contemporary contexts do affect attitudes under certain conditions, such as after exogenous shocks to an area's racial composition (Hopkins 2010, 2012; Enos 2016)—evidence complemented by findings from experimental studies (Enos 2017; Enos and Celaya 2018). I recognize that the distribution of Black and White Americans across contexts reflects longstanding patterns in racial geography and associated culture rather than sudden changes. Therefore, rather than try to explain context *causing* attitudes, I use quantitative methods to illustrate systematic variation in White Americans' racialized preferences—and draw on qualitative insights from Baton Rouge to understand this variation as a function of White people's shared perspective.

A second complication presented by the racial threat hypothesis concerns whether the patterns scholars identify in White people's behavior are overly sensitive to the level at which "local" is measured (Cho and Manski 2008;

Fotheringham and Wong 1991). I will address this complication in more detail in Chapters 4 and 5, where I primarily operationalize context at the metropolitan area level but also investigate variation at the county and congressional district level. For now, note that I choose to focus on the metropolitan area as a proxy for White individuals' general milieus: the areas they move through on a daily basis, and in which they are likely to be aware of current events, racial demographics, and economic conditions (Fossett and Kiecolt 1989; Wilcox and Roof 1978). Urban areas also serve as key units in American political life (Stone 1989; Trounstine 2009), and as a result have been central sites for reproducing racial, economic, and spatial inequality through both segregation and unequal public goods provision (Alesina, Baqir, and Easterly 1999; Rothstein 2017; Trounstine 2018; see also Harvey 1985). More than acknowledging the debate over how to measure geography and its effects, my interest in White people's local field of vision brings me to a third issue with the racial threat hypothesis—one that informs my critique of it.

The third complication relates to the question of whether White people actually perceive the contextual cues that scholars use to operationalize threat. This is a key but infrequently tested assumption in much of the literature on racial threat. On the one hand, people do appear perceptive of factors such as immigration levels and unemployment in their ZIP codes and counties (Newman et al. 2015). On the other hand, there is a frequent disjuncture between what an officially defined context (such as a census tract or county) contains and what people perceive, particularly when it comes to racial demographics (Wong et al. 2012). I draw on both of these insights. People should be aware of their surroundings on some objective level, while also liable to operate based on subjective understandings of those surroundings. When the people in question are White Americans, we further have to remember that their perspective is not just subjective, like any other group's. It is also conditioned by their privileged position in the racial hierarchy.

What's the Matter with Threat
To be fair, most applications of the racial threat hypothesis implicitly recognize White subjectivity, even if they do not often emphasize White privilege. For example, it is commonplace to analyze racial threat as a partly psychological (rather than purely pragmatic or instrumental) response to a Black outgroup (see Enos 2016, 125–126). Psychological approaches are broadly consistent with Key's original argument that fear led White people to exaggerate the true threat posed by Black people. Some applications of the threat hypothesis also have explicitly investigated White subjectivity, like I

seek to do here. A prominent example comes from Marylee Taylor (1998), who asks whether the effect of "percent Black" (i.e., the local percentage of Black residents) is mediated by White people's subjective perceptions of a threat. Taylor finds no evidence to support this hypothesis and, along with reflecting on the difficulty of operationalizing the feeling that one's group is threatened, concludes that her findings "should encourage some skepticism about equating the effect of percent black with economic or political threat" (527).

The challenge is that even when empirically interrogating the workings of White subjectivity, scholars (often White themselves) tend to subtly position White people as victims, or hesitate to assign them an active role in the workings of the threat hypothesis. Similarly, researchers typically use a Black population as a proxy for a threat while remaining silent on the lived experience that the threat hypothesis represents: one of Black suffering as a result of White fear. As a result, even when scholars nod to threat as a product of White people's psychology, we nonetheless are left with a body of literature that could be interpreted by an ignorant reader (or a White supremacist reader, for that matter) as a canon documenting *White* suffering as a result of Black fearsomeness.

Consider, first, many scholars' tendency to defer to—or even to display—the "fragility" (DiAngelo 2011) of the White psyche by tacitly characterizing White people as victims of a threat. Kinder and Sanders (1996, 90), on the one hand, directly recognize the symbolic nature of threat as they argue: "Threat is not so much a clear-eyed perception as it is an emotion-laden attitude." On the other hand, the authors use passive language when they explain that White people simply "are predisposed" to "feel racially threatened," and "to look at the world [and] see danger and risk." Such passive language minimizes White individuals' agency in perceiving Black people as threatening and acting on those perceptions. Another sort of minimization of White agency appears when authors are seemingly hesitant to refer to White people in racial terms when analyzing political behavior (see Harris-Lacewell 2003, 230–231). There are, of course, exceptions to this trend.[15] But take Hersh and Nall (2015), who argue that local racial context conditions the link between income and partisanship. Although the authors examine registered voters of all races, they repeatedly refer to "voters" in the aggregate (or simply to "income-based voting") when explaining their findings—despite the fact that it is primarily *White* citizens' party identification that they find to vary across local context. Specifically, affluent White people are more Republican when they live in proximity to poor Black people; Black voters' partisan affiliation does not vary at all according to racial context in Hersh and Nall's analysis—only the presence of Black voters does.

A second, related tendency also appears throughout scholarship on racial threat: the tacit definition of Blackness as inherently threatening. This was on display, for example, in the language from Kinder and Sanders (1996) referenced in the previous paragraph, from which we deduce that the "danger and risk" White people see in the world are embodied by Blackness. In another example, an often cited paper by Giles and Evans (1985) asks whether there is a link between actual threat and perceived threat. While this approach does engage with White people's subjective perceptions, the authors plainly define "actual" threat as a Black presence. In their words: "In the United States the principal threat to white dominance has come from blacks" (51); it is unclear when exactly Giles and Evans believe Black Americans posed a credible threat to White dominance (as opposed to simply making gains against deep inequality). The authors nuance this take over the course of their discussion,[16] but they nonetheless endorse the threatening nature of Blackness as something to be *dis*-proven. To see Black spaces and by extension Black people as threatening, as sources of harm, ultimately is dehumanizing. As Hunter et al. (2016, 32) poignantly argue, the necessity of an "otherwise obvious assertion—that 'Black Lives Matter'" is partly a product of the scholarly (and media) portrayal of Black communities that "so rarely captures the life that happens within them, and thus the matter of black people's humanity."

In more recent applications of the threat hypothesis (Baybeck 2006; Weber et al. 2014), authors focus more closely on psychological mechanisms, using the language of "activation" or "stimulation" of stereotypes or racial attitudes, much as I do throughout this book. Still, leaning into the (seeming) neutrality of scientific rhetoric can be problematic when not also acknowledging the power dynamics or lived realities within the contexts we are studying.

Ultimately, when failing to acknowledge the privileged position from which White people perceive a threat, scholarship commonly reproduces a White viewpoint in analyses of racial politics, positioning White people as victims and Black people as threats. In other words, scholars easily themselves slip into, rather than analyze, White Americans' experience of racial politics as a spectacle.

Spectacles are capable of deeply engaging people's emotions even when an issue has little material impact on their lives, thanks to being based more on imagery than on reality (Debord 1967; Edelman 1988). Imagery has been central to the racialization of geography, manifest in the "iconic ghetto" in the minds of White Americans from which Black Americans are inseparable (Elijah Anderson 2012). Imagery also has been central to the racialization of politics, manifest in the overrepresentation of Black people in media depictions of the poor and resulting stigmatization of poverty programs (Gilens 1999). And of course, few themes have been more integral to Black literary, scholarly, and artistic traditions than how Black people appear—or do not—in the White gaze. The theme of Black (in)visibility largely descends from Du Bois's identification of White people's inability to see Black people in *The Souls of Black Folk*, and later was vividly developed by Ellison in *Invisible Man*. Invisibility has been used to explain how White Americans construct, subscribe to, and reproduce images of Blackness that tell us more about White people's own fears and insecurities than about Black people themselves. It was never meant to imply that White people did not *notice* Black people (as was evident in the recognition of slain police officer Montrell Jackson at the LSU vigil, in contrast to Alton Sterling). In the White gaze, Blackness can be hyper-visible at the same time as ignored. And as writer and artist Claudia Rankine (2014, 24) laments, "[N]o amount of visibility will alter the ways in which one is perceived."

I do not dismiss the value of the psychological mechanism of threat in understanding racial politics. As I have said, the fundamental idea that White people will defend their dominant position implies that perceived challenges to that position will be accompanied by feelings of threat. I also follow the convention in the literature of using Black population share to measure racial context. However, I strive not to equate "percent Black" with "threat," and not to posit nearby Black bodies as entities liable to inflict harm while White people remain innocent and vulnerable. In reality, *Black* residents of counties with the highest support for the Southern Democrats in Key's original study were at greater risk of suffering racialized harm than were the White residents who were "threatened" by the local Black population—as Key himself acknowledged.

Thus, to better engage with the racial power imbalance in the racial threat hypothesis, this book assigns White people responsibility for the construal of threat by drawing on standpoint theory's fundamental point that no vision is neutral: everything is seen from somewhere.

How: The Situational Activation of Racialized Behavior

I have so far situated this book within theories explaining White people's political behavior as shaped both by their proclivity to defend their racial group's dominant position, and by concerns in their local surroundings. Two points should emerge from these discussions. First, I build on the work of those who understand racial attitudes to operate in defense of White people's group interests, but I do so while also emphasizing the diversity of feelings that might serve this purpose. Second, I draw on the insights of racial threat literature regarding where White people are most likely to feel that their group interests need defending, but I do so while rejecting the paradigm that assigns neutrality to the White perspective and subtly posits Blackness as threatening.

Accordingly, this book conceptualizes White people as viewers, with diverse beliefs and surroundings but a common racial viewpoint. The contours of this viewpoint emerge in detail over the course of my conversations with White Baton Rougeans, despite—and more striking in light of—deep disagreements among them over the case of St. George. Thanks to the concentration of both Black residents and poverty in the larger Baton Rouge area, amplified by the fight over St. George and the killing of Alton Sterling, my White respondents' racial attitudes were what we can call "activated." I understand racial attitudes to be activated when they are readily accessible, or more easily called to mind, and thus likely to influence someone's other political opinions. This understanding draws on psychological research into racial priming, which shows that racial attitudes are more influential in political decision-making when someone is exposed to a stimulus related to race (Mendelberg 2001; Valentino, Hutchings, and White 2002). To apply these insights to geographic variation in White public opinion, I posit local geography as indicative of the stimuli related to race and class that are present in a White individual's surroundings.

Geography therefore serves as a source of what John Zaller (1992, 25) might call "contextual information" for the residents of a given metropolitan area. Whereas Zaller posits levels of political knowledge as reflective of the objective information different people possess, I posit local demographics as indicative of the subjective understanding people might have about the status of the races in their surroundings. In other words, features of local geography tell us about the different landscapes people see when they take stock of their surroundings—or the "different worlds" in which people live (Lippmann 1922; see also Enos 2017). In a setting other than Baton Rouge, for example, with a different story of race and class, White residents would draw on different contextual information and likely behave differently as a result.

These differences come to light in my quantitative analyses of White Americans' activated racial attitudes in local contexts across the United States. While the activation of White racial attitudes is one of the core findings of existing literature on racial threat, examining this dynamic as a function of

White people's perspective from the top of the racial hierarchy complicates—and modernizes—the story beyond racially hostile White people reacting negatively to (assumedly) poor Black people. Here lies the analytic value of asking both who is the viewer, and what is in their field of vision.

Asking about White people's field of vision pushes us to interrogate the different landscapes White Americans see today and thus to engage with diversity along the material color line. Most pointedly, this book highlights the capacity for White people to perceive a threat in the form of a nearby Black middle class—a group often assumed to be viewed positively by White Americans. More broadly, this book will explore how White people react differently depending on the racial and class demographics of their surroundings, and whether segregation makes those demographics more or less visible from the point of view of White households. After all, just as White people's racial vantage point shapes their interpretations of their surroundings, residential segregation—a system built and maintained primarily by White Americans—literally shapes the version of geography that many White people see in cities across the United States.

Turning to the question of who is the viewer, it is similarly important to engage with diversity along the attitudinal color line. There is both coherence and variation among White Americans today: they share a vantage point on racial politics from atop the racial hierarchy, but not all will bring the same beliefs to bear when forming opinions. In this sense, my approach does more than reject the equation of Blackness with threat; it also adds depth to White people's views. Not all White people will see a Black population as threatening, or will do so for the same reasons, depending on the beliefs a particular individual holds. Most practically, this casts racially tolerant White people in a complicated light. On the one hand, we must appreciate that White Americans are not a monolithic group, uniformly likely to see the same stimuli as threatening—many might respond *positively* to the salience of race. On the other hand, we still must appreciate how prejudice can inform even the most tolerant White people's viewpoints.

The Methods and Organization of This Book

I draw together multiple methodological approaches to assign White Americans the role (and thus the agency and responsibility) of viewers in the racial threat hypothesis, and to explore how they interpret their fields of vision in localities across the United States. This section details the logic behind my qualitative and quantitative approaches, in turn. It also introduces the various racialized policy debates and associated times and places within which I situate my analyses, and that demonstrate the expansive reach of Whites' racialized vantage point in shaping their political behavior.

Illuminating the White Perspective: Schools, Segregation, and the Case of St. George (Chapters 2 and 3)

Chapters 2 and 3 of this book represent my qualitative, interpretive study of White attitudes in Baton Rouge—in contrast to the quantitative, positivist approach more commonly used to study racial threat. The quantitative literature generally requires understanding context and attitudes in aggregate terms, examining the preferences of large numbers of White Americans living in many different metropolitan areas—or, in more localized studies, large numbers of White Americans living in one city or state (e.g., Baybeck 2006; Weber et al. 2014; Enos 2016). I seek to deepen the insights contributed by this existing literature by critically examining White people's viewpoint and racialized preferences—not as measured through survey questions, but as expressed in everyday actions and speech.

Three key choices define my qualitative approach: why I chose to study White residents of Baton Rouge; why I took an interpretive approach to analyze what I found there; and how standpoint theory informs my interpretive analysis identifying a shared White perspective.

Why Study White Perspectives in Baton Rouge?
My time in Baton Rouge in 2016 coincided with a state-mandated waiting period in the years-long St. George incorporation effort, brought into effect after a 2015 petition to bring the cityhood issue to vote failed to get enough support. Just as many had promised me they would, the organizers launched a new effort in 2018 and ultimately were successful: as of October 2019, a proposal to incorporate a smaller, but still sizable area as the new city of St. George passed with a majority of 54% (although the incorporation is still stalled in the courts at the time of writing).

Irrespective of the ultimate outcome—the fight over St. George reflects the deeply racialized and economically unequal geography of the Baton Rouge area. This geography is similar to cities across the country but was exacerbated in Baton Rouge by a federal school desegregation lawsuit that lasted almost 50 years, accompanied by considerable White flight. The tragic shootings of July 2016 only threw this spatial inequality into harsher relief, offering an unexpected, tragic, and theoretically rich background for research.

My selection of this case partially reflects a pragmatic consideration: I had access to and knowledge of South Louisiana thanks to my family's roots there. However, two interlinked theoretical reasons more crucially motivate my study of Baton Rouge. The most obvious one is situational: the ongoing case of St. George as of 2016 (and the accompanying, if coincidental, racialized violence) brought to the surface reflections among White residents about race and class in their local geography that would have been harder to access otherwise. Talking about the St. George effort and the July shootings offered me an opportunity to understand White residents' perceptions of the local geography of Baton Rouge, and to study how these perceptions were shaped by their racial identity. Additionally, the stark divide in public opinion on St. George offered an ideal opportunity to analyze White opinion when polarized over a racialized issue, making Chapter 3's evidence of their common perspective on racial politics that much more striking.

The second reason for my case selection is foundational to the first: a debate like the one over St. George likely would not have emerged in a place where the attitudinal and material dimensions of the color line were not so salient. Thanks to a large Black population, and a high poverty rate at the same time as a considerable Black middle-class presence, White residents' complex beliefs about race and class are chronically activated in Baton Rouge. This makes the area a valuable setting in which to study dynamics likely to emerge in other places, too, when White beliefs about race and class are similarly activated, whether chronically or situationally. In other words, Baton Rouge presents an example of the sort of setting that will play a key role throughout this book's analyses: one where White people's attentiveness to the color line is sharpened.

There are obvious limits to how much one should generalize from my analysis of a midsize city in the Deep South where the population is nearly evenly split between Black and White. However, the goal of my analysis of White opinion on school desegregation and municipal incorporation in Baton Rouge, as with my studies of welfare and affirmative action, is not to write an authoritative account of a particular policy issue. Rather, it is to demonstrate how White Americans' racial identity shapes their perceptions of their local geography when forming racialized preferences, including the interpretation of certain demographics as threatening. Such a task requires situating my analysis within the particular parameters of Baton Rouge, both historically (e.g., the collective memory of a desegregation lawsuit of fifty-plus years) and geographically (e.g., the racial segregation of the parish and its schools). The task also requires study of not just *what* White people think as captured on a survey, but also *how* they develop and express those thoughts when interacting with others. It is for these reasons that my approach to analysis in Baton Rouge is an interpretive one.

An Interpretive Approach

One of the best recent examples of interpretive political science comes from Katherine Cramer (2016). Cramer's study in rural Wisconsin identifies a "rural consciousness," or an attachment to place and belief in fundamental differences between rural and urban America, which helps explain the centrality of resentment to her research subjects' interactions with politics. As Cramer puts it, the goal of her interpretive study is not to show that X causes Y, but "to show, convincingly, that a particular perspective is influential for the way some people think about politics . . . [and that it] screens out certain considerations and makes others obvious and commonplace" (23). My similar task in Chapters 2 and 3 is to show what it looks like when a particular perspective is influential for how people think about politics— in this case, to show how White residents' racial identity influences their understandings of the geography of Baton Rouge and the related issues of municipal incorporation and school desegregation.

Because interpretivism is underutilized in the study of prejudice and place, it is worth explaining some underlying tenets in more detail. In more technical terms, an interpretive methodology is one that "privileges local, situated knowledge and situated knowers" (Schwartz-Shea and Yanow 2012, 5–6).

Seeking to "privilege" a certain kind of knowledge reflects interpretivism's basis in social constructivism. Rather than assume a single, objective reality of race relations in Baton Rouge, I assume there to be multiple realities depending on who is doing the telling. I further understand these different truths to be constructed through social interaction, shaped by culture and history, and inextricably tied up with power (Burr 2003). This means that, while I point out factual inaccuracies in respondents' arguments as appropriate, my goal is not to critique their knowledge but to consider *why* particular "facts" are known and cited over others (much like Cramer investigates how rural consciousness screens out some considerations but not others).

It also means that I assume the presence of a researcher in conversation with a research subject inevitably shapes the data collected. In Cramer's case, this requires noticing how respondents react to her status as an urbanite (albeit also a lifelong Wisconsinite). In mine, it requires noticing how White respondents react to a Black interviewer (albeit also someone with Louisiana roots). In the next chapter, I will discuss norms of race-matching in qualitative interviews, challenge the assumption that only White interviewers can glean valuable insight about White attitudes, and argue for the potential benefits of conducting research from a non-White perspective. It is undoubtedly the case that my interview data would have differed were it collected by a White researcher. Yet, that researcher would have no less obligation to reflect critically on the role her race played in influencing the nature of knowledge produced in the interview setting.

Returning to the aforementioned definition of interpretive methodology—what does it mean to privilege "local" knowledge? Local knowledge comes from a specific context. By working with a small, nonrepresentative sample, the close study of my participants' reflections is not an attempt to represent population-level variation in White or Black attitudes. Instead, my analysis shows how coherent viewpoints are created by specific individuals using the resources available in their environment. This does not mean that the insight generated by an interpretive study is applicable *only* to the context from which it was gleaned. Cramer emphasizes that hers is a study conducted in Wisconsin, not of Wisconsin (Cramer 2016, 23; see also Geertz 1973), and I could say the same for my work in Louisiana. It is my responsibility as a researcher to present my analysis as the product of the specific context of Baton Rouge in the tumultuous summer of 2016, while also drawing connections to a broader understanding of the role of White actions and attitudes in upholding the color line.

Finally, a focus on "situated knowledge and knowers" reflects the interpretivist emphasis on embodied understandings of the world, meaning how people conceive of the world based on their own subjective perspectives and lived experiences. This concept largely originates in feminist scholar Donna Haraway's (1988) critique of so-called objective knowledge—one that crucially informed both the development of standpoint theory and my use of it.

Standpoint Theory and the White Perspective

Far beyond pointing out that all perspectives are subjective, Haraway calls out the workings of power and its ability to prioritize certain perspectives over others. This informs the basis of standpoint theory, the approach developed by feminist scholars like Haraway as they sought to explain knowledge production as contingent on the structural position (i.e., standpoint) of the knower, and to prescribe that research engage critically with the "conceptual practices of power" (D. E. Smith 1990). Feminist standpoint theory in particular challenges the assumed neutrality or omniscience of the dominant (male) subject. In doing so, it emphasizes the insight that the *subjugated* (female) subject has into the workings of power. bell hooks (1992, 165), for example, writes about the long tradition of Black people "[sharing] with one another 'special' knowledge of whiteness gleaned from close scrutiny of white people"—a necessary practice for survival in a White supremacist world. The argument here is that the workings of a system of power are the most visible to and often best understood by subjects who are oppressed by that system—whether the system is one of gender domination or race domination (or an intersection of the two).

In my application of standpoint theory, I focus on the perspective of the *dominant* (White) residents of Baton Rouge. Although standpoint theory is less frequently used to critique the perspectives of subjects who occupy dominant positions, there is some precedent for this approach. One example is Ruth Frankenberg's (1993) *White Women, Race Matters*, an early contribution to conceptualizations of Whiteness (at least by White academics; see also McIntosh 1988). Frankenberg invokes feminist scholarship to conceptualize what she calls a "White standpoint," explaining how White women's structural position keeps them from seeing how race shapes their lives.

Frankenberg and McIntosh were writing as scholars were shifting from studying White ethnic identity (e.g., Waters 1990) and how the boundaries of Whiteness had been contested over time (e.g., Brodkin 1998; Roediger 1999), to focus more closely on the coherence of a White American racial identity. This brought a wave of research that broadly characterized Whiteness as "a core set of racial interests often obscured by seemingly race-neutral words, actions, or policies" (Hartigan 1997, 496). Central to this definition was the idea of Whiteness as "obscured," whether intentionally or unintentionally so. Research in this paradigm illuminated the "colorblind" language White people use to avoid sounding racist (Bonilla-Silva 2002) or to discursively distance themselves from practices that perpetuate racial inequality in which they themselves nonetheless engage (DiTomaso 2013). Research also highlighted (dis)comfort as a core concern governing how White people speak about race, exemplified by White people's avoidance of mentioning race when a Black person is present (Norton et al. 2006). More recently, scholars have noted a shift toward more active identification as "White" among White Americans (Jardina 2019). Correspondingly, scholars have challenged the passivity implied by theories of colorblindness, instead emphasizing White people's effortful pursuit of racial ignorance in order to preserve their dominance (Mueller 2020). We will see a combination of both evasive and active engagement with Whiteness play out among White residents of Baton Rouge (although I emphasize White agency throughout).

My concern, however, is not what Whiteness is as much as how being White—and thus inhabiting a dominant position in the racial order—is related to both the opinions White people hold and the ultimate consequences of those opinions for politics. Accordingly, the key insight standpoint theory offers my analysis in Baton Rouge is that, as anthropologist David Graeber (2015, 72) puts it, hierarchies produce "highly lopsided structures of the imagination." Those at the top of a hierarchy are required to do considerably less interpretive labor, and give considerably less thought to the experiences of those at the bottom, than vice versa.

Note that, unlike Frankenberg, I do not propose that a shared "standpoint" exists among White residents of Baton Rouge. Although Frankenberg's artic-ulation of a White standpoint is consistent with standpoint *theory* and the premise that dominant subjects are limited in their perspective, her use of "standpoint" as a *term* contradicts the consensus among standpoint theorists that a standpoint is something that must be achieved. That is, it takes inter-pretive effort to turn an oppressive feature of a subordinate position into a critical understanding of the workings of power (Harding 2004). Accordingly, I identify, in more neutral terms, a White "perspective" or "vantage point" that is evident among White people in Baton Rouge.[17]

My analysis should not assign individualized blame to White people for tending to have a limited capacity for imagination, empathy, or under-standing when it comes to racial politics. On a group level, however, these limitations stem from White people's place in a hierarchy that they have collectively built, maintained, and benefited from. Such is the consequence of the epistemology of ignorance on which White dominance is built— producing what Mills (1997, 18) calls "the ironic outcome that whites will in general be unable to understand the world *they themselves have made*" (emphasis added). Mills's reference to "whites . . . in general" recognizes that some White people are in fact deeply committed to better understanding the world they have made. Yet, commitment alone does not necessarily bring insight into the workings of power. For example, White individuals who identify as antiracist are nonetheless prone to express racial identities that are remarkably similar to those of White nationalists (Hughey 2010). As Nancy Hartsock (2004, 36–37) puts it, "[T]here are some perspectives on society from which, however well-intentioned one may be, the real relations of humans with each other and with the natural world are not visible."

In Chapter 3, bringing an interpretive lens and the insights of standpoint theory to my conversations about St. George allows me to show how White residents negotiate between both outgroup and ingroup-oriented feelings of prejudice in the present day. They work hard not to seem to embrace anti-Black (i.e., outgroup-oriented) animus but are less cautious about prioritizing White interests. Although the views of White residents who fought *against* St. George illuminate the possibilities of motivating racially tolerant individ-uals to action, I ultimately identify a shared perspective across the polarized sample. This emerges in the form of four common discursive practices: (1) denying racial motivations behind White attitudes or actions (such as the St. George incorporation effort); (2) minimizing the relevance of racial categories to material outcomes; (3) centering White concerns and leaving Black ones invisible (unless referencing Black bodies, and often Black children, as sources of harm); and (4) defending the social order, particularly through a belief in "togetherness" that does little to challenge White dominance. In other words, even as what the White respondents *say* varies, what they *do* is reproduce the same practices that reify the color line—as both a metaphorical and physical divide—in Baton Rouge. From their privileged position in the racial order, not to mention their privileged position within the geography of Baton Rouge, the White respondents claim authority to explain the workings of the color line (or at times to deny its existence) and reveal little appreciation that their viewpoint is conditioned by their dominant position.

What about the standpoint of the Black individuals I encountered in Baton Rouge? Earlier in this chapter, I noted that reflections collected from Black residents provide a valuable contrast to the White residents' views as well as offer additional ethnographic insight into the workings of Whiteness in Baton Rouge. Yet, as I also noted, the perspective of Black people in Baton Rouge merits more attention than the scope of this book allows. I therefore do not claim to have illuminated either the coherence of or the diversity within a "Black perspective" in Baton Rouge, or to have fully demonstrated the extent to which Black residents have achieved the standpoint of nondominant subjects—tasks that would require closer study of the Black residents on their own terms. The evidence this book *does* share from my Black interviewees nonetheless will illustrate the understanding they have gained of the racial order through their lived experiences—and will serve as another reminder that White opinion on St. George and related issues is consequential not for its own sake, but because White Baton Rougeans have a disproportionate amount of power to impact the lives of their Black neighbors.

Revisiting Racial Threat: White Opposition to Welfare and Affirmative Action (Chapters 4 and 5)

My study in Baton Rouge ultimately shows what activated attitudes look like in a specific local context; the variety of responses we can expect when race is salient; and the color line's ability to stay intact—evident in the constraints of White vision, even among those working to dismantle the color line's physical manifestations. Turning to quantitative methods in the latter part of the book allows me to explore these dynamics across different settings, each with their own manifestations of the attitudinal and material color lines. And crucially, returning to the well-worn path of investigating racial threat via survey data allows me to demonstrate how explicitly recognizing White viewership in the process both theoretically reframes the relationship between prejudice and place and encourages new empirical findings.

Moving Beyond Baton Rouge and the Case of St. George

Chapters 4 and 5 focus on two paradigmatically racialized policy areas that, like schooling and municipal incorporation in Baton Rouge, fundamentally concern the distribution of social goods, opportunities, or benefits—thus prompting debate about what both Black and White Americans deserve. Because welfare powerfully provokes imagery of "undeserving" Black people, whereas affirmative action prompts White people to reflect on their *own* deservingness of access to jobs, these two issues demonstrate the coherence of White people's vantage point across both outgroup- and ingroup-oriented prejudices, much as was the case in Baton Rouge.

In each chapter, I focus on a time period when the racialized issues at hand would have been salient across the United States, just as the context of the St. George effort offered a valuable time to explore White Baton Rouge residents' attitudes on local schools. Chapter 4 turns to one of the most quintessential examples of a racialized policy at a time when it was particularly salient—following the 1996 reforms that sought to "end welfare as we know it" but failed to de-racialize welfare policy. It is therefore in the wake of debates that used imagery of the Black poor to stigmatize welfare that I investigate White responses to the visible stigmas of welfare in a given local context. Chapter 5 is set against the backdrop of the 2007–2009 recession— when unemployment was increasing rapidly, and Obama's election offered at least one prominent example of a high-status Black American. This offers a compelling setting in which to consider how reducing racial inequality and improving race relations do not necessarily go hand in hand, exploring localized White fears of Black Americans "catching up" in economic standing and the effect of these fears on opposition to affirmative action.

Tracing the White Perspective Through Quantitative Study

Throughout these analyses, I follow the classic approach of the racial threat hypothesis by pairing survey data with location data. I primarily leverage the location files of the General Social Survey (GSS), and I pair these files with data on racial demographics, economic conditions, and segregation to analyze White policy preferences in light of where White individuals live across the

United States.[18] I also supplement my analyses by replicating my results with data from the American National Election Study (ANES).

Importantly, I understand context as more than a "stand-in for clusters of variables," a critique that has been levied against the prevailing approach in contextual research (Gieryn 2000, 466). With insight gained from Baton Rouge, I assume that White residents of cities across the United States interpret and assign racialized meanings to their surroundings. Accordingly, whereas Ryan Enos (2017, ch. 2) interrogates what he calls "the demagogue of space" in shaping attitudes (including as Enos explores and manipulates space in the context of a laboratory), I am interested in something closer to *place*. By place, I mean space that is invested with meaning or value, space that is lived and felt and understood (Gieryn 2000, 465)—places like the one this book visits, in Baton Rouge, where racial identity is interwoven with geography. My analytic approach still resembles a positivist one in technical terms, and does not afford detailed exploration of the construct of place as it relates to meaning and power (i.e., the work of poststructuralist geography; see, e.g., Bourdieu 1990; Lefebvre 1991; Soja 1989). Nonetheless, the distinction I make between space and place helps ground the distinction between conventional applications of the threat hypothesis and this book's novel approach.

Specifically, the appreciation of the White vantage point gained from my analysis in Baton Rouge informs my quantitative analyses of White welfare and affirmative action preferences in two key ways. First, it demands we reject the framing of White people as victims and reckon with the power dynamics of White vision in any quantitative application of the racial threat hypothesis. Ignoring the position from which something is seen leaves the seer "unable to be called to account" (Haraway 1988, 582–583)—a point that should apply to White research subjects as well as to (typically) White researchers.

Second, appreciating the White vantage point helps highlight the varied ways White people might (or might not) construe their surroundings as threatening. Just as St. George critics were moved to action against the incorporation effort, might we see the activation of racially *tolerant* attitudes around prominent policy issues in other contexts? Just as the St. George opponents nonetheless displayed striking similarities to the St. George proponents in their outlooks, can we tease apart the kinds of "threats" that will activate the defenses of racially hostile and tolerant White people alike? This is an analytic approach that, as Matthew Hughey (2010, 1306) would put it, is "sensitized to both white homogeneity and heterogeneity;" and these are the questions I explore—while also striving to reject the typical conceptual practices of power in the study of racial threat—in Chapters 4 and 5.

My first quantitative application revisits the oft-identified relationship between outgroup-oriented prejudice and opposition to welfare spending, the archetypically racialized policy area that White Americans have long associated with undeserving Black beneficiaries. Chapter 4 introduces the concept of White viewership to the classic racial threat hypothesis.[19] Building on research that has demonstrated people's responsiveness to both racial and economic geography, I ask how the demographics White people see in their surroundings inform the opinions they express on welfare. I show that racial attitudes are more predictive of welfare preferences not simply where the stigmas of welfare are salient due to a large Black population or high poverty rate, but more specifically where residential segregation makes Black or poor households more visible from the viewpoint of White households. In addition to endorsing the importance of theorizing White viewership, this analysis also recognizes the diversity of views *within* White Americans' positionality, much as was the case in Baton Rouge. Though they look through a shared racial lens, Chapter 4 shows how White people's perception of their surroundings varies according to the different kinds of prejudices that they hold—or that they reject. While a proximate Black population may indicate threat to some White viewers and exacerbate opposition to welfare spending, it can simultaneously activate racially tolerant behavior in other viewers, making tolerant White people more likely to *support* welfare spending.

The second quantitative application in Chapter 5 turns to affirmative action, a quintessential case that requires White people to consider what they believe their ingroup deserves—and invites greater recognition of class diversity within and among the Black populations that may be interpreted as threatening by White viewers. In investigating White Americans' ingroup-oriented prejudices in settings beyond Baton Rouge, I identify a novel status threat response among prejudiced *and* tolerant White individuals: perceptions of a rising Black middle class exacerbate local opposition to affirmative action in employment, whereas White people who feel their status over Black people is secure are more supportive of affirmative action. Calling out White people's positionality and how it leads to defensiveness of White privilege supports my identification of the possible threat White people perceive in a rising Black middle class—a population often described as nonthreatening. My analysis further reveals that White people were most likely to sense a status threat from the Black middle class in areas hit hardest by rising unemployment during the 2007–2009 recession. In such settings, prejudiced and tolerant White people alike tended to believe that Black people were getting *richer*, while White people were getting poorer, despite the devastating effects of the recession on Black Americans. These findings highlight the subjectivity of White vision in construing Black people as threatening, and the consistency of the White vantage point, even among racially tolerant White people—as was the case in Baton Rouge.

•

The specific findings of each of my qualitative and quantitative studies could stand on their own. It is together, however, that they bring a critical lens to the typically positivist study of prejudice and place, traversing a breadth of topics to show the wide potential of explicitly conceptualizing White Americans' subjective, racialized perspective. And it is together that I hope these studies contribute to a conversation about the theoretical and empirical imperative to be clear about to whom exactly Black Americans are visible or invisible.

My argument should not imply that racial identity deterministically informs public opinion on racial issues. In addition to emphasizing the diversity of racial attitudes held among White Americans, throughout the book I consider how class status and partisanship shape opinion. Moreover, my focus on the Black–White divide neither should minimize the multiethnic diversity of the United States and the shared experiences of many people of color, nor should it essentialize "Black" and "White" as fixed categories that are homogenous and unchangeable rather than constituted by a specific political moment (for more on these topics, see Hochschild, Weaver, and Burch 2012). Rather, my focus reflects and recognizes that the racial identity of Black Americans has proved to be remarkably durable, and that Black Americans' experiences of inequality and discrimination have been remarkably severe.

Ultimately, by not losing sight of Black people's experiences when studying White attitudes, this book forwards an approach that insists on recognizing the duality of the color line to explain its durability. To emphasize the color line as both attitudinal and material is not new. Frederick Douglass himself recognized this duality in his original usage. He writes: "The color is innocent enough, but things with which it is coupled make it hated ... servility, poverty, dependence, are undesirable conditions. When these shall cease to be coupled with color, there will be no color line drawn" (Douglass 1881, 575).

Much literature in American racial politics operates on a similar optimistic assumption: that material and attitudinal progress will go hand in hand. This is hardly surprising. Research seeing racial inequality as a problem worthy of study naturally orients itself toward an end point where skin color does not determine life chances. I by no means challenge this ultimate goal. Yet, the analysis presented in this book suggests a thornier path ahead. My findings offer optimism about the activation of racially tolerant White people at the same time as pessimism about even some of the most tolerant White people's capacity to reflect on, and to take responsibility for, their racialized viewpoint. In other words, even as Blackness slowly dissociates from some of the worst social conditions, and as White Americans drop some of their old prejudices, we still should expect the color line to put up a fight. This may come in the form of "White rage" (C. Anderson 2016) or "White backlash" (Hughey 2014; Abrajano and Hajnal 2017) in the face of non-White people's advancement—but it can also come in the form of continued White blindness, ignorance, and complacency.

This is less a pessimistic proclamation than an honest one. Douglass went on to point out the "inconsistencies of the color-line feeling" as evidence of racism's "hollowness" (576). It is hollow indeed, but if we are to have any hope of breaking down the color line, then we must appreciate racism's inconsistencies as part of its strength as well as its vulnerability. This is why I name the color line's flexibility: to identify where it is likely to harden, to keep us vigilant when it seems to have receded, and to contemplate the potential of helping the line bend toward inclusion, and maybe, one day, break.

2
The Case of St. George and the Outsider Within

Although Baton Rouge is the state capital of Louisiana, locals will tell you that it feels more like a big small town than a small big city. Its largely suburban population of 800,000 is spread across 4,000 square miles. In contrast to its illustrious neighbors of Cajun country in Lafayette and the Creole and cosmopolitan New Orleans, Baton Rouge seems content to be known for family, faith, and, most importantly, football.

A certain lack of cultural distinctiveness makes Baton Rouge an easier setting to introduce. Though a thoroughly Southern city, it nonetheless resembles many others across the United States: cleanly divided into Black and White, poor and rich, north and south.

What motivates this book's focus on Baton Rouge, however, is the St. George incorporation effort that unfolded around 2012 and achieved success at the ballot box in October 2019. The victory represented the culmination of an initiative by residents of the unincorporated parts of East Baton Rouge Parish to break away from the current consolidated city–parish governance structure and create a new municipality. Leaders of the effort made clear from the start that their top priority was to create a new, independent school district for residents of the southeastern part of the parish.

For those familiar with Baton Rouge's troubled history as home to the longest school desegregation lawsuit in the country, the St. George effort raised a red flag. The incorporation of St. George would create one of the richest and Whitest cities in Louisiana, severing the area's existing ties with the city of Baton Rouge and the larger East Baton Rouge School District— both of which are majority-Black and disproportionately impoverished. Race constantly lurked in the background (and sometimes entered the foreground) of debates over St. George. Moreover, while the St. George effort focused residents' attention on a specific, racialized debate about education—a convenient topic to explore through interviews—race is potentially salient anywhere and on any given day in Baton Rouge. This salience was only heightened following the killing of Alton Sterling by police in July 2016, and

How the Color Line Bends: The Geography of White Prejudice in Modern America. Nina M. Yancy,
Oxford University Press. © Oxford University Press 2022. DOI: 10.1093/oso/9780197599426.003.0002

arguably also heightened when White people were in conversation with me as a Black interviewer.

In this chapter and the next, I take a deep dive into the racialized setting of Baton Rouge to interrogate the White perspective and how it helps explain White political behavior when race is salient. I will show that White Baton Rougeans' behavior illustrates outgroup-oriented animus toward Black people (or, in today's world, efforts *not* to appear to express such animus) as much as ingroup-oriented concerns for White people's deservingness of certain advantages (such as access to superior education). These are the same concerns this book later explores by analyzing welfare and affirmative action preferences, where a shared racial vantage point on local geography again is evident in the opinions White people express. However, my analysis in Baton Rouge first lays a critical foundation by showing how White individuals' preferences—as revealed and rationalized in ordinary conversation, and within a particular, local world—reveal the constraints of their viewpoint from atop the racial order. Chapter 3 will present evidence from my conversations about St. George. Before that, this chapter sets the scene in Baton Rouge, introduces the St. George effort, and addresses my own positionality as researcher in such a setting.

Baton Rouge's long road from segregated schools to court-ordered integration to de facto *re*-segregation illustrates the flexibility of White attitudes and actions as they have evolved to maintain White privilege—particularly against the prospect of the "threat" of integration. In a sense, St. George presents a post-threat scenario: White people in East Baton Rouge Parish are no longer facing the active "danger" of Black students integrating into White schools. Rather, St. George supporters hope to formalize an arrangement resulting from decades of White flight, and to do so by drawing a new city boundary that happens to closely track the color line.

To be clear, the St. George incorporation effort worked hard to defend itself against claims that it was racially motivated. This shows how far Louisiana has come since the unambiguous racism of Huey Long in the 1930s, or since Southern White voters first led V. O. Key to identify the geography of threat in the 1940s. Yet, this chapter also will suggest what has *not* changed in Louisiana, including persistent Black–White inequality as well as White Southerners' skill when talking about—or around—race. What Gunnar Myrdal (1944) commented of his encounters with White Southerners in the 1940s arguably remains true today: "Everything can be said in the South if it is said 'in the right way'" (36).

Here lies the importance of appreciating the perspective from which White Americans view racial politics: a perspective that informs them of the "right way" to say things, and a perspective that, even with good intentions, tends to center White interests. Heeding standpoint theory's lesson that everything is seen from somewhere, I close this chapter by reflecting on my own perspective as an "outsider within" Baton Rouge—both in literal terms as a visitor to the area (albeit with deep connections to it), and in theoretical terms as a Black woman researcher in conversation with mostly White (and some Black) research subjects (see Collins 1986). But to begin, I trace the history that motivates my study of the area, and map out the racialized geography that made the St. George effort possible in the first place.

A Divided Parish

Besides college football and the Christian church, it is hard to think of many institutions more visibly central to life in Baton Rouge than the Interstate. Interstates, to be more precise, as East Baton Rouge Parish is home to several, along with uncommonly bad traffic. TomTom Traffic, a major international index, ranked Baton Rouge 11th among all American cities for congestion as of 2019—one of the highest rankings for a midsize urban area. Particularly in the bustling southeastern part of the parish, congestion is prominent but complaints about it even more so. A complaint about long evening commutes, which in Baton Rouge take 1.7 times longer than if traffic were free-flowing, is appropriate to throw into almost any conversation.

Whether or not the traffic deserves the amount of attention it gets, the topic evokes a point journalist Robert Samuelson once made: "To understand America, you must understand highways."[1]

My own effort to understand Baton Rouge in the summer of 2016 began on the highway, with a rainy drive on Interstate 10 (I-10) on my first morning in town. I had picked up a rental car in Prairieville—one of the distant but rapidly growing bedroom suburbs of Baton Rouge, located in neighboring Ascension Parish—which gave me several miles of bayou to traverse as I headed northwest and crossed into East Baton Rouge Parish (see map in Figure 2.1). As the sparse scenery grew denser, I passed the Country Club of Louisiana, home to some of the state's most expensive real estate; the buzzing Mall of Louisiana, the parish's biggest source of sales tax; and, nearing the city center, the urban lakes behind which lies the sprawling campus of Louisiana State University (LSU). So far, Baton Rouge appeared to be a relatively prosperous metro area.

Things changed drastically when I merged onto Interstate 110 (I-110), just past the exit for Florida Boulevard—a street my interview subjects would

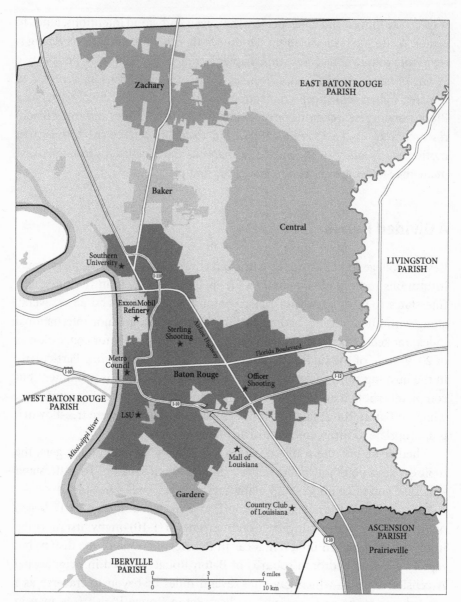

Fig. 2.1 Map of East Baton Rouge Parish

Map uses census TIGER/Line shapefiles for county and city boundaries, major roads, and water, based on the 2010 census. At the time of writing, the East Baton Rouge School District encompassed the entire parish except for the cities of Baker, Central, and Zachary. The boundaries of the St. George incorporation and school district proposed in the 2015 vote would have encompassed most of the lighter-shaded, unincorporated land in the southeast part of East Baton Rouge Parish, as well as the area labeled Gardere (a census-designated place). The St. George incorporation that eventually passed in October 2019 represents a considerably smaller area in the southeast. For the official boundaries of the proposed city of St. George in both the 2015 and 2019 votes, see Figure 2.2. Note that the Baton Rouge city boundaries shown here, as well as the 2019 St. George boundaries in Figure 2.2, have remained in flux, while parts of the proposed St. George incorporation have been annexed into Baton Rouge—a practice that started in opposition to the 2015 incorporation effort and that has persisted as the 2019 vote continues to be contested.

later describe as the "equator," "Mason–Dixon line," or "great dividing line." Whatever it's called, Florida Boulevard is understood to be the border of North Baton Rouge (NBR), which used to be the heart of the blue-collar White community but is now over 90% Black. My journey took me a bit further north through blighted neighborhoods before I found a parking spot on the campus of Southern University, a historically Black institution. I was there for a funeral.

Thousands of other people had made a similar journey that day to attend the funeral of Alton Sterling—the Black man killed at point-blank range on July 5th, 2016, by two White members of the Baton Rouge police force. I may not have realized at the time, but almost every part of the story this chapter tells about race, class, and geography was on display in the 30 miles I traveled to NBR: the disrepair evident on Southern's campus compared to the gleaming grounds of LSU; the location of the I-10/I-110 junction at the center of what used to be a vibrant Black neighborhood before the highway was built; the wealth of the southeastern part of the parish embodied in the Mall and Country Club of Louisiana; Prarieville's reputation as either a "White flight" community or a place known for "good schools," depending on who you ask; and the highway-facilitated sprawl that had me traversing 30 miles in the first place.

Baton Rouge's sprawled, segregated, and car-dominated landscape is far from unique among American cities. In that sense, it offers a paradigmatic setting for a qualitative study of White Americans' racialized political behavior as contextualized by local geography. The particularities of Baton Rouge's geography, however, are key to understanding the effort to create the city of St. George.

The Racialized Geography of Baton Rouge

East Baton Rouge (EBR) Parish has had a consolidated city–parish (i.e., city–county) government since 1947, with a Mayor–President and Metro Council presiding over both the city of Baton Rouge and the larger parish. The city had little incentive to annex land as the area grew in the following years: for decades, the city–parish distinction was of little significance. Residents may have known whether the EBR Sheriff's Office or Baton Rouge Police Department would have answered an emergency call, but few could tell you exactly where the jagged boundary line was.

The past several years have made that line drastically more meaningful as a result of the St. George effort, which in its original 2014–2015 campaign

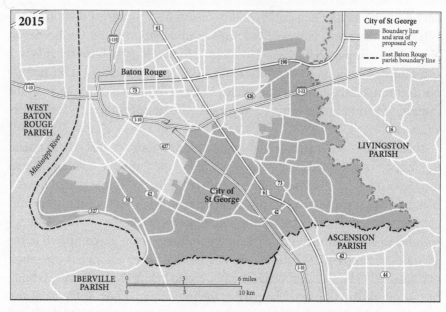

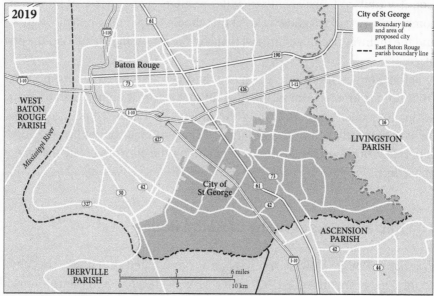

Fig. 2.2 Maps of Proposed City of St. George

Figures drawn based on maps that were created by organizers of the St. George incorporation effort and provided on their official website (www.stgeorgelouisiana.com; accessed November 10, 2019).

proposed to include all the unincorporated land in the southeastern parish in a new city, complete with its own school district. If the campaign culminating in 2015 had been successful, 107,000 people who lived across 85 square miles of unincorporated EBR Parish would have become residents of the city of

St. George. The new city would have been 70% White and 23% Black—in contrast to the population living within the city lines of Baton Rouge, which is 40% White and 55% Black.

When the effort relaunched in 2018–2019, the organizers proposed to incorporate a smaller area, with 86,00 residents across 60 square miles— notably eliminating a number of predominately Black neighborhoods originally included within the proposed boundaries (meaning these neighborhoods were no longer eligible to vote on the incorporation). An official St. George spokesperson explained this to the local media as a nonracial, strategic move: "Demographics are irrelevant to me. We wanted the votes, and we went where the support was located" (J. Clark 2019). In practical terms, this meant that the second map the St. George organizers drew was even wealthier and Whiter than before. The city that voters in the area ultimately decided to incorporate in 2019 is only 12% Black in a majority-Black parish.

In formalizing the previously perfunctory border between the southern part of the parish and the central city, the creation of St. George separates the area with the highest level of human development in Louisiana from the area with the lowest (Burd-Sharps, Lewis, and Martins 2009).[2]

Table 2.1 summarizes these disparities across the larger Baton Rouge area based on a state-wide study. Between the area encompassing St. George and NBR, there is a four-year difference in life expectancy, an almost 20 percentage-point difference in high school diploma attainment, and a 30 percentage-point difference in bachelor's degree attainment. The similarities between St. George and South Baton Rouge city further illustrate that the city boundary is much less consequential for life outcomes than the line traced along Florida Boulevard, marking the boundary of NBR.

Such a landscape, where creating a new boundary could drastically change the official demographics of the areas on either side, is a product of longstanding trends. The White population in the city of Baton Rouge has been declining since 1980 as White households have left the central city for suburbs.[3] White households also have been moving out of EBR parish entirely, with a net migration of 13,574 native-born residents leaving EBR between 2010 and 2016 (see Figure 2.3); EBR's population increase of around 7,000 during these years is attributable to births and a small amount of international migration. By contrast, the population of neighboring Ascension Parish grew by 14,393, representing a 13.4% increase between 2010 and 2016.

In the process, the area has become more segregated on a macro level. As White along with affluent Black households moved away from the central city, NBR became disproportionately Black and poor. The construction of highways facilitated this racial and economic sorting, not only by easing travel

Table 2.1 Human Development in the Baton Rouge Area

Area	Encompassing Parish Group	Rank in state	Human Development Index	Life expectancy (years)	High school diploma (%)	Bachelor's degree (%)	Median earnings (2007 dollars)	Black population (%)
St. George	E. Baton Rouge (South)-W. Baton Rouge	1	5.73	77.3	91.2	40.6	32,631	23
South Baton Rouge (city)	E. Baton Rouge (South)	3	5.12	76.7	90.6	45.7	23,841	26
Northern EBR Parish	E. Baton Rouge (North)	8	4.47	76.0	85.8	18.8	26,935	42
North Baton Rouge (city)	E. Baton Rouge (North and Central)	36	2.51	72.7	73.3	14.2	16,398	88

Data drawn from "Portrait of Louisiana" Human Development study (Burd-Sharps, Lewis, and Martins 2009). Parish groups reflect the units used in the study; as one of the state's most populous parishes, EBR was divided into smaller units for analysis, and its unincorporated areas (i.e., the St. George area) were grouped with a neighboring parish, West Baton Rouge, whose population is only about 25,000. The divide between "South Baton Rouge" and "North Baton Rouge" roughly follows Florida Boulevard (see map in Figure 2.1).

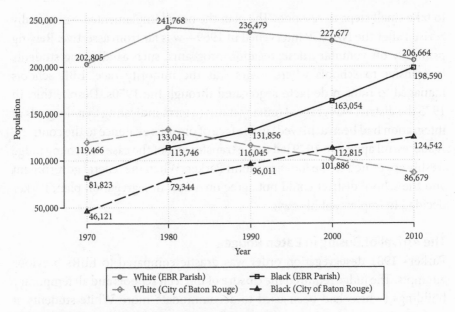

Fig. 2.3 Demographic Shifts in the Baton Rouge Area

Figure illustrates the declining White population and growing Black population in both the city of Baton Rouge and EBR Parish. The city is now majority-Black, and the parish is nearly half Black.

Source: U.S. Census, 1970–2010.

to the periphery of the parish but also due to the placement of I-10 through the heart of Old South Baton Rouge, a historically vibrant, Black neighborhood that began a precipitous decline when construction of the highway started in the late 1950s. My father's childhood home was one of the countless that were taken by eminent domain, and for which little compensation was given. This story is one of many examples of the demolition of Black neighborhoods nationwide in the name of urban expansion and renewal.[4] Baton Rouge similarly is reflective of national patterns when it comes to the reason that the disproportionately wealthy and White southeastern part of the parish wanted to form a new city in the first place. Its stated primary goal was to break away from the EBR public school system—the defendant in the longest federal desegregation lawsuit in the country.

Desegregation and the Fracturing of EBR Schools

The EBR Parish School Board's long battle with desegregation began in 1956 when, in light of Baton Rouge's starkly segregated schools following the 1954 *Brown v. Board of Education of Topeka* decision, the Justice Department filed a lawsuit against the EBR school board. Only in 1963 did the school board begin to take small steps to respond. The plan the board implemented—minimally revised after the NAACP intervened in 1969—was far from assertive. Relying primarily on voluntary desegregation programs, such as allowing students to transfer to schools where theirs was the minority race, EBR schools managed to remain de facto segregated through the 1970s. Despite this, in 1975 the district was granted unitary status (a term indicating that the goals of integration had been achieved) in the face of obvious evidence to the contrary. A successful appeal in 1979 led to the transferring of the case to a young judge freshly appointed to the judiciary, John Parker. When the federal government and the school district could not agree on a new desegregation plan, Parker decided to implement his own.

The Arrival of Busing in Baton Rouge

Parker's 1981 desegregation order was drastic compared to EBR's previous attempts. The judge required the closure of thirteen schools and all temporary buildings (which had been used to accommodate more White students at majority-White schools so they could avoid transferring to majority-Black schools). Parker also required that the school board gain court approval for any changes that would affect the racial distribution of students (Cowen Institute 2010). Most notable, however, was the decision to reassign students to schools across the sprawling district, to which students would travel by bus in order to achieve a racial balance.[5]

Parker's plan was similar to contemporaneous "busing" initiatives across the country that sought to address a persistent racial imbalance in schools following the *Brown* decision. Civil rights leaders at the time, as well as historian Matthew Delmont (2016) more recently, pointed out that busing itself was a fabricated issue: children traveling to school on buses was hardly a new innovation. White children in particular had always been more likely to enjoy a bus ride to school than Black children, who were more likely to walk. The debates that emerged over busing and "neighborhood schools," Delmont argues, allowed White people to oppose school desegregation in race-neutral terms, all the while centering the feelings of White families rather than the constitutional rights of Black ones.

Needless to say, busing was deeply unpopular among White Americans: in the early 1980s, when Parker brought busing to Baton Rouge, the GSS found that 82% of White people nationwide opposed mandatory busing, even as 88% said that Black and White students should attend the same schools (similar to the seemingly contradictory opinions many White people have expressed about affirmative action and welfare, as we will see later in this book).[6] Beyond the approximately 50% of White students reassigned to predominately Black schools who simply did not show up for the first day of class, school districts that enforced mandatory desegregation programs lost an average of 13% of their White student populations overall (Rossell 2010).

These national trends suggest how the busing order was to play out in Baton Rouge. In the fall of 1981, enrollment in EBR public schools fell by 4,722 pupils (7%) (Marcus 1981). One state representative at the time (who would go on to be a public proponent of the St. George movement) successfully sponsored a bill removing virtually all requirements for home schooling, in order to "[give] people an escape from a bad system" (par. 4). And private schools swelled to absorb more students. It is hard to precisely measure private school enrollment before the Private School Universe survey began in 1989. But, as one of my respondents told me, many in Baton Rouge believe that "the Catholic Church has been the biggest beneficiary of the desegregation suit," citing memories of how quickly Catholic schools grew as White students left public schools in droves throughout the 1980s. A case study of Boston during this period estimated that students transferring to Catholic schools accounted for 20% of the school district's loss of approximately 2,000 White students (J. T. Hannon 1984; for a broader discussion of race and the public–private school divide, see also Fairlie and Resch 2002; Reardon and Yun 2006). Amidst all this, Judge Parker, himself a White graduate of EBR public schools, received death threats, was socially ostracized, and for years traveled with a U.S. marshal for protection.

The busing era still looms large in the collective memory of Baton Rouge. As we will see in the next chapter, nostalgia for pre-busing "neighborhood schools" or "community schools" features prominently in the rhetoric of many White residents who support initiatives such as St. George. The majority of Black residents I encountered in Baton Rouge had mixed feelings about desegregation, recognizing its necessity but also lamenting its negative impacts. One Black respondent lamented not being able to attend the same school that generations of his family had attended. Two retired Black school principals were similarly melancholy when recounting the loss of their most talented teachers, when the effort to achieve a racial mix at the staff level sent the top-performing Black teachers to the traditionally White schools and the weakest White teachers to the Black schools. When I asked my own father about his experience (which dates to the years of half-hearted integration shortly before Parker's order), he said plainly: "They took what was good from us." All the while, the flood of White students out of the parish continued, taking human, social, and economic capital with it.

By the 1990s, when it was clear that busing had not succeeded in desegregating the district, the school board began to pursue unitary status via a new plan. A 1996 consent decree (i.e., a settlement without admission of liability) brought a return to community-based attendance zones in Baton Rouge. The decree also created "magnet" schools with special focuses, intended to attract high-quality students of all races from across the district. Magnet schools were (and still are) seen by many to be a more sustainable and successful way of achieving desegregation goals, although others have long pointed out their potentially negative effects on equity across districts (Price and Stern 1987) as well as within magnet schools themselves (K. C. West 1994). In the case of Baton Rouge, magnet schools have been high performing on the whole but could hardly be credited with desegregating the district. In 2016, over half of White students in the district attended a magnet school (and most of the rest attended "A" or "B" graded schools) compared to 30% of Black students attending magnet schools.[7] The district's flagship Baton Rouge Magnet High School offers an example, at 33% White and 45% Black, and with 50% of its students classified as economically disadvantaged.[8] Though not a homogeneously White or wealthy school, it stands out in a school system that is 11% White and 81% Black, and also 81% economically disadvantaged.

Judge Parker quit the case in 2001, exercising his right as a senior judge to do so. Shortly after, the school district petitioned for unitary status, ahead of the deadline of 2004 that Parker had set. More out of fatigue than any sense of success, the desegregation litigation was finally brought to a close through a settlement agreement in 2003.

From Busing to Breakaway Districts

Although the district officially remained under court oversight until 2007, rapid changes followed the settlement agreement. These developments made Baton Rouge a vivid example of the pattern of school districts across the country resegregating as they were released from court orders in the 1990s and early 2000s. This happened in seventy districts during the Clinton administration, and double that during the second Bush administration (Reardon et al. 2012).[9] After decades of frustration, deterioration in EBR's facilities while the district was prohibited from building new schools, and the departure of White and middle-income students, the end of federal oversight saw three parts of the EBR school system break off and form independent school districts.

First were the cities of Baker and Zachary, two small municipalities that were founded in the northwestern part of the parish in the late 1800s but had historically been part of the EBR school district. Parents in both areas had been agitating to form their own districts well before the lifting of Parker's order and, after 2003, finally were able to do so. Central, LA, an unincorporated suburb in the northeast of the parish, soon followed suit. Central incorporated as a city in 2005 and then formed a new school district in 2007.[10] Central's departure from the district reduced EBR's White student population to its current standing of 11%. In 1980, before the busing order, the White population of EBR schools stood at 60% (Nossiter 2003).

This brings us to the present era, and to my time in Baton Rouge in 2016. The Louisiana Department of Education ranked the Zachary and Central school districts at #1 and #2 in the state as of 2016. In the #3 and #4 spots were Livingston Parish and Ascension Parish schools—both major destinations for people leaving EBR. By contrast, the EBR district was ranked #60 out of seventy-three districts statewide in 2016. These disparate rankings are not surprising when we consider the different demographics of the school districts (Table 2.2), given the correlation between academic performance and economic disadvantage at both the individual and school level—and the undeniable overlap between economic disadvantage and race (Caldas and Bankston 1997).

The disparity between school districts further helps introduce the grievances vocalized by the St. George effort, and echoed by many Baton Rouge residents regardless of their interest or investment in issues of education. It is commonplace to hear Zachary and Central cited as models of excellence.[11] It is similarly commonplace for St. George supporters to ignore Baker when pointing to examples of prior breakaway school districts (Baker's population changed drastically, from majority-White to majority-Black and lower income, by the time it secured its own district).[12] And when it comes to EBR schools, a resounding chorus claims that the system is "broken" and "failing." Especially when compared to Zachary and Central, EBR school district employees are likely to point out that the previous breakaway districts took with them a sizable chunk of high-performing EBR students and their associated funding. The breakaway districts also took school facilities that used to belong to EBR, along with revenue streams to support the pensions of retired teachers who had taught in those schools. Had a St. George school district been formed in 2015, it would have displaced over 8,000 students, representing a further loss of resources to EBR (Together Baton Rouge 2014, 3).

The successful 2019 incorporation, though smaller (an area home to 86,000 as opposed to over 100,000), still is estimated to displace around 3,600 students if the new district's boundaries follow the new city's. EBR school

Table 2.2 Snapshot of School Districts in East Baton Rouge Parish, 2016

District	Rank in state	2016 District letter grade	Students in district	Free/reduced lunch	Proficiency on state exams	Per capita income	Racial makeup
Zachary Community Schools District	1	A	7 schools 5,335 students	43%	75%	$76,154	45% Black 51% White
Central Community Schools District	2	A	5 schools 4,315 students	53%	75%	$74,986	19% Black 76% White
East Baton Rouge Parish School District	60	C	82 schools 42,334 students	81%	50%	$47,164	81% Black 11% White
City of Baker School District	67	D	5 schools 1,753 students	81%	39%	$44,236	94% Black <5% White

Data from Louisiana Department of Education. Exam proficiency refers to student performance on "end of course" tests required for high school diploma. In the 2017–2018 school year, a family of four at 185% of the federal poverty line (earning less than $45,510 annually) would qualify for reduced price meals at public schools, and would qualify for free meals at 130% of the poverty line (earning less than $31,980 annually), according to the U.S. Department of Agriculture.

officials are estimating a loss of $85 million in annual revenue. They also expect EBR's White student population to shrink to 8% from 12% (Lussier 2019).

In keeping with rhetoric dating back to the pre-*Brown* era, St. George advocates argued for the positives of creating "neighborhood schools" with reference to the damage busing had done, and with concerns that EBR was "still busing kids all over the parish." The reality, however, is that the only students still bused outside their attendance zones are bused voluntarily— either to attend magnet schools or, for students in underperforming schools, to attend higher-performing schools as space allows. It was the latter of these student populations, composed of virtually no White students, that community groups fighting against St. George were worried was being inaccurately represented. Far from floods of Black students from within the city lines traveling to the unincorporated area to attend school, 91% of the students who traversed the city line as of 2014 did so in the opposite direction: living in the unincorporated area and attending schools in the city of Baton Rouge, rather than vice versa (Together Baton Rouge 2014).

For students who previously crossed the city line, the success of the incorporation vote will mean reassignment to different schools in students' new districts (either Baton Rouge or St. George, depending on a student's home address). If ultimately realized, the creation of St. George will deal EBR the loss of a student population that is largely White, nonpoor, and high achieving—crippling the district's already limited ability to meet the needs of its overwhelmingly non-White, disadvantaged population.

Although this potential outcome was downplayed in the messaging of the St. George campaign, it did not escape the notice of people concerned by the incorporation effort—or of the Public Broadcasting Service (PBS). The case received limited attention in national media outlets during the first incorporation effort, but one exception to this was a PBS "Frontline" documentary released in July 2014 entitled *Separate and Unequal* (Robertson 2014). The documentary foregrounded issues of race and class in its telling of the story. In response, the St. George organizers released a statement saying it was "unfortunate" that PBS chose to focus on the desegregation lawsuit and to paint the effort as racially motivated: "This movement has NOTHING to do with class or race," the organizers argued. "It has everything to do with parents (black and white, rich and poor) who are fed up with the current education, or lack thereof, in the public schools in East Baton Rouge Parish."[13] Whether someone agreed with the PBS angle or accepted the defense made by the incorporation effort, race was an explicit topic in debates over St. George.

"You Can Only Run So Far"

The legacy of school desegregation in Baton Rouge helps explain the relevance of race to the fight over St. George—but this is only half of the story. The other half concerns the fact that the St. George organizers were not just working to form a new school district. They were working to form a new city.

St. George's Fight for Cityhood

Forming a city may seem like a roundabout way to form a school district. It was not the first approach the organizers tried, having launched the effort in 2012 under the banner of "Local Schools for Local Children." The original goal was to lobby the legislature to create a Southeast Community School District, considerably smaller than what would be later proposed as the St. George district. A key source of support for the group was State Senator Mack "Bodi" White, who had helped pass the legislation establishing the school districts in Zachary, Baker, and Central. After a failed first attempt in 2012, a bill sponsored by Sen. White authorizing the creation of the Southeast district (SB199) passed the House in March 2013. However, the bill that would have amended the state constitution to *fund* the school district (SB73) failed to win the two-thirds vote it required.

As St. George organizers explained the situation to me, legislators told them that cityhood status was what separated their situation from that of Zachary. The organizers felt this argument was an attempt by state law-makers to dismiss the St. George effort and consequently decided to pursue incorporation as a means to achieve the school district after all. The official wording on the St. George website as of the 2014–2015 campaign reflected the stance they ultimately adopted, explaining that the shift to the incorporation strategy ensued when "[t]he character of the opposition to [the first] effort set in motion a larger discussion among grassroots citizens dissatisfied by the quality of governance from the Powers That Be in East Baton Rouge Parish."[14]

Louisiana has lax requirements for municipal incorporation compared to many other states. Only 25% of registered voters in an unincorporated area must sign a petition supporting the effort, and then, in a special election to be called by the governor, a simple majority vote among residents of the area is required for the motion to succeed.[15] The law also specifies no time limit within which organizers must collect signatures for a petition. And more, there are few avenues to oppose an incorporation effort in Louisiana, other than discouraging residents from signing the petition, particularly for opponents who are not residents of the proposed incorporation. Although Central went through this process on the way to forming its own school district, St. George raised the stakes considerably. With a population of about 86,000, St. George would displace Lake Charles as the fifth most populous city in the state, dwarfing nearby Baker (pop. 13,700), Zachary (pop. 16,900), and Central (pop. 28,500). The footprint of the new city also is geographically comparable to the city of Baton Rouge, encompassing 60 square miles compared to 76 in the capital city. And, as I have mentioned, St. George would be only 12% Black in a parish with almost equally sized Black and White populations.

There remains disagreement over what it will take to build up and open a large school district in St. George. One report estimated that up to a dozen new schools needed to be built to accommodate students in the originally proposed boundaries (Together Baton Rouge 2014), and updated estimates for the 2018–2019 effort indicate that at least six new schools will be needed to accommodate the 2,400 students who reside in St. George but do not attend schools located in the new district (One Baton Rouge 2019). On the other hand, St. George organizers and supporters insisted the number would be closer to three or four buildings even when St. George's proposed boundaries were larger, and that temporary buildings would ease the construction process (Bethencourt and Lussier 2014; Robertson 2014). However much new construction may be required, St. George will benefit from its relative wealth within EBR Parish, with a mean household income around $90,000— about $30,000 greater than the mean income in the city of Baton Rouge. Consequently, a team of LSU economists showed that the per pupil net revenue of around $9,600 in EBR public schools (as of 2013) was projected to fall to $8,870; meanwhile, per pupil funding in the new district was projected to rise to $11,686 (Richardson, Llorens, and Heidelberg 2013).

The economists' report was commissioned by the Baton Rouge Area Foundation (BRAF) and Baton Rouge Area Chamber (BRAC), two local institutions with interests in the economic health of Baton Rouge.[16] The BRAF/BRAC report had a major impact on the 2014–2015 St. George debate, reaching far beyond the impact of the new city on local public schools. The report estimated that the creation of the new city would take $85 million, or 30%, from the annual revenue of the East Baton Rouge Parish General Fund due to the loss of sales taxes generated in the unincorporated area. The release of these findings in December 2013 spurred a wave of new annexations by the city of Baton Rouge, including the Mall of Louisiana, the southern part of LSU's campus, the L'Auberge casino and hotel, a major film studio, and several hospital sites that were located in the unincorporated area.[17]

The annexations drew sharp criticism from St. George supporters, as each annexation hurt the feasibility of the organizers' repeated claim that no increase in taxes should be needed to support a new city. They planned to pursue a "21st-century model" of city governance, with few public employees and broad privatization of city services. The organizers argued that this model had already been proven successful, frequently referencing the example of Sandy Springs, GA. Notably, they did not reference Sandy Springs' long and racialized road to incorporation—from resisting annexation by Atlanta in the 1960s while promising "to build up a city separate from Atlanta and your Negroes," to ultimately incorporating as its own city in 2005 (Kruse 2005).[18] The 2018–2019 St. George incorporation effort ironically also happened to coincide with Sandy Springs announcing in early 2019 that they would be abandoning privatization and bringing most of their contracts in-house after realizing this would save them about $14 million over five years (Ruch 2019).

In the lead-up to both the 2015 and 2019 votes, opponents and proponents continued to spar over the feasibility of the proposal to run St. George as a fully privatized city. Another report commissioned by BRAF and BRAC in 2014 highlighted serious shortfalls for St. George based on lost tax revenue following the annexations; the portion of legacy costs St. George would have to assume for the benefits of retired EBR employees; and the feasibility of St. George's plan to spend less than half as much per capita compared to average spending for similarly sized cities (Faulk & Winkler LLC 2014). Similar issues were highlighted in a 2018 report, arguing that the proposed $34 million budget for St. George was likely $14 million too low based on expenditures of comparable cities (Richardson and Llorens 2018). The St. George committee disputed most of these findings, including by commissioning their own research (e.g., Carr Riggs & Ingram 2015). Yet, in conversation, the organizers recognized how much the annexations hurt their plans and expressed frustration that this strategy had been promoted by the "Powers That Be" (i.e., BRAC, BRAF, and the Metro Council) to undermine their efforts.

So far, I have highlighted the practical impact the new city would have had on life in the parish, but the St. George organizers' choice to pursue cityhood had legal dimensions, too. Municipal incorporation tends to be a strategic move to increase local control over resources, often on racialized terms, by shrinking the circle that benefits from a given community's tax dollars. Legal scholarship on municipal incorporation further illuminates the issues at play.

The Fallacy of a "Right" to Local Governance

First, despite the tendency for communities to make reference to a "right" to local self-government or municipal identity, no such federally protected right exists. Instead, as legal scholar Christopher Tyson (2014, 654) explains, "[S]ocial developments and the law have reified and legitimated broadly held expectations about the ability of individuals and groups to withdraw from the redistributive obligations and legacy burdens of cities." This point does not deny the legality of the process by which the St. George organizers pursued the incorporation of a new city. Rather, it emphasizes that deference to local control is often reflective of subjective interpretations of the law.

Take, for example, *Milliken v. Bradley* (1974), in which the Supreme Court deferred to a "deeply rooted" tradition of local control over schools to strike down a desegregation plan in Detroit, despite Michigan law clearly stating that education was a matter of statewide—not local—concern. A commitment to deeply rooted tradition rather than the law similarly pervaded debates about St. George. Proponents often argued for the benefits of "community schools" of the pre-desegregation era, making no reference to the fact that for at least two decades these schools served all-White communities that were in blatant violation of federal orders to desegregate.

The Tautology of Using Geography to Define a Community

A second insight on municipal incorporation is that cityhood is often fought for on the basis of a community's identity—but to define a community's identity with reference to boundaries inevitably verges on tautology. As critical legal scholar Richard Thompson Ford (1994, 1860) has argued, to say that people comprise a community because they live in a particular area is to give space itself a seemingly objective or even primordial role in defining the community. Such statements rarely engage with why only area X, rather than area X plus area Y, is the most valid definition of the community.

In the case of St. George, the slippery nature of defining a new community with reference to a geographical boundary—and a nonsalient boundary at that—was apparent in the ambivalent opinions expressed about the identity of the proposed city. Some ardent St. George backers, for example, spoke enthusiastically about a new municipal identity based on good schools and privatized services. Yet, they would minimize the importance of this identity when trying to downplay the effect the incorporation would have on the larger area: "I mean, I don't think anything changes ... it's like a suburb," one St. George organizer told me, explaining that the area would still identify as part of Baton Rouge.

Respondents were typically assertive in embracing the identity of being from "Baton Rouge" (irrespective of where in the larger area a respondent lived). Multiple Black residents of the unincorporated areas told me they would have moved into the city boundaries had the 2015 incorporation effort succeeded. One volunteer who had helped with grassroots efforts to oppose St. George described a group of "older White ladies [who] were like, 'I live in Baton Rouge; I've been born and raised in Baton Rouge; my address is going to *say* Baton Rouge'"—and then petitioned on their own to be annexed into Baton Rouge in order to eliminate the possibility of being included in the proposed city of St. George.

The Dilemma of Who Decides

A final insight from scholarship on incorporation follows from the challenge of defining communities with boundaries, and goes on to ask—who decides? This question illuminates what legal scholar Richard Briffault (1993, 1132) calls the local boundary problem: "Boundaries exclude people who may be interested in or affected by the decision made within the boundaries." Localities tend to make decisions in their short-term economic interests, seeking to attract residents and firms that contribute more in tax revenue than they cost in service consumption (Hirsch and Hirsch 1979; Schneider 1989). In the long term, however, localities' economic well-being depends on areas outside their boundaries. Not only does the economic health of a region suffer when inequality between the city and the suburbs is greater (Savitch et al. 1993), but large income disparities also hurt employment and population growth regionwide (Briffault 1993). Even if St. George were to be a thriving city, a weakened and impoverished city of Baton Rouge would be a detriment for the health of the larger metropolitan area, including St. George, in the long term.

Some opponents of the effort made arguments along these lines. "The better it is in these other areas," one St. George opponent told me, the "healthier, happier, and safer" her own community would be. "If you've got hurt here (*she pointed to NBR on a map*), it spills over everywhere." Proponents of the St. George movement, on the other hand, were more likely to argue that competition from St. George would push Baton Rouge to improve. I lack the scope to investigate what the incorporation of St. George could mean for the area in the long term. Yet, it is clear that the St. George effort offers an example of the local boundary problem in action. Aside from the efforts of city institutions like BRAF and BRAC, there were limited avenues for nonresidents of the proposed new city to voice an opinion on St. George.

As a result, concerned Baton Rogueans mounted a grassroots countereffort to try, as they described it, "to keep the community together."

A Failed Petition, a Successful Vote, and the Waiting Game in Between

When a nascent St. George effort was still trying only to establish a school district in the southeast, a parent-led organization called One Community, One School District (OCOSD) played a major role in lobbying the legislature to preserve the unified school district. As the strategy to incorporate a city developed, OCOSD pivoted to fight this, too. Further institutional opposition came from local organizations such as BRAC and BRAF in sponsoring research into the effects of St. George. Putting incorporation on the table also gave the Metro Council the option of annexing unincorporated territory into the city to reduce St. George's potential tax base.

Another major opponent emerged from a multifaith community organization called Together Baton Rouge, which formed a spinoff group to fight the 2014–2015 campaign—Better Together, also known as Residents Against the Breakaway—to focus exclusively on fighting St. George. In the 2018–2019 campaign, Better Together evolved into a community organization called One Baton Rouge. Throughout, this citizen-led opposition sought to educate residents of the St. George area about the implications of the incorporation. Particularly in the first incorporation effort, opponents also worked to fight what they saw as a widespread misconception that signing the petition only indicated willingness for the issue to be voted on, rather than a signatory's official support for the effort (many signatories had also been unaware that their names would be publicly accessible). In 2014–2015, Better Together competed with the St. George organizers by going door-to-door to talk about the petition, but in this case to inform residents that they could *remove* their signatures from the petition if they chose. The 2018–2019 One Baton Rouge campaign further increased efforts to facilitate annexation into the city of Baton Rouge for any property owners adjacent to existing city limits— efforts that they continued in the transition period following the successful incorporation vote in October 2019, seeking to reduce the land that would ultimately become St. George.

Mixed Support for the Incorporation Effort

As illustrated by Figure 2.4, public opinion over the issue was deeply divided. In the first incorporation effort, nearly half of EBR voters opposed the St. George petition, driven by strong opposition from those who did not live in the proposed incorporation. More support was found among voters living in the St. George area—although nearly as many residents of the area opposed the petition. Keep in mind that the demographics of the "Not in St. George"

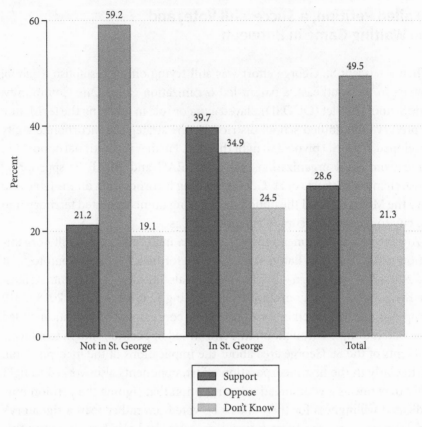

Fig. 2.4 Public Opinion on the St. George Incorporation Effort
Source: LSU Public Policy Research Lab (Climek and Means 2013); *n* = 1,097.

and "In St. George" categories differ drastically. Among those surveyed about the St. George issue by LSU's Public Policy Research Lab, residents of the proposed new city were 78% White and 50% Republican, while those residing elsewhere were 36% White and 18% Republican.

There were still several notable points of agreement between residents and nonresidents of St. George. First, St. George area residents were only marginally more likely than other residents to cite education as the biggest issue facing the parish (33% as opposed to 28%). This similarity suggests that limited concern about education might have made it hard to rally further support for the St. George effort.

Second, residents of the St. George area were equally likely to say that the creation of a new city would have a negative effect on the city of Baton Rouge (62% as opposed to 63% of nonresidents). Relatedly, though St. George residents were less likely to say that the incorporation would negatively impact the larger parish, still more than half agreed that EBR likely would suffer (53% of residents agreed, in comparison to 63% of nonresidents). These numbers suggest that at least some supporters of St. George felt the incorporation would hurt their neighbors, but perhaps considered this beyond their concern.

Third, more than half of all those surveyed as of 2013, whether residents of the St. George area or not, incorrectly believed that the area was already part of the incorporated city of Baton Rouge. These misconceptions were a source of frustration for the organizers of the incorporation effort, who felt they were mischaracterized as trying to "break away" from a city that they never belonged to in the first place. At the same time, these misconceptions reemphasize the extent to which the official boundary separating the city from the unincorporated areas has historically held little meaning for residents of the area, and the corresponding difficulty of appealing to a distinct identity of the unincorporated area.

On October 20th, 2014, the St. George organizers turned in a petition with over 18,000 signatures for the parish Registrar of Voters to count. While signatures were being verified, the organizers were allowed to collect more; the opposition effort was able to continue reaching out to people to remove signatures, too. In June 2015, however, the petition was ultimately declared short by a mere seventy-one signatures.[19] After a state judge quickly dismissed the lawsuit the St. George campaign had tried to bring against the Registrar's Office—a dismissal that organizers considered deeply unfair—the 2013–2015 campaign officially ended in defeat. State law mandated a two-year waiting period before another incorporation attempt could be launched.

As many St. George supporters assured me would happen, in early 2018 the effort relaunched. This time, they were given nine months (as opposed to no timeline) to collect the nearly 13,000 required signatures on a petition to hold a vote on the new, smaller incorporation. With the necessary signatures collected by November 2018, the issue was brought to vote on October 12, 2019. A majority of registered voters in the proposed new city turned out to vote, and 54% of those, or a total of 17,422, voted to create the new city.

At the time of writing, the exact path forward for St. George has yet to be determined. This is primarily because Baton Rouge Mayor-President Sharon Weston Broome and two other local leaders brought a lawsuit against the St. George effort in late 2019, citing the financial harm the incorporation poses to EBR as a parish.[20] While debate continues over the lawsuit, a steady stream of businesses and some subdivisions have continued pursing annexation into the city of Baton Rouge, winnowing down the St. George tax base. Moreover, in the event of a successful incorporation, ultimately the state legislature would have to approve a new St. George school district.

All the same—based on the October 2019 vote, the support of St. George voters to establish their own city has been made clear.

Where the Present Study Begins

The waiting period between the first and second St. George incorporation efforts was the background of my research in Baton Rouge. As of the summer of 2016, the sentiment around St. George was what one might expect—mildly evocative of Montgomery, AL, in the months following the bus boycott as Baldwin (1961, 641) described it: "aimlessly hostile, [...] having inherited nothing less than an ocean of spilt milk."

The mix of suppressed anger and tenuous relief that the initial St. George effort failed was suddenly disrupted by the violence of early July. The police killing of Sterling on July 5th, the video footage of the event, and the protests that followed stunned many residents of EBR Parish. Sterling was far from the first to suffer from racialized policing, but he was the first in decades to bring race-related violence in Baton Rouge into the national spotlight, and to bring wider attention to the dire social conditions in NBR that contextualized Sterling's life and premature death. As one White LSU student described the aftermath of July 5th, "There was probably 24 hours where everybody, even the Whitest, frattiest, Greek guy was like, 'that was bad.'"

Beyond the immediate shock of Sterling's murder, however, support for the police began to emerge. No one could have expected how that support would be amplified after five police officers were killed in a sniper attack in Dallas on July 7th, let alone what would happen after a Black Marine Corps veteran from Missouri, Gavin Long, was spotted with an assault rifle outside of a convenience store on one of Baton Rouge's major streets, around 8:40 a.m. on Sunday, July 17th. Long fired forty-three rounds over the next fourteen minutes, ultimately killing two Baton Rouge Police Department officers, Montrell Jackson and Matthew Gerald, along with EBR Sheriff's Deputy Brad Garafola. Two other deputies and one additional police officer sustained injuries in the attack.

What did these tragic events mean for my research into White public opinion in Baton Rouge? I had planned to study opinion on the St. George issue long before the shootings. When I conducted my first interviews on Monday, July 18th, the mood was a starkly different one than I had anticipated (see Figure 2.5 for photos of Baton Rouge in the aftermath of both violent incidents). Yet, I found that respondents' reflections on the shootings touched on the same themes raised by the St. George issue. The location of

Fig. 2.5 Memorials to Alton Sterling and Local Law Enforcement Officers

Photos taken by the author in July 2016. The memorial to Sterling was located at the Triple-S Food Mart in NBR where he was murdered. The memorial to the officers was located near the site of the gunfight between Long and local law enforcement, not far from the intersection of Airline Highway and Old Hammond in the middle of the parish. See map in Figure 2.1.

Sterling's shooting in a ghettoized part of NBR, the sentiments (ranging from scorn to support) surrounding the Black Lives Matter protests that followed, the frequent implication that those who mourned Sterling and those who mourned the officers were (or should have been) mutually exclusive—all of this led respondents to reflect on race more openly than they might have if the appalling violence had never occurred. Race became too large an "elephant in the room" to ignore. And at least some St. George supporters cited the shootings as even more reason to create their own city. As one told me, "Where Alton Sterling was shot is a *war zone*," he said. "I mean, you will get straight up murdered in that part of town."

The respondent made this comment when explaining why Baton Rouge was going in the wrong direction, and why drastic moves such as municipal incorporation were necessary. He did not condone the officers' killing of Sterling. However, Sterling's killing was consistent with the St. George supporter's conception of the local geography. If anything, Sterling's killing affirmed this respondent's understanding of NBR as a "war zone" and the St. George area as, needless to say, not a war zone. The events of early July thus seemed to affirm the rightness of formally establishing a separate identity for the unincorporated area.

In short, both the St. George case that drew me to Baton Rouge in the first place and the unforeseeable turmoil that enveloped the city in July 2016 provoked reflection on the racialized and unequal geography of EBR, and informed opinion on what, if anything, was to be done. The tragedy of the shootings therefore further illuminated Baton Rouge's deeply wrought color line—the metaphorical and physical divide between Black people and White people in the area. As the next chapter will show, the reflections of White individuals who supported *and* those who opposed St. George make evident the capacity of their community's color line to endure, over sixty years after Baton Rouge was first brought to court for excluding Black children from White schools.

One Black respondent reflected on how long it had been for White people to still be attempting to avoid integrated schools: "We need to figure out how we can live together, work together, go to school together, as opposed to simply segregating ourselves." He sounded exasperated. "You can only run so far."

Studying St. George as an Outsider Within

The history recounted in this chapter demonstrates how White people's avoidance of sharing a public school system with their Black neighbors has evolved to fit the time and place. Creating a new city, in a sense, represents the culmination of White flight in EBR Parish. Baton Rouge and the case of St. George also offered me an ideal landscape, as discussed in Chapter 1, in which to analyze deeply polarized opinion among White residents and to investigate the nonetheless common ways in which they perceive their local geography. It was in this setting that I undertook the critical, interpretive task of tracing the boundaries of White Americans' perspective on racial politics from their position atop the American racial order.

Other considerations when choosing Baton Rouge as a field site had less to do with the place itself and more to do with me as the researcher, and my ability to bring the richness of the case to light. In particular, two notable features of my own positionality that I have briefly mentioned so far merit further discussion: my family ties to Louisiana, and my identity as a Black interviewer of (primarily) White subjects. This section discusses both these features in greater detail. In doing so, I hope to acknowledge how my presence in the research setting intersubjectively shaped the knowledge produced—arguably in some valuable ways—and to hold myself to the standard I have advocated: recognizing that no vision, mine included, is neutral.

My discussion proceeds in three parts. First, I elaborate on how my Louisiana background shaped my connection to the field site and to my interviewees, regardless of race. Second, I discuss the reality that I was a *Black* person with a Louisiana background interviewing White Louisianans, introducing so-called race-of-interviewer effects and related concerns that White respondents would not reveal the "truth" to a non-White interviewer. Third, I respond to these concerns by reflecting on the specific circumstances of my project and argue for the value of its findings.

The Displaced Southerner

I introduced my Louisiana roots in Chapter 1 as a pragmatic reason for my case selection. While true, pragmatism alone does not capture the full story. As one of my interviewees said of what she called the "displaced Southerner": "There's always a homing instinct: I will eventually go home." Indeed, a strong sense of place is core to the Southern American identity; in Louisiana, 78% of residents were born in the state—the highest percentage in the nation.[21] This is relevant to my research because a sense of "home" was as central to my interviewees' understanding of why I was there as it was to my own.

Though raised in Texas myself, my family roots run deep in Louisiana (and on my father's side, in Baton Rouge specifically; it was his grandparents who were sharecroppers there; his ancestors before that were both enslavers and enslaved). I still remained an outsider during my fieldwork, in several ways. Besides not having grown up there, I was at the time a graduate student at the University of Oxford, an overtly elite institution a world away from Baton Rouge. My appearance also hints that my mother's side comes from the more eclectic New Orleans, where I have a thoroughly Creole background. These outsider characteristics undoubtedly shaped my reception in Baton Rouge, as I will elaborate on shortly. But at the end of the day, my familiarity with the field site, access to local knowledge, and general cultural fluency greatly improved the feasibility of my research.

Even more, as another interviewee told me: what it meant to be "from" Baton Rouge was to walk into a meeting where you knew no one in the room, but where you could still march up to the new faces and ask, "Where are you from? Who's your mom?" The fact that my answers to these questions all led back to Louisiana—and that I myself was a displaced Southerner who had come home to conduct fieldwork—was part of what made my presence in Baton Rouge readily accepted.

I did not take that acceptance lightly. Sociologist Shamus Khan (2011) has noted that anonymity often protects the researcher more than the subjects of research, explaining his decision to use the real name of the elite boarding school at which he based his research on privilege, and his corresponding commitment to "get things right" in his analysis. Concealing the identity of the St. George effort as located in the Baton Rouge area was not a practical option for me, given unique features of the case (e.g., the city–parish structure, the Baton Rouge desegregation lawsuit) as well as its publicity. All the same, by naming the site as Baton Rouge and being open with my respondents and readers about my connections to the place, I am holding myself accountable to get things right, too.

Part of getting things right includes emphasizing that—while I may identify what I argue are racially harmful ideas or behaviors among White respondents—none of my critique concerns whether any of the White respondents is a "good" or "bad" person. Indeed, any focus on individual goodness misses the point. Another sociologist of privilege, Rachel Sherman (2019, 27), points out how we ultimately "legitimate [class] privilege by representing some rich people as 'good' while others are 'bad.'" Similarly, focusing on what makes a good White person risks legitimating racial privilege and the violent hierarchy on which it is based. It is for that reason that I hope to focus my critique on the hierarchy itself, and on the actions and attitudes that often serve to legitimate it.

None of this should minimize the extent to which I regard each of my respondents with respect and am deeply grateful for their generosity with their time and thoughts. But neither should it minimize the agency and responsibility each one has to critically reflect on whether they are defending the racial order or dismantling it.

This responsibility applies to me as the researcher, too. Indeed, throughout the process of writing this book I continued to notice—or to have my attention astutely drawn to by readers—the ways in which my own language or analyses were demonstrating the same epistemological biases that I seek to critique. Even as I am sure some such biases remain, I am appreciative of the self-awareness I have built through the process, and I hope this book encourages self-awareness among others as well.

Race Matching in Qualitative Interviews

My connection to Baton Rouge would stand regardless of my race, but it is now worth more directly considering the implications of my racial identity for my research in Baton Rouge—and by extension, for a book on White Americans' racial attitudes and policy preferences.

I should not overstate the need to explain or justify one's research focus—something rarely expected of the stereotypically White, male, heterosexual and/or cisgender academic, for example. My discussions of interpretivsim in Chapter 1 also should make clear that the question of the researcher's positionality would be germane to the analysis of this chapter and the next irrespective of my particular identity: an interpretive study explicitly concep-tualizes knowledge as produced through the interaction of researcher and participants. It is unconventional, however, for Black researchers of racial politics to conduct interviews with White respondents (and certainly less conventional than the quantitative study of White public opinion by Black researchers—my approach in Chapters 4 and 5).

It is not entirely surprising that few Black researchers conduct interviews with White research subjects about race. There is, of course, a persistent underrepresentation of Black Americans in the academy (Hussar et al. 2020). Race may also influence someone's access to research subjects, or raise valid concerns about a Black researcher's safety or well-being and thus compli-cate the idea of interviewing White subjects. But, another reason few Black researchers of race work with White research participants is that many valuably choose to turn a lens on Black people rather than White people, challenging the long tradition of studying Black people through a White lens (Zuberi and Bonilla-Silva 2008)—and, in some cases, addressing a foundational concern of literature on "race-of-interviewer" effects.

Early investigation into the effects of an interviewer's race was rooted in the concerns of mid-20th century researchers that Black people felt less comfortable speaking to White survey researchers.[22] In the 1990s, qualitative interviewers—particularly White feminists—also began to contemplate how the racially dominant position of White people would limit their ability to interact with and understand the experiences of Black interviewees (for a review, see O'Brien 2016). The standard strategy to minimize such race-of-interviewer effects has been to match interviewers and respondents by race (and/or gender)—a particularly valuable approach when working with marginalized groups (Few, Stephens, and Rouse-Arnett 2003).

As much as these efforts have been promoted as a way to challenge assumptions of White neutrality and objectivity in conducting research, it is striking that the "problem" of race-of-interviewer effects is almost unquestionably framed as one that arises when White people study Black people. This leaves the norm that White interviewers should interview White respondents unchallenged. There are some exceptions to this.[23] Nonetheless, my approach in Baton Rouge offers a valuable opportunity for further reflection on the integrity of data gleaned from White subjects by a Black researcher.

The Perspective of a Black (Woman) Researcher

When I was seeking feedback on my research design, one distinguished White political scientist told me I should "make a bug a feature" when it came to being a Black person talking to White people. Putting aside the assumptions laden in identifying my race as a "bug" to begin with, her statement demonstrated the conventional wisdom that White people should be interviewed by White researchers. It also suggests a way to unpack the significance of my race in the interview setting: beginning by responding to two of the most common reasons one might see my race as a "bug" in the present study of White attitudes, then discussing two "features" that, I argue, my positionality brings to this project.

"White People Won't be Willing to Talk to You About Race"

When planning my research in Baton Rouge, the most common response I received upon describing my project in academic settings was that White people would not be willing to talk to me about anything related to race. This is an understandable concern. Yet, I argue now, as I did then, that it was easy for those offering me feedback to ignore both the details of my project and the possible biases of their own perspectives.

First, the goal of my interviews was not to ascertain White respondents' underlying racial attitudes, or to have sustained conversation about their feelings toward Black people. Rather, I was exploring White Baton Rougeans' positions on the locally salient policy issues described in the first part of this chapter. The racial dimensions of these issues (along with my presence in the interview setting, as I will discuss shortly) certainly brought race into the conversations. Yet, my targeted questions about much publicized issues such as St. George and EBR public schools were by no means traversing taboo issues. The violence of early July was a more sensitive topic—but respondents themselves almost always brought up the shootings, often in processing what had happened or defending Baton Rouge as a calm, friendly place. In other words, far from asking uncomfortable questions about race or inequality, my interviews covered standard topics of conversation given the time and place. This is not to say that a Black researcher could not interview White people about more sensitive topics related to race, but it is important to be explicit about the nature of my interviews.

Second, I primarily was warned about White reticence by scholars (from both the United States and abroad) who appeared to have little familiarity with the South—where White people, generally speaking, are known for their ability to comfortably coexist in close physical proximity to Black people. Baton Rouge certainly is full of barriers between the races, particularly when it comes to where people live, go to school, and go to church. But with such a large Black presence, the area also is full of what Jane Jacobs (1961) would call "seams": places where the Black and White worlds are enmeshed in one another. This is not to say the color line does not still hold at the seams. Instead, one must appreciate that a major legacy of Jim Crow is White people's knowledge of how to maintain social and emotional distance from Black people despite physical proximity (Ritterhouse 2006). Thus, White people in Baton Rouge, a context where Blackness is never far away, are adept at either talking about race or deploying the rhetoric of colorblindness where needed. The Southernness of this feature might contribute to the specificity of my case study more than its generalizability—but, combined with my ties to Louisiana, it valuably contributed to the fluidity of my conversations.

So, far from my academic colleagues' predictions that White people would refuse my interviews, the White residents I spoke with were generally warm, welcoming, and happy to discuss the issues I raised. Even a respondent I refer to as Randy, whom we will soon meet in Chapter 3 and who initially expressed suspicion toward me, was remarkably open once we sat down for a coffee. Randy will be an excellent example, in fact, of someone who has supported initiatives that stand to disproportionately harm Black people in Baton Rouge and who endorses a number of racial stereotypes—but who also moves fluently through interracial settings and energetically discusses his racial views (e.g., how people too often blame things on race). Other dynamics were at play in my conversation with Randy, but he certainly illustrated the comfort that I expected from White individuals who live in a parish that is almost half Black.

"White People Will Only Say What They Think You Want to Hear"
Related to the concern that White people would not speak to a Black interviewer was the concern I frequently encountered that any comments shared with me would be biased due to respondents' fears of seeming racist.

There undoubtedly was some social desirability bias at play among my interviewees, leading them to take more care in their wording than they would have with a White interviewer. For example, there were times when my respondents caught themselves having "slipped" (e.g., when one respondent realizes that she has referenced a "White restaurant," as described in the next chapter). There were other instances in which respondents worked hard to convince me that they liked Black people, had Black friends, were not scared to go to NBR, and the like. These tendencies may reflect Kinder and Sanders's (1996) findings that White people are more likely to express liberal views on racial issues when speaking to Black as opposed to White interviewers (see also Finkel, Guterbock, and Borg 1991).[24]

However, it is unlikely that pressure to appear racially tolerant or progressive was so enhanced by my race that it distorted my findings. For one, norms around discussing racial issues have evolved in the two decades since Kinder and Sanders wrote, changing what might be considered acceptable to say even to a White interviewer (in live conversation, at least; the trend has gone in a different direction in online spaces; see Daniels 2013; Keum and Miller 2018). Research into racial politics need not rely on White respondents confessing their deepest and darkest feelings about race in the first place—but, assuming such feelings exist, even a White researcher may have to navigate a "rhetorical maze of color blindness" to get to any confessions in conversation (Bonilla-Silva 2006).

More fundamentally, a core premise of interpretive methodology is that researcher influence not only is inevitable but also is a *valuable* part of the research process. As Erving Goffman (1978) famously argued, we all perform "frontstage" identities that are distinct from our "backstage" ones, but neither identity is inherently more "real." Appreciating that I collected the reflections respondents *chose* to share with a Black interviewer should frame my discussion, not invalidate it. We also should question why, much like Whiteness is often assumed to be neutral or immutable, it is assumed that White respondents do not also perform to White interviewers. Ultimately, if knowledge in the interview setting is always produced intersubjectively, then any version of truth produced should be appreciated as one of many valid performances an interview subject could give.

Raising the Salience of Race

I now turn to two of the benefits of my racial identity in conducting this research. Building on the interpretivist argument that a researcher's presence can be valuable—this can be particularly true when a researcher's presence violates the norms of a situation and thus brings to the surface dynamics that may not otherwise reveal themselves (Schwartz-Shea and Yanow 2012). In one of few examples I could find of a Black researcher in conversation with White individuals about race, Kirby Moss (2003) explains that he "strategically [cast himself] as a social actor" in the field, recognizing that his presence would racialize his conversations with low-income White respondents, but being open about this and contextualizing his observations accordingly. I would not categorize my entry into the field as similarly "strategic," but my presence almost certainly made my respondents more likely to bring up issues of race, which I would refrain from mentioning until respondents did first.[25]

Respondents' awareness of my race was clear in many instances, some of which I have referenced, such as when White respondents tried to demonstrate their rejection of racial stereotypes more strongly than they might have to a White interviewer. It was also evident when White respondents would make non sequitur references to race (i.e., bringing up race when the conversation was quite far from the topic), or would occasionally use phrases such as "people like you" to make reference to (presumably) middle-income Black people.

In short, I brought race into the room. This undoubtedly reflected in the data I collected. But, the truth is that race is no less in the room when a White researcher speaks to a White respondent. Moreover, in a setting like Baton Rouge—where race was already a prominent feature of life and the issues we were discussing, particularly so in the summer of 2016—my subtle racialization of the interviews arguably served as an illuminative rather than "contaminating" addition to the research settings.

Being an "Outsider Within"

Fourth and finally, my identity as a Black woman researcher recalls Black feminist scholarship on the status of Black women in academia. Patricia Hill Collins (1986, 1999) has called this position that of the "outsider within," based on the tension between the Black female experience and the "White male insiderism" of the academy. Collins (1999, 85) uses the concept of the outsider within to understand the social locations of individuals "caught between groups of unequal power," as well as to argue for the insights to be gained from Black women's perspectives. This argument, one that has significantly informed standpoint theory, endorses the value to be gained from supplementing academic concepts with one's lived experiences of systems of power.

Considering my particular "outsider within" status in Baton Rouge offers another way to think about my role as an interviewer. On the one hand, certain features increased my proximity to the position of "insider." As I have noted, I had the requisite cultural competence to interact with Southerners as a Southerner myself, even if not a White one. My speech and presentation also read as "White" to many audiences, particularly when paired with a medium brown skin tone that reflects my mother's Creole background—both of which almost certainly improved my reception by the White people I encountered. (The racialization of speech and presentation, along with colorism, are their own weighty topics, none of which I can do justice here; see, for a start, Dixon and Telles 2017, 407–409; see also Hunter 2007; L. Hannon 2015.) Furthermore, I occupied a position of authority in the interview setting as the person asking the questions, and with the legitimacy afforded to a researcher coming from an elite university.

On the other hand, I am a member of a subordinated gender, a subjugated race, and a younger age group than most of my interviewees. These nondominant group identities arguably complemented the other factors I have mentioned to produce my status as an outsider within. My age and gender in particular shaped the power dynamic in the interview setting: while it was at times challenging to navigate remarks on my relative youth or references to gendered stereotypes, it was beneficial that my persona was not one that my White respondents were inclined to see as particularly threatening (as too often is the case with Black men) or accusatory. On the contrary, my age and gender, as well as my race, may have made some White respondents more prone to "explain" things to me—ranging from what it is like to have a mortgage and kids (to be fair, I have neither), to how schools are funded in Louisiana (whether the respondent was citing correct information or not), to what the experiences of middle-class Black Baton Rougeans entail (which often sharply contrasted what my Black respondents themselves said).

Moreover, while my affiliation with Oxford no doubt helped me be taken seriously as a young woman, Oxford was not of particular interest to most respondents and occasionally was viewed with confusion (or even suspicion; these were instances when it was particularly helpful to explain that I had family ties to Baton Rouge). My general experience in Louisiana, and in my home state of Texas for that matter, has been that Oxford's foreignness often outweighs its status—meaning that, while still conferring a certain amount of prestige and assumed class identity, it seemed to mark me less as an elite and more as someone who had traveled a long way to get to Baton Rouge. After all, elitism is contingent on the society that a particular elite rules. Therefore, my position as a foreigner who was nonetheless approachable offered some of the capacities of the "stranger," to use sociologist Georg Simmel's term— someone whose insight comes from "a peculiar composition of nearness and remoteness, concern and indifference"; who often elicits comments that someone might not confide in one of their peers; and who has the ability to see patterns it would be harder to identify if immersed in the situation (qtd. in Collins 1986, S15).[26]

It is possible that my White and/or male equivalent—a young researcher with roots in Baton Rouge but having left to study at Oxford—could have played a different sort of stranger had she or he conducted this research. There are multiple ways to strike a balance between proximity and distance. Yet, it also is possible that my hypothetical counterparts would have encountered challenges that I did not. Would my Black male counterpart have suffered from different stereotypes, such as those of Black men as aggressive or dangerous? Would my White female counterpart have had to find ways to ask more directly about race, rather than waiting for respondents to bring it up?

There are obvious, problematic issues underlying these rhetorical questions, which reference racial stereotypes and gender norms that shape many social interactions. But my point is that the influence of a researcher's identity is inevitable, and the influence of mine, in this case, brought advantages as well as disadvantages. In another version of this project, someone might have hired a White research assistant to conduct interviews, systematically conducted a portion of interviews by phone for comparison; or otherwise investigated the potential influence of my race.[27] I maintain, however, that the research as it stands should be considered no more biased, certainly no less "true," and potentially more interesting than had the project been conducted entirely by a White researcher.

To pose a final rhetorical question, would my White male counterpart have ignored or even rejected the premise that those at the top of a system of structural violence do not have to engage with what life is like for those at the bottom? As Collins (1986, S29–S30) argues, the creativity of the marginal space occupied by Black women in the academy is realized when exploring these sorts of premises—or when "experienced reality is used as a valid source of knowledge for critical sociological facts and theories" at the same time as "sociological thought offers new ways of seeing that experienced reality." This point is as relevant to my qualitative investigation in Baton Rouge as it is to my critical reinterpretation of the quantitative study of racial threat that will follow in Chapters 4 and 5. Although I cannot claim to have mastered the sort of creativity Collins names, she offers a goal to work toward, and inspires confidence in the value of bringing underrepresented and often disregarded perspectives to light.

The Black Respondents

Finally, while this book does bring my own underrepresented Black voice to light, it does not fully achieve the same for Black residents of Baton Rouge due to my focus on the White vantage point. Still, I will draw on some of the insights that Black residents shared with me—and just as White-on-White research settings are not necessarily "pure," neither are Black-on-Black ones.

My positionality in relation to my Black respondents was no doubt also shaped by elements of both affinity and foreignness. I was more an insider with this group in clear ways, my race being the most obvious one. My family history in Baton Rouge is more similar to that of my Black research subjects as a result; all of our pasts are somehow marked by slavery, sharecropping, and segregation, stories about NBR's Plank Road in its glory days, connections to Southern University (or its HBCU rivals), Sundays at the same churches.

But of course, small differences sometimes can stand out more than large ones. Among my Black respondents, I no doubt seemed more lacking in ties to communities in present-day Baton Rouge, rather than past. My Black respondents also would have had their own reactions to my appearance, presentation, and Oxford affiliation. Granted, my Black interviewees were generally skewed toward middle-income and had higher educational backgrounds (partly reflecting my sampling approach, which I will discuss in the next chapter). This means my own signifiers of class and educational attainment may have contributed more to a sense affinity than foreignness among the Black respondents. Yet, it also serves as a reminder that the voices this book does not bring to light are those from backgrounds more similar to Alton Sterling's.

In the end, we should assume that each of my Black Baton Rouge respondents offered a particular version of themselves when in conversation with me. Yet, it also seems fair to assume the Black respondents were less consciously performing than would have been the case for many of the White respondents. My conversations with Black residents ultimately stood out for their frankness, and for giving me the sense that they were observing the White respondents along with me.

In the next chapter, I report on conversations I had with Black and White residents alike, amidst tension over St. George, schools, and Sterling's killing. I focus, however, on the discourses deployed by White residents—demonstrating their common vantage point on local racial politics, even when deeply divided, and thus the flexibility and strength of the color line in Baton Rouge.

3
The White Perspective in a Divided City

I was surprised not to have gotten a flat-out rejection sooner. "Now listen here: I've been around a long time." I grimaced with the phone held to my ear. I hadn't been told to "listen here" since I was a teenager; the term does not usually preface good news. "Why would someone come all the way from Oxford to ask about St. George if not to try to expose it as some sort of 'racist' effort?" This chilly response came from a St. George supporter and colorful persona named Randy.[1] His reply exposed how central race had become to the conversation around St. George: supporters were actively on the defense to demonstrate it was not racially motivated.

It is a testament to how small a midsize city can feel that, less than a week later, I found myself squeezed into a 12-year-old-sized desk next to none other than Randy himself. We were both attending a school board event at a local middle school. He had arrived shortly after the meeting started. The only open seat was right next to me. He, of course, had no idea that I was the researcher who had "come all the way from Oxford," where I was a graduate student at the time.

Both of us blended into the mix of attendees at the meeting: older White graduates and younger Black ones of the same nearby high school, whose racial demographics had flipped drastically in the mid-1980s, but for which the group was organizing a multi-decade alumni event. Randy's persona in this setting was opposite from what I had experienced in our tense first exchange. He was congenial and inclusive, emerged as a natural leader in the biracial group, and clearly was respected by the others for his commitment to the school. I introduced myself to him once the meeting ended. Having spent the last hour sharing a copy of both the meeting agenda and the LSU and Southern football schedules (lest the group accidentally schedule a future event that clashed with a game), Randy was probably more inclined to believe that I had some legitimate interest in the Baton Rouge community than he had been on the phone. Afterward, we ended up sitting down to talk for an hour and a half.

Though an outspoken supporter of the St. George effort, Randy not only lives outside the boundaries of the proposed new city but is one of few White

How the Color Line Bends: The Geography of White Prejudice in Modern America. Nina M. Yancy,
Oxford University Press. © Oxford University Press 2022. DOI: 10.1093/oso/9780197599426.003.0003

holdouts in North Baton Rouge (NBR). He still lives in the historically White, blue-collar neighborhood where he grew up and has experienced its changing demographics firsthand. During his interview, Randy slightly overestimated the Black majority within the city lines to be 65%, about 10 percentage points too high; but he maintained, "Black–White doesn't play into it, to me, very much."

•

My encounter with Deborah got off to a very different start. In response to my first question, which was simply to tell me about the area, she took a deep breath. "Let me just tell you some of my background … because I don't want to throw your data off." Deborah is a social worker for an organization that provides special education services to children under age 5. "A lot of social workers literally choose the nice area by zip code," Deborah told me before explaining that she would work anywhere in the parish where her services were needed. "I've been in lots of parts of Baton Rouge that most people, middle-income people, probably have never been," she said. Underneath Deborah's words are racialized meanings—"nice" and "middle-income" being code for predominantly White areas and a predominantly White income bracket—but what she was trying to communicate to me was clear. Unlike many White, middle-income residents of the parish, Deborah was intimately familiar with the social ills plaguing the area north of Florida Boulevard. As an active member of the community organization Together Baton Rouge, she had vehemently opposed the St. George effort and volunteered time to campaign against it.

Deborah was realistic about the severity of racial inequality in Baton Rouge, but she spoke with pride about how much Together Baton Rouge has brought Black and White residents together. "The race crap is gone," she said with elation, in reference to the community group's gatherings. "That is not an issue." As opposed to other settings around town where the topic of race might be avoided, "at Together Baton Rouge, we're comfortable. We've used those words enough with each other. We can talk about it."

•

On the surface, Randy and Deborah look like polar opposites. Randy is proudly conservative, a bold supporter of St. George, and adamant that race is of little significance in Baton Rouge. Deborah falls at the other end of the spectrum in both her politics and her stance on St. George, and believes that racial inequality is a major issue in the parish. Yet, the conclusions Randy and Deborah reach have something in common. Whether "race doesn't play into it" or "the race crap is gone," both reveal an understanding of race relations in

Table 3.1 Four Discursive Practices, Four Feelings of Prejudice

Discursive practice	Feeling of prejudice
Outgroup-oriented	
1) Denying racial motivations	*Subordinate race inspires fear and suspicion*
2) Minimizing racial categories	*Subordinate race is intrinsically different*
Ingroup-oriented	
3) Prioritizing White concerns	*Dominant race is superior*
4) Defending the social order	*Dominant race has claim to privilege and advantage*

Table synthesizes the discursive practices engaged in by White residents of Baton Rouge with the feelings of prejudice articulated by Blumer (1958).

which racial group interests are largely irrelevant to shaping one's perspective, priorities, or motivations. Even as Deborah believes that race is a powerful structural force shaping life outcomes in EBR, she argues that racial categories can be superseded when it comes to sharing stories and perspectives.

This chapter explores such instances—when similar logic underlies the speech of White residents of Baton Rouge despite the range of political opinions they express, revealing a shared perspective descending from White Americans' place atop the racial hierarchy. I offer evidence for the influence of this common perspective in the form of what I call four "discursive practices" that structure the reflections of the White respondents. These practices include (1) a rejection of racial motivations as a basis for White attitudes or actions in Baton Rouge in general, or in the St. George effort in particular; (2) an equation of Black and White based on a depoliticized understanding of the racial divide; (3) an acceptance of White concerns as legitimate and a silence around Black suffering; and (4) a defense of or deference to the social order.

These practices revisit the duality of prejudice as made up of both positive feelings about one's ingroup and negative feelings about an outgroup (Table 3.1). The first two discursive practices are engaged in denying that the outgroup-oriented feelings govern political, economic, and social relations in Baton Rouge. I find a broad avoidance of expressing beliefs traditionally understood to be prejudicial. White respondents openly reject the idea that fear or suspicion of Black people is at play, or that Black people are intrinsically different from White people.

On the other hand, the second two discursive practices positively embrace the ingroup-oriented feelings of prejudice—feelings that White respondents are less likely to consider prejudicial, but that are equally important in upholding the racial hierarchy. I find a broad lack of concern about implying the superiority of White people or their claim to certain privileges. With little hesitation, White respondents prioritize White interests (except for the sharpest critics of St. George), and they defer to and validate the racial status quo (St. George critics included).

In the background of all of this is the starkly segregated geography of Baton Rouge. The concentration of Black poverty in NBR and in public schools keeps it out of sight while also hyper-visible to many White residents, adding a layer of racial meaning to my White respondents' reflections on place and politics. This local landscape suggests why White residents would share a common perspective, and also reveals the limitations of this shared perspective—how much they do not see, or do not admit to see, from their vantage point.

After briefly explaining my approach to locating, interviewing, and analyzing the reflections of Baton Rouge residents, this chapter discusses the discursive practices that reveal my White respondents' aversion to appearing to hold anti-Black animus. I then discuss the discursive practices that reveal White respondents' *absence* of aversion to centering White people in their outlook on the world. Much of the rhetoric and reasoning that comprise these practices is in keeping with literature on contemporary White attitudes. In identifying these practices across the spectrum of opinion on a policy issue like St. George, however, I shine new light on the flexibility of the White perspective to uphold the color line. There exist many ways White Americans reinforce the racial divide even as they seek to minimize its significance.

Collecting and Analyzing Baton Rougeans' Perspectives

In July and August of 2016, I interviewed forty-eight residents of the greater Baton Rouge area that were located via a stratified, purposeful sampling approach (Patton 2002). The sample was stratified in that I aimed to capture a variety of perspectives on the St. George movement and life in Baton Rouge more generally; and purposeful in that it was constructed in order to include people likely to have opinions on St. George, although I also sought out more neutral observers of the movement. I began by contacting respondents I could easily access, across a range of categories—public figures that had been associated with the movement or the various sources of opposition; people connected to the school district or to the Catholic Church; residents I found through my local network—and then snowballed from there. I asked each respondent for recommendations of other people to interview, or events to attend. I also encountered a number of respondents by spending time at coffee shops, school board meetings, or around LSU's campus, following the example of Cramer (2016) and other ethnographic researchers.

A full list of respondents is provided in Appendix A. For the purposes of analysis, it is helpful to think of respondents as falling into five categories.

- **St. George supporters** ($n = 8$): White residents of the Baton Rouge area who actively supported the St. George incorporation effect, whether as volunteers on or leaders of the campaign, signatories to the petition, or outspoken advocates.
- **St. George opponents** ($n = 8$): White residents who were engaged in efforts to fight the incorporation of the new city and/or establishment of the new school district, whether via grassroots or institutional means.
- **School affiliates** ($n = 5$): White residents connected to the public school system (e.g., affiliated with schools or the school board).
- **Observers** ($n = 15$): White residents of the area who ranged from critical of to sympathetic to St. George, but who had not been actively involved with either the movement itself or the opposition to it.
- **Non-White respondents** ($n = 12$): Black residents of the area, including one mixed-race, Black-identifying respondent. Some were connected to the grassroots opposition to St. George, some were connected to the school system or other local institutions, and others were simply observers.

All my Black respondents were opposed to St. George, though I cannot claim that there was zero support for the incorporation or the school district among Black people in the area. There are some notable examples of Black support (such as Tea Party activist C. L. Bryant, who is based in Shreveport, LA, but was a public advocate for St. George). However, I did not personally encounter any Black residents of the unincorporated area who supported the petition. It also is important to note that, while I was intentional about including Black residents in the sample, when in the field I primarily was focused on learning about the impacts and legacy of Baton Rouge's desegregation order from Black residents' point of view, and on having a point of comparison to the White respondents. At the time, I was not necessarily planning to analyze the Black respondents' reflections in interpretive detail (see my discussion in Chapter 1 for more on my research scope). Thus, while I did interview several Black residents who held positions in local institutions comparable to some of the White respondents or who were similarly proximate to the St. George effort, my selection of Black respondents nonetheless lent toward convenience sampling. A different sampling approach could have highlighted greater diversity in Black perspectives and experiences in Baton Rouge. The penultimate section of this chapter will demonstrate the value they add to this analysis notwithstanding.

My sample tended to be older (M = 52 years, $S.D.$ = 15 years), included thirty males and eighteen females; twenty respondents had school-age children (42%). My sample also contained virtually no low-income individuals. These trends reflect the purposive sampling approach that led me to the disproportionately male, middle-aged, and middle-income individuals who hold positions of influence in Baton Rouge (including within the St. George movement, though to a considerably lesser extent among the opposition). The skew of these demographics should be kept in mind when reading my analysis. At the same time, contextuality, not representativeness or generalizability, should be the goal of an interpretive project such as this. I therefore describe the makeup of my sample, just as I described the particular context of Baton Rouge in Chapter 2, in order to show how my findings "work in context" and equip readers to think about how the findings might work similarly or differently in another context (Schwartz-Shea and Yanow 2012, 48).

All interviews were conducted in person, with the exception of three conducted over the phone.[2] Interviews lasted an hour on average and took place in a variety of locations: many in cafés, public libraries, or respondents' workplaces. I began by asking respondents to describe EBR Parish and offered them a map of the area as a visual aid. I then followed my interview script (see Appendix A), diverging if the respondent wanted to, but centering conversation on the St. George movement, schools in Baton Rouge, and broader issues facing the city–parish. In almost every case, the conversation naturally wandered to the events of early July.

I recorded, transcribed, and then analyzed interviews in a three-stage process (Braun and Clarke 2006; Weiss 1994). The first stage was open coding, or an initial review to identify general features that appeared throughout the data—such as references, figures of speech, particular arguments and opinions, or descriptions of events. I then arranged codes into larger themes, thinking about how the patterns that appeared throughout the interviews spoke to broader concepts. In this second stage of analysis, I created a data display, or a visual organization of the data that helped me categorize codes in the process of sorting them into themes (Miles and Huberman 1994). In a final stage of analysis, I considered the relationships between these themes, often used to express opposing views on a given topic, to identify four common *discursive practices* engaged in by the White respondents. I argue that these practices structured the reflections of White respondents across the sample, despite their polarization in opinion on a range of racialized issues.

Linguistic Patterns as "Discursive Practices"

The term "discourse" has been given a variety of definitions and thus is prone to vague usage. I understand discourses to be mechanisms of power that determine what is and is not said—whether a discourse takes the form of a version of events, a particular understanding of a social phenomenon, or some other interpretation of the "truth."[3] All of these serve as frames of reference on which individuals base their ideas and understandings. A quintessential example is colorblindness, the contemporary frame of reference that considers overtly racist language unacceptable but still provides White people with a language for justifying racial inequality (Bonilla-Silva 2006).

My use of the term "discursive" intends to describe what respondents are doing in the literal sense (i.e., talking to me). It further recognizes that their speech reflects not merely their own opinions, but also the interpretive resources (i.e., discourses) they are using to describe the world around them.

More central to my analysis is the term "practices." Shamus Khan's (2011) ethnography of privileged American youth emphasizes a disjuncture between what elite boarding school students *say* (espouse meritocracy) and what they *do* (entrench privilege). Similarly, I am interested in how my White respondents reproduce a number of discourses by espousing varied (and at times contradictory) points of view that nonetheless achieve similar ends. White people in Baton Rouge *say* a range of things, but, as I will show in this chapter, they *do* four things: deny racism, minimize racial categories, prioritize White concerns, and defend the social order. All of these, I argue, serve to legitimize the color line in Baton Rouge.

To say the White respondents are engaging in discursive "practices" also references the work of Pierre Bourdieu, whose theory of practice explains the social world as a dialectic relationship between social structures (e.g., state and economic institutions, cultural norms, and language) and human agents. Central to this interplay is Bourdieu's concept of *habitus*.[4] Habitus refers to the embodied, durable dispositions that inform how an individual interprets the world—one's "feel for the game" of social and political relations (Bourdieu 1990, 66–68). Scholars of race relations have previously proposed the idea of a "White habitus" to reference the common ways White people are socialized based on their position in the racial hierarchy, and thus the common ways White people tend to see the world (Bonilla-Silva 2006; DiAngelo 2011).

Because habitus descends from (even as it dialectically shapes and often reproduces) one's place in the social structure, it is a helpful concept when revisiting the logic of interpretivism and thinking about how White people's positionality would reveal itself in action. Each of my White respondents would have entered the interview setting with an intuitive understanding of how to move through the local world of Baton Rouge, including what is appropriate to say and how to say it, shaped by their racial identity. Each one's understanding would have informed their instinctive decisions in conversation with me. Close analysis of my interview data therefore offers a chance to consider the White respondents' choices in offering a particular interpretation of events, emphasizing certain arguments, or at times correcting themselves for having seemingly misspoken.

Of course, a semi-structured interview is not the way most people converse on a day-to-day basis. My presence as a researcher therefore created an instance in which the White respondents' "feel for the game" was put into practice in an unfamiliar setting. How a system works, however, is often revealed just as much by its stumbles as by its smooth operation. This means that even if the setting was unnatural, the way White respondents grappled with, went back and forth on, and ultimately came to answer my questions was revealing of what they thought to be the "right" or "true" understanding of their local world in Baton Rouge. And even if my presence as a *Black* interviewer influenced White respondents' speech, the same underlying habitus— shaped by life in a high-density Black area—would have guided their instincts about how to speak to me.

I now turn to what was said, addressing each of the four discursive practices in turn. In my discussion of each practice, I generally move across the spectrum from St. George support to opposition as I identify themes in the White respondents' reflections.

Denying Racial Motivations

"It's already the #1 area in the country for private school attendance," Wayne said with frustration, explaining why he had little faith that Baton Rouge's schools could be saved. The Baton Rouge metro area in fact ranked fourth in the country at the time, and it is not an outlier in a state with particularly high private school enrollment rates—but with 19% of children enrolled in private or parochial schools, Baton Rouge nearly doubles the national rate of 10%.[5] Wayne continued: "There's a reason for that, and it's not because White people don't like Black people."

Wayne was young and enthusiastic, had helped organize the 2014–2015 St. George campaign, and evidently had experience in defending the initiative against accusations of racism. While his denial that anti-Black sentiment holds sway in Baton Rouge today is a particularly explicit example, everyone I encountered who was sympathetic to the St. George effort—and many who were critical—offered a similar argument. Given the racial overtones of the public debate about St. George, the recent racial turbulence, and likely also my presence as a Black interviewer, the White respondents regularly denied that that racism explained either the incorporation effort or social outcomes in Baton Rouge—without me making any mention of race.

Playing by the Rules of the Game

According to the St. George advocates, trying to not appear racially motivated was an official part of their strategy in the 2014–2015 effort, evidenced by their decision to include *all* of the contiguous unincorporated land in the parish within the boundaries of the proposed city. Kenneth, a middle-aged small business owner close to the effort's leadership, explained why he believed this decision was necessary.

> **Nina**: Did it seem like there was already a distinct identity among the unincorpo-
> rated parts?
> **Kenneth**: Well, you've got to be very careful when you draw your boundaries, okay?
> Because if you just go picking and choosing …you can't do that. For one thing, you
> are going to be challenged in court, and it's not going to pass. You can't just pick and
> choose. So, we said to eliminate any thought—which it didn't *(Kenneth laughed,
> shaking his head)*—about this being racially or economically motivated, we said,
> okay we'll just take the unincorporated area, no argument there. So we took all,
> what some may consider good and bad areas. We took the high-crime areas along
> with the affluent areas.

Residents of the "bad," "high-crime" areas are implied to be Black on the basis of those code words alone, but also thanks to Kenneth's explanation that these areas were strategically included to demonstrate that racism did not motivate the effort. Equating this strategy with being "very careful" in order to avoid a legal challenge, as well as using the language of what you "can" and "can't" do, suggests the St. George leaders' understanding that there are rules for avoiding accusations of racism—rules that they felt they were following by including Black neighborhoods. Others made this point more explicitly. Randy, for example, cited a neighborhood called Gardere that is notable for having a concentrated, low-income, Black population south of Florida Boulevard. Randy remarked: "They didn't want to be charged with discrimination, like, 'oh well, you left out Gardere [...], it's going to be lily White.'" Conspicuously, Gardere was among the majority-Black areas that *were* left out of the revised boundaries for the 2018–2019 St. George campaign.

It is worth noting that Randy's logic also resonated among observers (rather than organizers or supporters) of the St. George effort. One respondent, for example, mentioned Gardere as a "huge African-American area," and then continued, "so, there are sects that would be included, so I don't know if it was necessarily..." He trailed off before finishing his sentence. "I think people just wanted to have more control over their public schools," he concluded, having avoided the uncomfortable topic of whether anti-Black sentiment was behind the effort.

In addition to saying that the effort was not about race, the St. George advocates described the incorporation effort in a manner at odds with polling that showed a stark racial divide in opinion on the issue: 44% of White residents supported the effort, in comparison to 8% of Black residents (Climek and Means 2013). The White respondents who supported St. George frequently echoed the disparaging tone of the official St. George website that criticized the "Powers That Be" in Baton Rouge (i.e., BRAC, BRAF, and the Metro Council). Respondents closest to the effort, however, expressed the greatest animosity toward White parents of students enrolled in EBR's magnet schools. These parents were characterized as among the few who benefit from an underperforming school system. The fact that many of these parents were critical of the St. George effort, and often on the grounds of its potential racial impact, was a source of deep frustration.

> **Randy:** What the magnet schools are basically is the liberal White parents—this is their way to say, "Hey, I'm with the public schools." Yeah, they're with the public schools, but they're not with *these* public schools. They're with Baton Rouge High which is—it's a rose garden."
>
> ...
>
> **Wayne:** It's always some lily-White mom whose kid goes to the foreign language academic immersive program. I mean, not that there's anything wrong with that, but it's like, "really? Really? Your kid is just getting a private school education for free." The hypocrisy is sickening.

It is true that magnet school parents had a stake in the St. George fight: 27% of the students who would have been displaced by the 2014–2015 incorporation effort were in magnet schools (Together Baton Rouge 2014). Yet, this group—and its White members, as Randy and Wayne both specified—

received nearly all the attention of the St. George advocates when they described who in Baton Rouge would suffer as a result of the incorporation. Randy and Wayne thus shifted the conversation away from St. George's racial impact. The tacit argument was that because White families are the ones who benefit from the current system, White families are the ones with something to lose, and therefore changing the current system would not hurt Black families.

Besides obscuring the impact the incorporation would have had on the majority of students who do not attend magnet schools (a population of over 27,000 that is less than 8% White), the narrative criticizing the White magnet parents was tinged with a sense of betrayal. Feeling the efforts they took to include Black people within the new city were not appreciated, the St. George advocates retort with the same labels—such as "lily White"—which they felt had been wrongly applied to them. If "you can't pick and choose" city boundaries, it is unfair that the magnet schools are allowed to choose the best students and create a "rose garden." With these comments, the St. George advocates reveal an expectation that other White people play by the same rules of the game of avoiding the appearance of racism. When White individuals opposed to St. George call the effort "racist," they violate these expectations and instead subvert the norm of what Kristen Lavelle (2014) calls White protectionism: a shared commitment to depicting other White individuals as fundamentally good (and, by extension, nonracist) people.

The moral outrage that emerges when the rules of White protectionism are violated, evident in Wayne and Randy's comments, tells us two things. First, it demonstrates that the expectation to play by the rules operates as a sort of unspoken "pact" between White people. The common sense that White people should not accuse one another of racism is maintained *transactionally*: had the St. George organizers not felt they were accused of racism by magnet school parents, they would not have made accusations of hypocrisy in return. Second, Wayne and Randy's anger offers insight into how they understand "racism" in the first place: it is located in bad intentions. Further, if one's intentions are *said* to be racism-free, they should be taken as such.

This understanding of racism as something to be either admitted or denied is also evident in instances where the pact is being upheld. A young lawyer named Chad, for example, described the incorporation effort as "a stupid and obtuse" way to address school quality. But, Chad is the parent of a young child, was thoroughly disappointed with his public school options, and had signed the 2014 petition reluctantly. He was clear that schools, and not race, were his only motivation, and believed this was the case for others, too: "Not a single person that I ever talked to, even when they were as honest as they could be, over beers or whatever, no one ever communicated this was about getting away from the Black part of the city."

Chad characterizes the (implicitly White) people he spoke to about St. George as fundamentally good by emphasizing that, even in the most candid of situations "over beers," no racial intentions were admitted. Contemporary norms make it unlikely that these people would have explicitly told Chad they were trying to "get away from the Black part of the city," even if this were true. All the same, Chad's willingness to divulge details of these interpersonal exchanges—which, at face value, appears frank— in fact highlights his commitment to upholding White protectionism and illustrating the innocence of his fellow St. George supporters.

Even more, it highlights the pact I identify related to St. George as an example of Mills's (1997) "Racial Contract" in action. As with all contracts, the Racial Contract comes with duties: specifically, it requires White people to agree to the "correct" view of the world in order to take up their privileged place within it. The correct view required by the Racial Contract, however, is a deliberately *incorrect* one: an "inverted epistemology" or "cognitive dysfunction" that "precludes self-transparency and genuine understanding of social realities" (18). This is the basis of Mills's epistemology of ignorance— the epistemology that underlies Chad and his friends' deep-seated agreement not to admit, suggest, or even acknowledge in oneself the possibility of racial motivations.

Ignorance and Innocence

It was hardly surprising that the St. George advocates defended the effort as nonracially motivated. Moving along the spectrum toward opposition to the effort, however, I again find a hesitance to identify racial motives—even if White respondents' engagement with the pact not to call St. George racist is slightly different. Chad upheld the pact by claiming *knowledge* of the effort's motivations (i.e., as being nonracial), while nonetheless revealing his and his friends' commitment to racial *ignorance* as an epistemology that "evades and distorts racial reality" [quoting Mueller's (2020, 148) reformulation of Mills]. Other White respondents were more explicit in declaring either their own ignorance or the ignorance of St. George supporters as a means to uphold the pact—and, on the few occasions where the pact was violated, they found other ways to defend White innocence.

Consider the perspectives offered by Baton Rouge residents connected to the local school system or to city organizations: both categories in which White respondents tended to express concerns about the impact St. George would have on EBR schools and city finances, but who were not particularly close to the grassroots opposition to the effort. One of these respondents was Nancy, who has spent her whole career in the public school system, including working at a school in the southeast when mandatory busing was first implemented. She cited this experience with authority when explaining her position on St. George, which was one of the most sympathetic among respondents affiliated to public schools. "We don't want our kids bused," Nancy said, adopting the pronoun "we" as she argued that St. George was fundamentally an effort to regain the control parents had lost under Parker's desegregation plan. Despite the racialized history this conjures (and, of course, the fact that involuntary busing ended over twenty years ago), Nancy said of St. George, "It wasn't racial. It was we just want our kids closer to home." She added: "That's basically what I know." Nancy casts herself as someone with both intimate knowledge of the perspective of dissatisfied school parents, and limited knowledge of their motivations in the present day. She vouches for the St. George supporters as not racially motivated, but deflects much further consideration of the topic.

Other White respondents connected to the school system repeatedly made claims of not knowing what motivated the St. George supporters, and further suggested that the supporters of St. George themselves were limited in their knowledge, too. A school district employee named Joanne said of the southeast, "They just don't know what's really available, or they won't believe it—I don't know." Another school district employee criticized the media for failing to cover positive stories about EBR but reliably airing coverage of fights or other incidents. "They don't put it out in the media when it happens at Catholic High, or in Livingston Parish, you know what I'm saying? It's like EBR's got this cloud over it. I don't know what it is." A leader at one of Baton Rouge's major civic institutions refrained from making a disclaimer about his own knowledge but explicitly called out ignorance among the general populace: "Ignorance is the biggest challenge we have. People don't understand there's some super-cool things going on in Baton Rouge."

In these examples, claims to ignorance work as a shield in two ways. On the one hand, these respondents argue that it is only a lack of knowledge, rather than racialized perceptions or fears, that leads residents of the southeast to be critical of EBR schools. On the other hand, ignorance also is invoked to shield the respondents themselves. Even as Joanne suggests parents "won't believe" the good things about the school system, she concludes her reflection by commenting on the limits of her own knowledge. If there are racial motivations behind the effort beyond what she knows, she cannot be held accountable for them.

White respondents unconnected to the school system or city institutions (the "observers" of the St. George effort) were less likely to suggest that ignorance about what EBR had to offer was driving the St. George supporters to pursue the breakaway district. In contrast to the "insider" opinions of school district employees, for example, the observers generally believed that the public school system was underperforming and unsafe. Yet, the observers nonetheless supported the characterization of the St. George supporters as oblivious, this time to the racial implications of their campaign. As a recent college graduate named Isabel put it, "They just want to amputate the stuff that doesn't concern them and build something that will help them and their family, not necessarily the city of Baton Rouge." Amputation is a strong metaphor to invoke, which Isabel seemed to recognize when clarifying: "I don't know if their goal was to—this makes it sound so bad—if their goal is to make [the schools] more White." She hesitated. "I feel like that's not what they intend to do."

Other White observers repeatedly cited "selfishness" or "self-centeredness" as the motivation behind St. George. Only one observer, however, considered the *consequences* of the effort as well as its motives. This was a reporter who had covered some of the news around St. George, and who called the effort "naive": "They hated that they were being attacked as racist," she said. "But it's like, they were absolutely ignoring the fact that it was going to have racial implications. I don't think that they were all racist, but they were ignoring that." The reporter engaged with the topic of racism more straightforwardly than did any other White observer I encountered—but still used the language of ignorance to characterize the effort as well intentioned, even if naively so.

I should note that while talking *around* the word "racism" was most common, two White respondents stood out for being less hesitant to directly call St. George supporters "racist." Both were laypeople who had endorsed St. George opposition efforts (but did not lead or actively participate in them), and took pains to distance themselves from other "racist Whites" in Baton Rouge, both geographically and ideologically. One respondent, Kathy, said she called those who had left the city or parish "the White flighters" and shared her suspicions that St. George supporters were racially motivated. Another respondent, Susan, said "I'm pretty sure it's all racist," and then emphasized her distance in part by sharing, "I don't think I know anybody . . . well, I might know one couple living there."

These deliberate distancing efforts are a notable diversion from most White respondents' hesitance to make claims of racism in relation to St. George. However, also notable was what accompanied the delivery of these comments, and how White respondents like Kathy grappled with the implications of calling St. George a racist effort. For example, Kathy dramatically lowered her voice to a whisper (despite the fact that we were already in a private discussion room at the local library) when referencing St. George supporters as "some people I think who are racist, closet racists; not all of them, but some of them." Kathy's whisper indicated that she recognized her statement violated the pact and thus should be shared discreetly, even as she added the caveat, "not all of them." She also went on to reference someone she did consider to be among the "closet racists," but emphasized that they had "a nice, polite churchgoing relationship—so we've got that church love." This reference to "church love" again serves the purpose of morally distancing Kathy from racist White behavior, while also softening her critique of her "polite, churchgoing" acquaintance. (We also will see later in this chapter how Kathy fails to transfer her concern about White racism being behind St. George to the Black children and households who stand to suffer most from the incorporation.)

Finally, White respondents who were more engaged in or helped lead the grassroots opposition to St. George were more likely to talk about racism in institutional terms, openly expressing concerns about the role of racism in shaping the demographics of Baton Rouge schools and neighborhoods. Nonetheless, a reluctance to identify individual racial motivations within this system was clear. One respondent, Elizabeth, recounted a conversation she had with a St. George organizer, trying to explain to him the racialized impact the incorporation would have: "I told him, 'Look, okay you're not a racist—and besides, racism is only possible *institutionally*.'" Another respondent, Tammy, who was involved in the grassroots opposition, said, "I've always tried to always be careful that I'm not saying that race was the motivating factor, but there were inevitable consequences for race that could not be ignored."

Both of these comments direct attention to the racial consequences of the St. George effort. This is the same approach I myself took in telling the history of the effort in Chapter 2, rather than try to arbitrate the influence of racial fears or prejudices. Yet, both respondents also reveal an avoidance of engaging with the possibility of racist motivations at the individual level. Consider Elizabeth: it is evident that she has put effort into learning about the insidious effects of racism as it operates within institutions, and she was confident in sharing her knowledge with the St. George organizer. However, she has embraced a structural framework for understanding racism to the extent that she argues racism existing at the individual level is impossible. In a similar vein, Tammy admits that she has "always tried to always be careful"—echoing Kenneth's warning that "you've got to be very careful when you draw your boundaries." The resonance between these two phrases suggests that even the racially progressive White respondents are following implicit rules about not calling other White people racist.

A final example comes from Deborah, the social worker introduced the start of this chapter, who admitted that she had sensed hesitance from White people to stand behind the claim that the St. George supporters were racist—even as she herself wavered in drawing the same conclusion. "Everybody kind of came down to 'they are racist' . . . but everybody had friends over there," she said. Deborah assigned herself and other critics of St. George the authority to adjudicate claims of racism, claims that were dismissed in most cases on the grounds that the St. George supporters were "nice people" and "friends they liked." It is worth noting that Deborah stands out among respondents as a White parent whose children attended traditional public schools. "Don't you think you're abusing your daughter?" she recounted once being asked by a White, private school parent who was aghast that Deborah would send her children to EBR schools. Reflecting on that experience, Deborah shared her disbelief: "that prejudice was so strong." But she soon retracted this claim: "I don't know that it's really prejudice, if that's the right word. They are scared."

Deborah's constant vacillations between portraying other White people as either racially prejudiced or sympathetic show White protectionism at work even among those most critical of St. George. In contrast to the protectionism Lavelle (2014) identifies among White people who work to portray their close family members as good people, however, Deborah and the other critics of St. George hesitate to criticize White people on the opposite side of a contentious debate. This hesitance speaks to the power of the shared understanding among the White respondents that the influence of anti-Black animus should be denied or minimized (unless pointing it out in others to demonstrate oneself as nonracist by comparison). Even as the St. George opponents express concerns about the racial impacts of the incorporation effort, they, too, reveal a conception of racism—or, at least, the sort of racism for which an individual can be held accountable—as located in ill will toward Black people. More than an individualistic and moralistic definition of racism, this conception further grants the White respondents authority to adjudicate whether or not racism is at play, based on whether their White peers admit to having prejudicial intentions or instead seem to be "nice people."

The St. George effort raised red flags in a parish with a fraught history of desegregation. The racial dimensions of the incorporation effort may have been more salient in the presence of a Black interviewer, but they had been significant enough to make the idea that the St. George supporters were "racist" something that Deborah felt "everybody kind of came down to" in the opposition to the effort; something that Baton Rouge insiders as well as observers of the effort felt they had to delicately address and should claim no knowledge of; and something that the St. George supporters felt they had to actively fight. In each of these diverse arguments, I find a readiness to defend the St. George actors as not racially motivated, or to attribute what looks like racism to ignorance, selfishness, or fear. These common instincts, coming from people with diametrical views on the issue, therefore offer evidence for the first element of the shared White perspective in Baton Rouge: the denial that racial considerations are behind White people's actions or attitudes.

Equating Black and White

In response to headlines that had referenced the St. George effort along the lines of "Wealthy Whites want to break away from Baton Rouge," Wayne shared his disbelief.[6] "Huh? It's like, wait, that's *way* more segregated," he said, referencing the affluent neighborhoods of South Baton Rouge that are sprinkled around LSU's campus. "You stand at the top of your tower and chastise us, when you're more segregated than North Baton Rouge—which is predominantly Black!"

Wayne's use of the word "segregated" departs from a pattern that other researchers have identified (e.g., Bonilla-Silva 2006, 112) and that most of my sample followed: because all-White neighborhoods have been normalized, a "segregated neighborhood" is often a euphemism for a Black neighborhood. In that regard, Wayne is more accurate than most in recognizing that a majority-White neighborhood can in fact be "more segregated" than a majority-Black one. At the same time, Wayne reveals an understanding that single-race spaces are "bad." A segregated neighborhood invites criticism, and "segregated" thus serves as a useful adjective for *deploying* criticism targeted at White critics of St. George. Still, Wayne reveals little appreciation that what segregation means for an all-White space is drastically different for an all-Black one. For Wayne, segregation exists as a discursive weapon, rather than a system of exclusion that has wrought deep harm on many Black communities, while concentrating privilege among many White ones.

Wayne's comment offers one illustration of how racial difference is depoliticized among the White respondents—by which I mean racial difference is understood in isolation from the history that produced and the power relations that govern the present-day divide between Black and White people in Baton Rouge (W. Brown 2008). Beyond taking care not to identify anti-Black sentiment, as discussed in the previous section, the White respondents take care not to imply that Black people are fundamentally different or lesser than White people. I by no means argue that they *should* do so. Yet, in tracing the ways the White respondents work to demonstrate the irrelevance of racial categories, I identify a common practice of constructing a false equivalence between Black and White.

Two Takes on Race and Class

Among St. George supporters, the false equivalence of Black and White was evident in a central argument made by the campaign: that smaller, community school districts invariably lead to better outcomes for students. The St. George advocates I spoke with specifically emphasized that smaller districts would be better for students not only in the southeast but also in the predominately Black neighborhoods of NBR.

I should note that, today, there are multiple lines of discourse around "community schools." One concerns longstanding, racialized debates over local control (e.g., descending from the busing era). The other concerns more recent, socialized debates over the role a school should play in a community, typically emphasizing the importance of school–community partnerships to provide holistic services to students and families, particularly in disinvested neighborhoods (and at times, with neoliberal intentions).[7] The former of these two interpretations of community schools is most relevant to my analysis in Baton Rouge; whether EBR schools should provide more social services was not a subject of great concern. However, the arguments of St. George supporters may have subtly benefited from the fact that calls for "community schools" have been made in the interest of both privileged (typically White) neighborhoods and underprivileged (typically non-White) neighborhoods.

Kenneth, for example, argued that each smaller school system could "focus on the needs of its immediate community." Wayne reported that this was what people in NBR wanted, too: "They're like, 'please get this done, because if you do, we want to create an independent school district here.' " I do not wade into the debate over the ideal size of a school district.[8] I also do not wade into the nuanced topic of how, at times, Black communities have argued for greater local control over schools, too, seeking self-determination in reaction to the harms of desegregation and disinvestment.[9] Instead, I make two observations about *how* St. George supporters argue for smaller districts in Baton Rouge.

First, there is a noticeable silence around the fact that there already exists an example of the kind of community school district that it is claimed would benefit NBR—the City of Baker School District, located immediately north of NBR (see map in Figure 2.1). Although Baker was 84% White when it began agitating to break away from EBR schools in the 1980s, outmigration left Baker with a 46% White population by the time it was finally able to create its own district. Baker was 76% Black as of 2016, with a student body that was 94% Black and 81% eligible for free or reduced lunch. Despite its small size—one-twentieth the size of EBR—in 2016 Baker trailed EBR as the 67th-ranked school district in the state. While Zachary and Central are regularly cited by St. George advocates, Baker is never considered in the context of the "smaller is better" argument. Only Randy mentioned Baker on accident, saying, "I love Baker and Zachary [schools]," but quickly correcting himself to replace "Baker" with "Central." No other supporter of St. George ever brought up Baker.

It is understandable that the St. George organizers point to successful examples of prior breakaway efforts to justify their cause. Yet, they conspicuously ignore the most proximate example of the solution they argue would be better for students in a disproportionately Black and low-income area like NBR. Randy's slip suggests that behind this silence was a shared understanding that Baker—a close neighbor to NBR with comparable demographics—was best left unmentioned when praising the benefits of small school systems.

Related to the silence around Baker, a second trend in the St. George supporters' arguments for smaller districts was turning a blind eye toward the immense burden of poverty in NBR. The larger silence here is around the well-documented relationship between both individual- and community-level socioeconomic status and school performance (for a review, see Sirin 2005). The burden of poverty in NBR most often simply went unmentioned, although Randy at one point slammed his hand on the table and announced, "It's not the money!"

Wayne's only engagement with the question of school funding in NBR was to suggest that corporate taxes collected from NBR's ExxonMobil petroleum plant would support the schools. This idea was considered irrational, or even offensive, by other Baton Rouge residents—and not without reason. Louisiana is famous for offering lavish subsidies to corporations, and to ExxonMobil in particular, through mechanisms such as long-term property tax abatements granted by the state (with local governments having little say); these mechanisms have been estimated to cost Louisiana schools $600 million each year (Litvinov 2019). Although there has been recent progress in dismantling this system,[10] Wayne's research into the financing of the St. George district almost certainly would have made him aware that corporate taxes do relatively little to fund education in Louisiana. Proximity to petroleum refineries is also a severe environmental hazard for the disproportionately Black and low-income communities who live near the plants spread along the

Mississippi River between Baton Rouge and New Orleans, in what is known as "Cancer Alley" (Baurick, Younes, and Meiners 2019; see also Cole and Foster 2001). Even if we put aside these concerns, Wayne's suggestion shows that he recognized some financial disparity between NBR and St. George, but he dismissed the importance of this disparity with his reference to nonexistent corporate tax revenue.

In addition to minimizing the resource differential that parallels the color line in Baton Rouge, the St. George supporters tended to defer responsibility to Black communities for Black problems. "Let them run their schools," as Randy put it. One local politician who had supported St. George revealed a similar sentiment when explaining the need for development in NBR to encourage more "Black professionals" to move back. "I mean, they expect amenities and services and shopping and a doctor's office," he said. "They expect everything everybody else has." The politician's racially coded use of "everybody" necessarily leaves out the communities in NBR where, as he himself noted, there is a considerable lack of grocery stores, let alone other amenities and services. He further equates Black professionals with White professionals while also implying that the Black professionals have a partic-ular obligation to return to NBR.[11] This is similar to the argument that NBR would be just as likely as the southeast to benefit from a smaller school district, and should be granted sole responsibility over the challenge of creating one. Race is downplayed as a category that shapes material outcomes, while also reified as a category that determines who is naturally responsible for whom.

At least one critic of St. George, another school district affiliate, similarly assigned responsibility to the Black middle class to bring their capital to lower-income settings. "I don't mean to sound prejudiced," she said, going on to cite "middle-class African-American families" as "the low-hanging fruit" to be drawn back into the public schools and back to NBR. More common among those either neutral about or critical of St. George, however, was support for the argument that class identity mattered more than racial identity. While this meant they were much more likely than the St. George advocates to recognize poverty as a significant problem in Baton Rouge, this recognition served as yet another way to conceptualize the racial divide in depoliticized terms.

A common way that White respondents minimized race and argued that class was more important was invoking their own middle-income Black friends. A respondent named Brian cited his Black neighbors' opposition to building a basketball court in the neighborhood as an effort to show "how much they valued *not* valuing street culture stuff." He went on, "because, culturally, it all gets so homogeneous when you get up to these upper levels of income." Brian's story touches on dynamics that appear in scholarship on middle-income Black Americans, who often face tenuous economic situations as well as have to negotiate between their racial and class identities—particularly in more advantaged, suburban settings.[12] Yet, Brian gave little thought to the complexities that might have informed his neighbors' preferences. He instead laughed as he told this story, as if cultural difference between middle-income White and Black households was a comical suggestion—and as if I, an assumedly nonpoor Black person myself, could only concur.

Another respondent, James, worked for one of the downtown institutions that had fought against St. George on the grounds that it would negatively impact the well-being of the whole parish. He had a polished persona and sharp wit, but also a relaxed presence. He told a story that his Black friend, Don, had once recounted about an unpleasant traffic stop with a Baton Rouge police officer. James laughed off his friend's concern that things might have been even worse had Don's Black teenage son been at the wheel. "His son's an honor student at Catholic High School. I mean, give me a break, you know?" James explained his thinking in further detail:

> Unfortunately, in the South and in Louisiana, poor folks are Black folks. It looks like a racial issue, but it's really not. My Black professional friends go into North Baton Rouge, and they don't get treated well. "You don't know anything about where we live, who we are, what challenges we face." So I will say at first is a class issue, and secondly, is a race issue. That's where I tier it. It's really fascinating and interesting.

Even as James is more explicit than most White respondents in appreciating the burden of poverty that falls on Black people in Louisiana, he doubts that race itself has explanatory power. "There is no White community, there is no Black community," James later said of Baton Rouge, explaining that it only *looks* like this is the case. By citing his Black friends' experiences in NBR—after having explicitly dismissed Don's own take on his experience as a Black man in Baton Rouge—James grants himself the authority to speak on the "fascinating and interesting" topic of whether race matters. In doing so, James exemplifies the tendency of the dominant subject to claim to "see everything from nowhere," while also characterizing racial inequality as a "fascinating" issue into which he has more authentic insight than Don and other Black individuals.

On the surface, arguments such as James's contradict the St. George advo-cates' dismissal of socioeconomic status as a factor that limits the oppor-tunities of many Black people in Baton Rouge. Yet, emphasizing that class is the most important category does the same work of depoliticizing race by disregarding the role that race and racism have played in creating (and continue to play in maintaining) a system where the "poor folks are Black folks." Moreover, the St. George opponents and supporters are equally likely to claim authority to explain the importance—or lack thereof—of racial categories.

The naturalness with which race is consistently discounted therefore offers evidence of a coherent perspective among the White respondents. The St. George advocates treat the racial divide as natural (in assigning responsibility to Black communities for their own problems) but also as insignificant in shaping outcomes. And while those critical of St. George instead treat the racial divide as irrelevant (in respect to class identities), this line of thinking, too, concludes that race is insignificant in shaping outcomes. In both cases, the White respondents invoke the words of Black people, whether citing NBR residents who want their own school district or recounting stories about Black friends. But, the White respondents reveal no understanding of their Black peers as agents with their own subjective experiences and perspectives—let alone a group better positioned to understand how racial categories impact life in the parish. Instead, Black views are cited only to support White respondents' own points.

Taken together, the White respondents' effortlessness in minimizing race shines light on the habitus, or embodied logic, that guides them through life in EBR: as long as the consequences of racial categories remain unseen, the color line remains intact.

The Color Line Goes Both Ways

So far, we have seen that when White residents of Baton Rouge deem race irrelevant to outcomes, they also tend to imply that race has no meaningful impact on one's perspective (e.g., claiming just as much authority as their Black friends to comment on Black people's experience of racial discrimina-tion or inequality). White residents' reflections on the July shootings further illuminated this denial that racial identity affects subjective experiences.

Randy, for example, said, "Black people a lot of times in public, I would feel like they didn't *see* me; and I think a lot of Black people feel the Whites don't see them." While contradicting his initial argument that "Black–White doesn't play into things very much," Randy expressed sincere concern about this lack of interracial recognition. He spoke enthusiastically, however, about his feeling that there had been richer interracial exchanges since the shootings: "Now, suddenly—we're seeing each other!"

Many others echoed Randy by emphasizing that racial tensions impact White people as much as Black people. As one supporter of the St. George petition told me, "It's not only stuff with White people—Black people, they need to let go of how they feel about Whites. And it's definitely understandable, but it's gotta go both ways." A rising senior at LSU who was relatively neutral on the St. George issue offered another example: "You've got bubbles in all the neighborhoods," he commented. "I mean, there is a bubble in North Baton Rouge that doesn't understand what's going on in South Baton Rouge," suggesting that learning needs to happen on both sides. Finally, even among White respondents who were most vocally committed to racial progress, concerns about the role of Black residents in sustaining a racial divide appeared. A leader of Together Baton Rouge reflected, "That wall of racial distrust can work both ways." He went on to offer the example of Black communities often being suspicious of new initiatives intended to help them: "I mean, a proposal for schools? Well, immediately [someone] starts to say, 'are they trying to take over?'"

My point here is not to absolve Black residents of any role to play in bridging the racial divide, or to deny that White residents perceive distrust from their Black neighbors. I instead note that White residents frame the relationship between the races in Baton Rouge as one in which both players have equal agency in determining whether the relationship is friendly or antagonistic, and equal responsibility for its present-day form (let alone its present-day imbalance). One final exchange illustrates this sentiment. I was speaking with Larry, a mild-mannered and friendly shopkeeper. He thought the idea of incorporating a new city was "not fair" and that the effect it could have was "scary," but he also believed that racism was primarily a thing of the past. He recounted stories about tensions following the advent of busing as if they were amusing anecdotes from years past. "That just goes to show you how things change," Larry said as he laughed.

Larry's upbeat view of how much things had changed was at odds with the climate in Baton Rouge when I was speaking to him, only two days after the shooting of the officers and thus at the end of two of the most racially inflammatory weeks Baton Rouge had experienced in years. He did comment on the shootings, however, to say, "The races have to get along a little bit better." He spoke in scattered thoughts as he continued on this point, explaining that he loved all of his Black customers, and that he knows all of his neighbors by name, even the Black neighbor whom he's never met. He went on to tell a story about this "older Black fellow":

> **Larry:** Every time I go by, I always wave, and he turns his head down. And I told my wife, I said, 'one day he's going to be out cutting the grass, and I'm going to go over there, and I'm going to say, I've been here 16 years and I don't know your name.' Actually I do know his name, but I'll tell him that I don't—the only reason I know his name is because I got a piece of his mail by mistake *(Larry laughed)*. But it's pretty isolated, at least where I live . . . I bet it's a lot more common in the city. People have just got to get along . . . though it's so much easier said than done.
>
> **Nina:** What do you think keeps people from going up and introducing themselves?
>
> **Larry:** I don't know. Maybe they have pre-conceived notions about us . . . or me.

Although Larry jumps to explaining why the neighbor has never introduced himself to Larry rather than vice versa, Larry takes some responsibility for having never said hello, too, thinking that he should one day do so. But Larry quickly finds himself in unfamiliar territory when reflecting on how "they" (Black people) might view "us" (White people)—"us" being his first instinct to reference, before adding "or me." When probed, Larry makes a tentative step toward imagining what the mindset of the Black man might have been, but he loses the ease with which he previously commented on how much things had changed in Baton Rouge. No longer speaking with upbeat certainty, Larry struggles to do the kind of interpretive work that is rarely required of him, and to think of how Black people view White people.

This section, "Equating Black and White," has presented a range of arguments from White respondents built on the premise that there is no power differential that tracks the color line. Paradoxically, in *minimizing* the significance of race, the White respondents also *reinforce* how starkly the racial divide presents itself in Baton Rouge. The St. George advocates present racial categories as irrelevant to outcomes, but also immutable: the challenges facing Black communities are those that Black leaders should address. And in suggesting local schools as a solution for Black communities, the St. George advocates ironically only highlight Baton Rouge's stark segregation. St. George critics differ in their approach to minimizing race—they reject that racial categories are immutable—but they still highlight how race functions as a dividing line in Baton Rouge. For instance, when James says, "It looks like a racial issue, but it's really not," he has to admit how things look (i.e., deeply unequal) before working to minimize the importance of race. Finally, in the aftermath of the July shootings, the consensus that "the races have to get along better" highlights the existence of a racial fault line, even if it is then depoliticized by the argument that *White* residents are suffering from a lack of trust and recognition.

Beyond reducing the racial divide to a question of whether people "get along," the depoliticization of racial categories further demonstrates the White respondents' ignorance about the workings of racial power. This ignorance stems from White people's privileged position, from which they can easily navigate life with little understanding of how race functions as a category of oppression. Because White people benefit from this ignorance, they also have an interest in maintaining it—whether in overtly claiming no knowledge of whether anti-Black animus motivates White action, or simply revealing no knowledge of the limited life chances of Black people in Baton Rouge.

Taken together with the denial of racial motivations discussed in the previous section, the false equivalence of Black and White demonstrates how White residents of Baton Rouge make different arguments but engage in the same practices of negating traditional feelings of prejudice directed at Black people. In conversation with a Black researcher, but almost certainly in other facets of their lives, too, the White respondents operate with a conception of the world in which anti-Black sentiment does not (or should not be said to) influence White people's actions, and the Black–White divide does not (despite how it looks) influence outcomes. In the next section, I shift focus from discursive practices concerned with negating any ill will or ill fate associated with Blackness, to practices that positively assert or defend White people's privilege and superiority in the racial hierarchy.

The Superiority of White Concerns

There are probably few harder places to be a visiting team than "Death Valley"—or LSU's Tiger Stadium, as less ardent football fans might call it.[13] The stadium roared so loudly one Saturday night in 1988 that the nearby Louisiana Geological Survey registered it as an earthquake. The Tigers' impressive win record at home may or may not have anything to do with a longstanding tradition of greeting the visitors with a live tiger on the field— a tradition retired only in 2016. Purple and gold paraphernalia pervades the closets, lawns, and cars of EBR year-round. "It's not that Baton Rouge is 'sports fans,' " one respondent told me. "It's that Baton Rouge *is LSU*."

The intensity of LSU spirit can make it hard to believe that only 10 miles up the Mississippi River lies another campus with a ritualistic-like following. Southern University is the largest historically Black college or university

(HBCU) in Louisiana. It has only about 7,000 students to LSU's 31,000, and is severely underfunded (though all public higher education in Louisiana suffered cuts under Governor Bobby Jindal). All the same, many of the Black people I encountered in Baton Rouge talked about Southern with just as much passion, if not more. Southern even had its own live mascot, a jaguar, for some time—the only HBCU to do so.

The comparison between LSU and Southern helps introduce the third discursive practice engaged in by the White respondents, and the first one that primarily reveals an ingroup-oriented feeling of prejudice. It is not that White people in Baton Rouge are likely to say that LSU is "superior" to Southern, per Blumer's articulation of superiority as one of the feelings comprising prejudice as a sense of group position. Rather, they are unlikely to say anything about Southern at all. The most common reply when I would ask White respondents about Southern was that they did not know where it was located. One LSU alum who had a vague idea where Southern was explained the social distance between the two universities as a product of physical distance: "Not that they're close," he said. On second thought, he added, "Well, I guess they are. It's what, like, 10 miles? [Southern's] not easy to get to; traffic in Baton Rouge just sucks. That's really what it comes down to." This is the view of Southern from LSU—not easy to see in the background, or, at the very least, "not easy to get to."

I should not overstate the LSU–Southern comparison, on several accounts. LSU is the state's flagship university; Black Americans are certainly among its fans and alumni, and make up about 12% of LSU's student body today. It also is not a given that greater White awareness of or engagement with Southern would be a positive thing, given that creating primarily non-White, non-assimilationist spaces is part of HBCUs' value proposition for Black students and alumni (see Kim and Conrad 2006; on how this value proposition is evolving, see also Gasman 2013). Finally, keeping in mind the skew in my Black respondent sample toward older residents, many of them knew the LSU of prior generations and may have a different orientation toward the two universities than younger Black Baton Rougeans do (although more than one Black respondent pointed out to me that a purple and gold version of the Confederate flag can still reliably be spotted at LSU tailgates—indicating not everything has changed).[14]

All the same, the attention and legitimacy my White respondents granted to LSU, while ignoring or occasionally criticizing Southern, are in some ways illustrative of the attention and legitimacy most of the White respondents granted to the concerns of majority-White communities. It is understandable to focus on issues that matter to oneself and one's immediate community.

But when life is as segregated as it is in Baton Rouge, this focus perpetuates a dynamic of ignoring the problems plaguing the majority-Black, low-income student population of the public schools, or the residents of North Baton Rouge—or else strategically invoking the problems that affect these communities only to illustrate White people's own hardship.

The Plight of the Southeast

About halfway through my conversation with Randy, he insisted on stopping to show me a video. "It will help you understand, maybe, why some people don't want to send their kids to public school," he said. The video was entitled "Behind the Curtain" and had been produced several years prior by the precursor to the St. George effort (Local Schools for Local Children 2014).[15] It opens in silence, with black text against a white background, introducing a montage of videos. "Sadly, for the majority of students who attend public schools in East Baton Rouge Parish, this is their reality," the text reads. Fourteen clips follow, drawn from either newsreel or cell phone footage and depicting grim scenes: most are violent fights in school hallways or cafeterias, with a cast that is virtually all Black. The video reverts to text at the end:

The East Baton Rouge school system can no longer effectively manage its schools.
They are failing our children.
The citizens of Southeast Baton Rouge want to take accountability for their schools.
Let the people vote.
EVERY student deserves a quality education.

Despite the surface-level inclusivity of some of this language—"our children," "the people," and "EVERY"—the clear goal of the campaign is to improve outcomes for a particular "we:" that is, the "local children" of the "citizens of Southeast Baton Rouge."

The St. George supporters I encountered revealed a similar understanding of "we." Take, for example, Elise, an amiable and chatty accountant-turned-homemaker who now lives in the lush Country Club of Louisiana. A strong believer in Catholic education, Elise had no firsthand experience of the public schools but proclaimed that "public schools are terrible:" "I'm just saying what everybody, you know, from what I hear," she told me. "We never had anybody in the public school system here." Chad, the young lawyer, said it took him only a few months after arriving in Baton Rouge for law school to figure out the same common wisdom: "If you had parents that were involved and concerned, and you had any sort of academic prowess or ability, then they were going to have to recruit you into a private school or leave the parish."

Chad's comment seemingly condemns those parents who *do* send their kids to public schools as either uninvolved or unconcerned, acting against what "everybody" knows. It is more likely, however, that Chad, as well as Elise, simply did not understand "everybody" to extend to the disproportionately Black population of EBR students and parents.

Wayne suggested that a similar logic drove his thinking: "No one's going to send their kids to these [traditional] schools, and you don't have enough magnet schools, and that's not fair." Wayne's comment is based on an implicit divide between "them" and "us," but in which "us" becomes equivalent to "everyone." To him, it makes sense to identify the families of 28,000 EBR students in nonmagnet schools, of whom less than 8% are White, as "no one." In a striking contrast to the earlier emphasis the organizers put on the inclusion of the low-income Black neighborhood of Gardere within St. George in the 2014–2015 effort, Gardere now escapes mention. Public school attendance was over 90% in Gardere in 2016 (compared to around 40% in Elise's neighborhood, and between 40–60% across the southeastern parish, according to census estimates). Thus, even if the St. George supporters claim that "us" is geographically defined as the unincorporated area, they still dismiss as "no one" the (disproportionately Black) residents of the unincorporated area who utilize the traditional public schools. Moreover, Wayne does not call for an improvement of the whole system—despite the message concluding the "Behind the Curtain" video being that "every" student deserves a quality education. He instead argues that what would be fair would be having enough magnet schools for "everyone" (read: "us") to attend.

Putting aside White respondents' ahistorical understanding of why the school system has struggled, it makes sense that parents would not want their children in the scenarios depicted in the video. Yet, the severity of the school situation for implicitly *White* parents is communicated with stories featuring almost entirely *Black* casts—whether in dramatic examples such as "Behind the Curtain," or in the more quotidian references to the "failed," "dangerous," or "horrible" school system. On the rare occasions that EBR students are referenced directly (rather than subsumed into "the school system"), they most commonly appear as objects of danger.

Elise, for example, empathized with how hard it must be for teachers in EBR who "have so many bullies that they're scared of their students." A comment made by Randy achieves a similar end: "The students there were horrible," he said when explaining why a friend of his quit his teaching job. Randy said it was understandable: "Teachers are put in an impossible situation." This was the only way students of traditional public schools ever featured in the comments of the St. George advocates: as undisciplined troublemakers, with "different educational needs," or for whom "the damage is already done." The disproportionately Black students of the EBR system are thus invoked as sources of harm, and ignored as the ones who acutely suffer from the much elaborated shortcomings of the school system. This understanding supported an acceptance that some collateral damage might result from the incorporation effort, at least in the short term. As Wayne told me, "What [opponents] will say is, 'You're going to kill public schools by doing that.' I will argue public schools are dead." Kenneth echoed him: "It's almost like you have to get worse before you get better." Never did the St. George supporters recognize the experiences or perspectives of the students and families for whom things would "get worse" in the process of establishing St. George to offer "better" options for a smaller slice of the Baton Rouge community.

Beyond a silence around public school students themselves, the St. George advocates were explicit that their concern was for parents who have no other choice but to send their children to private schools if they do not want to leave the parish. It is true that many parents feel this way. Chad, for example, had reluctantly accepted that he would move to another parish in order to send his infant son to public school one day. "It's not what I want to do. I don't want to live in Ascension Parish . . . [but] that's going to be the only option." Even Joanne, the school district employee worried that parents in the southeast would not believe the good things about EBR schools, used the rhetoric of necessity. As she said of people who had moved to Zachary and Central, "They no longer have to send their kid—'have to,' notice how I say that—send their kids to Catholic schools and pay tuition." Joanne "noticed" that she had instinctively slipped into the language used by the St. George effort. But rather than correcting herself, she simply commented on it, as if to admit the pervasiveness or naturalness of this language. In a sense, this is a form of self-correction. Yet, it also reveals Joanne's inevitable identification with, or similar perspective to, a group of mostly White parents.

Vignettes about the struggles of being a middle-class family in Baton Rouge often accompanied comments like Joanne's, generally describing a young couple with a "pretty good" income of $100,000 per year (in the top 14% of the income distribution in EBR); after various bills including private school tuition, the couple was "living paycheck to paycheck." These vignettes were often accompanied by comments about me not yet having a family of my own. "You will see one day," one observer sympathetic to St. George told me. It was clear that effort was being taken to make sure that I, as a young person and an outsider, understood that private school tuition was an unfair but *necessary* expense for these households. Similarly, many White respondents echoed the refrain that St. George was "certainly not rich."[16]

Fitting with this sympathetic portrayal was the argument that the financial hardship of St. George supporters was even more unfair in light of the tax revenue the southeast contributes to the city–parish. As discussed in the previous chapter, this revenue comes primarily in the form of sales taxes generated by people coming from across the parish to spend at venues in the southeast, rather than taxes paid by residents of the southeast alone. All the same, the St. George supporters felt the southeast had not received its fair share of public investment in return.

Elise put things more bluntly than the campaign organizers did: "We're South Baton Rouge, we have a huge tax base," she said. "So we had that big advantage, and that's why they won't let us go." Elise vocalizes what is insinuated by the effort's concern with painting itself as "not rich" but rather middle-income: they know that St. George is advantaged compared to the larger parish. Being relatively advantaged does not make it impossible that individual families face financial strain, or that the tax structure is unfair. However, the St. George effort is argued to be justified on the grounds of the area's advantage—despite the time taken to explain residents' *dis*advantage. Randy offered one of the most colorful statements on this point when he referenced the St. George organizers' discovery that sales taxes generated in the unincorporated areas went into an "unincorporated fund" that funded services across the parish (rather than only for the southeast):

> When people [realized this], they said, "What? We're being screwed. This is like colonial India with the British coming in and just taking it all for themselves!" Then people said, "What do we not get in St. George?" Well, one of the things, if you drive around in South Baton Rouge, you know the traffic is horrible. And much of that is in St. George, because the infrastructure has not been built in the southeast part of the parish to deal with the traffic. Well, that's the biggest thing that hasn't been done.

The comparison to British colonialism is hyperbolic, but it captures the sentiment that the St. George effort was an uprising by people who had been treated unfairly. It was at other times called a "revolutionary" or quintessentially "American" struggle. [This rhetoric continued into the 2018–19 incorporation effort; for example, an official spokesperson for the effort said of St. George's refusal to "subsidize" the rest of the parish that "Britain told America the same thing [and] we got tired of that too. It worked out pretty well for us, America" (qtd. in J. Clark 2019).] Throughout these discourses, White people in East Baton Rouge parish are centered as victims of an unjust or undesirable set of circumstances.

Randy naming traffic as "the biggest thing that hasn't been done" in the St. George area points back to the frame with which Chapter 2 began. When viewed from the southeast, traffic is much like the school system: an ahistorical phenomenon, unconnected to White flight or racial inequality, and whose impact on the White majority is amplified in a manner that overshadows other concerns in the parish.

Elise's complaints about traffic segued into exasperation with the city's lack of attention to landscaping, and its weak efforts to attract new retail—the two things that Elise regularly referenced as features of "nice" neighborhoods. She cited the frustrations of her friends who had tried to work on city beautification projects, and commented on the weeds and litter she often saw on the side of the roads. She told stories about stores and restaurants—a home goods retailer, a Lafayette pizza chain—that had tried to open in Baton Rouge but found negotiating with local government so frustrating that the plans were dropped. "They're just not forward-thinking," she said of the amorphous "Powers That Be" in Baton Rouge, and explained that her family was thinking of moving to Lafayette. Lafayette, Elise said, was more "progressive": it has more museums, more parks, more restaurants, prettier streets. ("Even the races tend to get along better in Lafayette," Elise added at one point.)

Improving traffic flows, beautifying the built environment, and providing amenities are important to quality of life in any city. However, these issues dominate the perspective of someone like Elise. Issues that remain invisible include the upward of 100,000 residents of the parish who live in food deserts,[17] and a shortage of emergency healthcare in NBR, which only in November 2017 regained an emergency room after going almost five years without one.[18] Elise occasionally referenced NBR as a place where she was "scared to death" to go—purportedly because of "those people that have crime problems or just, you know, records," as she put it. Unsurprisingly, then, the needs of "those people" or their potential frustrations with city government were absent from Elise's comments. Instead, concern for her own safety functioned as a barrier that justified Elise giving little thought to the residents of NBR as anything more than threats.

As Graeber (2015, 101) puts it, "[M]ost of the time, power is all about what you *don't* have to worry about, *don't* have to know about, and *don't* have to do." Of course, the luxury of what Elise does not have to worry about comes from her economic as much as racial privilege (our conversation took place amidst visible wealth, inside the gates of the Country Club of Louisiana). The same can be said for many of the middle- and upper-income supporters of the St. George effort. However, in Baton Rouge, as in the United States more generally, wealth dovetails with race and reinforces the role of the color line in limiting many White Americans' circle of concern.

"Understanding" and the Normalization of Separate and Unequal

So far, supporters of St. George have characterized the southeast as the recipient of an unfair deal when it comes to schools and other city services. White respondents who were critical of St. George generally rejected this portrayal. Critics were much more likely to describe St. George supporters as "wealthy people" without claims to financial hardship.

Even so, the St. George critics often granted legitimacy to the concerns of majority-White communities—for example, related to schools and traffic— while a silence remained around the concerns of majority-Black communities. This practice of centering White people in conversations about race offers evidence of what is instinctive to the White respondents (i.e., sympathizing with other White people). Moreover, it demonstrates the capacity of White instincts to also serve White interests: it is easier for White people to have comfortable and polite conversation about racial inequality when the subjectivity of Black people themselves is never mentioned.

For example, consider the White respondents connected to the school district, who usually expressed concerns that the St. George effort would have hurt EBR. Many in this group expressed empathy for the parents supporting the St. George effort, but not one mentioned the impact it would have had on the remaining student population and their parents. In contrast to the repeated claims among these respondents that they "didn't know" much about the motivations of the St. George supporters, here the school affiliates repeatedly claimed that they nonetheless "understood" the St. George supporters' perspectives. As Joanne said, "I worked very, very closely with those people in the area, and I like them. I understand their issues; they understand my concerns." Nancy said almost the same. From these positions of "understanding," both women argued that the concerns of the St. George effort should be taken more seriously.

Nancy went further in suggesting that a debt was owed to the parents behind St. George when she referenced Parker's busing order. Adopting the first person plural as she did earlier, Nancy said: "We were left out. We were not treated fairly. That residual anger is there." Nancy's reference to fairness resonates with Wayne's earlier complaints about the unfairness of the limited supply of magnet schools. Yet, to say that the forced integration of Baton Rouge's schools "left out" the White parents blatantly ignores the impetus for integration being to include Black children in the schools from which *they* had been left out by law.

Joanne more explicitly called for attention to be given to the present-day demands of residents of the southeast, saying, "You have to listen to some of the people's concerns, and you have to meet them at some point, at least halfway." In Joanne's view, the St. George effort stands on legitimate enough ground to be met *at least* halfway—and if this did not happen, Joanne's only vocalized concern was that EBR would lose the existing school facilities in the southeast if the new district successfully formed. Her concern is understandable: EBR lost valuable facilities when Central, Zachary, and Baker broke away from the district. Then again, for someone with deep knowledge of the school system, it is notable that Joanne never mentions any impact the creation of St. George would have on the remaining, even more disproportionately Black EBR student population. The same silence was present among all the White respondents connected to EBR schools.

Critical White observers of St. George were less likely than White school district employees to join in the sympathetic portrayal of parents behind the incorporation effort, but they fell short of giving attention or legitimacy to issues facing majority-Black communities. Critical White observers instead collectively normalized the status quo. As one LSU student council member summed things up, "If you are a White kid you go to a Catholic school. If you are a Black kid you go to a public school. And that's just how it is." The young college graduate Isabel called the public and private schools systems "like night and day." One parent who sent her children to Catholic schools explained many parents avoid traditional schools "because they're afraid that the student body is not going to be ... the student body that they want their kids to be in." Over and over, observers of the effort signaled that the division of Black and White students into two systems of education was common knowledge—simply the way things are, the natural state of affairs. At most, observers suggested the divide was reflective of race-neutral desires about what kind of student body would be best for a given child.

Even among some of the White respondents who were loudest in their criticism of St. George, there is evidence of a collective blind spot around the needs of majority-Black students in the system. Take, for example, Kathy, who volunteers with her church at a local elementary school. The experience led her to say of the St. George supporters, "In their defense, the schools are horrible." She went on:

> Despite all the volunteer work that my church does, whenever that school makes above an F, I sometimes think oh, how did they do that? I mean, I'm disappointed in the quality of some of the teachers. I'm disappointed in the quality of the administration. Now, I'm not *at all* disappointed in all the things my church does.

Kathy's experiences in this school, which led her to the "defense" of the St. George parents, have opened up little space for further thought about the depth of need in the community where she volunteers. "I'm not sure why, but [there's] a lot of hopelessness from some people," she says of the impoverished area surrounding the school. Kathy recognizes the level of poverty but puts little interpretive labor into imagining why such poverty might be accompanied by hopelessness.

An important note in regard to this third discursive practice is that the White grassroots opponents to St. George I encountered largely abstained from centering White concerns. These were the few White respondents who had been most likely to comment on the racial impact (rather than intentions) of the incorporation effort. In doing so, they emphasized that the real harm done by St. George would fall primarily on the shoulders of the majority-Black school population. This was the greatest diversion in my sample from the "structured blindness" that the Racial Contract typically requires (Mills 1997, 19). In contrast to other White residents, the grassroots opponents displayed considerable self-transparency in reflecting on how the needs and experiences of Black children in EBR schools were being downplayed compared to those of White children. Tammy, for example, commented on the fact that per-pupil funding at her children's magnet school was about two-thirds the funding at a nearby traditional (and majority-Black) school, saying, "[that] is exactly what I want. Because that school is full of children who have enormous barriers to education and payment, and they need extra resources to overcome those barriers so that they can be successful." Tammy stops short of directly engaging with race, instead emphasizing the economic circumstances of certain students. Elizabeth did similarly, in saying, "to me, the most egregious injustice was that you would take money from poor kids' schools so that you can show how you can make a good school." But still, these two women clearly diverge from the majority of the White respondents, in whose comments the children who would most suffer from St. George were all but invisible.

With the exception of the few like Tammy and Elizabeth, there is an implicit hierarchy of needs subscribed to by most White respondents. It is not common sense to extend empathy to Black students of EBR schools or Black residents of the parish, who instead fade into the background of concerns relevant to majority-White communities. The White respondents may not claim their racial ingroup to be "superior," per se, but they do reveal a perspective that operates on this assumption unless challenged to think more broadly (e.g., as part of a community organization such as Together Baton Rouge).

The class positions of my White respondents undoubtedly contribute to their constrained insight into life in EBR. Yet, when class overlaps with race as much as it does in Baton Rouge, the narrowness of a middle-income perspective only reinforces the tendency to legitimize White concerns. Although the White respondents lean into this tendency in a variety of ways—from Randy's hyperbolic comparison to colonial India, to Joanne and Nancy's subtler "understanding" of parents' concerns—they nonetheless reveal a common habitus informing their strategic choices to give minimal thought to the needs, experiences, and perspectives of their Black neighbors.

Upholding the Social Order

I have now reported three practices engaged in by the White respondents that reveal the influence of a shared White perspective. The fourth and final practice follows from my discussion under "The Superiority of White Concerns" by demonstrating White respondents' understandings of their ingroup, as opposed to engaging with and rationalizing their orientations toward Black people as an outgroup. Here, I report evidence for the myriad ways the White respondents, including grassroots St. George opponents, engage in a defense of the social order—an order in which White people have certain privileges and advantages over Black people. This deference to the status quo is produced in two ways: either through expressed desires to return to a sense of calm and order located at some time in the past, or through endorsement of the importance of "togetherness" for Baton Rouge's future in a manner that admits little need for White people to make any concessions to achieve the inclusion of Black people.

Returning to Order

The most explicit endorsements of the racial order came from St. George advocates and sympathizers, and primarily in the form of nostalgia for a time when that order was stacked even more in White residents' favor. We saw this nostalgia in St. George's origin story as told by Nancy, who cited not wanting their kids bused as one reason the St. George effort had begun. It was surprising that Nancy, as a school district employee, would not be clear that mandatory busing had ended long ago when reciting claims made by St. George supporters that implied otherwise. This blurring of busing-era sentiments and present-day frustrations with the school system was a common pattern, however, among other White respondents. Several supporters of St. George called busing a "mistake" and indicated that some parents still had to "ship kids up" to North Baton Rouge.

Some St. George supporters did distinguish mandatory from voluntary busing. Yet, revisiting the strategy of citing Black hardship as an argument for improving the system in White people's favor, they tended to lament that students from majority-Black areas were waking up early and traveling "way down here" to schools in the southeast, all for the sake of "diversity." As mentioned in Chapter 2, the voluntary busing programs today are not diversity initiatives but rather a way to give students in underperforming schools the option to attend stronger schools if space allows. The idea of "busing" has nonetheless taken on a meaning as something destructive to communities, rather than implemented to rectify EBR's stark segregation almost three decades after *Brown v. Board.*

Only one of the St. George supporters made mention of the busing order as provoked by EBR's blatant violation of federal orders, rather than a destructive initiative that both motivated and justified St. George's efforts to reestablish "community schools" in the southeast. In spite of the St. George effort's self-understanding that it was rebelling against the status quo—rejecting downtown power interests, challenging the privilege of the magnet school parents, creating a 21st-century city—this also revealed the effort's commitment to reasserting something supporters felt had been lost.

White respondents critical of St. George were less likely to speak about pre-busing days in romantic terms, even if they shared an understanding of the order as fundamentally destructive (it is worth remembering that Black communities, too, felt they were hurt by the order). Where the St. George supporters and critics were often indistinguishable, however, was in portraying the July shootings, much like Parker's busing order, as something that had "ruptured" the previously whole community. Sterling's killing in particular was portrayed as creating racial tensions where none previously existed, rather than making visible the tip of an iceberg of racially discriminatory policing and governing that has affected Black people in Baton Rouge for years. The White respondents repeatedly emphasized that Baton Rouge was a fundamentally friendly place that simply needed to quiet down and return to normal. Baton Rouge, they would say, was "not going to be another Ferguson or Baltimore."

One recurring refrain was the argument that people from "out of town" were giving Baton Rouge a bad image. This invoked the longstanding trope of the "outside agitator" who has come to fuel protests, rooted in the civil rights–era myth that radical outsiders were importing trouble and rousing the sentiments of otherwise content Black Southerners. Despite being long disproven, and in multiple ways [see, e.g., Fogelson (1971, 29–30) on 1960s-era protests in Los Angeles, or Feinberg and Johnson's (1988) computer simulation demonstrating the unfeasibility of outside agitators being able to mobilize a moderate crowd in the first place], the trope has continually been used to both deny local culpability for the cause of a protest as well as to justify harsh treatment of protestors (see Fortin 2020, for a recent overview).

In Baton Rouge, these comments were often pointed at Gavin Long, the Kansas City resident who killed the three officers, as well as at the Black Lives Matter protests following Sterling's killing. As a local politician who had supported St. George told me, "A lot of people, I don't think they understood that a lot of this, things that went on—it wasn't the people from Baton Rouge." He was frustrated that the media had put a "blemish" on the city. He continued: "We may fight, we may argue, but it's like brothers and sisters— we get over it. Do you understand?" To compare racial tensions to a brother-sister relationship paints the divide as natural, like one between siblings; but it also minimizes the severity of the debates brought up by Sterling's murder to relatively trivial bickering between children.

More common than emphasizing troublemakers coming from out of town was the language of "fracturing" and "healing." Many White respondents were optimistic that in a year or so, the harm done in July would be healed. They occasionally commented on Black residents' role in the healing process. Randy, for example, said that a local Black female leader whom he normally considered "kind of loud" had surprised him by being "very responsible" in calling for peace after Sterling's killing. But the larger pattern among the White respondents was to state a belief that Baton Rouge would return to its "pre-Alton Sterling" trajectory. Rarely did the White respondents reflect on what the process of healing would entail, let alone whether the state of affairs to which they hoped to return was a positive one.

While I would not endorse the common portrayal of Sterling's killing as a cause, rather than consequence, of trouble in Baton Rouge, there *was* a state of calm before the shooting in comparison to the tumult that followed. The question is whether calm reflects deep harmony, or the forces of a social order that means most White people do not have to think about the tangled web of factors that shaped Sterling's life (and death) in the first place. Sterling's murder was hardly an unprecedented incident of racially discriminatory policing in Baton Rouge, even if Baton Rouge had been relatively quiet about the issue before July 5th.[19]

One critical observer of the St. George effort, Luke, was more direct than most in speaking to the racial tensions the shooting had unleashed and his frustration with the affluent, White community in which he grew up. "Sometimes I wonder, like, am I betraying the part of town I grew up in?" he said. Luke was in his early twenties and had recently finished a year working as a teacher's assistant in a traditional public school. He expressed frustration at the comments he would get from family friends when sharing some of the perspectives he had gained over the year.

> I think it happens sometimes, for social justice. People point out legitimate issues, and they're villainized. Like if you think about Black Lives Matter, you say "this is an issue," and they say, "oh, no, no, you're hurting the social order." I think sometimes that happens with South Baton Rouge. Like, they don't want to change their status quo, and so if you point it out, it's like "you're just ungrateful for where you came from."

Luke indicates that the calm and quiet in Baton Rouge do not come naturally, but rather are the product of an agreement not to question the way things are.

A more neutral observer of St. George named Greg explained his discovery of this tendency to silence comments that criticize the way things are in Baton Rouge upon moving there from the Midwest. "It's kind of, *(putting on a soft voice)* 'bless your heart.' You know, underneath that bless your heart, there's that 'go to hell' comment." Greg's experience of moving to Baton Rouge required navigating these comments to learn what could and could not be said in polite company. When I asked if he had any thoughts about the upcoming mayor's election, for example, Greg got up and closed the door before continuing in hushed tones to explain that he did not identify as a Republican but had learned that "Democrat" was a "dirty word."

Although this chapter lacks the scope to dive into questions around partisanship in a place like Baton Rouge, Greg's comment illuminates the norms that maintain the quiet to which so many White respondents hoped the city would return. Moreover, even as Greg and Luke express frustration about the policing of polite conversation in Baton Rouge, they are both ultimately deferent to those norms. Luke worried about "betraying" his "part of town." Greg felt he had no choice but to adopt the right way of saying things—or at least, to only break the rules behind closed doors. In both cases, Luke and

Greg ultimately endorse an unequal and racially divided social order in Baton Rouge, even as they make some effort to critique it.

Togetherness in Talk and Action

The final discourse I identify among the White respondents is also the one on which there was the strongest consensus, irrespective of their views on St. George, race relations, or any other matter. Virtually every White resident I encountered agreed that the way forward was "togetherness."

One take on togetherness came from frequent references to the July shootings as "Baton Rouge's 9/11," in reference to the 2001 attack on the World Trade Center, as a way of commenting on how much the community had "come together" since the deaths of the officers. (The White respondents were less likely to reference the death of Sterling.) Another take echoed Randy's claim that the races were "seeing each other" in the wake of the shooting, and cited the benefits of increased interracial interaction. Elise, for example, referenced an event some churches had organized to get both Black and White residents to "mix, and come together, and just make a new friend." As Elise described the event, "You talk to this person, and [say] 'what are your issues? How do you feel? You know, why aren't we getting along?'" For Elise, progress was equivalent to conversation, or to the mixing of the races. She cited, for example, that when going out to eat in Baton Rouge recently, she was seeing "more Blacks than we have ever before in the White, in the White, you know, I say the White restaurant." Elise noted this as a positive change, saying she would like things to be "more that way."

It is worth noting that Elise had at least one close Black friend: though she implicitly recognized that there was a lack of meaningful interracial interaction in Baton Rouge without formalized means, she herself was not totally isolated from Black people on an interpersonal level. But, having a close Black friend does not preclude Elise from centering White people in her understanding of Baton Rouge's physical and social geography. And when her instinct is to explicitly identify certain restaurants as "White" ones, Elise suggests that she sees the racial divide as more fundamental than something that can be bridged by conversation alone.

Although some White respondents had more experience reflecting on and talking about race relations than did Elise, virtually no one in the sample challenged the equation of interaction with progress.[20] Some explicitly argued that increased Black–White interaction would be the best way to move forward slowly and carefully. An LSU student government member named

Mark encapsulated this sentiment when recounting his experience of working with Black members of the student council—a process that had convinced him that a gradualist approach to achieving change was the "most effective."

> It may be "progressive" to jump out and say we are supporting everything Black Lives Matter. We want to get that out there, but at the same time, we need to recognize that unity and just simply understanding someone who looks different from you, and shaking hands with someone who looks different from you, may be a more appropriate first approach than asking someone to completely shift their opinion.

Mark explained that he was wary of asking people who were "gung ho Blue Lives Matter" (i.e., pro-police) to take too large a step. What he described may indeed be the most pragmatic way to get White people to engage with Black people's experiences, which in turn could be an essential step toward progress in Baton Rouge. However, Mark reveals that he understands "unity" and "understanding" as distinct from asking (implicitly White) people to change an opinion; the power lies with White Baton Rougeans to decide what togetherness looks like, and to decide whether or how to change their minds.

This is not to minimize the importance of the experiences Mark has had working with his Black peers. "What flipped the switch for me was hearing smart Black intellectuals talk about how they view the world," he said. "I didn't necessarily agree with everything that everyone had to say, but then they made me think about it, and I think a lot of people just don't think about it every day." What Mark described might have been the start of a process of reflecting on his limited perspective from a position of privilege in the racial hierarchy—certainly a positive change. At the same time, Mark says that the "most important thing" his Black peers can do is "coming to the table and talking." In doing so, Mark implicitly acknowledges his own powerful position: he already has a seat at the table and believes he should retain his seat. Mark further assigns his Black peers the responsibility (and additional interpretive labor) required for his own education—echoing the logic of the color line "going both ways" that we encountered in the section titled "Equating Black and White". Ultimately, Mark reinforces the idea that interracial conversation is the sort of progress that Baton Rouge needs.

White respondents critical of St. George were more likely to shift emphasis from merely talking to instead building meaningful relationships that would compel cooperation and action. One grassroots organizer named Fred explained his commitment to building civic and social relationships in Baton Rouge: "Justice doesn't just happen at the Supreme Court level. I mean societies have to have relationships capable of sustaining that." Deborah spoke about her own experience of building these sorts of relationships as a "powerful" one, explaining that she had heard Black members of Together Baton Rouge "talk about the boycotts of the 60s and what it was like to go to school in the 50s." She added, "I don't remember the exact people . . ." but reflecting on the overall experience of sharing these stories, she concluded: "It's not that it's behind us, because you don't forget that kind of stuff; but we are moving on; we are there for a reason. It's like a drug."

To call the spirit of togetherness in these settings "a drug" speaks to the meaning Deborah draws from the interracial space Together Baton Rouge has created. It also indicates the importance that many people active in the community attribute to the process of engaging Black and White people to work together on the same issues. No one better represents a commitment to this process than Elizabeth, who worked tirelessly in both the 2014–2015 and 2018–2019 efforts to fight St. George. She had huge faith in the power of showing White residents of the southeast what life looked like north of Florida Boulevard.

Elizabeth recounted a story from a previous Together Baton Rouge campaign that sent volunteers to knock on doors around NBR. "They started meeting the people in these neighborhoods," she said. "And it became 'wow! They're kind of like me.'" Elizabeth argued that, during this process, "a new transformation occurred—and doors opened and they went in each other's homes and they shared water with each other." This transformative phenomenon, as Elizabeth described it, was not attributable to abstract ideals of togetherness but rather to a process of community activism. Elizabeth spoke with pride about former Attorney General Loretta Lynch's trip to Baton Rouge following Sterling's killing, when Lynch commented that Baton Rouge could be an example for the rest of the country. "Baton Rouge!" Elizabeth exclaimed. "I dare to say it's because of Together Baton Rouge, because we've had Blacks and Whites working together. If we didn't have that, we'd all be divided still. I mean we have a heart that we want to be together, but you need a mechanism. You need a process, and we have that."

Elizabeth goes further than most White respondents in thinking beyond opinions to actions. She expects more from her White peers than vaguely defined efforts to "understand" Black people. What Elizabeth does not engage with is the question of sacrifice beyond a few hours on a Saturday morning to knock on doors, or to otherwise volunteer time on a community initiative. I by no means seek to criticize these activities or to suggest that Elizabeth or any of the other White respondents are insincere in their belief that togetherness will lead to progress. The question is instead what progress means.

For many of the White respondents, progress was defined in reference to the way things were, either before busing or before Sterling's killing. People like Deborah and Elizabeth, on the contrary, are knowledgeable about policy issues related to racial inequality in Baton Rouge: their volunteer work with Together Baton Rouge has brought them into debates about issues ranging from public transport to food deserts to local elections. All the same, their optimism about the work they are doing reveals the extent to which their service for the community is, understandably, driven by their own self-concept— by the meaning they get out of the experience; by hearing each others' stories; and by the celebration of togetherness in which they are able to participate. On the one hand, this is simply an example of how having a positive experience of activism can powerfully motivate further engagement. On the other hand, it highlights the situated nature of White people's experience of racial politics. We should not necessarily equate White people's enthusiasm to volunteer or engage in conversation with their willingness to critically reflect on (let alone sacrifice) the privileges they enjoy at Black people's expense.

The optimism of the White respondents about race relations in Baton Rouge overall could be summed up with the words of one observer: "It's going to be really great when we get to the end of this transitional period of tackling the racial issues." With more or less nuance in their comments, and in their understanding of how long and transitional that period would be, virtually all White respondents shared a similar view. It may, and hopefully will, "be great" at the end of that process. Yet, the general acceptance of this idea in the absence of a discourse about White people's role in driving that process, or the possibility of sacrificing privilege along the way, suggests the limits of "togetherness" to change the subordination of Black Americans to White Americans in the racial hierarchy.

Interrogating the White Perspective

This chapter has shown that the White individuals I encountered in Baton Rouge engaged in four discursive practices, which direct attention one of two ways. The first two practices respond to the obvious salience of Black people as an *outgroup* in Baton Rouge and engage White residents in *negating* the relevance of race to White people's motives and attitudes (under "Denying Racial Motivations"), or to the lived experiences of Black people as distinct from White people (under "Equating Black and White"). The second two practices are instead attuned to White people as an *ingroup*, producing a *positive* embrace of attitudes that legitimize the needs of majority-White communities in Baton Rouge (under "The Superiority of White Concerns") and that defend White people's place in the racial hierarchy (under "Upholding the Social Order").

By identifying the same discursive practices among White individuals who express polarized opinions on contentious local issues, these practices illuminate a shared perspective among the White respondents that is derived from their position in the racial hierarchy. What they say varies, but what they do is reproduce the same set of practices that reify the metaphorical and physical color line. They seek to deny racism while also assuming White superiority. They seek to minimize racial categories while also upholding a social order defined by those categories. They choose what to see and how to see it—referencing Gardere and citing Black friends when convenient, but ignoring Black people entirely when the conversation could wade into uncomfortable reflection about those individuals' subjective experiences. The White respondents speak with little (if any) mention of the possibility that theirs is only one of many views on race and racism in Baton Rouge. Even— and perhaps particularly—White respondents most critical of St. George claim to see everything from nowhere: confident that racism and race itself can be transcended, and confident that togetherness is a tide that can lift all ships, White and Black alike. Underneath it all is a common habitus— a product of White people's privileged position, a "feel for the game"—that gives the White respondents the same instincts to be careful about claims of racism, depoliticize race as a category, legitimize White needs, and to defend the status quo.

What counterarguments would challenge the validity of this claim? I address some of these now.

Challenges to the Idea of a White Identity

Central to my argument is the premise, informed by group-based theories of prejudice and standpoint theory, that White people's position in the racial hierarchy shapes their view of racial politics. Two potential counterarguments to this premise include (1) that the perspectives of the White respondents reflect a group identity shaped by their class position more than their racial position, and (2) that the perspectives of the White respondents do not reflect a group-based identity at all, but rather individual self-interest.

A Common Class Identity?

First, is the evidence presented in this chapter representative of White respondents' class identity rather than racial identity? My sample was disproportionately middle- and upper-income. It is likely that my identification of White silence on issues impacting poorer areas of the parish partially reflects the respondents' insulation from the ills of poverty.

However, it is hard to deem race irrelevant to the material divide in Baton Rouge given the close correlation between race and poverty—true in many places across the United States, but particularly in Louisiana. There is virtually zero income overlap between Black people and White people across Louisiana's parishes: median incomes for Black Louisianans fall between $13,000 and $25,000, while White incomes fall between $25,000 and $37,000 (Burd-Sharps, Lewis, and Martins 2009, 27). The U.S. Human Development Index gives Black people in Tangipahoa Parish, which has the lowest median Black income in the state, a human development score comparable to that of the average American *in the 1950s* (15). Even if someone doubts that race plays a role in reproducing inequality in the present day, one cannot separate the dramatic disadvantage of Black Louisianans from the brutal history of slavery and Jim Crow, which should contextualize even a colorblind take on my findings. Thus, even if many of my White respondents reveal the limitations of an economically privileged perspective, more so than a racially privileged one, the two are deeply intertwined.

Individual Self-Interest?

A second challenge to my claim that a racial identity exists among the White respondents comes from the counterargument that the White respondents' views reflect their individual self-interest.

It is not my aim, nor, am I able, to determine whether the St. George effort itself was motivated by racial group interests, rational self-interest, or other considerations. I can note, however, that a slight majority (57%) of the White individuals I encountered, on both sides of the debate, did not have school-age children themselves. Therefore, the perspectives of the White respondents did not purely reflect the views of parents who were frustrated with the schooling options available to them, or who were trying to protect their children's access to EBR magnet schools. When White respondents sympathized with White parents of schoolchildren, or made reference to "us" or "everyone," in many cases these comments came from individuals who themselves would be unaffected by any change to the school district (Nancy's comments in "Denying Racial Motivations" offer one example).

It was also the case that many White individuals I encountered did not live in the proposed new incorporation. Granted, everyone in the parish would have been affected by changes in tax policy had the incorporation been successful (there was doubt on both sides as to whether St. George would succeed in keeping taxes low). And I certainly recognize that the White respondents drew on their individual-level ideologies and other opinions to form views that were shared with me. All the same, when White individuals with starkly different ideologies nonetheless embrace the same ways of talking (or not talking) about race and prejudice in their city, racial identity proves to be one critical thing they have in common.

The Potential Influence of Performance

Another challenge to the analysis presented in this chapter relates to whether White respondents were "performing" for me in the interview setting. In Chapter 2, I discussed the inevitability and potential value of performance within an interpretive framework. Having now presented my findings, however, it is worth briefly revisiting how an inclination to perform might have affected my conversations with the White respondents.

Most obviously, the care that White respondents took to neither appear racist nor identify any other White people as racist (the first practice) likely was amplified by the presence of a Black researcher and resulting salience of race in the interview setting. Some arguments made when equating Black and White (the second practice) likely also were amplified by my presence. This was where it was common for White respondents to reference what they perceived to be my class status in making arguments about the insignificance of race, or in alluding to middle-income Black people in Baton Rouge. One respondent tried to make the point that class mattered more than race by saying that just like he could "dress up and look like every bubba in the world" or could look "professional," I, too, could "probably dress up and look like any angry African-American woman. Or, you know, professional." The stereotype of the angry Black woman is, of course, one of the most infamous that has been used to denigrate Black women as well as Black feminism (and that has been powerfully explored and at times reclaimed; see Lorde 1984b; hooks 2000; Ahmed 2009). Its use by my respondent, however, certainly highlights his awareness of my race. I would argue that in the context of both the first and second discursive practices, this sort of awareness was valuable in leading to more direct commentary on race than might have surfaced otherwise.

The potential influence of either social desirability bias in general or of my race in particular may have been more nuanced in regard to the third discursive practice, or White respondents' silence around issues facing predominantly Black communities. Much like Myrdal (1944, 37) identified White Southerners' habit of speaking in polite, indirect terms in order to give themselves a "moral escape," it is possible that White respondents were prudently avoiding the thorny realities of racial inequality in Baton Rouge, and even more so than usual when speaking to a Black interviewer. Of course, it is also possible that some White respondents felt lacking in either the authority or the general knowledge to talk about certain issues, perhaps particularly to a Black interviewer, leading them to not mention anything in the first place.

Finally, in the fourth discursive practice, the dominance of togetherness talk seems unlikely to have been a product of the interview setting given the prevalence of this narrative around the city in the wake of the July shootings. It is possible that the defense of Baton Rouge as a calm and friendly place was expressed even more strongly to me as someone who, despite my connections to the area, was not a local. Yet, the pride with which my White respondents spoke about their belief in the power of unity was certainly echoed in forums far beyond our conversations, whether at town halls, in editorials in local papers, or at the vigil for Sterling and the officers where this book opened.

The Perspectives of Black Baton Rougeans

A final way to interrogate the claim that the White respondents' views were shaped by their racial identity comes from turning to the reflections of Black residents of Baton Rouge.

The Black residents I encountered in Baton Rouge deserve more space than I allot here. As I have noted, this book is explicitly focused on how White Americans perceive issues related to race in their local surroundings. This scope, and how I designed the research as a result, present limitations. I thus do not claim that my conversations with Black Baton Rougeans necessarily illuminate a shared perspective among them, or fully capture their experiences of their local world. I also emphasize that my sample was similarly skewed toward middle- and upper-income respondents (if not more so) among the Black respondents as it was among the sample as a whole, based on whom I was able to access. On the one hand, this should dampen concerns that the White views reported earlier in this chapter were merely reflective of a class identity, because middle-income Black people would share this identity, at least to a certain extent. On the other hand, this class skew should be kept in mind when considering Black respondents' views, both because of how it would have shaped their reflections and because of the silence it leaves around less privileged Black Baton Rougeans—for example, the one in four Black residents of EBR Parish who live below the poverty line, or those who live in NBR in particular and suffer from its blight. Their subjectivity, perspectives, membership in Baton Rouge's social fabric, and experiences of either inclusion or exclusion within it—all are owed more recognition than this book provides.

The truth is that I learned more from Black residents about White people than about the Black respondents themselves. There still is value in this, particularly in light of this chapter's aims. I will organize my discussion of Black residents' comments according to the four White discursive practices the chapter has identified. I make this choice not to imply that the same discursive practices structure the Black respondents' speech, but to demonstrate a notable contrast in Black and White respondents' perspectives that makes White respondents' engagement in the discursive practices all the more visible. More than playing foil to the White respondents, however, the Black respondents further develop and reinforce many of the arguments I have made in this chapter. That is, many of the Black individuals I spoke to demonstrate the ethnographic understanding of Whiteness that, as hooks (1992, 165) reminds us, has been cultivated and shared from slavery onward "to help black folks cope and survive in a white supremacist society." In sharing this understanding with me, Black residents also demonstrate their familiarity with (and at times, their conscious awareness of) undertaking the interpretive labor of imagining the dominant group's perspective, as is so often required of subordinate subjects (Graeber 2015, 58–68).

Denying Racial Motivations

Black respondents generally fell into two categories: (1) observers of the St. George effort, meaning those not actively involved with either the incorporation effort or opposition to it (although unlike the White observers, all the Black observers were critical of St. George); and (2) engaged opponents of St. George, whether via grassroots opposition efforts or through other avenues (e.g., one's work in local institutions). The opponents were often, though not always, more likely to cast their observations in structural terms or to make stronger social critiques. Across the board, however, the Black respondents were far from hesitant about discussing the question of racial motivations behind the St. George effort and often were forthright in characterizing the effort as racially motivated.

Particularly among Black observers of the effort, humor and cynicism often characterized their comments about St. George. Carol, a realtor in her mid-fifties, released a belly laugh when I brought up the incorporation effort, calling it "pathetic" and "obviously" driven by racism. Michelle, a healthcare worker with young children, laughed, too; when I asked what led her to think the movement was racially motivated, she exclaimed, "Look at a map! Common sense tells you that's what they were trying to do—they don't want their money to be used for the lower-income Black families that live in North Baton Rouge." When Diane laughed, she gave me a pointed look and said that, when the "rebel (i.e., Confederate) flag was flying" at one of the sites where signatures for the St. George petition were being solicited, it wasn't that hard to guess what was behind it. These comments reveal a different "common sense," to use Michelle's words, from the common sense that was evident among many White respondents.

These examples should not cast Black respondents' characterization of St. George in overly simplistic terms. One, Tonya, did not mention any suspicion of racial motivations behind it (Tonya also was the least familiar with the effort among the Black respondents). A few others admitted that labeling all supporters "racist" or "segregationist" would be "too harsh," and recognized the school system presented many parents with difficult choices. A more notable way several observers and particularly the St. George opponents complicated the characterization of the effort beyond simply being "racist" was to situate it within the context of Baton Rouge's long struggle with school desegregation. "Oh, this has been with us down through the years," Richard, a retired observer, put it. "It has its origin in the whole deseg. litigation," commented Lance, one of the St. George opponents, a professional in his late forties. Joshua, another professional several years younger than Lance and also an opponent, similarly described St. George as reflective of an evolution in White attempts to avoid sharing space with Black people.

Referencing this evolution suggests the lived and learned understanding some of the Black respondents have developed of White behavior in Baton Rouge, and of the history and present-day context that structures that behavior. Several went further to explicitly call out White residents' strategies to deny that St. George was racially motivated. Michelle's take was that "no matter how they try to sugarcoat it, that's the main motivation." Lance's was that "ours is an example of just supreme recalcitrance by people who *claim* Christ, people who *say* they're well intended, people who *say* they're not racist, and people who say, 'I just really want what's the best for my children'"—implying that these defenses would be revealed to be untrue if, as Lance said, "You peel back the layers." Both these comments display Black residents' awareness of Whiteness in action. Lance even nodded to the pact I have identified among Whites: he remarked that the challenge of engaging with arguments about wanting what was best for one's children was that "you do so at the risk of suggesting that this is about race." The word "risk" indicates Lance's sensitivity to unleashing the sort of White anger we saw in the St. George supporters' impassioned defenses of their motives.

In sum, these are the reflections of individuals who do not subscribe to the epistemology of ignorance. The Black respondents as a whole had little patience for coded language or beating around the bush, offering both a different interpretation of the role of race in motivating St. George and an awareness of the inverted epistemology that kept many White residents from coming to the same conclusion. As Joshua put it: "You have to be specific about this. We're talking about poor Black people, okay? We don't address White poverty the same. Poor Black and brown people are the ones [they] want to escape from."

Equating Black and White

Joshua's reference to "poor Black and brown people"—as well as Michelle's to "lower-income Black families"—brings up the question of class, and the perspectives Black residents of Baton Rouge offer on the second White discursive practice. This practice was the White respondents' habit, through various strategies, of minimizing the significance of race in shaping life outcomes in Baton Rouge.

The Black respondents collectively offer a more intersectional view of race and class than the White respondents. None rejected class as an important factor, in that each of them made some sort of acknowledgment of intergenerational Black poverty and its consequences, or referenced the deep income inequality among Black households in the area (roughly the same share of Black households in Baton Rouge earned less than $10,000 as earned more than $100,000 as of 2016 census estimates). Several reflected on their own class positions, or on their own journeys away from NBR.

Yet, almost all of the Black respondents also made some argument about the relevance of race across the class spectrum. One expression of this was occasional criticism of affluent Black people for trying to distance themselves from lower-income Black people, such as in moving to certain areas or seeking out private education as a status symbol. "Baton Rouge loves a ZIP code" was how Tonya put it when she described residents' concerns for living in the most "desirable" neighborhoods. If anything, though, criticism of this sort of behavior seemed largely to stem from the belief that it was futile for Black people to think they could escape their racial identity. As Lance said: "You know, in America, race is about class. It's naive to think that you can separate and distinguish the two."

Joshua said almost the same thing—and, even more explicitly than Lance's reference to naivete, Joshua criticized strategic references to class that minimized the importance of race. He argued that, for White people describing either White flight or the St. George effort, "it's always 'important' to point out" class demographics. "People say, 'Oh, it's about class not race.'" Joshua said. He continued, echoing Lance: "Okay. You know in America, race is about class."

Other Black respondents highlighted the relevance of race across the class spectrum with reference to their own experiences. In doing so, their reflections serve not just as a contrast to the White discursive practice or as a critique of White people using it, but also as a direct rebuttal to the idea that middle-income Black Baton Rougeans do not experience racism or discrimination. For example, Carol shared her frustrations in doing business, commenting on how often White potential clients would pull out of deals once discussions progressed far enough for them to realize she was Black. As Carol explained, "I'll send them correspondence, and they want to go with this," she said. But after seeing Carol's photo on the form her employer requires her to use when sending official quotes, "They'll say, 'well we decided to stay where we are.' And I'm like, you said five minutes ago send you the quote and you'll look it over and then we can move forward, and now you want to stay where you are?"[21] In another example, Diane shared that she had "stopped putting stickers on her car"—specifically referencing her old Southern University alumni sticker—after she came back from a trip and found her car vandalized in the airport parking lot, with explicit racial slurs and the comment "You probably supported Barack Obama" scrawled across it. Diane said she still believed it was "very important" to identify as Black and that she felt like a "coward" for removing her car stickers, but that, after that incident—"Yeah, forget it." (Remember that the White respondent James, by contrast, said, "Give me a break" on the topic of middle-income Black people being targets of racist behavior.)

I should note that a couple of Black residents did share views that, in a sense, resonated with the St. George advocates' and some White observers' deference to Black communities to solve their own problems—though in a different light. Michelle, for instance, remarked that some Black residents had concluded that then-Mayor-President Kip Holden was an "Uncle Tom" whom they had "given up on" because "although he's Black, he doesn't really support or help or assist any of the Black community"—a classic example of many Black Americans' sense of "linked fate" (Dawson 1994), which in this case assigns Holden particular responsibility for his Black constituents. Another version of this idea was more nuanced when Joshua argued that interracial coalition-building approaches like Together Baton Rouge's were "not equipped to deal with the trauma of intergenerational poverty." Joshua instead advocated for supporting local Black community organizations more explicitly focused on anti-poverty efforts.[22] In doing so, Joshua agreed with the principle of Black residents taking control of their own circumstances— but did so through direct recognition of the power differential between Black and White communities, and the danger of White interests either intentionally or inadvertently exploiting that differential. I lack scope to further explore Joshua's support for Black empowerment in contrast to other Black respondents' implied support for more integrationist approaches (i.e., the sort of contrasts interrogated in Dawson 2001 or more recently Dawson 2013). However, acknowledging these different positions is an important reminder of the diversity of opinion among Black Baton Rougeans that might have been masked by their shared opposition to St. George.

Prioritizing White Concerns

Let's now consider the third White discursive practice, where White respondents revealed tendencies such as characterizing White parents as the ones who were suffering most from the EBR school system, and only mentioning the children in the majority-Black system when citing concern for (presumably White) children's or teachers' well-being. The Black respondents offered a notable contrast by instead frequently drawing attention to social issues plaguing communities where many EBR schoolchildren live, and often expressing empathy or deep emotion when doing so. This is unsurprising, as many had grown up in NBR and/or attended Southern University, and nearly all of them attended churches in NBR—yet, it still speaks to how segregation impacts different racial groups' relationships to the local geography. Wayne was the White respondent who had told me that NBR was a "war zone" (as mentioned in Chapter 2). By contrast, Richard said to me, "Sometimes I go through there now and tears come out of my eyes," filled with sadness at how NBR had been slowly abandoned, disinvested from, and turned into a "wasteland."

Several Black observers again revealed a critical perspective on their surroundings when commenting on how segregation shaped White residents' circle of concern. Michelle, for example, agreed the traffic was a "nightmare" but also implied it was a problem of White residents' own making, thanks to the design of the city as a "segregated" one, full of "one-way in, one-way out subdivisions that people wanted to wall off." Another Black respondent more generally described the "invisible wall, both racial and economic" that crossed the parish and created separate worlds. "And you know, in the White world, you always have more choices," he said. Several others commented on how the geography of the area—such as where the highways were built, or the amount of space available for sprawl—facilitated the various routes White families had taken to "escape" Black families in their schools and neighborhoods; Joshua characterized St. George as simply the "most drastic exit option yet." These comments indicate that these Black residents understand the parish's geography to be deeply intertwined with race, and further indicate connections they have drawn between this racialized geography and White residents' actions and attitudes—as well as White residents' role in creating it.

It is also worth noting Lance's critique of White residents who would dismiss the majority-Black EBR student body as a lost cause and strategically reference EBR students (e.g., characterizing them as violent or underperforming) in order to make the case for St. George. "They would say things, like, 'no kids get a quality education there,'" Lance commented. "Those are just blanket indictments of a whole school system and all of the children in it. It's fairly ridiculous. And, quite frankly, uncharitable—and on many levels racist as far as I'm concerned." Note that, in contrast to those White respondents who had claimed that St. George supporters simply did not know about the good things in EBR schools, Lance characterizes this as willful ignorance and strategic disinformation. "Facts became unimportant," he said of the St. George leaders' portrayals of the school system, criticizing their hyperbole and selectivity in speaking about EBR students.[23]

Defending the Social Order

When it came to the fourth White discursive practice, the "all was calm before Alton Sterling" thesis was explicitly rejected by most of the Black respondents. As Pamela, a St. George opponent, put it: "[Racial] hostility has been more hushed than dissipating over time." She also laughed after she had initially commented on how Baton Rouge's shared identity was rooted in football and tailgating, then corrected herself: "Well, even that is divided, LSU versus Southern." Several respondents further commented on how White residents' positionality would have led them to the calm and order thesis in the first place. As Richard put it, "Most of them, those that I know, they have seen no racial divide. They think that everything is alright." Diane commented, in a similar vein, "Some people would see Baton Rouge as [. . .] a city on the verge of becoming great. And then there are other people who see it as the most racially intolerant segregated city I ever lived in. I would say that there's probably room for both of those. I don't think it's an either-or."

Pamela, Richard, and Diane's reflections all offer examples of Black residents' awareness of multiple realities in Baton Rouge—multiple experiences of their local geography as shaped, at least in part, by race.

On the topic of togetherness, the Black respondents offered somewhat more divergent perspectives. Some echoed themes the White respondents had cited, related to showing love to one another and building community. Carol commented approvingly, "Our churches and prayer organizations have invested some time in saying, 'Stop and try and smile at someone. Let's do some things to show some love.'" Two of the Black St. George opponents also commented on the importance of open conversation across racial lines: Pamela praised the Together Baton Rouge approach and called the organization "such a good role model," and Lance argued that, to get beyond racism, "the only way you do it is you've got to talk about it."

Critically, however, Pamela and Lance conceptualized conversation differently than most White respondents did, specifically by intimating the interpretive labor that would be required by White participants in discussions about race. Pamela commented, "If you talk about unifying a community, it has more to do with an attitudinal adjustment, right? You can't necessarily legislate unity . . . some intentional movement [has] to take place." Lance's approach was instead to call out that talking directly about race "probably makes some folks uncomfortable"—but that it was vital nonetheless, because "I live it. This is not some casual endeavor for me as a Black man in the United States of America—and particularly the South."

Several other Black residents agreed that the challenge facing Baton Rouge (and indeed, America) was no casual endeavor but rather hard work. "Get beyond the simple and irrelevant rhetoric," a Black pastor said. "This is hard work. This is real life. We're talking about things that are historical. They don't change immediately." Joshua even more directly addressed the discourse on "understanding one another." He criticized White politicians and business leaders in Baton Rouge for supporting policies that he believed were harmful to the Black community, even as those White people claimed to want to improve things for Black people.

So, that kind of kumbaya approach to this conversation? No one's interested in having that. No one is concerned about having White friends—not that there's anything wrong with having White friends, but that's not the issue. No one's concerned about understanding each other's experiences. That can help, but that, too, could be a distraction, right?

What we want is for you to stop doing this. Because this is hurting people. This is bad policy. This leads to these disastrous consequences for families' and individuals' lives. And if you stop that, regardless of whether you and I ever have a conversation, or you and I ever form some sort of interpersonal relationship—if you stop that, *that* will be progress.

Joshua's comments are nearly orthogonal to those of St. George supporters like Randy and Elise, but also to those of St. George opponents like Fred, Deborah, and Elizabeth—all of whom defined racial progress as primarily dependent on, if not equivalent to, improving interpersonal relationships and interracial understanding.

Joshua shared how draining it could be to get pulled into discussions with progressive White people in the parish, and how he would extract himself by offering to share resources or reading lists for them to tackle on their own. He said that he wasn't just "talking cheap" when he did this. He said, "It is to say that this is work—and so if I spent my life being forced into this work, and you have an attitude, then that is part of the problem. And so if you were really interested in understanding that problem, then one way to start that is to do this work." Joshua's take on "doing the work" is one that became a more common (if not always heeded) refrain in many circles after the racial unrest of the summer of 2020. But most notable for this analysis is the way he explains his expectations of his White peers: they are rooted in the fact that, as a Black man, he has felt "forced into" the interpretive labor of understanding America's racial order and the ways of White folks within it. And he has little patience left for White people who refuse to see this.

Conclusion to Chapter 3

Joshua, Lance, Pamela, and the pastor quoted in the previous section have given considerable thought to the nature of racial inequality in their home-town. They have put in interpretive work toward achieving the standpoint of a nondominant subject. They may not be representative of the larger Black population of Baton Rouge: their educational backgrounds and income levels set them apart from the disproportionately disadvantaged Black community. All the same, their view of race relations in Baton Rouge is drastically different from that presented by their White counterparts—even those who also have put effort into learning and thinking about racial inequality.

I do not question the dedication of these White people to the cause of improving race relations and fighting inequality in Baton Rouge. Neither should I downplay the efforts of groups such as Together Baton Rouge to mobilize voters, engage government officials, and achieve material improve-ments for the lives of many Black residents of Baton Rouge.

Yet, from an analytical perspective, we must recognize that these progressive White circles still engage in the practices of maintaining the color line. They reveal an aversion to calling out racism; a minimal recognition of the Black–White power differential; a value of "diversity" based on the positive experiences it can bring White people; and the assumption that White people *can* understand Black people's experiences, which is implied to be all that is needed to make progress toward racial equality. Even at sites of togetherness where White people seek to bridge the racial divide, they resist admitting their individual or collective complicity in maintaining the racial hierarchy, and do so following patterns similar to those used by the strongest advocates for St. George.

This chapter has thus identified striking similarities in the ways White residents of the Baton Rouge area, from the fiercest supporters to the strongest opponents of St. George, talk about local racialized issues. The results of my analysis resemble Matthew Hughey's comparison between a White nationalist organization and a White antiracist organization, both of which he argues were based on a fundamentally similar, hegemonic essentialization of Whiteness. Hughey's goal is to "destabilize the recent trend that overemphasizes white heterogeneity at the expense of discussion of power, racism, and discrimination" (Hughey 2010, 1289). My goal in this book resonates with Hughey's: to center "discussion of power, racism, and discrimination" in the racial threat hypothesis, doing so by theorizing the heterogeneity of White responses to context as nonetheless rooted in White people's common vantage point from the top of the racial hierarchy.

Recognizing the constrained vision of the most racially progressive White people in my sample is valuable because we tend to focus on how people who *support* policies with negative consequences for Black people help maintain the racial hierarchy. The analysis presented in this chapter prompts reflection on how White people who *fight* racially harmful policies and initiatives such as the St. George effort can still defend the color line—such as when centering their own experience in their activism, or when failing to recognize how privilege might constrain their vision.

I do not suggest that the racially progressive White people should feel guilty. After all, "guilt is a luxury," to use Baldwin's (1964, 62–63) words. "As long as you are guilty about something, no matter what it is, you are not compelled to change it." Empirical evidence suggests that Baldwin was right: although guilt on behalf of one's group might make group members more supportive of reparatory justice in principle, only feeling *anger* toward one's ingroup motivates group members to take action toward bringing about reparations (Leach, Iyer, and Pedersen 2006). The anger the St. George effort invoked among some White people who fought against it may be a good example of this sort of motivation to take action. Now, we could characterize such anger as not individual guilt but rather *collective* guilt (2019)—guilt by association with a group whose members have "'committed deplorable acts' against black people" (969, quoting Harvey and Oswald 2000), in contrast to individualistic remorse because of one's own actions. Whether conceptualized as collective guilt or anger at one's group, it seems clear that more White Americans experiencing such feelings, which require them to understand race relations in group-based terms, could represent a step toward accepting the structural nature of White privilege, White people's collective complicity in that system, and their responsibility to change it as a result.

In the end, calling for "togetherness" without questioning the dominance of a White perspective evokes Martin Luther King Jr.'s (1967, 93) warning about the White liberal who is "more devoted to 'order' than to justice, who prefers tranquility to equality." It is in heeding this warning that I critically reflect on the mobilization of racially tolerant White people in Baton Rouge. Feminist scholars of color including bell hooks, Audre Lorde, and Sara Ahmed have prominently challenged the premise that antiracism is "about making people feel better: safer, happier, more hopeful, less depressed, and so on" (Ahmed 2004, par. 30). Besides prioritizing White feelings as the ones that matter, Ahmed argues that this premise recenters the White subject by casting antiracism as a positive *White* attribute of which progressive White people could be proud. Thus, it may be of pragmatic value for organizers and activists to understand the motivations of White people who join efforts to fight racial inequality and discrimination—but the mobilization of these White people does not guarantee the subsequent dismantling of the color line.

A broader conclusion to draw from the present chapter concerns the importance of hearing the perspectives of nondominant subjects. For those who experience the double consciousness of life as Black Americans, it is harder to be ignorant of racial group interests. The Black members of Together Baton Rouge, for example, may be just as energized by the good work that organization is doing in the community. Yet, they are more likely to recognize the limitations to togetherness; to be skeptical of the value of White people trying to understand Black people; and to be realistic about the extent to which White interests will incorporate concern for Black communities. We should look forward to and support future work that further illuminates the nuances of Black opinion, including as it is shaped by and varies within local geographies (building on examples such as Bobo and Hutchings 1996; Gay 2004; and Gay 2006).

An Arab American with whom I spoke made a powerful statement along these lines. He passes as White in Baton Rouge, but pointed to his Middle

Eastern origins when sharing a perspective that I heard no other members of White society express. He said that even as someone familiar with the social problems that plague NBR, he has "no concept" of what life must be like there: "to be reminded every day not only of your race but your socioeconomic status. We even build freeways to avoid those places."

This comment contrasts sharply with the silence among virtually all of the White respondents around the possibility that there might be some things they could not understand in light of their position in the racial hierarchy. It also takes us back to where Chapter 2 began: on the highway, on a rainy drive through Baton Rouge to Alton Sterling's funeral. Returning to the highway is a reminder that the perspectives I have analyzed in this chapter and the St. George movement in the first place are contextualized by local geography: they reflect the racial politics of the specific geography of Baton Rouge as much as they reflect the attitudes of the individuals living there. Whether we consider White individuals' racial animus, ambivalence, or allyship—all of these are functions of people and politics, but also of place.

The chapters to follow will explore places beyond Baton Rouge where White people's attention to the color line is sharpened—thanks to a racialized issue salient at the time, and according to varying local demographics of race and class. But we will continue to see the dynamics I encountered in Baton Rouge come to light as I deploy and further develop this chapter's understanding of White people as diverse viewers with a shared lens.

4

The Geography of White Opposition to Welfare

For many Americans, the term "welfare" brings images of certain people and places to mind. Even though decades have passed since the peak of welfare's national salience in the late 1990s, it remains a quintessential example of a racialized policy area. In the minds of many White Americans in particular, antipoverty programs such as cash transfers and food assistance are stubbornly associated with Black recipients—and undeserving recipients at that.

"There's enough giveaway programs there," was how Kenneth, a St. George advocate, put it to me one morning in Baton Rouge, referencing a neighborhood a few miles away from the cheery café where we were meeting.

The association between race and welfare is not a random occurrence. Neither is the fact that the part of town Kenneth was referencing is both majority-Black and severely poor and segregated: the kind of place where welfare beneficiaries are thought to live. Far from random, welfare's racialization reflects the workings of the material color line as well as the metaphorical one. The real burden of poverty among Black Americans, descending from a history of discrimination, has all too easily sustained welfare's politicization as spending that fuels lifestyles of dependency among poor Black people at the cost of "hardworking" White people. Welfare therefore offers an ideal case in which to bring a consideration of power and positionality—and specifically, White people's vantage point—into the typical racial threat hypothesis.[1]

This chapter marks my turn to quantitative methods in order to investigate how White Americans interpret their surroundings in contexts beyond Baton Rouge, but incorporating key insights revealed there. What if we return to the classic racial threat hypothesis as explored via survey data, but conceptualize White people as viewers of their surroundings, not victims of a threat? What if we analyze the relationship between local geography and White opinion on racialized issues, but think of White survey respondents as real people like Kenneth—or, at the other end of the spectrum, like St. George opponent Elizabeth—rather than anonymous individuals? Chapters 4 and 5 will offer two examples of what happens when following the path these

How the Color Line Bends: The Geography of White Prejudice in Modern America. Nina M. Yancy,
Oxford University Press. © Oxford University Press 2022. DOI: 10.1093/oso/9780197599426.003.0004

Table 4.1 Two Dimensions of Prejudice, Two Quantitative Applications

Dimension of prejudice	Outgroup-oriented	Ingroup-oriented (addressed in Ch. 5)
Feelings of prejudice	Subordinate race inspires fear and suspicion Subordinate race is intrinsically different	Dominant race is superior Dominant race has claim to privilege and advantage
Discursive practices identified in Ch. 3	Denying racial motivations Minimizing racial categories	Prioritizing White concerns Defending the social order
Policy area explored in Ch. 4–5	Welfare spending (Chapter 4)	Affirmative action (Chapter 5)

Table synthesizes the feelings of prejudice articulated by Blumer (1958), discursive practices engaged in by White residents of Baton Rouge in Chapter 3, and the corresponding policy areas examined in Chapters 4 and 5.

questions prompt: when seeing White opinion not as the objective truth, but as White individuals' interpretations of reality filtered through a shared racial lens.

As summarized in Table 4.1, this chapter and the next explore White public opinion on two policy debates emblematic of the discursive practices encountered in Baton Rouge. Whereas welfare is an archetypal issue associated with the undeserving Black "Other," affirmative action is an archetypal issue that leads many White people to defend their own privilege. Together, these issues allow me to quantitatively demonstrate the reach of the White perspective across both outgroup- and ingroup-oriented feelings of prejudice— the same reach my qualitative methods illuminated in Chapter 3. Moreover, Chapters 4 and 5 will interrogate both the homogeneity and heterogeneity of the White perspective we encountered in Baton Rouge: that is, my quantitative investigations will center discussion of White Americans' shared power and positionality while also highlighting the varied ways White people might (or might not) construe their surroundings as threatening.

To begin, this chapter will focus primarily on White prejudicial feelings targeted at Black Americans as an outgroup: fear and suspicion of Black people, and the belief that Black people are intrinsically different. These are feelings typically associated with imagery of Black people as "threatening"— feelings broadly (and forcefully) denied as motivations behind the St. George effort, but nonetheless revealed by several White Baton Rouge residents when referencing majority-Black settings. "I'd be afraid to send my kid there," Brian, an observer, said of the majority-Black Baker, LA, school system. "That's a whole different animal," Kenneth said of the neighborhood he

thought received too many "giveaways," his use of the word "animal" subtly degrading and emphasizing the Otherness of the neighborhood's Black
residents.

These, of course, are the sorts of feelings powerfully implicated in debates
over welfare spending. Remember, however, that several White Baton Rouge
residents would have disagreed with Brian or Kenneth, and for different
reasons. Thus, Chapter 4 also will focus on the diversity of attitudes within
White people's positionality, as was revealed in Baton Rouge but can be
measured more directly in survey data.

In moving my attention from St. George to welfare spending in Chapter 4,
I shift to the second instance of racialization this book examines, and the
second historical moment. I begin by tracing the rise, decline, and ultimate
durability of Black residential segregation—introducing the topic of Black
poverty with an explicit emphasis on segregation, and White Americans'
responsibility for it, as one of the key structural forces that both produced and
stigmatized the Black ghetto. I set the scene of Chapter 4 in the year 2000, in
the era of welfare's peak national salience: following the heated debates of the
1990s that positioned the Black urban poor as a national symbol of idleness
and immorality.

I then outline and test a model of White welfare preferences that assigns
White people the role of active viewers of their local surroundings, rather
than passive recipients of a threat. As we will see, the relationship between
White individuals' racial attitudes and welfare preferences is stronger where
the stigmas of welfare are more visible—whether due to the presence of
a larger Black population or higher poverty rates, or due to the effect of
racial or income segregation in making such populations more visible to
White residents. This finding not only supports casting White people as active
viewers. It also highlights that, while White people may share a vantage point
that understands "welfare" in similarly racialized terms, different contextual
stimuli activate White opposition to welfare depending on the particular
racial attitudes a White individual holds.

Moreover, my analysis allows for populations seen as threatening by some
White people to be interpreted differently by others. The salience of race
or poverty may thus provoke greater support for welfare spending among
more racially tolerant White people—a possibility ignored by conventional
applications of the threat hypothesis, but endorsed by Chapter 2 and 3's
demonstration of the robust activation of opposition to St. George and
other salient, racialized issues in Baton Rouge. I replicate my results using
another dataset before discussing Chapter 4's larger lessons on the flexibility

of prejudice and the importance of theorizing White people's role in seeing racialized issues as threatening to White interests.

Segregation, Poverty, and the Racialization of Welfare

At the start of this century, the Texan town where I grew up might have been paraded as a model integrated community. A quiet Dallas suburb, DeSoto had a population of about 50,000 split almost evenly between Black and White residents as of the 2000 census. What this statistic conceals, however, is how many White families were already on their way out. By 2010, the Black population of DeSoto had risen to almost 70%, and the White population had fallen to less than 23%. As of 2019, the White population had dropped further, to less than 13%.

This is part of the same pattern that we saw in Baton Rouge. Consider the 70805 ZIP code—one of the more prominent majority-Black ZIP codes in North Baton Rouge (NBR) thanks to its association with high crime rates.[2] As of 1970, several neighborhoods in 70805 were 99–100% White, and no neighborhood in the ZIP code was less than about 80% White. By 2000, no neighborhood in the ZIP code was less than about 80% Black. Today, only one is less than 93% Black.

The White flight experienced by DeSoto, NBR, and other places is only one of the interlocking forces contributing to the persistence of racial segregation in the United States. DeSoto and NBR also demonstrate the range of Black neighborhoods that have been affected or created as a result: the Black families who have flocked to DeSoto since 2000 have been largely affluent, in contrast to NBR (median household incomes in my childhood ZIP code today are approximately $40,000 higher than in 70805). One thing is true across the board: Black Americans have experienced higher levels of residential segregation than any other group in U.S. history (Massey and Denton 1993).[3]

To be sure, we have made major strides toward integration since the 1960s. There is no longer a neat divide between "chocolate city" and "vanilla suburbs." Central cities have seen White residents return and new racial and ethnic groups arrive. Contemporary suburbs are deeply heterogeneous in both racial and economic terms (Oliver 2012; R. C. Johnson 2014; Ehrenhalt 2012). As further discussed in Chapter 5, middle-income Black families have had moderate success in moving to more advantaged areas. And all-White neighborhoods have virtually disappeared: one-fifth of urban neighborhoods housed no Black residents in the 1960s, but this is true for only one in 200 neighborhoods today (Glaeser and Vigdor 2012; see also Logan 2011).

Despite these signs of progress toward integration, as of 2010, one-third of all Black metropolitan residents still lived in a "hyper-segregated" setting—meaning highly segregated according to all five of the commonly used measures (Massey and Tannen 2015). At the current pace of change, Rugh and Massey (2014) predict that it will take another six decades for Black–White segregation to be considered "low." And while some authors have argued that Black segregation reflects the preferences of Black people themselves (W. A. V. Clark 1991; Patterson 1997), White people's aversion to living in racially mixed neighborhoods is significantly more prominent (Hwang and Murdock 1998; Quillian 2002; Krysan and Farley 2002). In other words, Black Americans are the most open to living in integrated settings, but also the most often avoided by White Americans—and Latinos and Asian Americans, too (Zubrinsky and Bobo 1996; Flores and Lobo 2013; Bader and Warkentien 2016).

Citing statistics, however, can only do so much to communicate the experience of segregation to those without firsthand knowledge. Far beyond the changing demographics of my hometown, the geographic isolation that millions of Black Americans experience is hard to imagine—and something that few White individuals I encountered in Baton Rouge tried to do. That is part of what makes segregation pernicious: it creates islands beyond the imagination of other area residents. These enclaves are easily ignored in the distribution of resources and opportunities, though often excessively attended to as sites of stigma and social control. Appreciating the continued existence of these enclaves, and the deprivation within them, offers two important lessons for this book.

Why Start With Segregation?

The first lesson to be drawn from a discussion of segregation concerns the role of both White citizens and the American state in creating and upholding this regime. The sort of White flight experienced by my hometown can result from even slight preferences for same-race neighbors (Schelling 1971; see also Shertzer and Walsh 2016). But this does not change the fact that White Americans have deliberately and violently avoided living with Black Americans. It was with the support of federal, state, and local governments that White people were able to do so with great success for most of the 20th century.

This history has been well documented (Massey and Denton 1993; King 1995; Cutler, Glaeser, and Vigdor 1999; Rothstein 2017; Trounstine 2018). As late as 1900, the average Black family still lived in a majority-White neighborhood, but the waves of Black people who left the South in the Great Migration—primarily as refugees fleeing Jim Crow's reign of terror—brought about a major shift in the racial makeup of the Northern and Midwestern cities where Black migrants began to concentrate (Wilkerson 2010). The 1934 creation of the Federal Housing Administration (FHA) brought the advent of redlining, or the practice of rating Black neighborhoods unsuitable for FHA-insured mortgages. Black veterans were later systematically excluded from the support for home ownership provided by Title III of the 1944 G.I. Bill (Frydl 2009). Both practices contributed to the federal government's effective subsidization of White wealth in the form of home ownership. This not only left Black families without equivalent government support. Locking them out of mainstream credit markets also enabled a "dual housing market" for Black buyers, where they were captive to exploitative and predatory practices that left them paying *more* for substandard housing—a phenomenon that reverberated throughout the 20th century and continues today (K.-Y. Taylor 2012, 2019).

For those Black families who were able to buy homes, racially restrictive covenants legally excluding Black people from certain neighborhoods were not outlawed until the 1948 case *Shelley v. Kraemer*, although they were enforced in practice long beyond that (Brooks and Rose 2013); indeed, racial restrictions still hide in many property deeds to this day.[4] White people also did not need covenants to resort to violence to keep Black families away, or to convince them to leave a neighborhood shortly after arriving (Seligman 2005; J. Bell 2007). In a survey of 9,000 Black urban residents in the 1990s, a majority (53%) cited fear of White hostility as a reason they would avoid living in all-White neighborhoods (Krysan and Farley 2002). Richard, one of the Black Baton Rouge residents we met in Chapter 2, brought this sentiment to life when recounting the process of buying a house in Baton Rouge the 1980s, and being warned by the realtor that he and his wife had "better be strong because there are people here who might put crosses in your yard" (they chose to move elsewhere). Richard shook his head, saying that similar dynamics remained "a problem that we have to respond to [. . .] even to this day." At minimum, subtler forms of "steering" of Black prospective buyers away from White neighborhoods persist (Choi, Herbert, and Winslow 2019) and are the reason I grew up in DeSoto, TX, in the first place, after my parents were blatantly steered away from Dallas neighborhoods closer to their workplaces (like Richard, they decided those were not places they wanted to live).

The built environment and availability of housing played a key role, too. From the 1950s onward, the interstate highway program had facilitated White suburbanization by subsidizing the cost of driving from distant locations into central cities, while offering little support for public transportation within cities themselves. This is not to mention the explicit destruction of Black communities by the government to build highways, as was the case in Old South Baton Rouge along with countless other places across the country (Avila 2014; Fullilove 2016). In 1968, the Fair Housing Act and the Housing and Urban Development Act sought to ban residential discrimination and create new integrated public housing, but both fell short of their promises as the state systematically sided with the interests of suburban White people (Bonastia 2006). The housing legislation did help some Black families move to the suburbs, yet this outmigration of more affluent Black people from central cities helped lead to concentrated Black poverty: the deindustrialization of the 1970s most heavily affected the lower-income Black laborers and their families who remained behind (Wilson 1987).[5]

This fact points to the second lesson that an appreciation of segregation offers for the present study. Segregation has been a central driver of racial inequality by reproducing the economic, social, and political disparities between Black and White Americans. As a result, segregation is ground zero for the maintenance of the material color line.

Although scholars debate the specifics of the relationship between racial segregation and the concentration of poverty among Black Americans, dense pockets of disadvantage increasingly appeared in segregated Black communities from 1970 to 1990 (Massey and Denton 1993; Jargowsky 1996; Quillian 2012). These pockets might be defined based on a number of factors, including high rates of poverty, unemployment, or welfare receipt, often in conjunction with a large number of female-headed households and high densities of children. Whatever definition of disadvantage is used, these neighborhoods have durable properties. Sociologists who study "neighborhood effects" tell us that negative social outcomes in certain areas do not merely reflect the choices of individuals who live there: the effects of deprivation are compounded when concentrated (Sampson 2012). Thus, when Black families have been systematically relegated to neighborhoods with inferior schools, low-quality housing, and a deficit of other resources, understanding the spatial logic of the neighborhood is central to understanding Black Americans' lagging social indicators in education, employment, and even life expectancy (see Sharkey 2009). And because outmigration never resulted in the full separation of middle-class Black people from poorer communities, the neighborhoods of Black households making between $55,000 to $100,000 annually are comparable (on measures of economic disadvantage) to the neighborhoods of White households making $12,000 to $30,000 annually (Sharkey 2014, 927; see also Reardon, Fox, and Townsend 2015).

In sum, Black Americans have had a residential experience categorically distinct from that of White Americans. Telling this grim history always comes with the risk of implicitly denigrating and dehumanizing all-Black spaces—making efforts to center the joy, life, and meaning that also emanate from Black spaces all the more important (see Hunter et al. 2016). At the same time, the story of segregation is integral to understanding the vantage point from which many White people would respond to questions about welfare spending. This is a vantage point that can easily ignore what Massey and Denton (1993, 2) articulate in their landmark study as the "fundamental fact" that segregation "constrains Black life chances irrespective of personal traits, individual motivations, or private achievements." A denial of this fact fueled much of the debate over welfare spending that began in the 1960s and continued throughout the late 20th century, against a backdrop of segregated cities and concentrated Black poverty, ultimately producing the visual stigmas still associated with welfare today. This is the history I turn to now.

Race and the Politics of Welfare Reform

Although there is a long American tradition of doubting the deservingness of the poor, the politicization of the term "welfare" in regard to the supposedly undeserving *Black* poor dates to the 1960s. The postwar boom was fading; poverty was reemerging as a national concern; and Black poverty was drawing new attention amidst civil unrest in cities across the country, as well as an emphasis by civil rights leaders on economic empowerment.

The disproportionate burden of poverty borne by Black Americans was hardly a phenomenon of the 1960s. What was new was the disproportionate number of Black people receiving Aid to Families with Dependent Children (AFDC), reflecting both the deleterious economic circumstances of many Black Americans and the fact that states had slowly dropped restrictions that had excluded many Black people from AFDC in its early years. Whereas in 1936, only 14% of AFDC beneficiaries were Black, by the time the nation turned its attention back to poverty in the 1960s, over 40% of AFDC recipients were Black (Turner 1993; see also M. B. Katz 1989; Fox 2012).

The racial composition of AFDC recipients was only a precondition, however, for a much more sudden shift Martin Gilens (1999) identifies in national media coverage of poverty. Black people featured in only 27% of images of the poor in 1964, but this percentage increased drastically to 49% in 1965, 53% in 1966, and 72% in 1967—ultimately projecting an image that was *double* the true proportion of welfare recipients who were Black. Correspondingly, racial attitudes and welfare preferences, which previously had been uncorrelated, became closely related after 1965 (Kellstedt 2003). The term "welfare" became code for cash and in-kind transfer programs (i.e., AFDC and food assistance) believed to benefit Black people at the cost of White people (Gilens 1996; Bobo and Kluegel 1993).

While the share of Black welfare recipients began to decline after 1969, the increase in dense pockets of Black poverty cited in the previous section only exacerbated welfare's associations with both race and the geography of the inner city. These associations were further entrenched by a new rhetoric of "poverty as pathology" in intellectual and political debates. One harbinger of this rhetorical shift was the now-infamous 1965 report by Daniel Patrick Moynihan. Then a junior employee of the Department of Labor, Moynihan highlighted endemic unemployment among Black men. But he also argued that the "fundamental source" of the economic gap between White and Black Americans was the family structure of lower-income Black households, calling it "highly unstable, and in many urban centers approaching complete breakdown" (Moynihan 1965, 5).

The issues the report discussed—high rates of divorce, children born to unwed mothers, and single-parent households—had long been a subject of debate and some pathologization, both in the academy and Black communities (e.g., Frazier 1939). Also predating Moynihan's report were the suspect gender norms he invoked. In what Ange-Marie Hancock (2003, 37) calls "a curious mix of race, class, and gender politics," many civil rights leaders subtly approved of Moynihan for echoing the refrain most Black churches at the time preached: that Black men should be assuming their proper places as the heads of Black families. This, Hancock argues, reinforced the idea that "female-headed households were countercultural and thus incompatible with the American lifestyle," furthering the stigmatization of single, poor Black women, including by their better-off Black peers (Hancock 2003, 37; Giddings 1996).[6]

Moynihan may have been well intentioned, but his take on these issues had a sensationalist impact when the report was leaked to the press. Its vivid discussion of the "tangle of pathology" that ensnared poor Black people far overshadowed its discussion of structural inequality. The report therefore both exacerbated longstanding stereotypes about the lesser morality and greater fertility of Black women (Collins 1998, 98–101), and dovetailed perfectly with growing ideas about the self-perpetuating values and practices that comprised a "culture of poverty" (O. Lewis 1966).

Conservative commentators such as Charles Murray (1984) and Lawrence Mead (1993) embraced these individualistic explanations for poverty with particular vigor, arguing that welfare only exacerbated things by offering perverse incentives. The idea of a culture of poverty also resonated beyond intellectual circles. It served as a powerful euphemism among the White public for Black people who behaved in ways unworthy of government support. Moreover, although welfare became one of several race-coded issues that powerfully drove racially resentful White Americans to the Republican Party (Carmines and Stimson 1989; Edsall and Edsall 1991), both parties used tropes such as the "welfare queen" as shorthand for Black, single mothers with a pathological dependence on welfare (Hancock 2004).

Being cast as undeserving, immoral, and lazy is much less likely to help welfare recipients find work than it is to negatively impact their psychological well-being and feelings of efficacy, thus undercutting welfare policy's ostensible goals (Fox Piven and Cloward 1971; Soss 2005; Campbell 2007). Yet, the image of the underserving welfare recipient fueled political debates for decades, culminating in President Clinton's pledge to "end welfare as we know it." The 1996 Personal Responsibility and Work Reconciliation Act replaced AFDC with Temporary Assistance for Needy Families (TANF), which eliminated cash assistance in favor of work requirements and time-limited welfare support. The reforms were meant to deracialize welfare, but stereotypes of Black recipients showed little change in the years after reform (Soss and Schram 2007). And as Kenneth's comment at the beginning of this chapter demonstrated, these stereotypes have survived into the present day, too.

As Elise, another one of the White St. George supporters we met in Chapter 3, told me with a sigh, "It all starts in the home, of course." Elise was reflecting on how, in her opinion, "the damage is already done" by the time many children in NBR reach school age. "A lot of them come from one-parent households; a lot of these kids don't have dads, or they live with their grandparents," she said. "You can just see some of the kids never had any work ethic."

It is true that between 30% and 40% of families in the census tracts comprising NBR are headed by a single female without a male partner present, compared to less than 3% of households in Elise's affluent and majority-White census tract. But beyond this accurate part of Elise's statement, she was powerfully illustrating the intersecting stigmatization of poverty, race, and gender. In both scenarios Elise mentioned, the Black mother is implied to be deviant—(willfully) single, absent, unemployed, and/or welfare-dependent—and thus implicitly culpable for her child's or children's "damage," even in a two-adult scenario where a child is raised by grandparents.[7]

Elise's understanding of intergenerational poverty in Baton Rouge ultimately reveals something that the liberal reformers who hoped for a new politics of welfare after 1996 failed to appreciate. Reforming AFDC as a program with material effects for a fraction of all Americans did little to change popular conceptions of welfare as a powerful political symbol. It has thus remained associated with the Black urban poor, whose poverty is often believed to be the product of individual behaviors or family values, rather than institutionalized segregation and structural inequality. When Black Americans continue to make up around a third of TANF recipients and in many instances remain concentrated in poor neighborhoods, the image of the Black urban poor that Chapter 4 examines easily is substantiated from the perspective of many White Americans.

Theorizing Racialized Preferences in Context

The fundamental disjuncture between the institutionalized segregation that has constrained Black Americans' life chances and the rhetoric of personal responsibility that has blamed Black people for their own poverty motivates this chapter's inquiry: one that centers White Americans' own responsibility in the construal of welfare as a threat to White people's interests. In taking on this inquiry, the present analysis represents this book's closest replication of the most common approach to studying racial threat, but bringing lessons from earlier in the book to bear.

Chapter 4 argues that White people's welfare preferences are more likely to be racialized—or predicted by White racial attitudes—in settings where the visibility of race or poverty raises the salience of welfare's image as a benefit to Black Americans at the cost of White Americans. As I discuss in this section, this argument diverges from many classic applications of racial threat (building on recent approaches such as Weber et al. 2014). I investigate not whether White welfare preferences are only more *negative* in certain contexts, but how certain contexts activate White people's racial attitudes—that is, White people's predispositions to oppose welfare spending on racialized grounds. Moreover, my analysis of welfare emphasizes the variety of White attitudes we saw in Chapter 3: the St. George effort activated White Baton Rouge residents both in favor of and in opposition to the incorporation, and based on different beliefs. In this chapter, I further investigate how different racial attitudes, held by different White individuals, are activated by distinct demographics White Americans might see in their local surroundings. Finally, Chapter 4 further explores the subjectivity of the White vantage point as revealed in Baton Rouge by highlighting how segregation makes certain demographics more or less visible from the average White urban resident's perspective.

In this section, I will explain why welfare's reputation as a benefit to the Black, urban poor invites an approach theorizing White people's awareness of either racial diversity or poverty in their surroundings. I then lay out such an approach, synthesizing individual- and group-level models of White policy preferences into an application of the racial threat hypothesis that casts White people as viewers, not victims. One important note before undertaking this task: in moving to quantitative study, this chapter shifts to the language of "variables," "probabilities," "effects," and so on—the sort of language that describes what a statistical model can tell us about a large sample of data. But this survey data come from White people like Kenneth, Elise, and Elizabeth, or their counterparts in other geographies. As was the case in Baton Rouge, geography can help us understand these people's opinions—that is, someone's field of vision can help predict the preferences they will express. But this should not minimize the extent to which White people are agents, not passive subjects, in drawing racialized meanings from urban geography and expressing racialized policy preferences as a result. Neither should the seeming neutrality of technical language minimize White Americans' collective responsibility for helping to create, sustain, and stigmatize economic realities that have had severe consequences for Black lives. I hope the history I have discussed related to the racialization of welfare helps us keep this in mind.

Revisiting the Classic Racial Threat Hypothesis

The history discussed in "Segregation, Poverty, and the Racialization of Welfare" also is of theoretical importance to the present study. Crucially, we can now appreciate the visual stigmas that featured in the racialization of welfare, as well as the durable conditions of segregation and inequality that sustained these stigmas. Images of poor Black Americans, and the blighted neighborhoods they inhabited, were central to welfare's construal as a threat to "hardworking" and implicitly White Americans. This reputation not only leads many Americans to drastically overestimate the scale of welfare spending and proportion of beneficiaries who are Black, but, importantly, it also frames welfare as an instance of racial group competition. Such framing helps explain why even White people with little personal interest in the matter might nonetheless oppose welfare spending in defense of White Americans' collective interests—or their "way of life"—per the insights of socio-structural theories of prejudice (e.g., Blumer 1958; Bobo 1983). Welfare was politicized in relation to place as much as race, further making it an ideal case in which to investigate how White people see a racialized policy issue in their local geographies.

In order to test my expectation that White people's expression of racialized welfare preferences varies across metropolitan areas, I synthesize individual-level and contextual models of preference formation. Specifically, I bring a fuller consideration of the racial attitudes literature into a racial threat approach. Although these are typically presented in isolation of one another, to consider them separately ignores that, as was vividly on display in Baton Rouge, White people express diverse viewpoints while also sharing interests on behalf of their racial group.

A prototypical individual-level analysis comes from Gilens (1995, 1999), who shows that the term "welfare" functions as a code word for means-tested transfer programs associated with Black recipients, namely food assistance and cash transfers. Gilens further shows that opposition to such programs is strongest among White Americans who believe Black Americans are poor due to an inherent lack of work ethic.

Examples from across comparative politics support Gilens's finding: social affinity with a policy's perceived beneficiaries plays a key role, distinct from economic self-interest, in determining individuals' attitudes toward redistribution (Alesina and Glaeser 2004; Cavaillé and Trump 2015; Klor and Shayo 2010). Though these approaches focus on individual attitudes, they are not divorced from the insights of structural, group-based theories of prejudice. Generally speaking, it is on the grounds that group members share a social identity, and prefer spending that benefits their ingroup, that White people are predicted to oppose spending associated with Black people.

What individual-level approaches ignore, however, is the possibility that White people's racialized welfare preferences reflect not only concerns about an undeserving outgroup but also geographically clustered beliefs about the threat welfare poses to White interests. This, of course, draws on the insights of the body of literature on racial threat. While I follow the convention of operationalizing threat with a measure of Black population share, I emphasize that threat is not a consequence of Black people's presence, but of White people's perceptions.

As noted in Chapter 1, previous work has recognized, to varying extents, that "threat" is a shorthand for what happens when White people react to a nearby Black population. Scholars such as M. C, Taylor (1998) have more explicitly asked whether White people who express perceiving a threat (on economic or political grounds) are more sensitive to the relative size of a local Black population; her conclusion is no: perceived threat does not heighten White people's responses to context. One explanation Taylor offers is that the threat perceptions she measures might be inseparable from negative sentiments White people already hold toward Black people. My analysis follows this line of thinking by focusing on those negative sentiments— White people's racial attitudes. These attitudes represent the beliefs that White people are likely to draw on when evaluating a policy that has been framed as a threat to their collective interests, and doing so within a particular context of racial diversity and poverty.

Understanding White people as viewers underpins my analysis, with dual implications for the relationship between a White individual and their sur- roundings: I recognize that individual-level prejudices are likely to affect how White people view their local geography, while also recognizing that welfare policy is likely to be viewed through a lens conditioned by White people's group-level interests.

I thus diverge from Oliver and Mendelberg (2000) who find that context predicts policy preferences within the geography in which a policy's benefits are distributed.[8] Though welfare is administered by states, to assume that White people are thinking specifically of their state's Black population when asked about welfare would ignore that welfare was politicized as an urban issue, and that political behavior often reflects local (i.e., substate) concerns (Tobler 1970; Reeves and Gimpel 2012). I therefore analyze White welfare preferences as they vary across metropolitan areas—specifically, according to the salience of race and poverty in these local contexts. Similar reasoning informs my conceptualization of racial diversity in Black–White terms; a focus on racial heterogeneity (such as that of Branton and Jones 2005) would be at odds with the extent to which welfare has been politicized in relation to Black Americans more so than other minorities.[9]

A Contextual Model of Welfare Preferences

I now outline a theory to test my conjecture that White welfare preferences will be more racialized where the stigmas of welfare are more visible. I theorize, first, the responsiveness of racial attitudes to contextual cues; and second, why different racial attitudes should be activated depending on the cue that is seen.

The Responsiveness of Attitudes to Racial and Economic Context

As introduced in Chapter 1, research in political psychology supports the idea that local context will affect the salience of race or poverty, albeit looking beyond a geographic definition of context. Studies of racial priming, for example, offer compelling evidence that racial attitudes become more influential in political decision-making when these attitudes are made more accessible—or more quickly and easily retrieved—after exposure to a stimulus related to race (Mendelberg 2001; Valentino, Hutchings, and White 2002). The psychological process at play here is one akin to Zaller's (1992) model of attitudinal formation, which identifies political awareness as the crucial link determining whether individuals' preexisting values and beliefs are translated into their political preferences. Zaller argues that whether a predisposition informs someone's survey response depends on whether the respondent possesses contextual information that connects the predisposition to the issue being surveyed.

Weber et al. (2014) extend this logic to the racial threat hypothesis by identifying a stronger relationship between racial stereotypes and policy preferences in racially diverse settings. These authors set a precedent for challenging the literature's conventional focus on how racial attitudes themselves vary across context, instead asking *in what circumstances* negative orientations toward outgroups are likely to be consequential for politics. This shift nods to research in political economy that has identified how context, or more specifically, the structure of a given welfare regime, conditions the relevance of individual-level factors to social policy preferences (Gingrich and Ansell 2012; Gingrich 2014). Investigating the conditioning effects of context also recognizes that racial attitudes themselves tend to be remarkably stable over time, whereas racial threat is a situational phenomenon (Hopkins 2011; Enos 2016; see also Velez and Lavine 2017).

When analyzing White people as viewers of their surroundings, however, we should expect more than racial context alone to play a role in raising the salience of welfare's racialized image. I will investigate White responses to racial *and* economic context on the understanding that either could indicate the salience of welfare's image. Because both Blackness itself and concentrated, urban poverty are visual stigmas of welfare use, measures of the Black population share or central city poverty rate should serve to indicate the salience of welfare's racialized image in a given setting. When that image is easily accessible, racial attitudes are more likely to be invoked in opposition to welfare spending, serving a White individual's psychological "need" to defend one's way of life (D. Katz 1960; Stenner 2005).

Although my argument implies that a White individual would possess the same racial predispositions regardless of setting, I am cautious in posing racial attitudes as exogenous to context. Similarly, it is possible that White Americans' orientations toward either Black Americans or public spending reflect regional or state cultures. I discuss how I account for these considerations when I turn to my empirical analysis. I argue that it remains necessary to question the frequent assumption that the *relationship* between racial attitudes and welfare preferences is exogenous to context. Furthermore, I expect that measures of Black population share or poverty rate will not independently predict a White individual's probability of expressing a particular welfare preference. The contextual measures should instead reveal their significance *in relation to* a White individual's existing racial attitudes, resulting in a heightened effect of racial attitudes when race or poverty is salient.

Two Measures of Racial Attitudes

What attitudes would be amplified by the salience of race or poverty? Because racial attitudes are multidimensional, more than one formulation of prejudice should operate in defense of White Americans' interests. Moreover, if racial attitudes are akin to predispositions in Zaller's model, then the attitude that is brought to bear on welfare preferences should depend on the contextual information that is provided.

Accordingly, I operationalize two racial attitudes that should lead White people to construe either a large Black population or a high poverty rate as a threat. The first follows from Gilens's finding that endorsing the traditional, insidious stereotype of Black people as lazy strongly predicts opposition to welfare (see not only Gilens 1999, 155–165, but also Kendi 2016 on this stereotype's origins).[10] Because welfare is associated with Black recipients, a White individual who believes Black people are inherently lazy is likely to think of welfare as money spent on the undeserving poor—or people who take advantage of "giveaway" programs to use Kenneth's term. Fellow St. George supporter Wayne's take on antipoverty policies in Baton Rouge was similar: "It's not helping move forward; it's handouts." To be clear, Kenneth and Wayne calling welfare a giveaway or handout does not necessarily mean they would endorse the stereotype of Black people as lazy. It is also worth remembering here that both men, along with most White residents I encountered in Baton Rouge, were careful to avoid expressing views that would be construed as racist. All the same, Kenneth and Wayne's understanding of welfare helps bring to life how someone who believes Black people are lazy might think.

The second racial attitude I measure is racial resentment, a more nuanced expression of prejudice, introduced by Donald Kinder and David Sears as "symbolic racism" (Kinder and Sears 1981) and later reformulated as "modern racism" (McConahay 1986) or "racial resentment" (Kinder and Sanders 1996; Tesler 2016a). All of these use the rhetoric of egalitarianism to normalize racial inequality, to oppose "special favors" for Black people, and to deny that discrimination rather than lack of effort explains why Black people remain disproportionately poor. White people holding these views would oppose welfare spending not because they think all Black people are inherently lazy, but because the term "welfare" recalls images of the Black poor who are believed to violate American values of self-reliance and discipline. This is a subtler view than a racial stereotype: it posits the prevalence of poverty among Black people, rather than their race itself, as a sign of Black people's lesser commitment to hard work. This view could manifest itself in comments similar to Elise's reflections on children who grow up in NBR. She cites the number of single-parent households, a common indicator of poverty, as evidence that kids grow up lacking "any work ethic." Again, I did not directly measure the racial attitudes of the Baton Rouge residents, hence the value of looking at racial attitudes measured on surveys, but Elise still helps illustrate how a racially resentful White viewer might interpret poverty in their surroundings.

Both racial resentment and the laziness stereotype hold that Black people have a substandard work ethic, whether intrinsically or just generally. Both attitudes have played pernicious roles in stigmatizing the Black poor. As a result, both should predict White opposition to welfare:

- **Racial attitude hypothesis**: Holding either traditionally prejudicial or racially resentful views will make a White individual more likely to oppose welfare.

Yet, these two attitudes are not identical. Consider how each attitude would respond to a middle-income Black family. White people who consider Black people inherently lazy would see this family as an exception to the rule (e.g., if the Black family's success is believed to be a product of hard work), or perhaps as evidence of success gained by disingenuous means (e.g., if the Black family's success is believed to be the product of manipulating the welfare system). White people who are racially resentful, on the other hand, would see the middle-income Black family as proof of their argument: if only more Black people would work harder, like this family has, then fewer Black people would be poor.

Where this descriptive difference becomes a functional one is in the unique relationships we should expect between each racial attitude and local geography. The laziness stereotype explicitly posits race as an indication of someone's work ethic and consequential deservingness of poverty assistance. If skin color functions as a cue bringing the idea that Black people are lazy to the top of a White observer's mind, then the salience of Black residents in a White individual's surroundings should predict the accessibility of this stereotype.

Taking the percentage of Black people in a metropolitan area as a proxy for the salience of a Black population, then agreement with the laziness stereotype should be more predictive of opposition to welfare among White people who live in settings with a larger Black presence.

- **Visibility hypothesis 1**: White people who hold traditionally racist views are more likely to oppose welfare in metropolitan areas where a larger share of the population is Black.

On the other hand, racial resentment uses the lower average economic status of Black people, rather than skin color itself, as an indicator of deservingness that explains inequality between White and Black Americans. Thus, racial resentment should be more accessible in settings where poverty, not race, is salient. In order to compare White people who live in settings with a similar Black presence, I control for the Black population share when positing a relationship between racial resentment and local poverty rates. However, it should not be necessary that *Black* poverty is salient in White people's surroundings for the salience of poverty in general to increase the accessibility of racial resentment when a racialized policy like welfare is in question. Poverty is a structural condition of the American racial order, disproportionately affecting Black Americans thanks to a history of oppression, and often viewed by White Americans through a racial lens. Even the salience of *non-Black* urban poverty should make the imagery of the Black poor more accessible, and thus make White people more likely to draw on racial resentment when evaluating a policy so closely associated with race.

- **Visibility hypothesis 2**: White people who hold racially resentful views are more likely to oppose welfare in metropolitan areas where the poverty rate is higher.

There has long been a lively debate around racial resentment (including in its earlier formulations, e.g., as symbolic racism). Some of the loudest critics, most notably Paul Sniderman and coauthors, have argued that what we are actually talking about is a principled, conservative belief about the appropriateness of government action to reduce racial inequality (Sniderman and Piazza 1993). In response to this claim, other scholars have demonstrated that principled conservatism fails to predict conservative stances on issues unrelated to race (Schuman et al. 1997; Sidanius, Pratto, and Bobo 1996). More recently, Cindy Kam and Camille Burge (2018) have pushed scholars to recast the racial resentment scale as one capturing structural versus individual explanations for Black Americans' social and economic standing. [Commendably, the authors develop this argument by including a focus on Black people's own attitudes and nod to scholars such as Dawson (1994), in whose footsteps they follow.]

Ultimately, my goal is not to enter the debate over racial resentment, but rather to understand the operation of a sentiment that tries to explain the intersection of poverty and race. Even if racial resentment captures conservatism or individualism more than racism, identifying the amplified effect of this attitude on welfare preferences in settings where poverty is more salient would be valuable. Such a finding would reveal that attitudes about inequality between racial groups—whether reflective of animus or not—are responsive to economic context.

Polarized White Welfare Preferences in Settings of Threat

I now put my hypotheses to the test. Is there a stronger relationship between White people's racial prejudices and their welfare preferences in settings of greater racial diversity or poverty? And does the contextual indicator that is relevant depend on the form of prejudice in question—or rather, the particular beliefs a White individual draws on when viewing the world through a racialized lens?

Choosing a Dataset and Measuring Attitudes

I draw on the General Social Survey (GSS) to examine non-Hispanic White Americans' evaluations of welfare spending as of 2000. Locating my analysis in this year offers contextual data and segregation measures based on the 2000 decennial census, as well as proximity to the 1996 reforms, when the national salience of welfare would have made welfare opinions more sensitive to contextual cues (Hopkins 2010). Using the GSS question asking whether the country spends "too much, too little, or about the right amount on welfare," I focus on the likelihood a White respondent expresses opposition to welfare by saying that too much is spent on it.

To measure the laziness stereotype, I control for White respondents' placement of Black Americans on a scale from "hardworking" to "lazy." I adjust this variable by each respondent's corresponding evaluation of White Americans as hardworking or lazy and rescale it between 0 and 10 ($M = 5.31$, $S.D. = 1.31$).

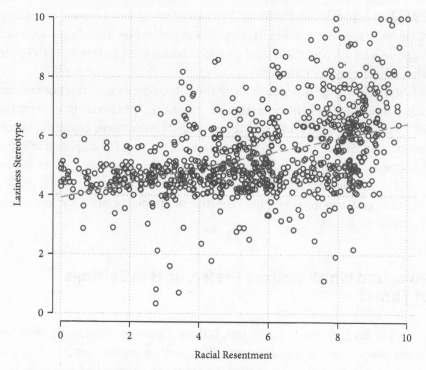

Fig. 4.1 Correlation between Racial Attitude Variables

Figure visualizes where White respondents in the GSS sample rank on measures of both traditional prejudice and racial resentment.
Source: 2000 General Social Survey (*n* = 1,224).

To measure racial resentment, I rely on a number of survey questions and conduct factor analysis to identify common variation in how people respond to these questions. This process is described further in the technical appendix for this chapter. The resulting racial resentment variable captures agreement with three beliefs. First, that worse outcomes for Black people are due to a lack of motivation to succeed; second, that Black people no longer face discrimination; and third, that Black people should "work their way up" as other minority groups have.[11] Like the laziness stereotype, I scale the racial resentment variable between 0 and 10, with higher values reflecting more resentful attitudes (*M* = 5.65, *S.D.* = 2.48).

Comparing the two variables supports my multidimensional approach to conceptualizing racial animus. Figure 4.1 illustrates that the laziness stereotype and racial resentment are correlated, at 0.47, but clearly capture different dimensions. The figure also illustrates the larger spread of attitudes on the racial resentment scale, including among the large number of White respondents who cluster around the middle of the Black laziness scale.

Besides controlling for racial attitudes, I also control for age, education, gender (male = 1), marital status (married = 1), and income (in 2000 dollars). I control for partisanship with dummy variables reflecting identification as a Democrat, independent, or Republican. I do not simultaneously control for ideology in order to reduce the collinearity or endogeneity of using self-placement on a left–right scale to predict a dependent variable that likely informs ideological self-definition in the first place (see Strolovitch 1998). There is a good chance that opposing government spending on antipoverty programs leads someone to identify as conservative rather than vice versa.

Measuring Local Contexts

I measure racial and economic context at the level of the metropolitan statistical area (MSA). Given the politicization of welfare in regard to urban, Black poverty, as well as the availability of the segregation measures I will later use, I focus on public opinion among nonrural White Americans.[12] The higher density of MSAs also makes them settings where residents would be aware of visually identifiable communities associated with welfare.

As discussed in Chapter 1, no study assigning a role to context is immune from the modifiable areal unit problem (MAUP), or the propensity for the relationship between variables to depend on the scale and shape of the geographic container used for analysis (Fotheringham and Wong 1991). Measuring context at the metropolitan level mitigates this concern on two accounts. First, MSA boundaries should be large enough to capture indicators related to the visibility of welfare's stigmas even if people are sorted into neighborhoods by race or income. Although concerns of self-selection even at the neighborhood level may be overstated, it is costlier to move to a new metropolitan area than it is to move to a more favorable neighborhood within the same area (Kaufmann and Harris 2015). Second, people are likely to cross county lines in their daily activities and be consumers of a media market that reports on issues in the wider area (Behr and Iyengar 1985). MSAs are therefore reasonable containers in which White residents would be aware of the presence of Black communities, as well as low-income communities.

I thus isolate the 1,569 White respondents in the 2000 GSS sample who are located in 95 MSAs. I incorporate racial demographics using the percentage of Black residents in each MSA as of the 2000 census, log-transformed to account for the variable's right-skewed distribution. I incorporate economic context with a measure of the percentage of individuals living under the federal poverty line in the central city of an MSA in order to capture the salience of urban poverty.

On the Overlap Between Racial Diversity and Poverty

The present study offers two ways of thinking about the relationship between prejudice and place, depending on how prejudice is defined. I have noted that White people who rank highly on one of my racial attitude measures are likely to rank highly on the other—but not deterministically so, as Figure 4.1 made clear.

This same logic holds when examining racial and economic geography across MSAs. As illustrated in the map in Figure 4.2, there is clear overlap between high-density Black MSAs and high-poverty MSAs, particularly in the South. Yet there is considerable divergence, too. A number of MSAs in the Southwest and West with large Latino populations have high poverty rates but small Black populations. Cases such as these offer the opportunity to investigate how the local salience of poverty can activate racial resentment even in the absence of a sizable Black population.

On the other hand, a number of MSAs in the Midwest, Upper South, and Mid-Atlantic have sizable Black populations but poverty rates that fall into the bottom half of the national distribution. These places offer a chance to

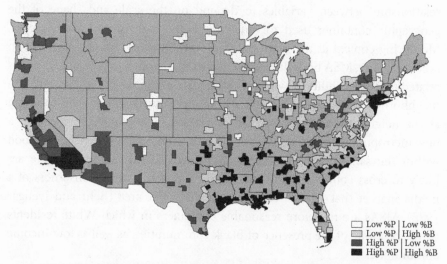

Low %P	Low %B
Low %P	High %B
High %P	Low %B
High %P	High %B

Fig. 4.2 Black Population Presence and Poverty Rates by Metropolitan Area, 2000

Maps use TIGER/Line Shapefiles and census data to illustrate poverty rates and Black population share across MSAs as of 2000. Poverty rates (%P) and Black (%B) population shares are defined as "low" or "high" by virtue of being below or above the median value. The median poverty rate across MSAs in 2000 was approximately 12% and the median Black population share was approximately 7%.

investigate how racial geography might activate stereotypes of Black people as lazy and thus inform welfare preferences, even in a setting where poverty is less salient.

Of course, if a White individual who is both traditionally prejudiced *and* racially resentful lives in a Southern MSA with high poverty rates *and* a large Black population share—we might anticipate considerable opposition to welfare from this person no matter what. The good news for this analysis is that the GSS sample includes White respondents with a range of racial attitudes across MSAs with different Black population shares and poverty rates (visualized in the technical appendix). This indicates that the findings to follow do not simply reflect clusters of racially hostile White people living in either the most diverse or impoverished MSAs.

Empirical Models

I now test the proposition that racial attitudes have a greater effect on White welfare preferences in settings with a larger Black population share or higher poverty rate, depending on the racial attitude in question. I use binary logistic regression to estimate the probability that a White individual believes that too much is spent on welfare. All results are reported as odds ratios with standard errors clustered by MSA.[13]

To begin, I corroborate the link between White racial attitudes and welfare preferences documented in previous research. As expected, the odds ratios reported in the first two models of Table 4.2 offer support for the *racial attitude hypothesis*: both racial attitudes are significant predictors ($p < 0.01$) of welfare preferences. In Model 1, moving across the interquartile range of the Black laziness scale (from 4.54 to 6.36) predicts a 10 percentage-point increase in the likelihood of opposing welfare. In Model 2, the equivalent move across the racial resentment scale (from 3.98 to 8.18) predicts an almost 20 percentage-point increase. These changes in predicted probabilities are second only to partisanship. The average White Republican has a probability of opposing welfare approximately 20 percentage points greater than the average White Democrat in the model controlling for the Black laziness stereotype, and 14 percentage points greater in the model controlling for racial resentment. Education is also a significant predictor of more positive evaluations of welfare in Model 1, consistent with studies finding that more educated White people are less likely to hold traditional stereotypes—even if they remain defensive of White interests in other ways (Glaser 2001).

Table 4.2 White Welfare Preferences in Context

Opposition to Welfare	(1) Individual Level	(2) Individual Level	(3) Laziness Stereotype and Context	(4) Laziness Stereotype and Context	(5) Laziness Stereotype and Context	(6) Racial Resentment and Context	(7) Racial Resentment and Context	(8) Racial Resentment and Context
Individual-level variables								
Laziness Stereotype	1.263*** (0.096)		1.264*** (0.097)	0.897 (0.150)	0.983 (0.234)			
Racial Resentment		1.225*** (0.073)				1.220*** (0.073)	1.105 (0.104)	0.792 (0.138)
Independent	2.121*** (0.569)	2.233** (0.725)	2.126*** (0.564)	2.145*** (0.581)	2.143*** (0.575)	2.182** (0.713)	2.226** (0.730)	2.292** (0.744)
Republican	2.418*** (0.570)	1.861** (0.517)	2.421*** (0.569)	2.407*** (0.575)	2.431*** (0.576)	1.840*** (0.515)	1.863** (0.523)	1.869** (0.534)
Contextual Variables								
Percent Black (log)			0.982 (0.084)	0.436*** (0.131)	0.984 (0.083)	1.019 (0.116)	0.781 (0.243)	1.015 (0.105)
Poverty Rate			1.001 (0.020)	1.001 (0.020)	0.931 (0.057)	1.025 (0.023)	1.026 (0.023)	0.891** (0.047)
Laziness Stereotype × Percent Black (log)				1.165** (0.069)				

	(1)	(2)	(3)	(4)	(5)	(6)	(7)	(8)
Laziness Stereotype × Poverty Rate					1.013 (0.013)			
Racial Resentment × Percent Black (log)							1.046 (0.045)	1.025** (0.010)
Racial Resentment × Poverty Rate								
Constant	0.444 (0.352)	0.360 (0.298)	0.450 (0.380)	2.513 (2.678)	1.655 (2.009)	0.228 (0.221)	0.360 (0.370)	2.332 (2.820)
Observations	512	361	512	512	512	361	361	361
p	0.000000656	0.0000324	0.00000275	5.15e − 08	0.00000595	0.0000880	0.000128	0.0000623
Log likelihood	−324.1	−224.3	−324.1	−321.7	−323.7	−223.6	−223.1	−220.0

Exponentiated coefficients; standard errors in parentheses; party base category is Democrat.

Table reports odds ratios from logistic regression estimating probability of White respondents saying too much is spent on welfare.

For concision, controls for age, gender, marital status, and income are not displayed.

Source: 2000 General Social Survey.

* $p < 0.10$, ** $p < 0.05$, *** $p < 0.01$.

I next add measures of context to the analysis in order to test the two visibility hypotheses. Models 3 through 5 of Table 4.2 include measures of local Black population share and poverty rate when controlling for White respondents' agreement with the Black laziness stereotype. As expected, neither contextual variable on its own is a significant predictor of welfare views in Model 3.

However, when controlling for an interaction between the laziness stereotype and Black population share in Model 4, I find that racial geography conditions the effect of the belief that Black people are lazy on the probability of a White individual opposing welfare spending. Model 4's significant interaction supports *visibility hypothesis 1*. In metropolitan areas with a negligible Black presence, the Black laziness stereotype is less predictive of opposition to welfare; but as the Black population share increases, so does the predicted effect of holding a traditionally racist stereotype.

To put this interaction in substantive terms, consider an unmarried White woman in the dataset, positioned at the means of all individual variables but at 7 on the 0–10 scale measuring the laziness stereotype. In a metropolitan area where only 5% of the population is Black, her odds of saying too much is spent on welfare are 41.1%. For an otherwise identical person living in a 25% Black setting, these odds would increase to 50.8%. To offer additional support for the argument that a larger Black presence makes the laziness stereotype more accessible to White people when the topic of welfare spending is mentioned, I test whether the laziness stereotype responds similarly in high-poverty settings. The results reported in Model 5 indicate that no significant interaction exists between these two variables: endorsing the stereotype that Black people are lazy does not predict a greater likelihood of White opposition to welfare in settings with higher poverty rates (holding Black population share constant).

I argued in "A Contextual Model of Welfare Preferences" that this finding makes sense if we understand the laziness stereotype to be primarily about race, not poverty. Another consideration regards the fact that high-poverty MSAs with small Black populations tend to have large Latino populations. It is possible that the salience of Latino poverty would make the connection between Black Americans and poverty less clear-cut—a question that merits investigation in future research. For now, the lack of interaction between the laziness stereotype and local poverty rate indicates that, in MSAs with high poverty rates and low Black population shares, poverty alone is not enough to make the Black laziness stereotype more accessible to White viewers.

In Models 6 through 8 of Table 4.2, I repeat the same analysis but instead control for racial resentment. I confirm in Model 6 that poverty rate does not independently influence welfare views; nor does it significantly interact with Black population share in Model 7. The interaction between poverty rate and racial resentment posited in Model 8, however, is significant ($p < 0.05$), offering evidence for *visibility hypothesis 2*. The effect of racial resentment on a White individual's welfare preferences is minimized for those individuals living in settings with very low poverty rates. In higher-poverty settings, racial resentment is more predictive of opposition to welfare.

Predicted probabilities again convey the substantive effects of the interaction term. Returning to the above example of the average single White woman in the dataset and placing her at 7 on the racial resentment scale, this individual would have a 38.4% chance of saying too much is spent on welfare if she lived in a metropolitan area with a 15% poverty rate in its central city. In a setting where 30% of the population was poor, this probability would increase to 59.3%.

Interpreting the Results: Polarized Preferences
The findings reported so far identify unique responses of the laziness stereotype and racial resentment to the local salience of either race or poverty. Taken together, the models reveal that White welfare preferences are more polarized by racial attitudes where welfare's racialized policy image is more accessible—whether due to the presence of a large Black population or a high poverty rate. Figures 4.3 and 4.4 visualize the two interactions between

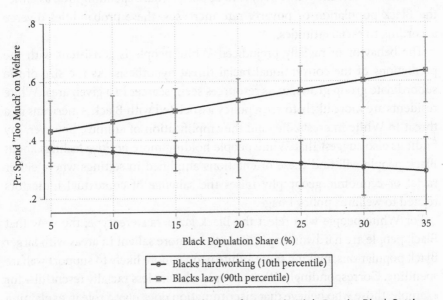

Fig. 4.3 The Polarization of White Welfare Preferences in High-Density Black Settings
Figure visualizes the interaction posed in Model 4 in Table 4.2. *Source:* 2000 General Social Survey ($n = 512$).

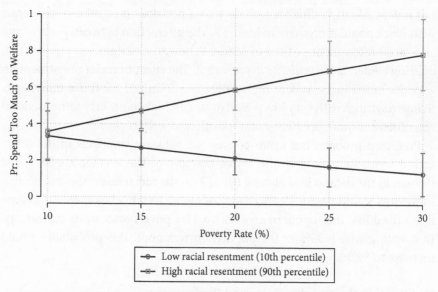

Fig. 4.4 The Polarization of White Welfare Preferences in High-Poverty Settings
Figure visualizes the interaction posed in Model 8 in Table 4.2. *Source*: 2000 General Social Survey (*n* = 361).

attitudes and context in order to visualize the different effects of geography on racially prejudiced and racially tolerant White people. In low-density Black or low-poverty MSAs, racially prejudiced White people are no more likely than racially tolerant White people to oppose welfare spending. Yet, as either the Black population or poverty rate increases, these probabilities diverge according to racial attitudes.

The behavior of racially prejudiced White people is consistent with the predictions of the conventional racial threat hypothesis. As the size of the subordinate group grows, or as resources seem scarcer in a given area, White residents are more likely to see a policy associated with Black Americans as a threat to White interests. Beyond the amplification of animus, however, my findings also suggest that White people holding more *positive* feelings about Black people will find these orientations amplified in settings where either racial or economic geography raises the salience of contextual indicators related to welfare's policy image.

For White people who reject the Black laziness stereotype, the view that Black people are hardworking is likely to be more salient in areas with larger Black populations, making these White people more likely to support welfare spending. Correspondingly, White people who are less racially resentful—for example, those who believe that discrimination does play a role in explaining racial inequality—are predicted to be more supportive of welfare in settings of higher poverty. In other words, what someone with high racial animus perceives as a threat may be interpreted differently by White Americans who are more sympathetic to Black Americans.

It is unlikely that White people with negative views of Black people seek out settings with larger Black populations or higher poverty rates, and thus unlikely that my results are the product of self-selection by racially prejudiced White individuals. On the other hand, it is possible that the behavior of the most racially tolerant White individuals in the sample reflects some degree of self-selection. Members of this category may be less averse to living near either racial diversity or poverty. Another important caveat is that few White people in the GSS sample hold expressly positive views of Black people. Only 6% of the sample rate Black Americans as harder-working than White Americans, whereas 49% evaluate the races as equivalent. The racial resentment scale also is weighted toward the racially prejudiced end. Therefore, the polarization I identify likely is driven by the amplification of prejudice more so than the amplification of tolerance—although the amplification of tolerance, even among a small share of White people, remains a notable finding.

Baton Rouge offered an example of this finding in practice: many St. George opponents I encountered strikingly illustrated the activation of tolerant White people against a racialized issue. My findings in Baton Rouge (as well as in Figures 4.3 and 4.4) also comport with prior quantitative findings. Tolerant White people often hold their positions even more strongly in diverse settings because fighting against the social norm (i.e., against White prejudice, often amplified in such settings) can strengthen one's views (Pettigrew, Wagner, and Christ 2010; see also Stein, Post, and Rinden 2000).

Importantly, the divergent behavior of both tolerant and prejudiced White individuals when race is salient does not negate the centrality of White people's shared racial lens. The tolerant White individuals in the sample still reveal their racialized understanding of the term "welfare" by being sensitive to a local Black population when expressing welfare preferences, even if these White viewers respond positively. Deborah, the White social worker we met in Chapter 3, showed this dynamic at work when commenting on her experiences visiting NBR:

> I see one Black man with droopy pants and kind of dark, in a hoodie—I'm nervous too. I know odds are he's just walking down the street, but I'm still going to be scared. And I'm giving him the benefit of the doubt more than most people my age and race and income level. I don't know. Guys are not helping themselves by appearing threatening. I don't know if you're trying to look threatening because you're mad at us *(Deborah laughed uncomfortably)* "Us," listen to me . . . wow.

Deborah reveals her racialized perspective in the instinct that Blackness "always already" presents a threat to White people (Butler 1993), and in her reference to White people as "us." But we can see the effort she makes to draw on her racially tolerant views: she is self-conscious about trying to give the Black man "the benefit of the doubt"; she justifies her fearful response by making a joke about why the man might have a good reason to be mad at White people in the deeply unequal Baton Rouge; and when Deborah uses the word "us" in making that joke, she calls herself out for doing so. In other words, Deborah comes to a different conclusion about issues related to race than many other (assumedly less tolerant) White people in Baton Rouge, but she reveals her racialized perspective in the process. Similarly, in Figures 4.3 and 4.4, racially tolerant White respondents express more support for welfare where race is salient, though based on a common understanding of the stigmas related to welfare's racialized image.

In sum, racial attitudes tell us the opinions White people are predisposed to express on welfare—but whether White people connect these racial attitudes to their policy preferences partially depends on contextual information making the racialized dimensions of welfare salient. Moreover, the relevant contextual information depends on the attitude in question. White people endorsing the Black laziness stereotype are more likely to perceive a Black population as an indicator of the threat welfare poses to White interests, whereas racially resentful White people are more likely to perceive a poor population as an indication of threat. The size of the effects I find caution against an interpretation that racially prejudiced White people in one metropolitan area are substantively different from their counterparts in other areas. But Figures 4.3 and 4.4 reveal that the *gap* between racially prejudiced and racially tolerant White people is likely to be substantively different in settings with a large Black population or high poverty rate, depending on which racial attitude is in question.

Considering Alternative Explanations

Several further investigations offer additional support for the findings presented thus far.

"Assistance to the Poor" Versus "Welfare"

First, I have argued that it is because of welfare's politicization in regard to Black, urban poverty that the presence of either a Black or poor population will be relevant to White people's opinions on welfare spending.

How important is welfare's racialized image in explaining this finding, rather than more general ideas about race and poverty? To explore this question, I repeat my analysis using another dependent variable that captures opinion on poverty assistance but uses the more race-neutral language of "assistance to the poor." Using a split-sample approach, respondents to the 2000 GSS were randomly asked about poverty assistance using either this wording or the more racialized "welfare."

The relative unpopularity of welfare is apparent in the GSS dataset: 39.45% of the sample says too much is spent on welfare, compared to 13.48% among those respondents who were instead asked about assistance to the poor. Still, both racial attitude variables are predictive of opinion regarding assistance to the poor (results included in Appendix B). In other words, White attitudes about Black people are implicated even when a less racialized term is used.

However, neither previously identified interaction between racial attitudes and context holds when White views on assistance to the poor is the dependent variable. Racial geography does not make traditional racial prejudice more accessible in regard to a race-neutral reference to redistribution, and economic geography is similarly insignificant in determining the effect of racial resentment on views about assistance to the poor. In a similar vein, party identification was a significant predictor of welfare views—reflecting the Republican Party's embrace of the argument that welfare incentivizes dependency—but is not significant in predicting White views on assisting the poor.

These results indicate the power of a policy narrative to make particular racial attitudes sensitive to contextual symbols associated with welfare: the term "welfare" calls to mind particular images that are not associated with the considerably less racialized term "assistance to the poor."

Partisanship

Having brought up the topic of partisanship, I now consider its relevance to this chapter's analysis. In keeping with research on the alignment between partisanship and racial attitudes that has emerged over the last several decades (Carmines and Stimson 1989; Hetherington 2009; Tesler 2016b), White Republicans in the 2000 GSS average slightly higher on the Black laziness scale (at 5.35 compared to White Democrats' 5.26) and considerably higher on the racial resentment scale (at 6.18, compared to Democrats' 5.18).

Stratifying the sample of White respondents by partisanship (Figure 4.5) reveals that the interaction between the laziness stereotype and context is notably stronger for Republicans in the sample than for Democrats. It is possible that this divergence reflects the Republican Party's stronger embrace

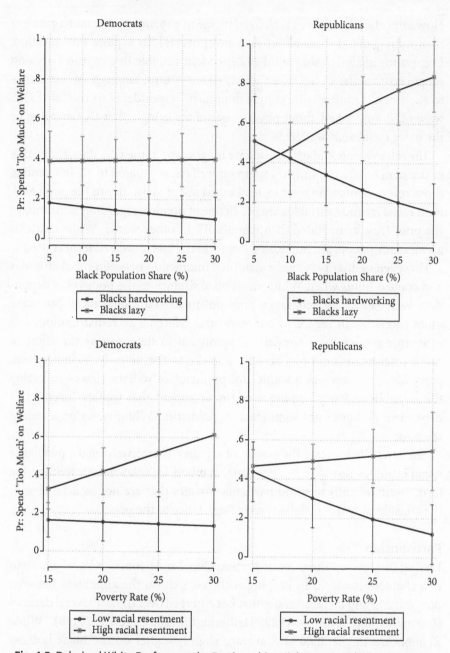

Fig. 4.5 Polarized White Preferences by Partisanship: High-Density Black Settings

Top figure visualizes the interaction posed in Model 4 in Table 4.2, but with White respondents stratified by party identification (*n* = 512). Bottom figure visualizes the interaction posed in Model 8 (*n* = 361). *Source:* 2000 General Social Survey.

of characterizations of welfare as a program benefiting lazy, Black recipients (i.e., Reagan's centering of the welfare queen trope in his 1980 presidential platform). By contrast, Republicans and Democrats are more similar when it comes to the responsiveness of racial resentment in higher- as opposed to lower-poverty settings. It is possible this similarity reflects that both parties embraced moralistic characterizations of poverty as the result of insufficient motivation, particularly in the lead-up to the 1996 reforms. Both parties also argued that welfare needed to be reformed to better encourage work. Further investigation is merited to investigate these differences according to partisanship.

Whatever explains the different partisan patterns between the two racial attitude measures, there is another notable finding when it comes to the bottom two graphs in Figure 4.5. White people whose attitudes diverge from the partisan norm are the most susceptible to having these attitudes amplified by context, whether Democrats with high racial resentment or Republicans with low racial resentment. This result affirms the idea that context serves as an additional source of information, offering cues to those cross-pressured partisans who may have beliefs that diverge from the party line.

Addressing Possible Confounders to Contextual Analysis

A third way to interrogate my findings is to consider factors that might confound my results, specifically related to conducting research into the relationship between attitudes and contexts. One challenge concerns the validity of positing racial attitudes as exogenous to context. We obviously should expect geographic patterns in racial attitudes, as research (including on racial threat) has shown. The question for the present analysis is whether Black population share is so strongly predictive of my racial attitude measures as to bias my results. This is unlikely based on the results reported in Appendix B. Even if White people in areas with large Black populations have slightly more negative racial attitudes to begin with, an MSA's Black population share more powerfully predicts the strength of the relationship between racial attitudes and welfare preferences.

A second challenge concerns whether the differences I identify between metropolitan areas reflect variation at the regional or state level. By repeating the analysis when controlling for the region in which each MSA is located, as well as building multilevel models that nest MSAs within states, in both cases the interactions between local context and racial attitudes remain significant. That is not to say that specific local cultures and histories do not play a role in shaping attitudes. However, even after accounting for such unobserved factors—such as when comparing two metropolitan areas in the same state—White welfare preferences are more likely to be influenced by racial attitudes where race or poverty is more locally visible.

A final challenge concerns my choice of geographic container, and whether my results are the product of how MSA boundaries are drawn. I have explained my focus on the MSA on the grounds that urban residents are likely to cross county lines in their daily activities and also to be aware of populations in neighboring counties. However, counties (as opposed to states or census tracts) are similar to MSAs as midsize containers. County-level data should therefore produce similar results when incorporated into the analysis, as is the case when repeating my analysis measuring geography at the county level (results included in Appendix B).

Segregation and the Visibility of Threat

The results presented thus far have used Black population share and poverty rates as proxies for White Americans' awareness of racial diversity or poverty in their metropolitan areas. A further investigation of my theorization of White people as viewers, however, comes from exploring how not only the presence but also the *patterning* of populations associated with welfare affects the salience of welfare's racialized image in a given context.

In this section, I revisit the relationship between attitudes and context while taking account of residential segregation in U.S. metropolitan areas. Segregation is a complicated phenomenon to measure. However, segregation indices based on the exposure of one population to another in residential settings offer a useful way to operationalize White people's awareness of racial diversity in their surroundings with a more literal focus on the visibility of these stimuli from White people's point of view.

How Segregation Shapes Perceptions

As the beginning of this chapter made clear, scholars have given considerable attention to segregation's deeply harmful effects on the life outcomes of Black Americans. The same is true for the social consequences of lesser intergroup contact in segregated spaces, descending from the work of Allport (1954). However, the benefits of small-scale, interpersonal interaction for reducing bias are not easily applicable to this book's analysis of attitudes across larger settings, such as metropolitan areas (Laurence 2014).

Furthermore, segregation's implications for an *experiential* outcome, such as interpersonal contact, seem to be distinct from its effects on a *perceptual* outcome, such as White people sensing a threat to their interests (Rocha and Espino 2009; Pettigrew, Wagner, and Christ 2010). Because the segregation of Black people may either remove them from the White public's eye (Blalock 1967; Spitzer 1975) or increase the salience of high-density Black areas (Stults and Baumer 2007), scholars have come to different conclusions regarding whether racial segregation increases or decreases White prejudice [e.g., see the contradictory findings of Kinder and Mendelberg (1995) and Taylor (1998)]. More clarity has come from recent work by Enos and Celaya (2018), who specifically investigate perception, rather than lack of interaction, as a mechanism through which segregation shapes attitudes; these authors experimentally demonstrate that the concentration of a group in space increases the salience of social categories, even when keeping interpersonal contact constant. The effect of income segregation on attitudes is more understudied; moreover, awareness of the poor may serve to inform people of the need for welfare support (Bamfield and Horton 2009), but it also may provoke more negative views of welfare recipients.

This lack of clarity partly reflects the complexity of measuring the spatial distribution of households by either race or income. Although researchers debate how to improve measures of racial segregation, it is agreed to be a multidimensional phenomenon.[14] The five dimensions typically identified include evenness, exposure, clustering, centralization, and concentration as related but distinct factors reflecting the residential patterning of racial groups (Massey and Denton 1988). Income segregation, too, can be measured in a variety of ways, accounting for either the clustering of poor households as opposed to affluent households; the overall degree to which households are sorted by income; or the intersection of income segregation with racial segregation (Reardon and Bischoff 2011; see also Quillian 2012).

I employ two indices that measure segregation as the amount of exposure between groups in residential settings—whether White households sharing neighborhoods with Black households,[15] or nonpoor households sharing neighborhoods with poor households. Both indicate higher exposure in metropolitan areas where neighborhoods are more mixed, and lower exposure where neighborhoods are more homogeneous in their racial or economic makeup. Both measures also are reflective of the underlying proportion of either Black or poor households, since exposure to any group is limited by how large the group is to begin with.

Investigating segregation as exposure sets my approach apart from analyses focused on the unevenness of a group's distribution across an urban space, regardless of the group's size. This common approach is a useful one, but my goal is to pair consideration of a group's size (as explored in *visibility hypotheses 1 and 2*) with its spatial patterning, in order to further consider how visible that group is from the vantage point of either White or nonpoor households.[16]

Although the logic of exposure can be applied to both the racial and income segregation measures, it is crucial to appreciate how the dispersal of lower-income households as opposed to Black households would affect the visibility of these respective populations. The visual stigmas of poverty are often environmental, stemming from signs of disorder related to disinvestment from poor communities (Sampson, Morenoff, and Earls 1999). Accordingly, low-income households are likely to be less visible when dispersed throughout mixed income areas, and the poor/nonpoor divide is likely to be less prominent [McPherson, Smith-Lovin, and Cook 2001; this logic also is consistent with the findings of Enos and Celaya (2018)].

Racial integration, on the other hand, does not make an individual Black household less racially identifiable. While Enos and Celaya's findings imply that White residents of an area might be more aware of a concentrated Black population than a dispersed one, psychological research has shown that Blackness is a powerful visual stimulus when only a single face is present (Eberhardt et al. 2004). We also should remember the long legacy of White violence toward Black families who moved into White neighborhoods, and what a powerful visual cue even one Black family could provide. Thus, when comparing areas with similar Black population shares, race would likely be more salient when a Black family lives in a White person's neighborhood than when that person is thinking of a concentrated Black community across town.

This reasoning informs my expectation that the effect of the Black laziness stereotype on welfare preferences will be amplified in settings where there is *greater* exposure of White households to Black households, while the effect of racial resentment will be amplified where there is *lesser* exposure of the nonpoor to the poor. In both cases, I expect a stronger relationship between racial attitudes and welfare preferences in settings where either racial diversity or poverty is more visible based on residential segregation. I summarize these expectations as follows:

- **Exposure hypothesis 1**: White people who hold traditionally racist views are more likely to oppose welfare in metropolitan areas that are *less* segregated by race.

- **Exposure hypothesis 2**: White people who hold racially resentful views are more likely to oppose welfare in metropolitan areas that are *more* segregated by income.

On Segregation and Endogeneity

The above hypotheses prompt another consideration of whether racial attitudes are endogenous to contextual measures, particularly in the case of racial segregation. Racial attitudes inevitably have some influence on White people's tendency to prefer majority-White neighborhoods—a key factor explaining the persistence of racial segregation (Quillian 2002; Krysan and Bader 2007). Thus, it is possible that the level of racial segregation in a given metropolitan area is, in part, a product of the racial attitudes of the White people who live there. While keeping this potential endogeneity in mind, two further considerations suggest that exploring the relevance of racial segregation to White welfare preferences remains a valid approach.

First, even in metropolitan areas where White people share neighborhoods with Black people, racial barriers often persist on a micro level (Logan and Parman 2017). This phenomenon reflects the difficulty of defining "segregation" in the first place. What it means for my analysis, however, is that the most racially prejudiced White people need not live in the most segregated metropolitan areas in order to avoid Black people in their most proximate residential surroundings.

Second, I expect to identify a stronger effect of prejudice on welfare preferences in the *least* racially segregated areas. This finding should not simply reflect greater welfare opposition among the most prejudiced White people because these people would, we assume, select into the *most* racially segregated areas. If anything, segregation may play a protective role, creating enclaves in which prejudiced White people avoid Black neighbors and give little thought to racial diversity in their surroundings.

It is also worth remembering that patterns of segregation are not liable to change quickly. The same is true for Black population shares and poverty rates, barring an economic shock or extenuating circumstance. Thus, I do not engage with research suggesting individuals' sensitivity to contexts that are rapidly diversifying or otherwise changing in a manner that signals a threat to majority group interests (Hopkins 2011). Akin to Zaller's focus on individuals with higher baseline levels of political knowledge, I investigate the effects of what Zaller might call a "chronic awareness" of race and poverty in one's surroundings. If racial attitudes are indeed more accessible in locations where White residents are chronically aware of the stigmas of welfare, then we should see a polarization in White welfare preferences according to racial attitudes in such places.

Measuring Segregation by Race and Income

I operationalize racial segregation using the exposure index (X), which includes a measure of White–Black interaction in residential settings. This variable reflects the proportion of Black households with which the average White household in an MSA will share a neighborhood.[17] This measure represents higher levels of segregation at its *lowest* values, where White households have a low probability of sharing neighborhoods with Black households. It reaches a maximum where the proportion of Black households in the average White household's neighborhood is equal to the total proportion of Black residents in the MSA. The exposure index is therefore correlated with Black population share while also adding a new layer of spatial information to my analysis. It is also worth emphasizing that "interaction" in the form of sharing census tracts should not necessarily be understood to reflect interpersonal engagement between White and Black people in such settings. It should, however, reflect the proportion of White people in an MSA who are likely to encounter Black people in residential settings.

I operationalize income segregation using an index capturing the percentage of families living in poor neighborhoods, defined as census tracts with median incomes less than two-thirds that of the larger metropolitan area (Bischoff and Reardon 2014). In a similar fashion to racial segregation and Black population share above, this income segregation measure reflects underlying levels of poverty because settings with higher poverty rates will tend to have higher proportions of poor neighborhoods. In order to match the logic of exposure of the nonpoor to the poor, I create an inverse version of the economic segregation index. This rescaled variable locates the areas that are *least* segregated by income at the *highest* values of the index, representing settings of greater exposure to the poor.

Figure 4.6 visualizes the logic of the two segregation indices I use, both of which intend to capture segregation from the viewpoint of the majority group (i.e., White households or nonpoor households). Whether the shaded squares are said to represent Black households or poor households, the hypothetical MSA on the left has those households clustered in only a few neighborhoods, meaning that the nonshaded households have little exposure to the shaded

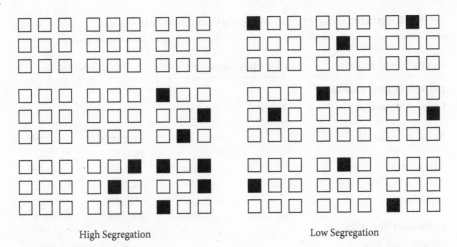

High Segregation   Low Segregation

Fig. 4.6 Visualizing Segregation as Exposure

This figure is adapted from an illustration used to explain the exposure index of racial segregation of White and Black households (see Iceland, Weinberg, and Steinmetz 2002). However, it is also useful in depicting the basic logic of income segregation when operationalized as the proportion of neighborhoods that have a mix of poor and nonpoor households.

households. The MSA on the right, on the other hand, is home to the same number of shaded households, but these are more dispersed across the area.

Empirical Models

To incorporate these measures, I begin by adding racial segregation to the model controlling for the laziness stereotype. Racial segregation is not significant on its own but interacts with the laziness stereotype in Model 2 of Table 4.3. The significant interaction ($p < 0.01$) indicates that greater exposure of White households to Black households amplifies the effect of racial attitudes on welfare preferences, offering evidence in support of *exposure hypothesis 1*.

Although the interaction in Model 2 resembles the relationship between the laziness stereotype and Black population share, it reveals previously unrecognized differences between MSAs with similar racial makeups but different levels of segregation. For example, the areas surrounding Detroit and Washington, DC, had similar Black population shares as of 2000: 23% and 27% Black, respectively. While Detroit's exposure score was 5.59, Washington's was more than twice that at 13.62. If the average White man in the dataset scored at 7 on the Black laziness scale and lived in Detroit, his odds of believing too much is spent on welfare would be 49.5%. If he instead

Table 4.3 Residential Segregation and White Opposition to Welfare

Opposition to Welfare	(1) Laziness Stereotype	(2) Laziness Stereotype	(3) Racial Resentment	(4) Racial Resentment
Individual-level variables				
Laziness Stereotype	1.260***	1.036		
	(0.097)	(0.120)		
Racial Resentment			1.227***	1.643***
			(0.075)	(0.252)
Independent	2.113***	2.066***	2.319**	2.436***
	(0.559)	(0.555)	(0.771)	(0.814)
Republican	2.406***	2.436***	1.899**	1.926**
	(0.563)	(0.581)	(0.530)	(0.549)
Contextual Variables				
Percent Black (log)			0.962	0.988
			(0.110)	(0.105)
Racial Segregation	1.004	0.864**		
	(0.012)	(0.052)		
Poverty Rate	1.000	1.001		
	(0.020)	(0.020)		
Income Segregation			0.916	1.290
			(0.050)	(0.220)
Laziness Stereotype × Racial Segregation		1.027**		
		(0.010)		
Racial Resentment × Income Segregation				0.945**
				(0.024)
Constant	0.429	1.236	0.662	0.0942*
	(0.365)	(1.200)	(0.623)	(0.128)
Observations	512	512	361	361
p	0.00000264	$1.33e-08$	0.000134	0.0000136
Log likelihood	−324.1	−321.8	−223.3	−220.5

Exponentiated coefficients; standard errors in parentheses.

Table reports odds ratios from logistic regression estimating probability of White respondents saying too much is spent on welfare; Party base category is Democrat.

For concision, controls for age, gender, marital status, and income are not displayed.

Source: 2000 General Social Survey.

* $p < 0.10$, ** $p < 0.05$, *** $p < 0.01$.

lived in Washington, with a higher chance of sharing a neighborhood with a Black household, those odds would rise to 57.4%. To be sure, Washington and Detroit are different places with different stories; yet, these results are robust to controlling for the region or state in which an MSA is located, and hold constant the individual-level factors that typically predict White welfare preferences.

In areas with small Black population shares, it is unlikely a White household will share a neighborhood with a Black household no matter how dispersed Black households are. Measuring racial segregation as exposure therefore has the most to add to our understanding of the spatial dynamics of threat in urban areas with substantial Black populations, in keeping with previous findings that segregation becomes more relevant to majority group attitudes as the minority presence grows (Rocha and Espino 2009). Nevertheless, the logic of exposure is applicable across the range of Black population share: where a Black population is more *visible*, based on the greater exposure of White people to Black people, traditional prejudice will have a greater effect on White welfare preferences.

Turning to income segregation, I follow a similar procedure to test *exposure hypothesis 2*. Exposure of the nonpoor to the poor is not itself predictive of welfare preferences, but it interacts with racial resentment to condition the effect of this racial attitude on welfare preferences. However, the direction of the effect is opposite to that of racial segregation: Model 4 in Table 4.3 indicates that the effect of racial resentment is weaker where there are more mixed income neighborhoods, or rather, where there is greater exposure of the nonpoor to the poor. Consider New York City and Atlanta, cities with poverty rates of 21.2% and 24.4%, respectively, as of 2000. Whereas the proportion of poor tracts in the greater New York area was 0.26, it was 0.13 in the Atlanta area. For the White man described above, were he to score a 7 on the racial resentment scale, his odds of saying too much is spent on welfare would be 59.2% in the New York area. These odds would fall to 45.0% if he lived in the less income-segregated Atlanta area.

Racial and income segregation thus have starkly different effects on the probability that the welfare preferences expressed by White people in a given setting are influenced by racial attitudes. These counterdirectional relationships are illustrated in Figures 4.7 and 4.8. While greater exposure of White people to Black people raises the salience of race and consequently amplifies the effect of traditional prejudice on welfare preferences, greater exposure of the nonpoor to the poor dampens the effect of racial resentment, as poverty becomes less salient when poor households are dispersed throughout an MSA.

These findings not only support my argument that White people's racial attitudes are more accessible where welfare's racialized image is more visible. They also highlight the subjectivity of the operation of racial threat. Even across MSAs with identical demographics, patterns of segregation could make the stigmas of welfare more or less visible, and White people's welfare preferences more or less racialized as a result.

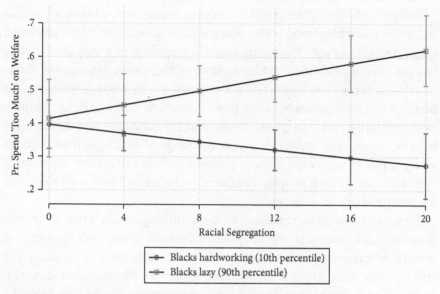

Fig. 4.7 Effects of Racial Segregation on White Welfare Preferences
Figure visualizes the interaction posed in Model 2 in Table 4.3. *Source:* 2000 General Social Survey (n = 512).

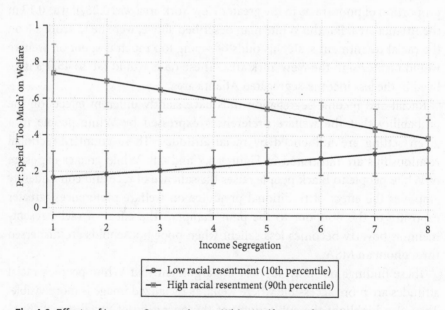

Fig. 4.8 Effects of Income Segregation on White Welfare Preferences
Figure visualizes the interaction posed in Model 4 in Table 4.3. *Source:* 2000 General Social Survey (n = 361).

Replication with ANES

My analysis of the 2000 GSS has offered three main insights. First, the likelihood that White people draw on their racial attitudes to inform their welfare preferences varies systematically across local contexts. Second, whether racial or economic context is relevant depends on the attitude in question—either the Black laziness stereotype or racial resentment. Third, we can theorize racial and economic context as indicative of whether welfare's racialized image is locally visible to White residents, due to either the presence of a Black or poor population, or the distribution of these populations according to residential segregation.

An external test of the robustness of these results comes from the replication of my analysis using contemporaneous data from the 2000 American National Election Survey (ANES). I locate the 1,393 White respondents to the ANES in their congressional districts as of the 106th Congress. Because congressional districts are apportioned by population, they are more variable in size than MSAs; nonetheless, districts allow me to measure racial and economic demographics at a more local level than states.[18] My variables are similar to those used in my analysis of the GSS. I construct an identical measure of the Black laziness stereotype, scaled between 0 and 10 ($M = 5.85$, $S.D. = 1.21$). I approximate racial resentment with views on whether Black Americans should "work their way up" as other minority groups have, also scaled between 0 and 10 ($M = 7.22$, $S.D. = 2.91$).[19] Data on Black population share and poverty rates at the congressional district level are drawn from the census. District-level segregation measures reflect weighted averages of the racial and income segregation indices across the MSAs that are partially or fully encompassed by a congressional district.

Table 4.4 reports odds ratios from binary logistic regression, clustering standard errors by district. The previously identified interactions between the laziness stereotype and racial context (Model 1) and between racial resentment and economic context (Model 3) are significant at the 90% confidence level (visualized in Figure 4.9). This borderline significant relationship between attitudes and context is strengthened ($p = 0.001$) when examining the behavior of the laziness stereotype according to White households' likelihood of sharing a neighborhood with a Black household (Model 2). The greater significance of the interaction of the laziness stereotype with racial segregation than with Black population share may reflect the influence of gerrymandering, which can produce artificially low- or high-density Black congressional districts whose populations do not reflect that of a larger area. The average level of segregation in an area (whether across the various

Table 4.4 White Welfare Preferences in Context: ANES Replication

Opposition to Welfare	(1) Laziness Stereotype	(2) Laziness Stereotype	(3) Racial Resentment	(4) Racial Resentment
Individual-Level Variables				
Laziness Stereotype	0.991 (0.111)	0.888 (0.085)		
Racial Resentment			1.069 (0.059)	1.212*** (0.069)
Independent	1.270 (0.267)	1.207 (0.255)	1.152 (0.243)	1.120 (0.237)
Republican	1.777*** (0.276)	1.728*** (0.275)	1.578*** (0.251)	1.549*** (0.248)
Contextual Variables				
Percent Black (log)	0.619 (0.217)		1.052 (0.075)	1.078 (0.076)
Laziness Stereotype × Percent Black (log)	1.108* (0.066)			
Racial Segregation		0.819*** (0.058)		
Laziness Stereotype × Racial Segregation		1.040*** (0.012)		
Poverty Rate	1.004 (0.015)	1.008 (0.014)	0.959 (0.034)	
Racial Resentment × Poverty Rate			1.008* (0.005)	
Income Segregation				1.462 (1.010)
Racial Resentment × Income Segregation				0.934 (0.084)
Constant	0.558 (0.433)	0.956 (0.679)	0.290** (0.167)	0.140*** (0.083)
Observations	858	852	872	867
Congressional Districts	290	291	288	290
Log likelihood	−556.2	−548.8	−551.8	−549.4

Exponentiated coefficients; standard errors in parentheses.

Table reports odds ratios from logistic regression estimating probability of White respondents saying too much is spent on welfare.

For concision, controls for age, gender, marital status, and income are not displayed.

Source: 2000 American National Election Study.

* $p < 0.10$, ** $p < 0.05$, *** $p < 0.01$.

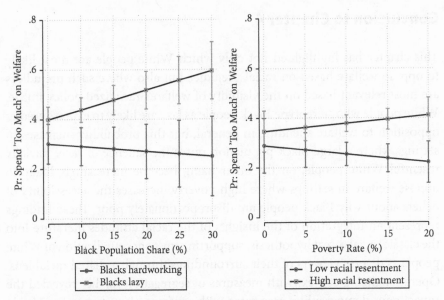

Fig. 4.9 Polarized White Preferences in the ANES: High-Density Black versus High-Poverty Settings

Figure on left visualizes the interaction posed in Model 1 in Table 4.4 ($n = 1,015$). Figure on right visualizes the interaction posed in Model 2 in Table 4.4 ($n = 1,033$). *Source:* 2000 American National Election Study.

MSAs located within a large congressional district, or in the larger urban area surrounding a small congressional district) would be less sensitive to gerrymandering. Together, Models 1 and 2 add confidence to the argument that, in substate geographies where a Black population is more visible, the traditional stereotype of Black people as lazy is more predictive of White opposition to welfare than in settings where race is less salient.

The ANES offers less conclusive evidence in regard to racial resentment. Beyond the moderately significant interaction between racial resentment and poverty rate in Model 3, Model 4 does not produce evidence for a significant relationship between racial resentment and income segregation. However, the direction of the relationship matches my findings in the GSS. The greater variation in size of congressional districts than MSAs also likely plays a role in explaining the insignificance of income segregation in the ANES, as well as the reduced significance of poverty rate. Concentrated poverty could be viewed from considerably greater proximity or greater distance, depending on the district. Although further research into the relationship between income segregation and White Americans' policy preferences is needed, my findings in the ANES are broadly consistent with my GSS analysis.

Conclusion to Chapter 4

This chapter has highlighted not only which White people are most likely to oppose welfare based on racial prejudice but also where such prejudices are most relevant based on the visibility of welfare's racialized policy image. White people who stereotype Black people as lazy are likely to express greater opposition to welfare spending in general, but this probability increases in settings where a large Black population raises the salience of race. Racially resentful White people, on the other hand, become increasingly likely to oppose welfare in settings where high poverty increases the accessibility of beliefs about why Black people are disproportionately poor. These findings represent an integration of the insights of the racial attitudes literature into the classic racial threat hypothesis, supporting my conceptualization of White people as diverse viewers of their surroundings through a shared racial lens. Operationalizing context with measures of segregation further revealed the capacity for demographics associated with welfare to be more or less visible depending on their distribution throughout an MSA. Accordingly, White welfare preferences are more likely to be racialized in a setting where a Black or poor population is more visible, even if the underlying size of either population is identical to that in another MSA with different patterns of segregation. This finding corroborates the role of White people's subjective interpretations of the different worlds in which they live—as Lippmann (1922) argued long ago; as more recent work has further theorized (Wong et al. 2012); and as my analysis in Baton Rouge brought to life.

Finally, these findings add a new dimension to the typical analysis of either White opposition to welfare or the geography of threat. The relationships I have identified here demonstrate the potential for a scenario commonly assumed to be threatening to White people to, in fact, amplify tolerant attitudes among tolerant viewers. Theorizing White people as the perceivers of a threat thus allows for the possibility that an individual viewer might perceive something entirely different, if they so choose. It also challenges the frequent implication by scholars that a proximate Black population necessarily must pose a threat to White people.

As I have discussed, there is obvious overlap between different forms of prejudice among White people, and between conditions of racial diversity and poverty across MSAs. Table 4.5 visualizes how we might think of the coincidence of these conditions. In the bottom right quadrant, or in places like Baton Rouge, we would expect both kinds of racial attitudes to be activated among White residents. Alternatively, in the top left quadrant, we would expect neither attitude to be activated.

Table 4.5 A Matrix of High-Density Black × High Poverty MSAs

		Percent Black (*Mean = 10.8%*)	
		Low	High
Poverty Rate (*Mean = 12.9%*)	Low	ex: Boise City, ID; Green Bay, WI	ex: Atlanta, GA; Richmond, VA
	High	ex: Eugene, OR; McAllen, TX	ex: Baton Rouge, LA; Miami, FL

Table illustrates possible combinations of the Black population size in a given MSA and the poverty rate in that MSA's central city. Means reflect average demographics across MSAs (rather than national statistics) as of 2000. Poverty rates and racial demographics for example cities were as follows as of 2000: *(a) Low, Low:* Boise City, ID: 9% poverty, 0.5% Black; Green Bay, WI: 6.9% poverty, 1.1.% Black; *(b) Low, High:* Atlanta, GA: 9.4% poverty, 28.7% Black; Richmond, VA: 9.3% poverty; 30% Black; *(c) High, Low:* Eugene-Springfield, OR: 14.4% poverty, 0.7% Black; McAllen-Edinburg-Mission, TX: 35% poverty, 0.3% Black; *(d) High, High:* Baton Rouge, LA: 16.2% poverty, 32% Black; Miami-Ft. Lauderdale, FL: 15.3% poverty, 19.4% Black.

MSAs along the opposite diagonal—those with high poverty rates or a large Black population, but not both—are where we are likely to see different responses among White residents depending on the prejudices they hold. This chapter's analysis implies that places like Atlanta or Richmond are where the Black laziness stereotype is more relevant to White people's welfare preferences, due to the high salience of race in conjunction with below-average poverty rates. Alternatively, places like Eugene or McAllen, with small Black populations but high poverty rates, are where racial resentment would be more relevant to White welfare attitudes. Highlighting this diversity in how White people are likely to respond to context, along with the possible activation of positive racial orientations, demonstrates the importance of theorizing *who* is viewing a given context rather than either assuming it is by default a threatening one or assuming that all White people will similarly see it as such.

The analysis presented here has two larger implications for racial politics. First, my analysis challenges the reliability of racial attitudes as predictive of policy preferences. Racial attitudes are less reflective of whether someone is "racist" than indicative of how a White individual will evaluate a political issue, especially when the issue's racialized dimensions are salient. This interpretation should not minimize White people's agency in holding and deploying racially prejudicial views, but rather should serve as a reminder that prejudice may appear irrelevant to politics in some circumstances only to be incited in others.

Second, my analysis of the GSS suggests that the dispersal of lower-income families throughout more affluent neighborhoods would reduce the visibility of poverty as a contextual stimulus related to a racialized understanding of welfare. Although the ANES offers limited support for this conclusion, it comports with the imperative of reducing income segregation in order to improve the life outcomes of the poor. In the case of racial segregation, on the other hand, my analysis indicates that the dispersal of Black families through-out White neighborhoods would not lower the salience of race as a factor influencing the expression of welfare preferences. This finding in no way questions the importance of fighting racial segregation and its harmful effects on Black communities. However, it should serve as a warning against equating residential proximity with either positive interracial contact (Laurence 2014; see also Enos 2016) or positive perceptual outcomes for White people in lived urban contexts (in contrast to, e.g., the laboratory-based findings of Enos and Celaya 2018). More broadly, my findings warn against advocating for racial integration as an end in itself, rather than a strategy to ameliorate racial inequality (Pattillo 2009).

There are clear avenues along which Chapter 4's analysis could be extended. For example, more research is needed to understand how racial and income segregation contextualize White people's racial policy preferences. Future work should also extend my analysis of welfare preferences following the 1996 reform bill to other racialized policy issues in other periods. And, in light of how many places with high poverty rates but low Black population shares (i.e., the bottom left quadrant in Table 4.5) have high concentrations of Latino residents, the question of how White attitudes toward Black people operate amidst other kinds of diversity merits further study.

For now, Chapter 4 has returned to the classic threat hypothesis and, while keeping White people in the spotlight, sought to interrogate White people's responsibility as agents of prejudice rather than victims of racial threat. Assigning White people agency as viewers highlights their capacity to respond positively—much like we saw among the White residents of Baton Rouge who oppose racially harmful policies. Yet, the example of Baton Rouge also reminds us that we should not equate this opposition with commitments to break down the racial status quo.

This proclivity to defend White Americans' position, and how it can shape even racially tolerant White people's viewpoint, is the focus of the next chapter.

5

Affirmative Action and the Threat of the Black Middle Class

"There's a couple of African-American male teenagers in our neighborhood, but nobody gives a crap." Brian was telling me about his subdivision in Baton Rouge. "Everybody makes good money."

Brian explained to me that, even if parties thrown at the homes of these teenagers would attract cars that "definitely will look different than the cars you're used to seeing," he and his White neighbors wouldn't call the police. "What it boils down to is that people just don't care about race so much when they know that their class protects them from everything that's . . . not that," he concluded.

Brian's reflections are laden with assumptions about race and evidence of his positionality, as we saw throughout my analysis in Baton Rouge. His comments further resonate with a common line of thinking, particularly in implying that middle-income Black people are nonthreatening. Consider abolitionist Frederick Douglass, whom I cited in Chapter 1 for having claimed that the disassociation of color from "undesirable conditions" would help dismantle the Black–White color line. In the same essay, Douglass (1881, 576) makes a claim similar to Brian's: "The higher the colored man rises in the scale of society, the less prejudice does he meet."

This book shares Douglass's (and, to some extent, Brian's) appreciation that race and class intersect to determine someone's status in American society. Much of racial politics scholarship further shares Douglass's belief that affluent Black people are less likely to be viewed negatively by White people. That is, reducing racial inequality and improving race relations are often posited as congruent or even interchangeable goals.

By contrast, this chapter considers the implications of Black economic improvement in a less optimistic light. This light has illuminated White people's capacity to react *negatively* to signs of Black advancement, through responses variously identified as "White backlash" (Abrajano and Hajnal 2017; Hewitt 2005; Hughey 2014), "White rage" (C. Anderson 2016), or

How the Color Line Bends: The Geography of White Prejudice in Modern America. Nina M. Yancy,
Oxford University Press. © Oxford University Press 2022. DOI: 10.1093/oso/9780197599426.003.0005

Table 5.1 Two Dimensions of Prejudice, Two Quantitative Applications (Revisited)

Dimension of prejudice	Outgroup-oriented (addressed in Ch. 4)	Ingroup-oriented
Feelings of prejudice	Subordinate race inspires fear and suspicion · Subordinate race is intrinsically different	Dominant race is superior Dominant race has claim to privilege and advantage
Discursive practices identified in Ch. 3	Denying racial motivations Minimizing racial categories	Prioritizing White concerns Defending the social order
Policy area explored in Ch. 4–5	Welfare spending (Chapter 4)	Affirmative action (Chapter 5)

Table synthesizes the feelings of prejudice articulated by Blumer (1958), discursive practices engaged in by White residents of Baton Rouge in Chapter 3, and the corresponding policy areas examined in Chapters 4 and 5.

"White protectionism" (Smith and King 2021; see also Jardina 2019).[1] One of the most blatant recent examples of this is the resurgence of racism spurred by Obama's presidency (see Tesler 2016b; or, more trenchantly put, Coates 2017). However, similar thinking has minimally been applied to the study of racial threat, or how localized perceptions of a Black middle class might inform White policy preferences. Instead, hidden in the assumption that a Black population is inherently threatening to nearby White people is an invitation to assume this Black population is either a poor (i.e., conventionally stigmatized) or otherwise "classless" one. This latter assumption had long felt problematic to me as a Black reader of political science texts; I became more motivated to challenge it after a summer spent in the geography of Baton Rouge, with its prominent Black middle-class presence.

To unpack the class assumptions in the typical racial threat hypothesis, I expand beyond Chapter 4's focus on welfare spending and the quintessentially "threatening" imagery of the Black poor, which illuminated White people's outgroup-oriented feelings of prejudice. As summarized in Table 5.1, Chapter 5 instead explores affirmative action and White perceptions of the Black middle class. In doing so, this chapter more closely interrogates White Americans' ingroup-oriented feelings of prejudice: a sense of superiority, and a feeling of entitlement to certain privileges. These are the feelings that came to life in the naturalness with which many White Baton Rougeans legitimized the problems of majority-White communities, while either ignoring the challenges of majority-Black communities (across the class spectrum) or strategically invoking those challenges to support the argument that White people were suffering. Ingroup-oriented feelings of prejudice also came to life after the killing of Alton Sterling as White residents—including some of the fiercest opponents to St. George—either explicitly called for a return to the racial status quo or put forth a vision of "togetherness" that implied the continued subordination of Black to White in the racial order. As we will see, similar feelings are at play not only in White attitudes on affirmative action but also in the relationship between affirmative action and localized White anxieties about the security of their economic status.

Specifically, Chapter 5 investigates the possible threat White Americans see in the form of locally rising Black status. I take advantage of a GSS panel that spans the 2007–2009 recession, when class anxiety was heightened for all Americans. Against this backdrop, I demonstrate systematic, contextual variation in White Americans' perceptions of the security of their economic advantage over Black Americans. Even more, these perceptions reveal the subjectivity of the White perspective: White people in the areas hardest hit by the recession were the most likely to think Black people were getting *richer* while White people were getting poorer—despite the fact that the recession had much harsher consequences for Black employment (not to mention Black economic well-being more generally).

In turn, the perception that Black people are catching up influences White opinion on affirmative action, a policy approach explicitly designed to speed Black economic advancement. Perceiving a status threat from Black people makes White people more likely to oppose affirmative action. By contrast, White people who feel their status over Black people is secure are more likely to *support* affirmative action. The main focus of this chapter is on affirmative action in employment, but I test the robustness of my findings by examining White opinion toward affirmative action in higher education as surveyed by the ANES.

Crucially, Chapter 5 shows that the effects of perceiving a status threat hold across the spectrum of White racial attitudes: racially progressive White people are just as likely to respond negatively to Black economic progress when it is perceived to threaten White people's status in a given local context. These findings are a quantitative manifestation of the similarities I qualitatively identified among White Baton Rouge residents, who were divided over St. George but still collectively defended the racial order. The results of Chapter 5 ultimately speak to the importance of conceptualizing the shared, racialized perspective that constrains White vision. Brian may be unlikely to call the police on his middle-class Black neighbors. But, when it comes to upholding the racial status quo in Baton Rouge, he is nonetheless likely to perceive middle- and upper-income Black people as a threat to the security of White privilege.

Theorizing a (Subjective) Status Threat

My analysis in this chapter proceeds in two stages. In the first half of the chapter, I investigate the relationship between local context and White Americans' likelihood of perceiving a racialized status threat from Black Americans. We will see that White people's perceptions of Black people's economic standing are distinct from a normative evaluation of where Black people *ought* to stand in economic terms, and are responsive to local racial and economic demographics. In the latter half of the chapter, I go on to investigate the relationship between these status perceptions and White opposition to affirmative action, highlighting the cases in which perceiving a status threat is most relevant.

To begin, it is necessary to introduce the Black Americans who might be seen to challenge White status. We should appreciate nonpoor Black people as a demographic meriting further study, while remaining realistic about the chasm that still exists between even upper-income Black people and their White peers.

A snapshot of the Black middle class

It's no secret that Black Americans suffer an inordinate burden of poverty, presenting a severe injustice that merits sustained scholarly attention. At the same time, Black Americans are an economically diverse demographic—among the *most* diverse, given that the Gini coefficient of inequality is higher among Black households than those of any other race.[2] And although inequality recently has risen steeply among all Americans in recent decades, it has historically been higher among Black Americans.

Sociological work by Black scholars in particular has long recognized the experiences of Black Americans who achieved a middle-class existence within structural constraints (e.g., Drake and Cayton 1945; Du Bois 1899; Frazier 1957). The 1960s and 70s, however, brought a new era of scholarship on Black class diversity, epitomized by the work of William Julius Wilson (1978, 1987). Wilson, too, was concerned with class variation among Black families, writing during an era when Black people were finally achieving greater representation in middle-class occupations. Yet, Wilson's largest contribution was to shine new light on the plight of the Black poor, whose neighborhoods slid into decline as better-off Black families outmigrated from central cities to suburbs. As Pattillo (2005, 306) puts it, middle-income Black people were important to

Wilson's analysis because of their *absence* from poor Black areas, rather than their presence at all.

More recent streams of research, including Pattillo's own work, have devoted more attention to the experiences of higher-status Black Americans. Research on racial segregation, for example, has questioned how much outmigration truly occurred, and whether it brought improved residential outcomes for middle- and upper-income Black households. The verdict here is mixed. Nonpoor Black families still live in neighborhoods drastically different to their White counterparts with similar incomes, considerably limiting social mobility for many Black people (Chetty et al. 2020; Mazumder 2014; Reardon, Fox, and Townsend 2015; Reeves and Rodrigue 2015). Majority-Black neighborhoods are just as likely to be economically disadvantaged today as they were 40 years ago (Sharkey 2014). Even more, the housing crash of 2006–2007 had a devastating impact on Black families' small amount of wealth, particularly given the concentration of foreclosures in the most segregated metropolitan areas (Rugh and Massey 2010).

These sorts of statistics are often unknown or ignored by those who believe that class negates considerations of race in today's America. As Greg, one of the White Baton Rouge residents we met in the last chapter, told me, the idea that middle-class Black people did not have the same choices of where to live as middle-class White people was a "trick question." He laughed as he went on to explain his opinion:

> Anyone with money—they are going to pick where they want to live. It isn't so much segregated . . . I don't believe that there's like a secret neighborhood with African American . . . you know what I mean. It's people who want a good school, period. I mean, someone sent you to a pretty decent school, right? And they said, this is important, and I'm sure you had a good place. You know what I mean?

Greg, of course, could not have known that my parents were steered away from affluent Dallas neighborhoods home to the city's most prestigious schools when they were looking to buy a house, but he left little room for the possibility of it. Greg also revealed his ignorance of the experiences of Black Baton Rouge residents like Richard, who was warned about burning crosses when looking for a house in a neighborhood not far from Greg's office.[3] While burning crosses may have faded, Black families "with money" (as Greg would put it) continue to be steered away from predominately White neighborhoods by real estate agents today (see Choi, Herbert, and Winslow 2019).

Despite all this, Greg's statement was not entirely incorrect. In Baton Rouge and across the country, middle- and upper-class Black families have increasingly moved to more advantaged, diverse, and suburban settings, putting distance between themselves and the Black ghetto.

Affluent Black people have less fully distanced themselves from the *iconic* ghetto, though. Both research (e.g., Feagin and Sikes 1994) and lived experience (e.g., that of my Black respondents from Baton Rouge, not to mention my family's and my own) document the persistence of racism even as Black Americans rise in status, complicating Douglass's claim that high-status Black people will necessarily be met with less prejudice. Again, White viewers are liable to contest this claim. As Brian put it in the same conversation that opened this chapter: "For middle class and above, race becomes so unimportant within that category. I mean, people just don't care." While this may be true in some instances, reams of scholarship suggest otherwise. In particular, research on middle-class Black people's negotiation between their racial and class identities emphasizes the "in-betweenness" of this group's experiences. They are caught between racial pride on the one hand, and the desire to distinguish themselves from negative stereotypes of the Black community on the other hand (Haynes 2001; J. L. Jackson 2001; Kefalas 2003; M. M. Taylor 2002; Pattillo 1999, 2008).

Less scholarly attention has been given to the perspectives of White people like Greg and Brian, or how middle- and upper-income Black people are *perceived* by White people. Specifically, less existing scholarship shares this chapter's focus on what significance the presence of nonpoor Black people has for White people's attitudes. One likely reason for this omission is the too powerful association between Blackness and poverty, as was evident in Chapter 4. Images of nonpoor Black people are often overpowered by the negatively framed images of lower-income Black people that dominate media depictions and political narratives in the present day. When scholarship has a tendency of centering White Americans' perspective and engaging too little with Black Americans' experiences, it is unsurprising that few scholars of White racism have investigated the particular racialization of middle- and upper-income Black people.

There are exceptions to this, such as the 1990s-era conversation about the fictional Huxtable family on NBC's *The Cosby Show*. Henry Louis Gates Jr. (1989) argued at the time that the show's focus on "the miniscule integration of blacks into the upper middle class [. . .] reassuringly throws the blame for black poverty back onto the impoverished." Subsequent research offered support for Gates's critique, finding that although White viewers recognized the Huxtables as atypical, White viewers also cited the Huxtables as evidence that Black people had equal opportunities in America, and that race-targeting

Table 5.2 Economic Characteristics of Black and White Americans

	Black Americans	White Americans
Education (Population 25 years and over)		
Less than high school diploma	**16%**	**8%**
High school graduate (includes equivalency)	31%	28%
Some college or associate's degree	33%	30%
Bachelor's degree or higher	**19%**	**33%**
Income (Households)		
Less than $15,000	**23%**	**10%**
$15,000 to $29,999	20%	14%
$30,000 to $49,999	20%	18%
$50,000 to $99,999	25%	31%
$100,000 or more	**12%**	**26%**
Occupation (Civilian employed 16 years and over):		
Management, business, science, and arts	**28%**	**41%**
Service	25%	15%
Sales and office	26%	25%
Natural resources, construction, and maintenance	5%	9%
Production, transportation, and material moving	15%	11%

Emphasis added to highlight disparities. *Source:* 2011–2015 American Community Survey.

or other initiatives to fight discrimination were unnecessary (Jhally and Lewis 1992; Lewis and Jhally 1995).

These findings inform my analysis. Yet, there remains scope to consider how perceptions of nonpoor Black Americans activate White Americans' feelings about their *own* racial group. Similarly, there is great scope to consider how these perceptions are contextualized by local geography, offering a new take on the racial threat hypothesis.

Table 5.2 offers a snapshot of class variation among Black people as compared to White people, with a focus on education, income, and occupation. I offer this comparison rather than draw strict boundaries around a "Black middle class," recognizing that how to delineate classes is a major debate in sociological literature. Simply surveying some of the most commonly used markers demonstrates the racial disparity: the "threat" of Black people collectively catching up to White people remains a far-off prospect. At the same time, the table reveals how much is obscured when debates focus only on the Black poor, or otherwise collapse variation in Black Americans' economic circumstances. In conjunction, Figure 5.1 visualizes how much the concentration of nonpoor Black households varies across metropolitan areas.

With this class diversity in mind, I turn to theorizing White perceptions of Black Americans' economic standing—positing these as an indication of the

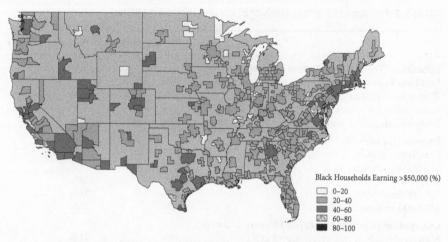

Black Households Earning >$50,000 (%)
- 0–20
- 20–40
- 40–60
- 60–80
- 80–100

Fig. 5.1 Black Households Earning >$50,000 Annually, 2015

Map includes all Metropolitan Statistical Areas. Higher concentrations of nonpoor Black households stand out where Black people are most populous, and where Black home ownership rates are highest (>40%). Examples of such places include Washington, DC, Baltimore, MD, and Richmond, VA, in the Mid-Atlantic region; Atlanta, GA, Miami, FL, and both Raleigh and Charlotte, NC, in the Southeast; and Austin, San Antonio, and Houston, TX, in the Southwest. *Source:* 2011–2015 American Community Survey 5-Year Estimates, Household Income (2015 Inflation-Adjusted Dollars).

perceived security of White people's economic advantage over Black people, and as partly informed by a White individual's proximate surroundings.

White perceptions of the social order

The relative positioning of the races is a foundational concern in group-based approaches to studying racial politics. Because dominant groups have a natural instinct to maintain a social order that places them at the top, animus toward Black Americans is unnecessary for White Americans to act in a manner that defends their interests.

But what tells White Americans how secure their interests are? I focus on White interests in economic terms. White Americans' dominant position does not stem from economic privilege alone. Yet, economic status is closely aligned with political power and social standing, and it offers an intuitive way of ranking groups in a social order. Literature from psychology and economics further indicates that individuals are sensitive to relative economic standing, especially their rank in an income distribution, when evaluating their well-being (Boyce, Brown, and Moore 2010; Luttmer 2005; Kuziemko et al. 2014). Similar dynamics should operate when evaluating a group's well-being, given that economic assessments are known to be more sensitive to "sociotropic," or group-level, considerations than to one's own economic standing (Kinder and Kiewiet 1981).

These insights motivate my focus on White perceptions of the economic positions of the races—operationalized as evaluations of whether Black people tend to be "rich" or "poor," relative to White people. I argue that these evaluations reflect the perceived security of White status by capturing the distance White Americans see between themselves and Black Americans on the economic ladder, and thus the prospect of Black Americans challenging White Americans' dominant position. Put differently, believing Black people to be relatively richer would mean a White individual perceives a smaller "status gap" between Black and White Americans; if Black people were believed to be relatively poorer, a White individual would perceive a larger status gap.

One potential challenge to my argument thus far concerns the possible influence of racial animus. Is it simply that racially hostile White people are likely to think Black people are poor—as well as lazy, violent, or in possession of other negative traits associated with pernicious racial stereotypes?

On the one hand, it is likely that endorsing traditional stereotypes will lead a White individual to evaluate Black Americans as poor. Particularly given that conceptions of poor Black people as lazy and thus undeserving have long underpinned the association between race and poverty (as discussed in Chapter 4; see also Gilens 1995, 1999), I expect that White people who believe Black people are lazy are likely to believe Black people also are poor.

On the other hand, it is not clear how White people with different levels of racial resentment would evaluate Black people's economic status. Remember that racial resentment is a moralistic attitude based on a "logically consistent view of Blacks' place in society" (Tarman and Sears 2005, 733), holding that Black people no longer face discrimination, and that their disadvantage therefore reflects lack of effort or weak commitment to American values.[4] White people with low levels of racial resentment might resist evaluating Black people as poor out of appreciation of class diversity within the Black community. Yet, they may also identify a large status gap between Black and White Americans based on awareness of contemporary racial disparities. Similarly, racial resentment could lead more racially hostile White people to express generally negative views about Black people and thus evaluate them as poor. Or, racially resentful White people might think Black people are relatively better off, based on the belief that Black Americans have already received enough "special favors."

Thus, while status perceptions are likely influenced by traditional stereotypes (i.e., the laziness sterotype), I expect they will *not* be predicted by a normative view about Black people's place in society (i.e., racial resentment). In other words, perceptions of the status gap between the races should be more reflective of how White people believe the world *is*—even if viewed through the lens of traditional prejudice—than how White people believe the world ought to be.[5]

- **Status perceptions hypothesis 1**: Endorsing traditional racial stereotypes will make a White individual more likely to think Black people are
  poor—but expressing racial resentment will not predict how rich or poor
  a White individual perceives Black people to be.

A White individual's placement of racial groups on the rich/poor spectrum undoubtedly reflects a range of individual-level factors besides racial stereotypes—from early socialization to media consumption. I control for factors such as education and income to account for some of these considerations (and shortly discuss the relevance of local context). My emphasis here, however, is that perceptions of Black people as poor relative to White people should not be reduced to a stereotype alone—if for no other reason than that Black people *are* poorer than White people on the whole. Perceptions of the gap between Black and White Americans in economic standing arguably offer insight into White people's subjective understandings of racial inequality rather than solely indicating a negative racial orientation.

Status perceptions in context

If White perceptions of Black Americans' relative status (henceforth, BRS) reflect White people's understanding of the racial economic order, one factor likely influencing these perceptions is local context. Scholarship on political geography, broader than the threat hypothesis alone, has shown that people's political behavior responds to local economic circumstances (Books and Prysby 1999; Reeves and Gimpel 2012; Tobler 1970). Blumer, too, in his original formulation of prejudice as a sense of group position, noted that this sense was shaped by environmental factors and liable to change over time. It therefore seems logical for perceptions of BRS to vary according to characteristics of White people's local surroundings. Investigating whether such geographic variation in perceptions of BRS exists also offers an opportunity to reexamine the threat hypothesis, and to theorize White people's agency and subjectivity in *perceiving* Black people as threatening (rather than "being threatened" by Black people).

Thus, I posit context as a source of information about the security of White people's economic advantage over Black people, based on the racial and economic demographics of a White individual's metropolitan area. Rather than seeking to identify a threat response in the form of heightened *animosity* when White people perceive a challenge to their interests, I identify a different sort of response, in the form of perceptions of Black people as relatively *richer*. The "threat" here, from the point of view of White people who are defensive of their racial privilege, is the threat of Black people catching up to White people economically.

A threat to a group's interests might be perceived on either objective or subjective grounds. In objective terms, White perceptions of BRS should be informed by the true relative standing of the races in a White individual's immediate geographic context. Even if White residents might not know the median incomes of Black and White households in an MSA, White residents likely will have a general sense of whether the income gap is large or small [besides the literature cited thus far, see examples such as Gay (2006), identifying Black people's sensitivity to their economic standing relative to nearby Latino populations]. I operationalize the true relative, local standing of Black and White Americans as a measure of the income gap between the two racial groups in a given metropolitan area.

- **Status perceptions hypothesis 2**: The larger the Black–White income gap in a White individual's surroundings, the poorer that individual will perceive Black people to be relative to White people.

Confirming *status perceptions hypothesis 2* would indicate that White people draw upon their local geographies when forming perceptions of BRS. To test whether White Americans' positionality plays a role in this process, I further theorize White people's *subjective* responses to context. Specifically, I expect to find evidence that White people often perceive a smaller status gap between the races than is warranted by local realities, whether considering racial or economic context.

Subjective responses to racial context
First, let's consider racial context. Following the predictions of the threat hypothesis (i.e., where a larger Black population share is associated with a greater threat response among White people), I anticipate that settings with a larger Black presence will be those where White people are more likely to believe that Black people are relatively richer, controlling for the true Black–White income gap. Similar logic leads me to investigate whether

White people in less segregated metropolitan areas—defined as those where White households have greater exposure to Black households in residential settings—are likely to see Black people as relatively better off than White people in more segregated settings, all else equal.[6]

These responses could reflect objective realities. Metropolitan areas with larger Black populations could be those where any Black middle-class presence would be more visible. For example, one Black Baton Rouge resident commented that "of course" White people in Baton Rouge were more aware of the area's Black middle class in light of the overall Black presence there (he added that it also helped to have prominent Black institutions, such as Southern University: "I mean, we live in a community where we have two- and four-year universities where you can get professional degrees and so forth"). Similarly, less segregated metropolitan areas, where there is greater exposure of Black households to White households, may be those where a larger share of Black people *do* rank closer to White people economically, particularly given that it is nearly impossible to isolate segregation's effects from its role in concentrating Black poverty.

However, if perceptions of BRS are predicted by Black population share and segregation measures even across metropolitan areas with the same Black–White income disparity, this suggests a subjective threat perceived by White people when race is more salient. The logic here is that White people will feel their privileged economic position is less secure when they are more aware of Black people in their surroundings.

Subjective responses to economic context

Next, let's consider economic context—where I expect the subjectivity of White people's reactions to context to be most apparent, particularly as economic conditions changed dramatically over the course of the GSS panel. I focus on local unemployment rates as an economic indicator that doubled between 2007 and 2009, and one that is closely tied to the economic standing of racial groups.

If settings of economic insecurity tend to cast race relations as a zero-sum game, then settings of high unemployment should be those where White people are more likely to sense a subjective status threat, in the form of perceiving a smaller gap between Black and White people in economic status. This means I expect Black people to be perceived as relatively *richer* in high-unemployment settings. Such a prediction seems illogical, given that Black people have consistently borne higher rates of unemployment than White people and suffered disproportionately during the recession of 2007–2009. Yet, an economic downturn would undoubtedly heighten the zero-sum framing of racial competition for resources, making it more likely that Black people would be seen to benefit as White people felt their own group suffer.

My predictions regarding White people's subjective responses to racial and economic context are summarized in the following hypotheses, both of which I expect to stand when holding the Black–White income gap constant:

- **Status threat hypothesis 1**: The greater the salience of race in a White individual's surroundings, the richer that individual will perceive Black people to be relative to White people.
- **Status threat hypothesis 2**: The higher the unemployment rate in a White individual's surroundings, the richer that individual will perceive Black people to be relative to White people.

Both status threat hypotheses posit White Americans to have a subjective, racialized perspective that shapes their interpretations of local context—but the latter hypothesis in particular inspires further reflection on racialized subjectivity. Specifically, the relationship proposed in *status threat hypothesis 2* resembles the psychological mechanism of scapegoating, or blaming an outgroup for an ingroup's suffering in the face of large-scale misfortune, such as a national economic crisis (Glick 2005). White people may not have explicitly blamed Black people for the recession; yet, scapegoating tends to draw upon culturally relevant symbols—such as the White–Black color line or the election of a Black president—and could have led many White Americans to believe that, if they were suffering economically, things must have been better for Black Americans. This (often irrational) "win/lose" logic has been central to the iteration of White backlash that Hughey (2014, 723–724) argues we see in the contemporary "postracial" period; it similarly has been demonstrated to be central to how people who most actively identify as White tend to think (Jardina 2019).

The predictions of *status threat hypothesis 2* also are in keeping with what White residents of Baton Rouge demonstrated they had a tendency to do in Chapter 3: to center White people as victims of events or circumstances that have left Black people in a far worse position. Whether in the case of White Baton Rougeans suffering from the struggles of a public school system that they have more or less abandoned, or White Americans believing the 2007–2009 recession hurt them more than Black Americans, who were hit much harder—these examples demonstrate what Jennifer Hochschild (1995, 68) has called "Whites' quandary." At the same time as White people have come to believe that discrimination no longer restrains Black outcomes and that Black people have the power to shape their own success, White people have also become convinced that their *own* prospects have deteriorated, that they are less able to succeed.

This spirit was captured, for example, by St. George supporter Chad when engaging in the discursive practice of prioritizing White concerns (while also denying racial motivations). Chad was remarkably direct in acknowledging racism in Baton Rouge's past: "50 or 60 years ago, it was a situation where the Blacks are contained, where we are trying to keep them down." He continued wryly: "Once they forced the desegregation, all of a sudden everyone became strong Catholics and wanted to send their kids to Catholic schools." Chad doubted, however, that these dynamics persisted: "I don't think that exists today; maybe the vestiges of that are still at play...but I don't necessarily believe in that." It was on these grounds that Chad emphasized the plight of southeast East Baton Rouge Parish and lamented that the "only option" for his child to attend a public school as Chad himself had done might be to move out of the parish. For Chad, the ideas that things had improved for Black residents and worsened for White residents went hand in hand.

The Effect of Local Context on Status Perceptions

Having laid out this chapter's first set of expectations—regarding how White perceptions of BRS will vary across contexts—I now put these hypotheses to the test. I begin by setting the scene of my analysis against the backdrop of the recession of 2007–2009, and particularly in light of an intriguing misalignment: White GSS respondents perceived *rising* perceptions of Black status during this time, even though we know the recession exacerbated racial disparities. Far from a coincidence, it was in fact in the places where race was most salient, and where unemployment was rising the fastest, that White people were most likely to believe Black people were closing the status gap.

Choosing a dataset and measuring status perceptions

This chapter takes advantage of a three-wave GSS panel survey conduced between 2006 and 2010, spanning what proved to be an economically volatile period, to measure White opinion on the economic status of both Black and White Americans. I focus on the GSS variables asking whether members of a racial group are either "rich" or "poor" on a 1–7 scale. I take the absolute value of the difference between a White respondent's evaluations of both Black and White Americans and then rescale the variable between 0 and 10 to create my

Table 5.3 Changing White Perceptions of White and Black Americans as Rich/Poor

	2006	2008	2010
White Americans	4.41	4.40	4.35
Black Americans	3.09	3.14	3.21
Δ	1.32	1.26	1.14

Labels reflect White respondents' mean evaluations of each racial group in a given year. Scale spans from "poor" = 1 to "rich" = 7 (reflecting the original GSS coding, rather than the perceptions of BRS variable I create and then rescale from 0–10). *Source*: 2006–2010 General Social Survey (*n* = 1,769).

measure of perceptions of BRS (*M* = 3.96, *S.D.* = 1.05). Higher values reflect evaluations of Black people as relatively richer, or, in other words, closer to White people in economic standing. Compared to the mean placement of Black Americans at 3.96 on the 0–10 scale, the average placement of White Americans is 6.04.

I have noted that evaluations of different racial groups' economic standings would inevitably be influenced by multiple factors, many of which I control for in the analysis to follow. One factor that merits further discussion here, however, is temporal context.

Status perceptions in a time of recession

Perceptions of BRS register a small but statistically significant increase (*p* < 0.05) among White GSS respondents from 2006 to 2010. Table 5.3 summarizes the change in the component parts of the status perceptions variable over the panel. The gap narrows by about 15% from a difference of 1.32 to 1.14, and is driven by perceptions of Black people becoming richer over the panel, and, to a smaller extent, perceptions of White people becoming poorer. To be fair, a shrinking gap between White and Black Americans has been the trend since the GSS introduced the rich/poor scale in 1990. But how logical is it for this trend to continue during the recession?

Although more than half of all American families lost at least a quarter of their wealth between 2007 and 2011, White households were considerably less likely to lose any wealth, let alone to fall into debt, compared to Black and other minority households. Overall, Black American families experienced a decline of 30% in their mean net worth compared to White families' 10% decline (Ackerman, Fries, and Windle 2012). Foreclosures played a central role in this process, reflecting the disproportionate targeting of Black Americans for subprime mortgage loans long before the housing boom of the early 2000s.[7] Unemployment also hit Black Americans harder, particularly when accounting for forgone employment—that is, not only jobs but also job *growth* lost thanks to the downturn. As of 2009, Black employment was down by 11.3 percentage points from the projected numbers in the absence of a recession, whereas White employment was down by 7.4 percentage points (Wall 2009). Increases in Black and White unemployment are illustrated in Figure 5.2. Especially because White families began to see gains in their wealth again beginning in 2009 and 2010 while Black wealth continued to slide (Burd-Sharps and Rasch 2015), the impact of the 2007–2009 recession is anticipated to be visible for generations to come.

Of course, Figure 5.2 also makes clear the economic setback that White families experienced relative to their standing before the recession, even if their wealth still dwarfed that of Black families. This situation is again reminiscent of some White Baton Rougeans' experiences: many *do* struggle to pay for private schooling rather than send their children to the (majority-Black) public schools; traffic *is* bad in the (disproportionately White and wealthy) southeast part of East Baton Rouge Parish. But these experiences easily obscure the considerably worse circumstances that many Black families in Baton Rouge face and paint an exaggerated picture of White victimization. Remember, for example, Randy's hyperbolic comparison of the relationship between St. George and Baton Rouge to that between colonial India and the British Empire.

Thus, while not minimizing the economic hardship the recession caused many White families, there is a clear misalignment between the recession's disproportionate impact on Black Americans, and White perceptions of rising Black status. This misalignment offers a valuable opportunity for further investigation—specifically into how those status perceptions are shaped by White people's subjective, local experiences of race and class.

Status perceptions under a Black president

A second temporal factor to consider stems from the fact that the GSS panel conspicuously spans the election of America's first Black president. It is certainly possible that having a nationally salient example of a high-status Black American led many White people to believe that Black people as a group were relatively richer. Would such an effect challenge the relationships I have hypothesized between local context and White perceptions? I suggest not, for three reasons.

For one, White people across the country would have had more or less equal exposure to a possible "Obama effect," justifying an investigation of how local context may have shaped White perceptions of BRS beyond any nationwide shift (see Welch and Sigelman 2011). Second, the subjectivity of a potential Obama effect would be similar to the subjectivity of White people seeing Black

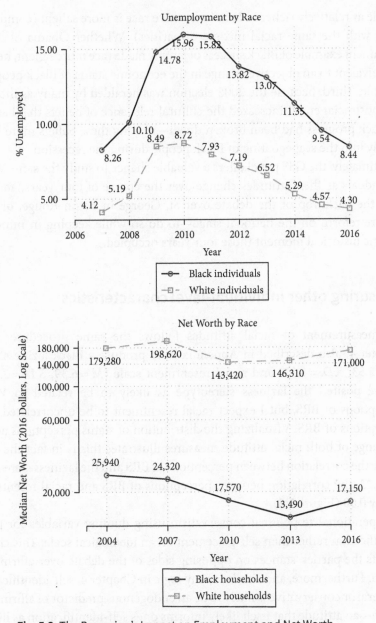

Fig. 5.2 The Recession's Impact on Employment and Net Worth
Top graph depicts annual average of seasonally adjusted unemployment rates
for both Black and White Americans (aged 16 years and over). *Source:* Bureau of
Labor Statistics, Labor Force Statistics from the Current Population Survey
2007–2016. Bottom graph depicts family net worth in 2016 dollars. *Source:*
Survey of Consumer Finances, Federal Reserve Bank Historic Tables 1989–2016.

people as relatively richer in locations where race is more salient (comparing areas with the same racial income disparities). Whether Obama offered a prominent example of Black success or simply made race more salient, neither is equivalent to an objective change in the economic status of Black people as a whole. Third, because the 2008 election was heralded by many as the start of a postracial era, it increased the cultural relevance of beliefs that barriers to Black progress had been broken down—making these beliefs more likely to play into the scapegoating of Black people during the recession.

Ultimately, the GSS panel offers a valuable chance to study the same White individuals as their attitudes change over the course of four years, and—as with the backdrop of the debate over St. George in Baton Rouge, or over welfare reform on the national stage—to do so while keeping in mind the specific historical moment those four years occupied.

Measuring other individual-level characteristics

My measurement of racial attitudes follows the same procedure as in Chapter 4, also described in Appendix B, to produce a Black laziness scale ($M = 5.53$, $S.D. = 1.12$) and racial resentment scale ($M = 6.39$, $S.D. = 2.37$).[8] I have posited the laziness stereotype as likely to be related to White perceptions of BRS, but I expect racial resentment to be uncorrelated with perceptions of BRS. Visualizing the distribution of status perceptions across the range of both racial attitude measures illustrates this is in fact the case. While the correlation between perceptions of BRS and the laziness stereotype is −0.23, the correlation between perceptions of BRS and racial resentment is only 0.08 (Figure 5.3).

I operationalize political conservatism using dummy variables for party identification rather than self-placement on an ideological scale. This choice reflects the parties' stances on opposing sides of the debate over affirmative action. Furthermore, and similar to my logic in Chapter 4, self-identification as liberal or conservative is likely to be an endogenous predictor of affirmative action—an attitude that itself likely informs one's self-identification as liberal or conservative. Other control variables drawn from the GSS include age, education, gender, marital status, and income.

Operationalizing urban contexts

With access to the GSS location files, I am able to locate the panel respondents in 117 MSAs and integrate MSA-level demographics into the dataset.[9] As in

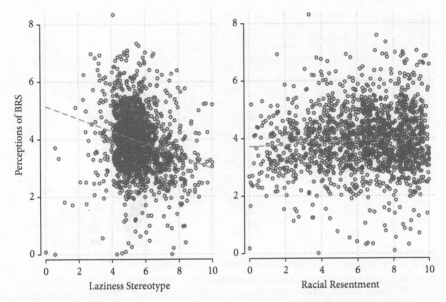

Fig. 5.3 White Racial Attitudes and Perceptions of Black Americans' Relative Status
Perceptions of Black relative status are measured on the *y*-axis; higher values indicate evaluations of Black people as relatively richer compared to White people, or rather, perceptions of a smaller status gap between the races. *Source:* 2006–2010 General Social Survey (*n* = 1,783).

Chapter 4, I focus on metropolitan areas as the day-to-day worlds Americans inhabit. MSAs also are the geographies in which people typically compete for jobs. While Chapter 4 affirmed that local context can be relevant to opinion on supra-local policies, the present chapter builds on previous findings that the MSA is a relevant geography in which to analyze White opinion on affirmative action (Oliver and Mendelberg 2000).

I measure the percentage of Black residents in each metropolitan area, transformed by the natural logarithm, using census estimates for each year of the panel. I also incorporate the exposure index of segregation to capture how residential patterns shape White people's experiences of racial diversity, based on the proportion of Black households with which the average White household in an MSA will share a neighborhood. Remember that areas that are *least* segregated by race take on the *highest* values of the exposure index, reaching a maximum where the proportion of Black households in the average White household's neighborhood is equal to the total proportion of Black households in the MSA.

Income data per year of the GSS panel are drawn from the census and adjusted by the Consumer Price Index to reflect 2010 dollars. To capture absolute economic status, I use median household income in an MSA for White and Black householders.[10] To capture the relative standing of racial

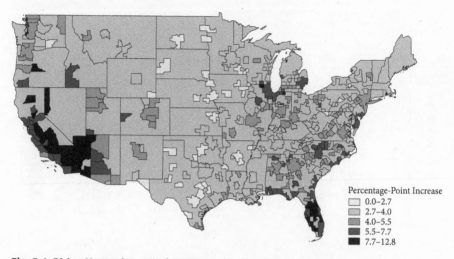

Fig. 5.4 Rising Unemployment by Metropolitan Area, 2006–2010

Figure depicts percentage-point increase in unemployment rates by MSA between July 2006 and July 2010. *Source:* Bureau of Labor Statistics, Local Area Unemployment Statistics, Seasonally Adjusted Metropolitan Area Estimates.

groups in an area, I subtract the Black median income from the equivalent measure for White households in each MSA and refer to this measure as the "Black–White income gap."[11]

Finally, MSA-level unemployment data are drawn from the Bureau of Labor Statistics as measured in July of each year of the panel. Figure 5.4 illustrates where unemployment rose the most between the start of the panel in 2006 and the end of the panel in 2010. These increases allow me to examine how perceptions of BRS respond to rapidly changing contexts: unemployment doubled over the course of the recession, even if the Black population of most MSAs has remained relatively stable.[12]

Analyzing longitudinal data helps address the danger of self-selection, as we can examine changes within the same White individuals as they respond to changing contexts. I also confirm that those who drop out of the panel do not skew the results: they are broadly similar to those who remain in the panel in terms of affirmative action views, party identification, and racial attitudes. But of course, there remains the possibility that my findings reflect respondents choosing to live in locations that reflect their preferences, rather than preferences being informed by their surroundings. It is not immediately clear why White individuals who think Black people are relatively better off would select into MSAs with larger Black population shares, or with higher levels of unemployment. But as in the previous chapter, I must emphasize that variation in perceptions of BRS should be more appropriately understood as reflective of place-specific experiences, including their histories and cultures, rather than direct "effects" of context.[13]

Empirical models

I begin my empirical analysis by identifying the individual-level and contextual factors that predict White perceptions of BRS. I use linear models to predict White respondents' perceptions of BRS on the 0–10 scale I created, reporting robust standard errors. The results of random-effects generalized least-squares regression in Table 5.4 reveal that the Black laziness stereotype is indeed a significant predictor of perceptions of BRS, but racial resentment is not. These results are consistent with *status perceptions hypothesis 1*. If anything, being racially resentful is associated with perceiving Black people as slightly closer to White people in economic standing. Although this relationship is not statistically significant, it is consistent with the idea that Black people have already gotten more help than they deserve; similarly, it is consistent with some White Baton Rouge residents' suggestion of creating "neighborhood schools" in majority-Black, impoverished parts of East Baton Rouge Parish while minimizing the economic barriers such schools would face.

The significance of the laziness stereotype leads me to use the first model in Table 5.4 as the base model for the remainder of my analysis of perceptions of BRS. This model also suggests that older White respondents and White males are more likely to think Black people are better off relative to White people, all else equal. It is possible that these demographics, tending toward more conservative or authoritarian stances, are more likely to subscribe to the idea that Black Americans' position has improved while White Americans' has worsened. My base model further indicates that more educated respondents rate Black Americans as slightly worse off, consistent with my expectation that evaluations of Black people as poor could be an informed position among some White people, rather than just a negative stereotype.

Finally, there is no significant difference in perceptions of BRS between White Republicans and Democrats, although White independent voters are likely to see Black people as slightly richer. Importantly, not only is the number of independent voters in the sample small, but independents also tend to be lower-information voters (Converse 1962) and thus may be more sensitive to events such as the election of a Black president. Thus, while not claiming that partisanship is wholly irrelevant to White Americans' perceptions of Black Americans as rich or poor, we can conclude that identification as a

Table 5.4 Individual-Level Predictors of White Perceptions of BRS

Perceptions of BRS	(1)	(2)
Laziness Stereotype	−0.242***	
	(0.032)	
Racial Resentment		0.0144
		(0.013)
Age	0.00680***	0.00467***
	(0.002)	(0.002)
Gender	−0.126**	−0.101
	(0.060)	(0.065)
Marital Status	0.0214	0.0231
	(0.062)	(0.065)
Education (years)	−0.0455***	−0.0292**
	(0.011)	(0.012)
Income (thousands)	−0.000294	−0.000356
	(0.001)	(0.001)
Independent	0.233***	0.247**
	(0.088)	(0.096)
Republican	0.0987	0.0421
	(0.060)	(0.069)
Constant	5.574***	4.022***
	(0.270)	(0.223)
Observations	1527	1422
p	1.08e−20	0.000197
R-squared (within)	0.0356	0.000173
R-squared (between)	0.123	0.0465
R-squared (overall)	0.103	0.0257

Standard errors in parentheses; table reports results of random effects GLS regression of White perceptions of BRS; party base category is Democrat.

Source: 2006–2010 General Social Survey.

* $p < 0.10$, ** $p < 0.05$, *** $p < 0.01$.

Democrat or Republican is not a primary determinant of perceptions of BRS among White respondents in the GSS sample.

The salience of race and the security of status

I next consider how White perceptions of BRS are predicted by local geography, incorporating measures of context alongside the individual-level variables to offer support for *status perceptions hypothesis 2*. Table 5.5 reveals that while simply living in areas with Black people that fall into higher income brackets has no significant effect on perceptions of BRS (Model 1), the size of the Black–White income *gap* has a small but significant negative effect on perceptions of BRS (Model 2). Moving from an MSA with a racial income

Table 5.5 Contextual Predictors of White Perceptions of BRS: Income and Race

Perceptions of BRS	(1) Black Income	(2) Black Income Gap	(3) Segregation
Laziness Stereotype	−0.246***	−0.249***	−0.248***
	(0.034)	(0.034)	(0.034)
Black Med. Household	0.00185		
Income (thousands)	(0.003)		
Black–White Income		−0.00998***	−0.00630**
Gap (thousands)		(0.003)	(0.003)
Percent Black (log)	0.119***	0.163***	
	(0.033)	(0.038)	
Segregation			0.0180**
(White–Black Exposure)			(0.007)
Constant	5.343***	5.565***	5.656***
	(0.306)	(0.294)	(0.292)
Observations	1406	1406	1406
p	1.43e−20	1.42e−20	1.37e−18
R-squared (within)	0.0378	0.0403	0.0401
R-squared (betwen)	0.127	0.136	0.121
R-squared (overall)	0.115	0.123	0.112

Standard errors in parentheses; table reports results of random effects GLS regression of White perceptions of BRS; for concision, controls for age, gender, marital status, income, and partisanship are not displayed.

Source: 2006–2010 General Social Survey.

* $p < 0.10$, ** $p < 0.05$, *** $p < 0.01$.

gap of \$19,000 (at the 25th percentile) to one with a more severe disparity of \$31,000 (at the 75th percentile) predicts an increase of 0.12 on the scale measuring perceptions of BRS (*S.D.* = 1.05). This finding is a straightforward one: where a local Black population economically lags further behind White residents, White perceptions of BRS reflect this lag. I find this effect when controlling for local Black population share, thus comparing MSAs with a similar Black presence but different income gaps.

An MSA's Black population share, however, also has its own significant effect on perceptions of BRS—but in the opposite direction. White respondents who live in high-density Black MSAs tend to think Black people are richer relative to White people, even though there tends to be greater income inequality between Black and White people in such settings. Among areas with the same size Black–White income gap, moving from an MSA that is 4% Black to one that is 17% Black (across the interquartile range) predicts an *increase* of 0.23 in a White individual's perceptions of BRS (which is about one-fifth of a standard deviation). What might be at play here?

The positive relationship between Black population share and White perceptions of BRS may reflect the greater likelihood of finding a visible Black middle class in an area with a larger Black population share, even if the median household income in that setting would not reflect this. After all, Black population share is negatively correlated with Black median income, although only at −0.05. This reflects that, much like Baton Rouge, higher-density Black MSAs in the GSS sample tend to have larger low-income *and* affluent Black communities, along with affluent White communities—hence the racial income disparity being greater in these settings.

In any case, the positive effect of Black population share indicates that, holding the Black–White income gap constant, White people are more likely to perceive a smaller status gap where race is more salient—or, I suggest, where the Black population is more visible.

I now turn to measures of segregation to further interrogate my hypothesis that the visibility of a Black population affects White perceptions. Model 3 replaces the Black population share variable with racial segregation to capture the probability a White family shares a neighborhood with a Black family. The segregation variable proves significant ($p < 0.05$), suggesting that White people perceive a smaller racial status gap in MSAs where there is greater exposure of White households to Black households.

Take, for example, the metropolitan area surrounding Milwaukee, WI. With a population of about 1.6 million, 17.4% of which is Black, and an exposure score of 5.91, White residents of Milwaukee are relatively unlikely to share a neighborhood with a Black family. Model 3 predicts that a White GSS respondent in such a setting, holding all other predictors at their means, would place Black people at 3.9 on the perceptions of BRS scale. Now imagine somewhere like the West Palm Beach/Boca Raton area (a division of the larger Miami metropolitan area). West Palm Beach/Boca Raton is similar to Milwaukee with a population of 1.3 million that is 17.5% Black—but also with an exposure score of 10.40. Holding the other variables held at their means, a White resident of an area comparable to West Palm Beach would place Black people around 4.0 on the perceptions of BRS scale (approximately one-tenth of a standard deviation higher).

Segregation measures reflect a number of factors, from the ability of local Black families to move away from isolated Black neighborhoods to an MSA's particular historical pattern of Black–White segregation. As I noted in "Status Perceptions in Context", there is also a possibility that Black–White income disparities are smaller in less segregated settings, given the role of segregation in concentrating poverty in Black communities and concentrating wealth in White ones. This might lead us to think that higher perceptions of BRS in less segregated MSAs are simply the product of Black people being relatively better off in such settings. For instance, the income gap between Black and

White households is smaller in West Palm Beach (approx. $20,000) than in the more segregated Milwaukee (approx. $35,000). However, the correlation between the segregation measure and the Black–White income gap is only 0.23, suggesting that the patterning of race in an MSA has an influence on perceptions of BRS distinct from any relationship between residential exposure and racial disparities.

Taken together, Models 2 and 3 offer evidence for *status threat hypothesis 1*. In settings where race is more salient—whether based on Black population share or residential exposure to Black households—White people tend to believe that Black people are richer relative to White people. The effects are small but statistically significant, and they hold when accounting for the true Black–White income gap in a White individual's MSA. My findings so far demonstrate that the logic of racial threat is applicable to the question of whether White people perceive Black Americans to be encroaching on White Americans in economic status.

Unemployment and the security of status

Do perceptions of BRS also vary according to economic context, per the economic dimension of the racial threat hypothesis? I investigate this question in Table 5.6. For reference, the first column revisits the model that identified the effects of the Black–White income gap and Black population share on perceptions of BRS in Table 5.5. Model 2 then incorporates a measure of MSA unemployment rates. Unemployment proves a significant predictor of the outcome variable in the positive direction. Across the interquartile range of unemployment rates (from 4.5% to 7.5%), perceptions of BRS increase by approximately 0.10. In settings where unemployment was highest during the recession, White people were more likely to think Black people, if anything, were *improving* in economic standing—despite the heavy weight of the recession borne by Black Americans.

I offer additional evidence for this relationship by accounting for an MSA's starting level of unemployment as of 2006 and measuring the proportional increase in Model 3: a 1% increase in the unemployment rate in an MSA is associated with a 0.18 increase in a White MSA resident's perception of BRS. While this effect is borderline significant ($p < 0.10$), taken together with the highly significant effect of absolute levels of unemployment, it demonstrates the robustness of unemployment's effect on perceptions of BRS.[14]

The effect of unemployment is the opposite of what we would expect if perceptions of BRS were a primarily affective orientation toward Black people, one that would be more "negative" in settings of economic scarcity (in which case, White respondents would evaluate Black people as poorer). Instead,

Table 5.6 Contextual Predictors of White Perceptions of BRS: Unemployment

Perceptions of BRS	(1) Racial Context	(2) Economic Context	(3) Dynamic Model
Laziness Stereotype	−0.249***	−0.246***	−0.283***
	(0.034)	(0.034)	(0.047)
Black–White Income Gap (thousands)	−0.00998***	−0.00864***	
	(0.003)	(0.003)	
Percent Black (log)	0.163***	0.151***	
	(0.038)	(0.039)	
Unemployment Rate		0.0320***	
		(0.011)	
Black–White Income Gap (%Δ)			0.0253
			(0.026)
Black Population Share (%Δ)			0.0120
			(0.053)
Unemployment Rate (%Δ)			0.182*
			(0.111)
Constant	5.565***	5.354***	5.769***
	(0.294)	(0.300)	(0.346)
Observations	1406	1406	775
p	1.42e−20	1.58e−22	9.84e−12
R-squared (within)	0.0403	0.0484	0.0350
R-squared (between)	0.136	0.141	0.164
R-squared (overall)	0.123	0.128	0.136

Standard errors in parentheses; table reports results of random effects GLS regression of White perceptions of BRS; for concision, controls for age, gender, marital status, income, and partisanship are not displayed.

Source: 2006–2010 General Social Survey.

* $p < 0.10$, ** $p < 0.05$, *** $p < 0.01$.

Models 2 and 3 support my conceptualization of White perceptions of BRS as responsive when local economic conditions paint race relations as a zero-sum game: as unemployment increases over the panel, losses suffered by White people are registered as gains for Black people. Table 5.6 therefore offers strong evidence for *status threat hypothesis 2*.[15]

Another way to look at these findings is to disaggregate the two components of the status perceptions variable as they changed over the course of the panel to produce a narrowing gap (Figure 5.5). Disaggregated analysis indicates that high local unemployment predicts the placement of Black people closer to "rich" on the rich/poor scale, and has no significance on White respondents' evaluations of their own group. On the contrary, it is large local Black population shares, or smaller local Black–White income gaps, that predict the placement of White people closer to "poor."

In other words, the true Black–White income gap in an MSA and the local salience of race are more predictive of White people's evaluations of their

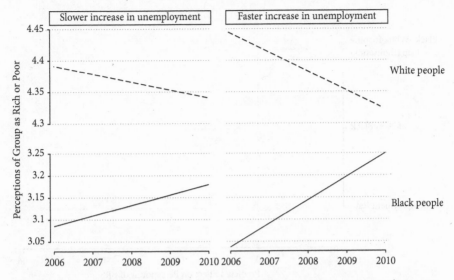

Fig. 5.5 Narrowing Perceived Status Gap among White Americans as Unemployment Rises

The figure depicts perceptions that White people were getting poorer while Black people were getting richer over the course of the panel. The trend holds across the panel but is exacerbated in settings where unemployment rose more quickly between 2006 and 2010: the graphs on the right depict status perceptions in MSAs where unemployment registered a greater than 60% increase. *Source:* 2006–2010 General Social Survey (*n* = 1,769).

own economic standing. Alternatively, contexts of economic insecurity are more predictive of White people's evaluations of *Black* Americans' economic standing in absolute terms.

The irony of White people perceiving Black people to have benefited economically in the MSAs hardest hit by the recession makes sense if we appreciate these as settings where race relations would most likely be cast as a zero-sum game. Yet, this finding only emphasizes the subjectivity of White Americans' vantage point on their local surroundings; remember that power brings the luxury of deciding what is seen and how.

Interpreting the results: Contextual variation in perceptions of the racial status gap

The findings reported thus far have demonstrated that White people see a smaller status gap between Black and White Americans in settings where race is salient, and where unemployment is high. I argue these findings illustrate the operation of a threat response among White Americans that appears not in the form of greater animus toward Black Americans, but rather in the form of perceptions of a narrowing gap between the races in economic status. This analysis therefore challenges the typical association of threat with negative

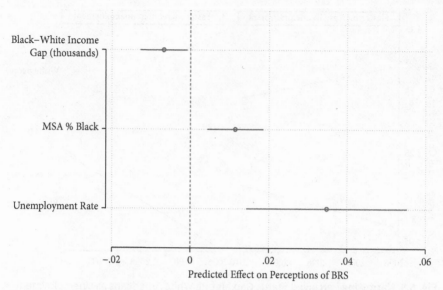

Fig. 5.6 Visualizing Effects of Racial and Economic Context on White Perceptions of BRS

Figure illustrates results of Model 2 in Table 5.6. Horizontal lines represent 95% confidence intervals. We can see that an MSA's Black–White income gap has a negative effect on White perceptions of BRS, whereas MSA % Black and unemployment have positive effects. None of the confidence intervals cross the vertical dotted line at 0 (i.e., representing a variable having no effect), indicating the significance of these relationships. *Source:* 2006–2010 General Social Survey (*n* = 1,406).

affect directed at Black people and instead draws attention to the ingroup-oriented dimension of prejudice as a sense of group position.

Figure 5.6 illustrates the key significant relationships that have emerged from my analysis thus far. Status perceptions might logically reflect realities in White people's surroundings, such as the Black–White income gap: if Black people are generally more disadvantaged in a given MSA, local White people's perceptions of BRS are lower. I also showed, however, that perceptions of BRS could reflect more subjective responses to context, as was the case with an MSA's Black population share—or even seemingly illogical responses, as was the case with unemployment rates. The amount of variance in perceptions of BRS explained by the models presented so far is small (the model with the highest R-squared value explains 13.5%). Beliefs about the relative status of the races are sure to be shaped by factors beyond one's local surroundings and personal characteristics. Nonetheless, it is possible to identify systematic variation in perceptions of BRS according to both racial and economic context.

Considering alternative explanations

Three additional tests offer further support for my interpretation of the relationship between context and perceptions of BRS.

Individual experiences of unemployment

First, is it simply White individuals who themselves are unemployed, or who become unemployed during the panel, who are likely to believe Black people are getting richer relative to White people? Including individual-level controls for respondents' current workforce status as unemployed, or for their experience of unemployment in the past ten years, indicates that the predictive power of MSA unemployment rate holds irrespective of White individuals' experiences of unemployment.

Economic mobility

Second, is it simply in places that were stagnant before the recession that White people are likely to think Black people are relatively better off? I repeat the analysis including measures of relative economic mobility by MSA, operationalized as the correlation between a parent and child's rank in the income distribution for children born 1980–1982 (data drawn from Chetty et al. 2014). This variable reflects economic opportunity in each MSA preceding the GSS panel, and further, is uncorrelated with unemployment rates. I find that the effects of unemployment rate in predicting perceptions of BRS hold across areas with both lower and higher levels of social mobility.

White population loss

Third, if perceptions of BRS approximate White people's evaluation of the security of their group's position, do noneconomic indicators related to the security of White status also predict perceptions of BRS? Following previous work on the relationship between demographic shifts and White insecurity (see, e.g., Hopkins 2010), I incorporate into my models a measure of the change in each MSA's White population between 2000 and 2010.

White population change itself does not predict perceptions of BRS. However, stratifying the sample according to White population change reveals that the statistical significance of the relationship between unemployment rate and perceptions of BRS is greater among White people in MSAs that saw more than an approximately 5 percentage-point decrease in White population in the last ten years. These White people also are the most likely to perceive Black people to be getting richer (rather than White people getting poorer) in response to rising unemployment. Future work should more closely investigate the relationship between White population change and status perceptions, but these preliminary findings support the interpretation that White insecurity about their racial ingroup is behind the effects I have identified thus far.

Status Perceptions and Affirmative Action Preferences

So far, we have seen that White perceptions of BRS vary systematically across local contexts—in some straightforward ways, but also in some subjective ones. In particular, economic insecurity leads many White people to believe Black Americans must be gaining on White Americans in economic standing. I now turn to the question of how this status threat response influences White opinion on affirmative action in employment—a policy approach that itself seeks to improve Black Americans' economic standing.

To be fair, the extent to which the presence of middle- and upper-income Black Americans today is a product of affirmative action policies is not clear. Multifold increases in the number of Black professionals during the post– civil rights era almost certainly were aided by changing practices for the admission of Black people to higher education; a similar point could be made about hiring practices. At the same time, research has attributed most of the economic gains made by Black Americans between the 1960s and 80s not to race-conscious hiring or admission practices, but rather to antidiscrimination laws, increased returns from education (particularly in the South), and the migration of Black Americans to urban centers in Northern cities (Donohue III and Heckman 1991; Heckman and Payner 1989; Thernstrom and Thernstrom 1998).

At the same time, affirmative action is one of the most prominent contemporary strategies to expand opportunity for Black Americans and thus is closely linked to the question of Black people's class status. Importantly, it is distinct from other racialized policies that are implicitly posed as threatening to White people because, as Charles Gallagher (2004, 154) puts it, affirmative action "[makes] whiteness both visible and a salient category of identification." In other words, affirmative action highlights *ingroup-oriented* concerns about the security of White Americans' position at the same time as provoking consideration of Black Americans' worthiness as beneficiaries (not dissimilar to themes implicated in debates over busing and school desegregation in Baton Rouge). Affirmative action therefore offers an ideal opportunity to demonstrate how perceiving a status threat goes on to inform White racial policy preferences, while also explicitly conceptualizing the multidimensionality of White Americans' feelings of prejudice that have been on display throughout this book.

Affirmative action and the defense of White interests

Affirmative action is the paradigm behind policies that aim to counter discrimination proactively rather than reactively. It seeks to increase the representation of minorities in higher education and employment by making structural changes to admissions and hiring practices. And in the decades since its creation, affirmative action has provoked heated debate in both the public sphere and the scholarly one.

John Skrentny (1996) calls it "ironic" that affirmative action emerged in the first place, given that it faced much public criticism and enjoyed little public support. Mainstream civil rights groups of the 1960s tended to advocate for colorblindness over race preferences, being sensitive to taboos around racial quotas. Even the Congress of Racial Equality was hesitant to stand too strongly behind its advocacy for the proportional hiring of Black candidates. In keeping with this hesitance, Section VII of the 1964 Civil Rights Act used only colorblind language to prohibit employers from discriminating on the basis of "race, color, religion, sex, or national origin" D.S. King (1995).

The more assertive idea of taking affirmative steps to recruit Black employees emerged from an executive order by President Kennedy in 1961, and was reinforced by another order from President Johnson in 1965. Skrentny argues both orders were a "crisis management" strategy by the White House, seeking to address racial unrest at home and to maintain American legitimacy abroad, particularly amidst growing concerns about human rights during the Cold War era. President Nixon's support of affirmative action can be seen as similarly pragmatic: it helped split his opposition by pitting labor interests and civil rights advocates against each other (see Frymer 2008). Tepid support from the courts ultimately helped make a controversial policy publicly acceptable, even if still hotly contested.[16]

The federal government remains a key player, particularly as affirmative action faces some of its greatest challenges in the courts at the hands of ideologically driven legislators and interest groups. Yet, affirmative action varies the most from state to state. Nine states have at some point implemented a ban on affirmative action; bans in place at the time of writing are summarized in Table 5.7 and in many cases were driven by debates around admissions to state universities. One important implication of these bans is that they would have

Table 5.7 States with Affirmative Action Bans

Year	State	Method	Policy	Voters in Favor
1996	California	Initiated constitutional amendment	Proposition 209	54.6%*
1998	Washington	Initiated statute	Washington Affirmative Action Ban, Initiative 200	58.2%
1999	Florida	Executive order by governor	Executive Order 99–281, the "One Florida" initiative	N/A
2006	Michigan	Initiated constitutional amendment	Michigan Civil Rights Amendment, Proposal 2	58.0%
2008	Nebraska	Initiated constitutional amendment	Nebraska Civil Rights Initiative, Measure 424	57.6%
2010	Arizona	Initiated constitutional amendment	Arizona Civil Rights Amendment, Proposition 107	59.5%
2011	New Hampshire	Statute	House Bill 0623	N/A
2012	Oklahoma	Legislatively referred constitutional amendment	Oklahoma Affirmative Action Ban Amendment, State Question 759	59.2%

Table lists the eight states that ban affirmative action in public employment and university admissions. Other state policies of note include a failed ballot initiative in Colorado in 2008, and a ban in place in Texas between 1996 and 2003. Also note that some states with no official affirmative action ban in place nonetheless have no universities that consider race in admissions.

*California's Proposition 209, the first legislation of its kind, has been challenged via multiple legal and legislative efforts during its existence; however, November 2020 represented the first time it was again presented to voters to either repeal or affirm it. Voters opted to keep the ban in place by a margin of 57.2% to 42.8%.

made affirmative action a more salient issue to state residents around the time the policies were put in place (or were being debated). While I ensure that my findings in this chapter hold when controlling for a White GSS respondent's state, it is no doubt the case that state context informed understandings of affirmative action during the period of the GSS panel.

Keep in mind, however, that I focus primarily on White views of affirmative action in employment. Although this realm affects many more Americans than university admissions do—and cases such as *Ricci v. DeStefano* (2009) have kept it in the national conversation[17]—affirmative action in employment tends to be less contentious than in higher education. This is potentially because it is easier to identify the positive effect affirmative action has had on corporate profit and performance (e.g., Bellinger and Hillman 2000; Hunt, Layton, and Prince 2015; Randle 1993) than on educational outcomes (but see Bowen and Bok 2000).

Whether considering education or employment, one thing is clear: White Americans have consistently viewed affirmative action for Black Americans less favorably than affirmative action initiatives targeting other groups (e.g., women), across a range of policy design and survey question wording (for a review, see Crosby, Iyer, and Sincharoen 2006). One example of such a finding comes from Lawrence Bobo and James Kluegel (1993), who demonstrate that White people's approval of affirmative action decreases when a policy's targeting of Black people becomes explicit. However, these authors also note that White people's approval *increases* when a policy is designed to emphasize equal opportunities rather than equal outcomes. Bobo and Kluegel's two findings thus highlight one of the fundamental points of contention in the debate over how to understand views on affirmative action: Is opposition to affirmative action the product of negative feelings toward Black people, or beliefs about the justifiability of group-based preferences? This debate is well worn, but I review it here to lay the groundwork for a discussion of racial policy preferences as operating in defense of White Americans' group interests.

Understanding White opposition to affirmative action

Some of the earliest approaches to conceptualizing opposition to affirmative action come from the racial attitudes literature that was emerging at the same time as affirmative action policies were taking shape in the 1970s and 80s. This approach was led by the scholars who argued that a new "symbolic" form of racism had emerged in the post–Jim Crow era (Sears and Kinder 1971). Sears and Kinder initially conceptualized opposition to affirmative action as itself a component of symbolic racism. This was justly criticized as a circular definition, given that symbolic racism was meant to *predict* opposition to race-targeted policies. Since then, however, a large body of research has identified anti-Black affect as at least one major predictor of White opposition to affirmative action (Bobo and Kluegel 1993; Bobo 1998b; Bobocel et al. 1998; Carmines and Layman 1998; Peffley and Hurwitz 1998; Sears et al. 1997; Sidanius, Pratto, and Bobo 1996; Strolovitch 1998).

An alternative argument is that the influence of racial animus on affirmative action views has been overstated, and that White opposition is based on

principles that are fundamentally race-neutral, such as a commitment to meritocracy. A popular version of this argument is the "principled conservatism"
hypothesis, which holds that race-targeting presents reasons for White opposition on grounds that cannot be dismissed as prejudice (Sniderman, Tetlock,
and Piazza 1991). Principled conservatism as applied to affirmative action
differs from its application to issues like welfare (as discussed in Chapter 4):
with an explicitly race-targeted approach like affirmative action, Sniderman
is more sympathetic to arguments that some degree of negative racial affect is
behind White opposition. Yet, the principled conservatism school maintains
that opposition to affirmative action is not simply a continuation of old racial
prejudices and fears, but rather "significantly departs from racial politics of
the past" (Kuklinski et al. 1997, 403).

Several studies challenge the logic of principled conservatism by presenting
empirical findings that contradict its claims. For example, scholars have
pointed out instances in which prejudice blinds people to whether or not
a policy violates their stated principles of justice (Bobocel et al. 1998), or
where beliefs about egalitarianism predict opposition to race-targeted policies
but not gender-targeted ones (Strolovitch 1998). In response, Sniderman and
coauthors argue that such inconsistencies in the principled conservatism
hypothesis tend to occur primarily among politically unsophisticated White
people (Sniderman, Brody, and Tetlock 1993). Politically sophisticated White
people, these scholars argue, are better able to draw upon their personal
ideologies to inform their policy preferences.[18]

Affirmative action, however, stands out among racial policies as one that
even politically sophisticated White people broadly oppose (Schuman et al.
1997). This finding has informed a third approach to explaining opposition
to affirmative action on the grounds that education makes White Americans
more adept in the "ideological refinement" of their policy preferences to
defend their privileges (Glaser 2001; Jackman 1978). Jim Sidanius and coauthors find that, while political ideology is indeed a stronger predictor of affirmative action preferences among sophisticated White people, conservatism
is also *more correlated with negative racial affect* among this group (Federico
and Sidanius 2002; Sidanius, Pratto, and Bobo 1996). These authors thus
agree with the principled conservatism school's premise that sophisticated
White people oppose affirmative action on ideological grounds—but they
see ideology as a tool equipping White people to explain their racial policy
preferences via arguments that defend "group superiority in terms that appear
both morally and intellectually justifiable" (Sidanius, Pratto, and Bobo 1996,
477; see also Wodtke 2016).

The ideological refinement hypothesis is located within the tradition of group-based theories of prejudice introduced in Chapter 1. The specific relevance of these approaches to affirmative action is perhaps best articulated by Bobo (1998a, 989): "Whites," he argues, "will oppose affirmative action, not so much because they see a race-based policy as contravening their highest values or because they have learned a new, politically relevant set of resentments of Black people, but rather because they perceive Black people as competitive threats for valued social resources, status, and privileges." In this statement, Bobo answers the question I posed to introduce this discussion: neither negative affect nor beliefs about group-based preferences explain opposition to affirmative action as much as White people's protectiveness of their own group interests.

The relevance of affirmative action to the present study

My analysis in Chapter 5 builds on Bobo's point. In focusing on affirmative action, it is not my aim to adjudicate on the influence of racial bias as opposed to race-neutral orientations on affirmative action preferences. Most scholars agree that both have some influence (indeed, the ideological refinement hypothesis sees the two as related). Neither is it my aim to offer an explanation that supplants any of these as a primary explanation of variation in White people's affirmative action views, especially given the stickiness of White opposition.[19]

Rather, affirmative action is valuable to study as a policy that inspires reflection on the security of White Americans' standing in the social order, as well as on the race *and* class of beneficiaries. To the first point, affirmative action offers an ideal background against which to demonstrate the relevance of White concerns about the security of their status over Black people. In addressing the historically privileged access White people have enjoyed to employment, affirmative action requires reflection not only on Black Americans as beneficiaries but also on White Americans' position in the racial hierarchy. More so than other policies, affirmative action prompts White people to "think about their own racial identity in relational terms" and reflect on what they stand to lose from granting more opportunities to Black people (Gallagher 2004, 154). This is the same kind of reflection that White residents of Baton Rouge engaged in through the latter two discursive practices identified in Chapter 3—assigning a greater importance to White communities' concerns than to Black communities', and defending the status quo of the racial hierarchy.

Moreover, because affirmative action is targeted not only at poor Black people but also at Black people further up the class ladder, it expands the typical focus on a threat posed by the "undeserving" Black poor (or an assumedly classless Black population) to consider a potential threat posed by middle- and upper-income Black Americans. Drawing on Chapter 3's insight into how White people's perspective is colored by their racial privilege, I will show how White perceptions of a local threat posed by nonpoor Black people, too, reveal the subjectivity of White Americans' vision.

The effect of status threat on affirmative action preferences

Why would perceptions of Black people's economic standing inform White preferences on affirmative action? Much like both income level *and* one's risk of falling below that income level predict an individual's demand for social protection (Rehm, Hacker, and Schlesinger 2012), I expect that both White Americans' group position *and* the perceived security of that position will predict White people's racial policy preferences. Although this idea has been implied in previous applications of the realistic group conflict and racial threat hypotheses, my measure of perceptions of BRS offers a novel, direct way to examine how beliefs about the security of White people's economic advantage will influence White opinion.

I anticipate that White people who perceive Black people to be relatively poorer—that is, who perceive White Americans' economic advantage as more secure—will be less opposed to affirmative action than White people who perceive Black people as relatively richer, posing a more imminent threat to White status. This interpretation need not paint all White people as hostile to Black improvement: benevolent motivations could lead White people to see a greater need for affirmative action when Black people are believed to lag behind, and less of a need if Black people have caught up. Either way, my emphasis is on White Americans' material interest in remaining higher up on the economic ladder. I expect that White people's evaluations of Black people's economic standing will have their own predictive power, even after controlling for more affective orientations that may serve a similar end, such as racial resentment and political conservatism.

Taking higher perceptions of BRS to indicate the perception of a greater status threat, I propose the following hypothesis:

- **Affirmative action hypothesis 1**: White people who believe that Black people pose a threat to White economic status will be more likely to oppose affirmative action, all else equal. White people who believe that

Black people do *not* pose a threat to White status will be more likely to *support* affirmative action.

Even though assertive White support of affirmative action is rare, this first hypothesis intends to capture the direction of the relationship between perceptions of BRS and affirmative action views. For example, believing that Black people do not pose a status threat might make a White individual simply "oppose" rather than "strongly oppose" affirmative action (i.e., potentially making a White person indifferent to affirmative action, but likely not supportive of it). All the same, a move toward indifference is notable for a policy approach that has attracted opposition as strong as affirmative action has.

Defending the operation of a status threat

I now consider two possible objections to *affirmative action hypothesis 1*.

Whether Black people "need" affirmative action

First, do White people who perceive a smaller status gap simply think affirmative action is less necessary? Consider an alternate interpretation of *affirmative action hypothesis 1*: perhaps it is not about Black people encroaching on White people's economic position, but rather that White people believe there is less need for affirmative action as they see Black people's collective economic status improve. This is the interpretation that Jhally and Lewis (1992) offer in their studies of reactions to *The Cosby Show*, discussed previously. I suggest that this interpretation does not make the rhetoric of White people perceiving a threat irrelevant.

For one, evidence of threat is already at play in the formation of White people's perceptions of BRS—perceptions that go on to inform views on affirmative action. If (1) White people become more opposed to affirmative action because they believe it is less necessary, but (2) that belief is a product of their reading the world through a racialized lens (e.g., believing Black people are getting richer as a result of rising unemployment and related insecurity about White people's economic status, then (3) opposition to affirmative action on "need-based" grounds is nonetheless liable to stand on subjective, racialized misperceptions of the world that are ultimately motivated by White Americans' defensiveness of their group position.

Furthermore, White people thinking affirmative action is "less necessary" when Black people are relatively richer supports the logic that White people want to maintain at least some advantage over Black people (and at minimum it confirms White people's sensitivity to the relative standing of the races). In support of this point, I will confirm that White perceptions of Black Americans' absolute status are not predictive of affirmative action views in the GSS panel; only a measure that takes account of the *distance* between White and Black people on a rich/poor spectrum will be predictive of affirmative action views. In other words, simply believing that Black people are poor does not motivate need-based support; a White person must believe Black people are poor *and also that White people are considerably richer*, and thus that Black people do not pose a status threat, in order to become more supportive of affirmative action.

Whether affluent Black people are threatening

A second challenge to *affirmative action hypothesis 1* concerns the logic of suggesting that White people would perceive higher-status Black people as somehow threatening. This logic not only challenges scholars and Baton Rouge residents like Brian who explicitly argue that class is more important than race (and thus that race should become increasingly irrelevant as Black Americans' status rises) but also challenges the more implicit assumption in literature on racial threat that better-off Black people will be seen as less threatening by White people.

One foundation for this argument/assumption comes from the work of William Julius Wilson, whose concern with the gulf between the Black poor and nonpoor leads him to focus on the absolute status of Black Americans. To be clear, Wilson does not deny the possibility of a threat posed by the Black middle class: he instead argues that the growth of employment opportunities for all Americans in the 1970s kept rising Black status from posing a competitive threat to White workers (see Wilson 1978, ch. 5). By arguing that Black people will most likely be seen to pose a status threat in high-unemployment settings, I make a complementary, though converse, argument to Wilson's original one.

However, Wilson has been cited in subsequent studies of the racial threat hypothesis as implying that affluent Black people are not threatening (see Quillian 1996, note 6). One prominent study has found that settings with higher-status Black people are associated with lower levels of perceived threat—arguing that improvements in Black people's status would not only improve life outcomes but also would "diminish threat, and hence, ameliorate racial hostility" (Giles and Evans 1985, 62). More generally, the literature on racial threat rarely engages with how both the race and class of a proximate Black population (in contrast to economic conditions across a given context) would influence the political behavior of White people.

There are exceptions to this. For instance, M. C. Taylor's (1998) study of the effect of local racial context on policy preferences argues that high- and low-status Black people are equally "threatening." Emerging scholarship on the relationship between state-level racial income disparities and welfare outcomes has also touched on the possibility of a threat response in reaction to improvements in Black status. Matsubayashi and Rocha (2012) find that a state's Black–White income disparity exacerbates the negative effect of a Black population share on the generosity of state welfare provision. Hero and Levy (2018) similarly suggest that "threats would presumably be more intense as majority and minority statuses become more equal, rather than less," although the authors do not test this hypothesis. (Instead, their analysis of state-level racial inequality and welfare spending preferences reveals a limited definition of threat, exemplifying the habit of equating a Black population with a threat and ignoring questions of power and positionality.)

Ultimately, few have considered the dynamics at play in White Americans' localized perceptions of nonpoor Black Americans, distinct from the idea that White people will construe their hypothetically undifferentiated Black neighbors as threatening. The Black middle class has grown considerably in the fifty years since Wilson wrote, and the macroeconomic context has changed. We also have seen various waves of White retaliation to Black progress during that time, notably in regard to the rolling back of Black Americans' civil rights (see, e.g., King and Smith 2016 on voting rights, or Beckett and Francis 2020 on criminal justice). In light of these currents, it is conceivable that White people would see a distinct threat represented by the Black residents in their MSAs who present competition for jobs—including, or perhaps especially, if those Black residents occupy positions higher up the income ladder.

When will perceiving a status threat come into play?

In theorizing a possible status threat response, I do not reject the premise that low-status Black Americans tend to be viewed negatively by White Americans, or the implication that high-status Black Americans will be less associated with the stigmas of poverty. Drawing upon literature emphasizing White Americans' racial policy preferences as multidimensional, I expect that White people will simultaneously evaluate affirmative action according to their concerns about the security of White economic privilege *and* their evaluations of Black people as "deserving" beneficiaries.

Such multidimensionality accords with previous research on affirmative action preferences and issue framing. Kinder and Sanders (1990) find that when affirmative action is framed as giving Black people an "undeserved advantage," racial prejudice is most predictive of preferences; alternatively, concerns about group interests are the strongest predictor when the frame emphasizes "reverse discrimination" against White people. These two frames recall the argument made by Cavaillé and Trump (2015) that preferences on redistribution "to" and redistribution "from" are distinct attitudinal dimensions. Resolving the conflict between competing predictions that views on redistribution are the product of either material self-interest *or* affinity with a policy's beneficiaries, these authors demonstrate that these concerns can exist simultaneously within a given individual's redistributive preferences.

Similar logic can help us understand affirmative action as redistribution both "from" White people and "to" Black people. Perceptions of BRS should be most pertinent to the "from" dimension: defensiveness over White Americans' own position should exacerbate opposition to affirmative action if Black people are perceived to pose a threat to White status. The "to" dimension of affirmative action preferences, on the other hand, would concern evaluations of Black Americans' deservingness as beneficiaries. Such evaluations would likely be influenced by a White individual's level of racial resentment, in keeping with White people's aversion to redistributing resources or opportunities to low-income Black communities characterized as undeserving of support. My aim in investigating the "to" dimension of affirmative action preferences, however, is to better understand the operation of a status threat response. *Under what circumstances* is perceiving a status threat most influential of White people's affirmative action preferences? My conjecture is that White people's status perceptions will be a second-order concern, revealing their effect after concerns about deservingness are minimized.

I test this conjecture by returning to my focus on material conditions in White people's local geography. On the grounds that low-status Black communities are likely to be deemed less deserving of support, I expect that White people living in proximity to these communities will be less likely to support affirmative action's distribution of employment opportunities to Black people. Correspondingly, White people living in proximity to higher-status Black communities should be more amenable to affirmative action, all else equal, on the grounds that nonpoor Black people are more likely to be deemed "respectable."[20]

For an example of this perspective, consider the reflections of a White resident of Baton Rouge who explained to me why Zachary, LA, a city within East Baton Rouge Parish known for having more middle-income Black residents, was different from a poorer majority-Black area:

> This area right here *(pointing to Zachary on a map)* is a predominantly African-American area—but it's not affluent at all. In fact the houses right there look a whole lot like the houses right over here *(pointing to North Baton Rouge)* on Chippewa St., okay? But the difference is most of these parents work. They may not make a hundred thousand a year, but they care about the community, they care about the schools, and they care about the kids getting good education. And most of these houses and these families, the kids stay at home with their parents, okay? I think that's the difference.

This respondent reveals his view that Black parents in Zachary are more "respectable" than those in North Baton Rouge (who are implied *not* to care about their community, schools, or children's education—as we saw in Chapter 3). If the average White person were to have only the image of the Black people who live on Chippewa St. in mind—a lower-income and often presumed to be "undeserving" Black community—it is unlikely this average White person would support distributing employment opportunities away from White Americans and to this group. By contrast, in a place with Black residents more similar to those in Zachary, we would expect a greater divergence between White people who feel their status is secure and those who feel it is insecure. White people who do not perceive a status threat from Black people would be considerably more supportive of distributing opportunities to the "respectable" Black community than White people who do perceive a status threat. These expectations are summarized in my final hypothesis.

- **Affirmative action hypothesis 2:**
  - In settings where the median Black income is low (and Black people are likely to be deemed "undeserving"), White people who feel their status over Black people is secure will nonetheless express similar opposition to affirmative action as White people who feel their status is insecure.
  - In settings where the median Black income is high (and Black people are likely to be deemed "respectable"), there will be a greater polarization in affirmative action preferences between White people who feel their status is secure, and White people who feel their status is insecure.

As authors ranging from Douglass to Wilson suggest, the primary hurdle to clear may be lifting the absolute status of Black Americans, bringing with it the benefit of dismantling racial stereotypes among White Americans. Yet, the theory presented in this chapter emphasizes the secondary hurdle beyond that if Black people's rising status *relative* to White people is seen to pose a new threat to White Americans' economic privilege, thus making even racially progressive White people less supportive of initiatives to close the gulf between the races.

Identifying Two Dimensions of Affirmative Action Preferences

In this section, I put my hypotheses to the test by showing how affirmative action can be understood as redistribution *from* White Americans that will draw greater opposition among White people who feel their status is less secure. I then discuss affirmative action as redistribution *to* Black Americans, and show that perceiving a status threat only comes into play as a significant consideration in settings where Black people are likely to be considered deserving beneficiaries of affirmative action in the first place.

Measuring opinion on affirmative action

The GSS surveys attitudes on affirmative action with the following question:

> Some people say that because of past discrimination, Blacks should be given preference in hiring and promotion. Others say that such preference in hiring and promotion of Blacks is wrong because it discriminates against Whites. What about your opinion—are you for or against preferential hiring and promotion of Blacks?

Responses to this question tend to be negative: 55–60% of White GSS respondents strongly oppose affirmative action in each wave of the panel, with 25–30% opposing and only 12–15% either supporting or strongly supporting it. For comparison, the ANES uses the same phrasing and finds similar opposition among White respondents. This widespread opposition is unsurprising given the aforementioned findings that the use of the language of "preferences" to describe affirmative action is more polarizing than "making extra effort" to hire and promote Black people.

In my analysis, I retain the categorical coding of the original variable (ranging from strong opposition = 4 to strong support = 1) to capture variation in both the strength and direction of a White respondent's views on affirmative action. I also create a binary version of the outcome variable (oppose = 1), which allows me to run a second iteration of my analysis including fixed effects for each White individual, adding confidence to my interpretation of the relationship between attitudes and contexts.

Empirical models

I use logistic models to estimate the probability of a White individual holding a particular stance on affirmative action, reporting robust standard errors in all cases. When modeling affirmative action preferences, I incorporate individual-level fixed effects. This allows me to analyze how variation in perceptions of BRS within a given individual is related to that person's views on affirmative action—thus accounting for unobserved variables at the individual level. I report the results of my fixed effects analysis along with random effects models, as both approaches offer insight: it is one thing to examine the effect of variation in one individual's attitudes or surroundings, and another to compare how particular attitudes or surroundings shape different individuals' political opinions. If I find significant effects of perceptions of BRS on affirmative action preferences not only between White people but also within a given White person, I can argue with greater confidence for the role status perceptions play in predicting White policy preferences.

Affirmative action as redistribution "from" White people

I first confirm that racial resentment is a more relevant measure of racial animus than the laziness stereotype in predicting opposition to affirmative action (Models 1 and 2 in Table 5.8). Model 3 next demonstrates that the perceptions of BRS variable is a significant predictor of affirmative action alongside partisanship and racial resentment. It remains significant when I control for individual-level fixed effects in Model 4, a linear probability model using a binary coding of the outcome variable (oppose affirmative action = 1, support affirmative action = 0).[21]

The status perceptions variable is the only predictor that remains significant in the fixed effects model, indicating that variation in a White individual's perceptions of BRS over the course of the panel is predictive of that individual's affirmative action views.[22] I further confirm that it is perceptions of *relative* status that predict affirmative action preferences: whether a White individual thinks Black people are rich or poor is insignificant (Model 5) if we do not account for where that individual also ranks White people (as in Models 3 and 4). These findings offer compelling support for *affirmative action hypothesis 1*.

Table 5.8 Individual-Level Predictors of White Affirmative Action Preferences

Opposition to AA	(1) Random Effects	(2) Random Effects	(3) Random Effects	(4) Fixed Effects	(5) Random Effects
Laziness Stereotype	1.101 (0.089)				
Racial Resentment		1.566*** (0.065)	1.559*** (0.064)	1.007 (0.006)	1.562*** (0.065)
Perceptions of BRS			1.182** (0.093)	1.029*** (0.010)	
Perceptions of Black Absolute Status					1.140 (0.102)
Independent	1.870** (0.530)	1.655* (0.472)	1.575 (0.450)	0.949 (0.039)	1.597 (0.456)
Republican	3.804*** (0.824)	2.642*** (0.557)	2.662*** (0.564)	0.997 (0.042)	2.647*** (0.560)
Constant				3.268*** (0.790)	
Cut 1	0.00939*** (0.008)	0.138*** (0.097)	0.296 (0.226)		0.247* (0.191)
Cut 2	0.0473*** (0.038)	0.706 (0.487)	1.515 (1.144)		1.259 (0.960)
Cut 3	0.703 (0.556)	10.58*** (7.282)	22.69*** (17.256)		18.74*** (14.356)
Observations	1492	1396	1389	1389	1389
Log likelihood	−1369.7	−1216.0	−1205.7	573.6	−1206.9
Adj. R-squared				0.0200	

Exponentiated coefficients; standard errors in parentheses; party base category is Democrat.

Table reports odds ratios from random-effects–ordered logistic regression of White affirmative action preferences, with the exception of Model 3, which reports exponentiated coefficients from a linear probability model including fixed effects.

For concision, controls for age, gender, marital status, and income are not displayed.

Source: 2006–2010 General Social Survey.

* $p < 0.10$, ** $p < 0.05$, *** $p < 0.01$.

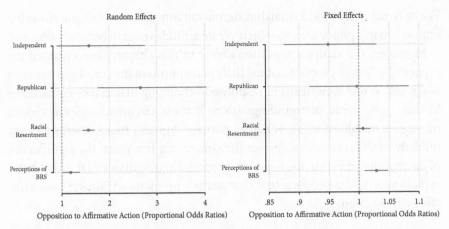

Fig. 5.7 Visualizing Effects of Status Perceptions on White Affirmative Action Preferences

Figure on left illustrates results of Model 3 in Table 5.8. Figure on right illustrates results of Model 4 in Table 5.8. Horizontal lines represent 95% confidence intervals; the vertical dotted line represents an odds ratio of 1 (which would indicate that a predictor variable has no effect on the odds of opposition to affirmative action). Although perceptions of BRS have a smaller effect than the other variables (i.e., with associated odds ratios closer to 1), they are a statistically significant predictor of White opposition to affirmative action in both the random and fixed effects models, as neither confidence interval crosses 1. *Source:* 2006–2010 General Social Survey (*n* = 1,389).

The implications of Model 1 are best understood in terms of predicted probabilities, which also help keep the effects of perceptions of BRS in perspective. A standard deviation increase in racial resentment (2.37) predicts an approximately 16 percentage-point increase in the likelihood that a White respondent strongly opposes affirmative action, holding all other variables at their means. Comparing a White Democrat to a White Republican predicts a 14 percentage-point increase in the same likelihood. By contrast, an increase in perceptions of BRS of one standard deviation (1.05) represents an approximately 2.5 percentage-point increase in the likelihood of strong opposition. Figure 5.7 visually compares these effect sizes. The degree to which a White individual perceives a status threat clearly does not outweigh the effects of partisanship and racial attitudes. However, given the typical focus on the latter two variables in discussing affirmative action preferences, it is valuable to appreciate a previously unrecognized predictive factor.

Ultimately, this analysis does not seek to offer a new primary explanation for why White people oppose affirmative action. It instead expands a group position framework and offers evidence for the operation of White people's racial group interests on economic grounds, irrespective of their racial attitudes. I reveal that a descriptive (rather than normative) evaluation—White people's perceptions of the economic distance between Black and

White Americans—has a small but significant influence in raising or lowering opposition in a policy area on which White attitudes tend to be firmly decided.

Moreover, the analysis presented earlier in this chapter demonstrated the capacity for White people to adjust their perceptions of the status gap between Black and White Americans in response to changing material circumstances in their geographic surroundings (even if these circumstances are viewed through a racialized lens). Whereas partisanship and racial resentment are unlikely to shift considerably over the course of a few years, the significance of perceptions of BRS in the fixed effects model highlights a variable that helps explain why White people might change their opinions on "sticky" issues like affirmative action.

Affirmative action as redistribution "to" Black people

I have argued that perceptions of BRS affect views on affirmative action by virtue of signaling the relative security or insecurity of White Americans' economic position—a consideration distinct from the deservingness of Black beneficiaries. My final analyses interrogate my conjecture that perceiving a geographic-based status threat will impact affirmative action views in settings where White people are not already predisposed to oppose redistributing employment opportunities to a local Black community that is perceived to be undeserving. I test *affirmative action hypothesis 2* in two steps.

The first step is to demonstrate the significance of an MSA's Black median household income in predicting variation in affirmative action views held by White residents—reported in Model 1 in Table 5.9. In Model 2, Black median household income remains marginally significant ($p < 0.10$) when incorporating individual fixed effects. Note that these models also control for the MSA's Black population share. Although this variable itself was a predictor of perceptions of BRS, I judge it appropriate to include because it has a relatively small effect in predicting BRS, proves not to be a significant predictor of affirmative action views, and allows for comparison among White respondents with similar lived experiences of racial diversity.

In Model 3 of Table 5.9, I further demonstrate that the predictive power of Black income does not merely reflect lower opposition to affirmative action in settings where White people themselves have higher incomes. Model 3 finds that an MSA's median White household income, although correlated to the median Black income at 0.71, is not on its own predictive of affirmative action views. This finding supports my conceptualization of Black median household income as a proxy for the extent to which a Black population will be seen as lower-status and thus less deserving, as opposed to appearing

Table 5.9 White Affirmative Action Preferences in Context

Opposition to AA	(1) Random Effects	(2) Random Effects	(3) Random Effects	(4) Fixed Effects
Contextual Variables				
Percent Black (log)	0.962	1.015	0.942	0.966
	(0.102)	(0.055)	(0.087)	(0.103)
Black Med. Household	0.981**	0.998*		0.912***
Income (thousands)	(0.008)	(0.001)		(0.027)
White Med. Household			0.995	
Income (thousands)			(0.008)	
Perceptions of BRS				1.019**
× Med. Black Income				(0.008)
Individual-Level Variables				
Perceptions of BRS	1.230**	1.033***	1.186**	0.592*
	(0.101)	(0.011)	(0.093)	(0.175)
Racial Resentment	1.573***	1.007	1.557***	1.590***
	(0.067)	(0.007)	(0.065)	(0.069)
Independent	1.719*	0.965	1.582	1.714*
	(0.518)	(0.033)	(0.454)	(0.517)
Republican	2.435***	1.035	2.654***	2.456***
	(0.527)	(0.042)	(0.564)	(0.533)
Observations	1279	1279	1389	1279
Log likelihood	−1113.5		−1205.0	−1110.2
Adj. R-squared		0.5987		

Exponentiated coefficients; standard errors in parentheses; party base category is Democrat.

Table reports odds ratios from random-effects ordered logistic regression of White affirmative action preferences, with the exception of Model 2, which reports exponentiated coefficients from a linear probability model including fixed effects.

For concision, controls for age, gender, marital status, and income are not displayed.

Source: 2006–2010 General Social Survey.

* $p < 0.10$, ** $p < 0.05$, *** $p < 0.01$.

more "respectable." My findings therefore show that White people are more supportive of affirmative action in MSAs where they are less likely to see images associated with negative conceptions of Black people as undeserving beneficiaries.

As in my individual-level models of affirmative action preferences, the effect I identify upon adding context explains only a small amount of variation in affirmative action views. For a standard deviation change in median Black household income ($11,000)—or, comparing otherwise identical individuals who live in MSAs where median Black income is either $30,000 or $41,000—the difference in one's probability of strongly opposing affirmative action is only about 3 percentage points. However, I go on to investigate whether the predictive power of Black median income offers the potential to identify the settings in which perceptions of BRS are most relevant to views on affirmative action.

The greater significance of perceiving a status threat as Black incomes increase

The final model in Table 5.9 poses an interaction between a White individual's perceptions of BRS and the Black median household income in that person's surroundings. The interaction proves significant ($p < 0.05$) and is visualized in Figure 5.8. We know that most White people oppose affirmative action. In settings where Black households are lower-income in absolute terms, it is unlikely that White people will reduce their opposition to affirmative action even if they do not perceive Black Americans to be encroaching on White Americans in economic standing.

But, if the stigma of Black poverty in one's local surroundings is minimal, then whether or not a White individual perceives a status threat will be more influential. Accordingly, White respondents with low perceptions of BRS (who think Black people do not pose a status threat) are more supportive of affirmative action in settings with higher Black incomes.

The interaction term also implies that White people with high perceptions of BRS (who think Black people pose a status threat) are even more likely to oppose affirmative action in high Black income settings, perhaps seeing Black people's absolute status in their surroundings as confirmation of the perception that Black people are relatively well off compared to White people. However, the interaction effect is driven primarily by those who think Black people are poor relative to White people, as illustrated by Figure 5.8. Predicted probabilities indicate that a White individual placed at 3 on the perceptions of BRS scale, holding the other variables at their means, has an approximately 10 percentage-point decrease in the probability of strongly opposing affirmative action as Black household income increases from $30,000 to $50,000. A White person placed at 5 on the perceptions of BRS scale, on the other hand, has only about a 1 percentage-point increase in the probability of strong opposition across the same range of Black income (a difference that is not statistically significant).

It could be the case that White people who are less opposed to affirmative action select into metropolitan areas where Black incomes are higher. These could be areas that are higher-status in general, raising the possibility that it is simply in higher-status settings that White opposition to racial policies is

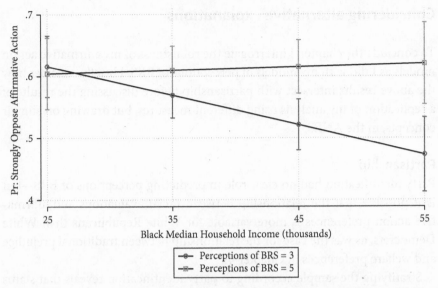

Fig. 5.8 White Affirmative Action Views in Areas with Low- versus. High-Status Black Populations

Figure illustrates interaction between a White individual's perceptions of BRS and the median Black household income in that individual's MSA (Model 4 in Table 5.9). On the left-hand side, where Black incomes are lower, there is little difference in affirmative action opinion among White respondents. As Black incomes increase, however, White respondents' affirmative action views diverge according to whether or not they believe Black people pose a status threat. *Source:* 2006–2010 General Social Survey (n = 1,279).

reduced (in line with some previous studies, e.g., Branton and Jones 2005; Oliver and Mendelberg 2000). However, neither having a higher income oneself nor living in an MSA with a higher median White household income is predictive of views on affirmative action, meaning that White people who favor affirmative action would have to select MSAs based on Black income for self-selection to bias my results. It seems unlikely that this is the case. What could instead be at play, however, is that White people who are less opposed to affirmative action select into more *integrated* metropolitan areas—where the negative effects of segregation have been minimized and Black incomes are higher as a result.

Although it is hard to eliminate the possible influence of self-selection, the fact that median Black income remains a moderately significant predictor of affirmative action views when individual-level fixed effects are included adds more confidence to my argument. Opposition to affirmative action is attenuated among White people who believe that Black people do not pose a status threat *and* who live near higher-income Black people—with the latter condition being necessary for status perceptions to be influential.

Considering alternative explanations

To conclude the chapter, I interrogate the robustness of my affirmative action models as I did with my models of perceptions of BRS. I briefly consider how the above results intersect with partisanship before discussing the results of a replication of my analysis using different measures, but drawing on similar concepts, in the ANES.

Partisanship

Party identification had no clear role in predicting perceptions of BRS—but is it possible that the relationship between racial evaluations and affirmative action preferences is more variable for White Republicans than White Democrats, as was the case for the relationship between traditional prejudice and welfare preferences in Chapter 4?

Stratifying the sample according to party identification reveals that status perceptions do indeed have a stronger effect on affirmative action views among White Republicans, who are typically associated with the firmest opposition to affirmative action. Revisiting Model 3 as reported in Table 5.8 but stratifying the sample by party reveals a greater significance and slightly steeper slope of the relationship between White Republicans' perceptions of BRS and their affirmative action preferences. The linear model predicts a 3.6 percentage-point change in the probability of opposing affirmative action for a change of 1 point on the perceptions of BRS scale among Republicans, compared to a 2.3 percentage-point change in the probability of opposing affirmative action among Democrats for the equivalent shift in perceptions of BRS.

These findings resonate with Taber and Lodge's (2006, 756) argument that people who feel strongest about an issue are most susceptible to strengthening their position on that issue "in ways not warranted by the evidence." High unemployment rates do not warrant an increased evaluation of Black people's economic status, but this response nonetheless goes on to predict greater opposition to affirmative action, particularly among White Republicans.

Replication with the ANES: The relative influence of Black people in politics

A final test of the arguments presented in this chapter comes from the replication of my analysis using data from the 2016 ANES. I take advantage of a set of questions on the ANES that ask respondents about how much influence Black people and White people have in American politics. Perceptions of a group's political influence obviously diverge from this chapter's central focus on economic status. A key distinction is that the GSS asks whether a group *is* rich or poor, whereas the ANES asks how much influence a group *should* have in politics (based on whether a group currently has too much, the right amount, or too little influence).

While keeping this difference in mind, there is a more fundamental similarity between political influence and economic status: both reflect the *power* a racial group wields in society. An analysis of perceptions of Black influence therefore offers another way to conceptualize White understandings of the security of their powerful position—and how these perceptions affect views on affirmative action.

Because the 2016 ANES surveys opinion about race-conscious university admissions, I shift focus to affirmative action in education. Accordingly, I limit my analysis to how perceptions of Black influence vary across racial contexts, rather than economic contexts. All the same: much like I conceptualized a perceived "status gap" between the races, we can think about a perceived "influence gap." White people who see a smaller influence gap between White and Black Americans are those likely to feel that White people's position is less secure (for more details on my construction of a relative influence measure, see Appendix B).

My contextualized analysis of White perceptions of Black influence shows that, all else equal, White people who live in places where race is more salient are more likely to think Black people have too much influence. As was the case earlier in the chapter, this is not a surprising finding: group size is one factor that can lead to greater political influence. However, there is also an element of subjectivity at play. For one, there are limits to the translation of minority group size into political power. Consider findings that lenient voter registration laws, often thought to amplify the voice of minority voters, in fact tend to amplify the voices of groups that are already advantaged (Matsubayashi and Rocha 2012). Moreover, the ANES asks about racial groups' "influence in U.S. politics," a phrasing that emphasizes the power a group exerts at the national level. In keeping with the principle that we draw on our proximate surroundings to form opinions about national-level issues, it is not surprising for White people to judge Black people's *national* influence in part based on the *local* presence of Black people. All the same, such behavior shows that the link between local group size and perceptions of national group influence is by no means clear-cut.

Note that, following my procedure from earlier in this chapter, I also control for the Black laziness stereotype when predicting perceptions of Black influence and find this variable to be significant. A White person who thinks

Table 5.10 White Perceptions of Black Political Influence: ANES Replication

Perceptions of Black Relative Influence	(1) Congressional District	(2) State
District Percent Black (Log)	1.083* (0.046)	
State Percent Black (Log)		1.206*** (0.064)
Laziness Stereotype	1.112*** (0.021)	1.108*** (0.019)
Independent	4.087*** (0.591)	4.081*** (0.560)
Republican	6.175*** (0.653)	6.163*** (0.584)
Age	1.011*** (0.002)	1.010*** (0.002)
Gender	1.121 (0.093)	1.120 (0.098)
Marital Status	0.986 (0.084)	0.984 (0.094)
Education	0.903*** (0.020)	0.903*** (0.023)
Income	0.992 (0.007)	0.993 (0.008)
Cut 1	1.535 (0.494)	1.964** (0.668)
Cut 2	34.26*** (11.253)	44.27*** (15.202)
Observations	2437	2437
p	2.83e84	2.85e121
Log likelihood	−2009.6	−2004.5

Exponentiated coefficients; standard errors in parentheses.

Table reports results of ordered logistic regression of White perceptions of Black Americans' relative influence in U.S. politics.

Party base category is Democrat.

Source: 2016 ANES Time Series Study.

* $p < 0.10$, ** $p < 0.05$, *** $p < 0.01$.

Black people are lazy may be more likely to think Black people also exert too much influence, even if that influence is minimal. The one other individual variable of note is education, which is associated with lower evaluations of Black influence. This matches my findings earlier in the chapter, suggesting that education brings awareness of true racial disparities, whether in terms of political power or economic capital.

Table 5.10 summarizes these results, supporting my core finding that White people who live in places where race is locally salient believe that Black people are more nationally influential. Although this finding holds with some significance in high-density Black congressional districts (the most granular geographies available in the ANES public data), the effect is most significant when taking account of the racial makeup of a White respondent's state. This finding makes sense given that someone in a low-density Black congressional district but high-density Black state would still be exposed to state-level racial politics in local media coverage. Moreover, the racial gerrymandering of districts means that, more so than MSA boundaries, congressional district lines may be artificial reflections of the salience of race in a given geographic container.

Next, do White perceptions of Black influence, as perceptions of Black economic status did, go on to predict White opinion on affirmative action, as a policy approach that seeks to address racial disparities? As mentioned above, the 2016 ANES surveys opinion on affirmative action in university admissions, which I operationalize by creating a binary variable measuring whether or no respondents oppose the consideration of race in admissions (1 = oppose, 0 = neutral or support). As a proxy for racial resentment, I use the question asking whether Black people should "work their way up" without "special favors."

The results of binary logistic regression show that believing Black people relatively influential predicts a greater likelihood of opposing affirmative action, all else equal. It mirrors the trend in the GSS panel of White people who perceive a smaller gap between Black and White Americans in economic status being more likely to oppose affirmative action, but the ANES further offers new insight into a key distinction. As illustrated in Figure 5.9, the jump occurs between White people who recognize only a small advantage for their group and White people who see their group as much more influential than Black people. As illustrated in Figure 5.9, White people in the latter category (at the far right of the graph) stand out as the most likely to support affirmative action.

In short, Figure 5.9 reveals that one indicator of whether White people will oppose affirmative action in higher education is whether they believe White Americans have considerably more political influence than Black Americans. White people who believe not only that Black people are disadvantaged *but also that White people are excessively advantaged* are the most likely to support race-targeted policies. When holding other variables at their means, there is a 14 percentage-point difference between a White Democrat and White Republican in the likelihood of opposing affirmative action. There is nearly as large a difference—12 percentage points—between a respondent who sees White people as much more influential in national politics than Black people, and one who sees White people as only slightly more influential.

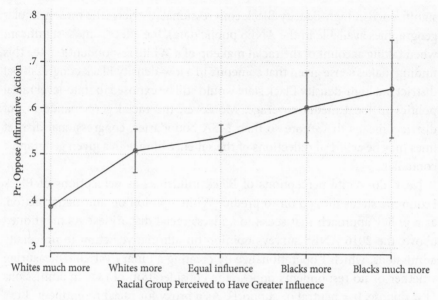

Fig. 5.9 White Opposition to Affirmative Action as Perceptions of Black Influence Increase

Figure visualizes relationship between White perceptions of Black Americans' relative influence (when coded as a categorical variable) and the probability of White opposition to affirmative action. *Source:* 2016 ANES Time Series Study ($n = 2,435$).

I have acknowledged the factors that differentiate my analysis of the ANES and GSS. In particular, believing that Black people have more influence in politics (albeit at the national level, per the ANES question's framing) may be a more logical conclusion to draw from greater exposure to a nearby Black population than the conclusion that Black people are richer relative to White people. The belief that Black people have "too much" power also is liable to blur with racial resentment, which I have shown is not the case with status perceptions. Nonetheless, my findings with perceptions of Black influence across racial contexts lend support to my conceptualization of status perceptions as a proxy for the perceived security of White Americans' position of relative privilege and power over Black Americans. This study of the ANES therefore further emphasizes the benefits of an approach that centers White people's defensiveness of their group position along with their subjective vantage point in explaining White opposition to racial policies. Finally, in revealing nuance among White people who characterize their racial group as either strongly politically advantaged or only minimally so, my analysis indicates the importance of not just whether but also the *degree* to which White people recognize their racial privilege.

Table 5.11 A Matrix of Status Threat × Local Black Income

| | | Black Household Income
(Absolute Status of Black Households) | |
		Low	High
Status Threat *(Perceived Relative Black Status)*	Low	ex: Twin Cities, MN	ex: San Jose, CA
	High	ex: Baton Rouge, LA	ex: Washington, DC

This table illustrates possible combinations of (a) the status threat a White individual perceives, predicted by both individual-level and contextual factors; and (b) the Black household income in that White individual's surroundings. White people who fall into the top right quadrant would be most likely to lower their opposition to affirmative action, seeing Black people as deserving beneficiaries who do not pose a threat to White people's status.

Conclusion to Chapter 5

The analysis presented in this chapter has suggested two seemingly contradictory consequences associated with Black economic advancement. On the one hand, my analysis supports the conventional expectation that improvements in Black Americans' *absolute* status will fight the image of Black people as undeserving beneficiaries. On the other hand, my findings indicate that improvements in Black Americans' economic status *relative* to White Americans' status will heighten the status threat posed by Black people, and thus increase White opposition to affirmative action. The subjective dimension of this threat becomes clear when we appreciate that, while White perceptions of BRS reflect the true Black–White income disparity in a given metropolitan area, they are also predicted by the local salience of race and local economic insecurity as perceived by White viewers.

Taken together, my findings suggest that White opposition to affirmative action is minimized in settings that fall into the top right quadrant in Table 5.11. This would be a metropolitan area where a Black community is seen as "respectable" by virtue of being higher-status in absolute terms, but also where White people's advantage over Black people feels secure: either because White incomes are considerably higher than Black incomes, the Black community is not too large, or economic anxiety is not too high.

One example of a setting that would fall into the top right quadrant as of 2010 (the end of the GSS panel) is the San Jose-Sunnyvale-Santa Clara, CA, metropolitan area, where Black residents make up only 3.2% of the population and have a median household income around $55,300—above the national median income, but considerably lower than the White median household income in San Jose of $94,700.[23] In the San Jose area, the minimal salience of the Black population combined with the nearly $40,000 gap between Black and White incomes would make White residents in this setting unlikely to perceive a status threat from Black people. In tandem with the likelihood that these White people would view the small local Black community as a relatively "respectable" and affluent one, White San Jose residents would be less likely to oppose affirmative action than their counterparts in an MSA that has a larger and poorer Black population, or an MSA where White residents have a less comfortable advantage over Black residents. Granted, White residents would likely have perceived a narrowing status gap as San Jose moved from an unemployment rate of 4.5% in 2006 to 10.4% in 2010. White residents would therefore have been more likely to oppose affirmative action in 2010 than they were in 2006.

We could also compare San Jose to a place like the Washington, DC, metropolitan area, which in 2010 had a similar Black–White income gap at around $40,000, and even more affluence among its Black and White populations (with a median White household income of just over $102,000 and a median Black household income of $61,800). But Washington is home to a larger Black population—27.3% of its population. In a place where race is considerably more salient, White Washington residents would be more likely than White people in San Jose to perceive a small status gap between Black and White Americans, edging Washington toward the bottom right quadrant of Table 5.11. White Washington residents would thus be more likely to oppose affirmative action than White people in San Jose. At the same time, a smaller increase in unemployment in Washington between 2006 and 2010 would likely not have exacerbated the perception of a status threat over the recession, as would have been the case in San Jose.

A third example comes from comparing Washington to a place like the metropolitan area around Minneapolis and St. Paul, MN (the Twin Cities). The income disparity between White and Black people in this area in 2010 was large, around $40,000. But the median White household income was $69,800, compared to a median Black household income of $29,000. The area's Black population is smaller than in Washington, at only 8.7%, meaning White people in the Twin Cities are likely to be less aware of the local Black population. The Twin Cities also saw a smaller increase in unemployment than San Jose between 2006 and 2010. While these factors may make White Twin Cites residents less likely to perceive a status threat from Black people, the Black population in their surroundings also is of low economic status in absolute terms, with a median income falling into the bottom quartile nationwide. Thus, the Twin Cities would fall into the top left quadrant in Table 5.11. Even the White Twin Cities residents who do not perceive a status threat from Black people would be unlikely to support affirmative action, in contrast to their White counterparts in cities where images of "undeserving," low-status Black people are less salient.

What might have happened in Baton Rouge during this time? With an income disparity of around $30,000 between White and Black residents, White residents likely would have perceived a smaller status gap than their counterparts in San Jose, Washington, or the Twin Cities. White residents would further be likely to sense a status threat thanks to the Baton Rouge area's large Black population share (35.7% in 2010), making race more salient. Unemployment also went from 4.3% in 2006 to 7.7% in 2010, which likely made White residents feel their status was even more precarious. On top of it all, Black Baton Rougeans' overall low economic status in absolute terms, with a median household income around $31,800, would make White people in Baton Rouge, as in the Twin Cities, likely to oppose affirmative action for "undeserving" Black people. These dynamics would place Baton Rouge in the bottom left quadrant of the table. In other words, with middle-income Black people in Zachary *and* low-income Black people on Chippewa St. salient in the minds of many White Baton Rougeans, it is unlikely many of these White people will see reason to lower their opposition to affirmative action.

Crucially, the above examples are based on my theorization of how local conditions will be *perceived* by White people. This chapter has shown that White people sometimes perceive their surroundings in straightforward ways, evidenced by perceived status gaps tending to reflect the true Black–White income gap in a given MSA. However, this chapter has also demonstrated the power of perception to be deeply racialized. White Americans' racialized perspective is inevitably at play when economic insecurity leads to the perception that Black people caught up to White people over the course of a recession that in fact widened racial disparities.

Ultimately, Chapter 5 offers this book a second application of the racial threat hypothesis that casts White people as viewers. I have used this conceptual shift to highlight White people's capacity to perceive the Black middle class as threatening, showing the relevance of a racialized, White vantage point to how White Americans view the Black poor and nonpoor alike— despite what Brian may have claimed in the opening to this chapter. In the process, this chapter also has expanded beyond the racial threat hypothesis's typical focus on fear, suspicion, or dislike of an outgroup by identifying a threat response rooted in White people's defensiveness of their ingroup's privileged position. By making this argument through a focus on material conditions, my analysis has further demonstrated the potential for a status threat response to operate across the spectrum of White Americans' political ideology and racial attitudes. These findings both have been motivated by and have reaffirmed a core finding of Chapter 3: that White Baton Rougeans most opposed to St. George nonetheless revealed a vantage point similar to that of St. George's strongest supporters.

I have cautioned that perceptions of BRS are surely influenced by sources not identified in this analysis; that the effect of status perceptions on affirmative action preferences is significant, but small; and that this analysis captures geographic variation in attitudes rather than the "effects" of geography. Nonetheless, this chapter envisages a winding road ahead as America makes slow progress in rectifying centuries-old disparities between Black and White Americans.

The results presented here have the potential to inform that path: for example, greater civic education about the extent to which Black people remain disadvantaged compared to White people might dampen policy opposition motivated by beliefs to the contrary. This sort of knowledge of racial disparities has been a key motivator for many White people working to fight racial inequality in Baton Rouge, not to mention for White people around the country who have increasingly become more aware of the injustices of police violence and brutality toward Black Americans. All the same—we should continue to expect defensiveness from White people as they see their racial privilege dissipate.

6

Visibility and Responsibility

> Irresponsibility is part of invisibility; any way you face it, it is a denial....Responsibility rests upon recognition.
>
> —Ralph Ellison (1952)

> We are all always awash in each other's lives, and for most of us that shared life, recorded as history, will be the only artifact we leave behind.
>
> —Danielle Allen (2004)

This book has examined the relationship between prejudice and place in contemporary America. It has done so by asking how the material Black–White color line shapes the expression of the metaphorical one—an old question, but one too commonly answered while minimizing the significance of looking at things from one side of the line versus the other. By contrast, I have explicitly theorized White Americans' particular, privileged perspective in the analysis of geography and racial politics. First, I qualitatively identified a shared White vantage point within the specific context of Baton Rouge, emerging in the form of four common discursive practices structuring the views of White residents, even when they were deeply divided over St. George. Then, I brought an appreciation of this vantage point to the more conventional, quantitative study of White opinion across contexts—exploring attitudes on both welfare spending and affirmative action in order to traverse the spectrum of outgroup- and ingroup-oriented discourses that were on display in Baton Rouge. Together, these studies of White attitudes within and across contexts have highlighted the subjectivity of White people's viewpoint and the constraints of White vision, while simultaneously recognizing the diversity of today's attitudinal and material landscape.

I have recognized the inevitability that geographic patterns in White public opinion reflect, in part, local cultures and histories: I have not been identifying the pure "effects" of context. We should be careful not to look to context for causality in the first place without theorizing White people's agency in reading their surroundings in certain ways. But of course, on methodological

How the Color Line Bends: The Geography of White Prejudice in Modern America. Nina M. Yancy,
Oxford University Press. © Oxford University Press 2022. DOI: 10.1093/oso/9780197599426.003.0006

grounds, it is difficult to analytically disentangle the influence of context from the choices people make to live in certain places (or to redefine the boundaries of a contextual container, as was the case in the St. George effort).

All the same, the empirical studies presented here endorse the power of geography to tell us about the different worlds White people inhabit when expressing opinions on issues related to race. Specifically, local geography structures White public opinion by providing a landscape in which certain factors are more or less salient. Whether the Black population share, the local poverty or unemployment rate, or the median incomes of Black and White households—these factors provide contextual information that White people draw on when expressing political preferences. Throughout, my focus on what White people "see" (rather than what "is") in their surroundings has been core to this book's theoretical and empirical contributions.

First, theorizing White Americans' fields of vision underpins my critique of the racial threat hypothesis for its failure to consider the positionality of White people who perceive Black people as threatening—a theoretical oversight that tacitly equates a Black population with a threat. Although White people remain at the center of my analysis (as too often is the case in scholarship on racial politics), I assign White people agency in viewing their surroundings through a racial lens. Local geography might structure what White residents of a given area are likely to see—but this does not excuse White people from responsibility in interpreting those visual cues as threatening (nor does it absolve White America of its complicity in creating and maintaining our segregated geography in the first place). Furthermore, I emphasize that White people's perspective not only is subjective, as is any racial group's, but also is *limited* in the insight it offers White people into the workings of the racial order. Chapters 2 and 3 illuminated both the subjectivity and constraints of the White perspective. The use of similar discursive practices by White Baton Rougeans, ranging from leaders of the St. George effort to its fiercest opponents, showed how White Americans' common racial identity influences their understanding of the world around them—and what they do or do not see from their position atop the racial order. Chapters 4 and 5 offered quantitative evidence to support this insight by highlighting the subjectivity of White people's responses to context. Chapter 4 identified the capacity of segregation to either highlight or hide an MSA's Black or poor population; and Chapter 5 identified the propensity of rising unemployment to make White people think their economic advantage over Black people is narrowing.

Second, theorizing White Americans' fields of vision helps highlight the empirical variation we miss when deferring to the trope of (racist) White people being threatened by (poor) Black people. Besides the implied passivity of White people in this trope, the simplicity it implies is increasingly hard to find in the world today. Baton Rouge offered an example of diversity along both the attitudinal and material color lines—motivating my quantitative investigations of how a Black presence could lead to polarization between racially hostile and tolerant White people (Chapter 4), and of how a Black *middle-class* presence could unite racially hostile and tolerant White people in the defense of their group's privilege (Chapter 5). In both of these investigations, theorizing White viewership is critical. In Chapter 4, conceptualizing White people as diverse viewers through a shared racial lens underpins my identification of unique relationships between the visibility of local demographics and the racial attitudes that inform White welfare preferences. In Chapter 5, a focus on White viewership is central to understanding how White people could perceive a threat in the form of rising Black economic status during a recession that ravaged Black economic fortunes.

The findings I have summarized offer reason for optimism and pessimism alike. This is perhaps epitomized in the promise of moving racially tolerant White people to action, contrasted with the persistence of a constrained White perspective even among this group. White Baton Rouge residents like Elizabeth, Deborah, Tammy, and Fred stand out for their commitment to fighting issues related to racial inequality. Yet, they still find ways to evade or soften the idea that White people can be racist ("racism is only possible institutionally"); they see antiracism as a positive *White* attribute and center themselves in their activism ("it's like a drug"); and they assume that they can (and do) "understand" Black people's experiences, and that this is the primary mechanism for achieving racial equity. To be clear—Baton Rouge undoubtedly *would* be a more equitable place were more White people to think and act as these individuals do. But appreciating the limitations of White vision even at this far end of the spectrum reminds us of the reach of the White vantage point across a range of racial attitudes. This reach was evident in Chapter 4, when both racially hostile and tolerant White individuals' welfare preferences were responsive to the salience of a nearby Black or poor population, albeit in different directions. This reach also was evident in Chapter 5, when both racially hostile and tolerant White individuals sensed a status threat from their Black neighbors, and adjusted their affirmative action preferences accordingly.

Ultimately, the diversity of behavior within White Americans' nonetheless shared positionality is a manifestation, I suggest, of the flexibility of the color line. In referencing the capacity of the color line to bend, I recall a line from St. Clair Drake and Horace Cayton's (1945, 101) classic *Black Metropolis*. "The color-line is not static; it bends and buckles and sometimes breaks." Often only this much of the quote is cited, but the authors continue: "This process results in tension; but the very existence of the tension—and even of the violence that sometimes results—is evidence of democracy at work." Optimism and pessimism aside, then: any study of the color line is a study of democracy at work; a study of our politics and society grappling with the full inclusion of the Black American; and thus a study of "the most obvious test" our democracy faces (Ellison 1970, 110).

From Racial Threat to White Vision and Visibility

It is worth remembering that V. O. Key (1949) had identified *fear* as what drove White residents of Black-belt states to work harder to suppress the Black vote, despite the fact that Black people were broadly disenfranchised at the time and thus presented little realistic threat. This line of thinking is not lost entirely in the research that followed Key—but neither is it emphasized. Acharya, Blackwell, and Sen (2018) thus fairly criticize scholars for defining the term "racial threat" as the effect of a Black population share, rather than appreciating "the cumulative effect of slavery, segregation, and inequality" on White Americans' attitudes, including White people's deep-seated fears (205). Although I continue the investigation of Black population share, I seek to do so with full recognition of the history that Key documented and that Acharya et al. reference. Specifically, I strive to reject the racial threat literature's tendency to reproduce the norms, language, and assumptions of the very phenomena (descended from slavery, segregation, and inequality, as Acharya et al. point out) that it seeks to understand.

This problem is not unique to racial threat. As feminist/queer theorist Sara Ahmed (2004, par. 9) has put it, "[T]he language we think of as critical can easily 'lend itself' to the very techniques of governance we critique." Much racial politics scholarship may not intend to be "critical" in the technical sense of the term. But we nonetheless should be vigilant regarding how power relations govern the terminology we use and the knowledge we produce—and how the scholarly project of understanding White Americans' racialized political behavior can itself both perpetuate and be limited by a Whiteness of perspective.

That Whiteness matters is not a new idea. But as Audre Lorde (1984a, 39) writes, "[T]here are no new ideas. There are only new ways of making them felt." Lorde argues for the importance of feeling and emotion—of subjective experience—in the epistemological value of the perspectives of women of color and other marginalized voices. This value was on display in the reflections of the Black Baton Rouge residents we met in Chapter 3, and in the humor, sadness, cynicism, and anger they evoked. I recognize that this book still has given much more attention to the White perspective than any marginalized one. But I hope that my own perspective, at minimum an underrepresented one in my field, has proved of value in emphasizing that White people's perspective is subjective, limited, and far from neutral, even if this is typically ignored in literature on racial threat. And thus I hope that this book has made Whiteness and its operation "felt" in a new way.

My approach to studying White people's vision is preceded by a rich tradition of Black scholarship about Black Americans' visibility (or invisibility) to White Americans. Yet, this book has been as much about White people's own visibility as about Black people's. After all, to critically examine the vision of the viewers is to point out that *they can be seen, too*. This is at the core of Haraway's (1988, 582) critique of the claim to universal knowledge, when she rejects the "god trick" of seeing everything from nowhere and insists on recognizing a viewer's positionality.

Even more, calling out White viewership both acknowledges one of Black Americans' sad inheritances and defies one of White Americans' habits that dates back to slavery. As hooks (1992, 168) explains: back when White people had total power over the gaze of enslaved Black people, who could receive severe punishment "for appearing to observe the whites they were serving," Black people learned to appear invisible for their own protection. This lesson has had clear staying power, evidenced in examples like the pursuit of political invisibility (i.e., invisibility from the state) by Black Americans who distrust government and fear its capacity for punishment (Rosenthal 2019; see also Cohen 2010). Importantly, enslaved Black people's invisibility also was in the interest of White slaveholders, making it easier for them to dehumanize and oppress Black people. As a result, White people came to believe they were invisible to Black people, too. Again, the staying power of this belief is evident today, particularly in White people's "amazement that black people watch white people with a critical 'ethnographic' gaze" (an amazement that, hooks argues, "is itself an expression of racism"; 167).

Despite the staying power I have noted, the dynamics of invisibility are no doubt evolving ones. In particular, White Americans today arguably are more aware of themselves as being "seen" as well as "seers" (an awareness that can be equally well displayed in aspirations for antiracism as in defiant shows of White supremacy). Yet, the imperative to challenge the god trick of the White gaze remains. Another way to think about the contribution of this book, therefore, is that it has *made White people visible* within the literature on the geography of prejudice, as the perceivers of threats from a subjective and powerful vantage point. This point has been made before, but it is rarely supported through the presentation of empirical evidence on the geographic dimensions of threat.

That I have put forth these ideas as a Black researcher is not irrelevant. Ahmed (2004, par. 2) points out that studies of Whiteness often situate themselves as making what is invisible, visible (see, e.g., Jardina 2019, ch. 2). But for those of us who do not inhabit it, Whiteness has always been visible. For those with the lived experience of being perceived as threatening, it arguably is hard *not* to see the subjectivity of the White perspective in the operation of racial threat. It is hard not to notice when scholars and commentators manage to avoid using the word "White" when talking about racist White people, or when talking about White people in general, for that matter. It is hard not to notice references to "Americans" that clearly do not include you.

Ahmed's critique points back to Lorde's comments above: Ahmed and Lorde together indicate that the task of research on racial politics and White Americans' role in it is not to make Whiteness seen. The task is to make it seen in a new way.[1] That is what this book ultimately has tried to achieve.

Limitations and Extensions

There inevitably have been limitations to the work presented here. For one, I have examined public opinion on three policy areas. As such, I have prioritized breadth over depth in illuminating the consistencies and complexities of the White perspective across local contexts. This multiissue, multimethod approach was motivated by a recognition of the broad reach of the White gaze, and a corresponding effort to illuminate White Americans' racial vantage point from a number of analytic perspectives. However, the unique dynamics identified in each case study invite deeper exploration. There is a longer story to be told about Baton Rouge and St. George, as well as about other places that have grappled with questions related to school desegregation or municipal incorporation (or police killings). Similarly, the relationships discussed in Chapters 4 and 5 should be interrogated in regard to other policy areas and other time periods.

Another obvious limitation of the book is its focus on the Black–White color line in the American context. My findings would be valuably extended to the study of White Americans' relations with other groups. Studies of racial threat among White people in proximity to Latino populations, for example, or in settings with high representation from multiple racial or ethnic groups, would benefit from a greater appreciation of White Americans' agency and subjectivity. Black Americans' experience is not incomparable (even if it does appear to be exceptional); rather, studying it should be seen as part of the larger project of understanding the American racial order (see, e.g., Fox 2012; King 2009).

Mentioning that Black Americans' experience appears exceptional prompts consideration of the idea that the United States is exceptional, too. I trust this book has safely avoided the self-congratulatory tone often associated with American exceptionalism—particularly given that one of the strongest challenges to American exceptionalism comes from scholars citing the hypocrisy of racial exclusion in a nation that considers itself the preeminent liberal democracy (R. M. Smith 1993). In light of the international reach of scholarship on racial threat (e.g., Kaufmann and Harris 2015; Quillian 1995) and scholarship on the consequences of living in diverse settings (e.g., Alesina and Glaeser 2004; McCarty 1993; Mueller and Murrell 1986), similar approaches to mine would valuably be tested in other national contexts, and in light of the power dynamics those contexts present.

A final limitation to revisit here is that—beyond the Black Baton Rouge residents—Black Americans minimally feature as subjects in my research. I have explained the theoretical motivations behind my focus on White opinion, which was further informed by considerations of scope and data availability. As a result, however, my argument for a conception of White subjectivity (rejecting an assumption of White neutrality) has left *Black* subjectivity largely ignored.

This is not a rare occurrence in debates about race. Kevin Quashie sharply points out that,"[a]s an identity, blackness is always supposed to tell us something about race or racism, or about America" (qtd. in Williams 2018). Thus we all too often deny Black people's individuality or inner life. As Patricia Williams (2018) points out, we celebrate the quiet strength of Ruby Bridges for integrating the William Franz Elementary School in 1960, but think little about the trauma the 6-year-old almost certainly suffered as a result. And thus I critiqued White residents of Baton Rouge for engaging little with the perspectives of their Black neighbors, while giving minimal attention to those Black neighbors myself.

In the end, I must recognize my role in reproducing certain norms even as I critique them. I must acknowledge the ongoing nature of the work of challenging one's own assumptions, language, and limitations—the inheritances, in my case, of occupying, surviving, and at times thriving in privileged, White spaces. And I must stress that this book be considered alongside other works that highlight the richness of Black life and more fully acknowledge Black agency, subjectivity, and humanity.[2]

Implications

I conclude by considering some of the implications of this book for political science, for policymakers and places, and for all of us who participate in democracy at work.

For Political Science

The first implication I consider stems directly from my findings regarding the constraints of the White perspective. As of 2010, 86.6% of full-time political science faculty members in the United States were White; 71.4% were men; only 6.1% were Black (APSA Task Force 2011, 41–43). The number of Black women political scientists as of 2010 was an appalling 1.7%, leading commentators to point out the fact that many undergraduates leave college having never been taught by a woman of color (Mershon and Walsh 2016, 462; see also Evans 2007).

I certainly should not minimize the contributions of Black scholars past and present. The numbers also would be different if we were to measure diversity among scholars of race and ethnic politics alone. All the same, the Whiteness of the academy undeniably has consequences for the research that is produced, for the recommendations political scientists offer to policymakers, and for the experiences of students and scholars.

Consider, for example, Charles Mills's (1997, 1) pivotal *The Racial Contract*, which he explicitly positioned as addressing the gap of "most scholarship being written and designed by whites"—a problem necessary to address because they "take their racial privilege so much for granted that they do not even see it as *political*, as a form of domination" (emphasis in original). Thus Mills challenged political theorists' broad dismissal of so-called violations to the social contract, and pointed out these violations in truth upheld the racial one.

Consider, also, Melissa Harris-Lacewell's (2003, 222) critique of research on American racial opinion for coming to the conclusion that "Black people don't matter," and asking the wrong questions as a result. Examples Harris-Lacewell points out include scholars ignoring the sizable share of Black

Americans who do not call for more federal spending or policies to help Black people, or who would prefer an approach more akin to Black nationalism over integration into the White world (see Dawson 2001; see also Kam and Burge 2018 for a recent example challenging the tendency of ignoring Black opinion—conducted by two non-White, women researchers).

Consider, lastly, this book's discussion of my own positionality as a Black researcher, particularly at the end of Chapter 2. How many White students of racial attitudes have been told by a (White) professor their race was a "bug" (i.e., a glitch) in their research, as I was? This offhand comment illustrated pervasive assumptions about White objectivity (e.g., that White people will only reveal the "truth" to a White interviewer), while also hinting at the uphill battle nondominant voices often face in being recognized as legitimate. In that section, I also expressed doubt that my hypothetical White male counterpart would have thought to interrogate the conceptual practices of power within racial politics scholarship in the first place. I made this conjecture based on my counterpart's likely positionality—but I also recognize there is a statistically small chance he would have been taught by or collaborated with many non-male, non-White scholars, which could have helped broaden his perspective.

In short, greater representation of marginalized groups in the academy undoubtedly would diversify the perspectives produced, and not just in the study of race and ethnic politics. There is a clear, continued imperative for universities to act to achieve that representation. The same could be said for public policy organizations, government, media, and other institutions that engage in the production and dissemination of knowledge.

Beyond addressing representation, there is a further imperative to challenge dominant ways of thinking among White members of the academy, and to acknowledge "the phenomenological bases of much empirical social science" (APSA Task Force 2011, 20)—including social science produced and taught by White scholars. Jennifer Mueller (2020, 159), in rejecting the idea that "progressive white people would do differently if only they could know differently," powerfully points out that "in fact, white actors need to 'not-know' in a certain way in order to 'not-do' (i.e., not make different choices)." This is why, Mueller argues, White people pursue racial ignorance—ignorance being "the *twin*...not the opposite of knowledge" (145, citing McGoey 2012, 3; emphasis added). In other words, ignorance and knowledge can be, and often are, pursued hand in hand. Even in the space of knowledge production, therefore, we should be vigilant about what the academy, and the individuals who occupy dominant positions within it, might be committed to not-knowing or not-doing.

For places and policy

A second area of implications regards this book's focus on material conditions. Specifically, this book has explored how material conditions in U.S. metropolitan areas shape the expression of White racial attitudes. Throughout, I have problematized White people's role in (mis)interpreting their surroundings, whether influenced by the racialization of policies, the segregation of cities, or the subjectivity of the privileged White perspective.

Yet, one obvious problem underlying the dynamics I have identified is the material conditions that exist in the first place. This is the problem of intergenerational Black poverty that politicians, pundits, and media pointed to as they stigmatized welfare in relation to the Black poor. It is the problem of longstanding discrimination against Black people that made a remedy like affirmative action necessary. It is the problem of the legalized exclusion of Black people from homeownership and the wealth it could have helped them build. In other words, it is the problem of the material color line. In a country that had better lived up to the promise of Reconstruction, we might not have landed here.

The metaphorical color line is, of course, inextricably interwoven with the material one: another problem underlying my analysis is White racism, whether manifested in lies about the laziness of an entire race or in the willingness to accept Black children in Baton Rouge as collateral damage. Yet, without the resource and power differential that exists between White and Black Americans, what White people thought about Black people would be considerably less consequential. Notice how relatively few studies there are about Black Americans' (or other racial groups') attitudes toward White Americans.

Hence, the findings of this book inevitably support the imperative to dismantle the color line. The strategies for doing so are far greater than I can address here, although my findings do offer some considerations to keep in mind along the way.

First, this book's quantitative studies offer some indications regarding how White people in a given area might respond, positively or negatively, to certain changes in their surroundings. Chapter 4 showed the potential for income desegregation to reduce the visibility of poverty's stigmas in a given metro area—making racially resentful White residents less likely to draw on their racial prejudices when asked about welfare, and thus reducing local White opposition to welfare on racialized grounds. We should celebrate this potential positive attitudinal externality of income desegregation efforts, particularly given the transformative effects for low-income families of all races who are able to move to opportunity (Chetty, Hendren, and Katz 2016; Ludwig et al. 2012; Sharkey 2008; see also Massey et al. 2013). Indeed, my findings regarding income segregation only further motivate the importance of expanding efforts such as the underfunded, federal Section 8 housing voucher program, and ensuring that vouchers enable recipients to secure housing in lower-poverty neighborhoods. On the flip side, Chapter 4 also highlighted the possible negative attitudinal externality among White people of *racial* desegregation, specifically the likelihood that greater exposure to Black people as neighbors would make traditionally prejudiced White residents *more* likely to express racialized opposition to welfare. This finding should serve as a reminder of what policymakers are up against, particularly where traditional prejudice is stronger, rather than any excuse for inaction.

Chapter 5 also highlighted some potential obstacles ahead. Here, my analysis broadly supported the idea that economic prosperity dampens prejudice—but it also more specifically demonstrated how improvements in Black economic status could be seen as threatening by White Americans, who have an interest in preserving their economic advantage. These findings should not lead to the problematic conclusion that policymakers should fight Black poverty without challenging White privilege. Instead, they offer another reminder that the road ahead will be a winding one, and emphasize the importance of challenging the zero-sum mindset that so often constrains debates about race (see McGhee 2021). Remember a critical point from Chapter 5: it was not actual changes in Black economic status but White people's insecurity-fueled *perceptions* of rising Black economic standing that led to greater White opposition to affirmative action.

Appreciating the centrality of perception recalls a point Lippmann (1922) famously made: we all act on the basis of "pictures in our heads" as much as the true "world outside." Those pictures come from somewhere. It was a *choice* by political actors in the late 20th century to focus policy on the de-concentration of poor Black neighborhoods, rather than the existence of all-White neighborhoods—legitimizing the concentration of White affluence and reinforcing the stigma against Black poverty, not to mention destroying the social cohesion of countless Black communities in the process (Fullilove 2016; Hunter et al. 2016). Similarly, it has been a choice by media outlets to present images of Black people that reify their location in the iconic ghetto, and a choice by political actors to subscribe to and build policy around these images (Elijah Anderson 2012; Hancock 2004). Much like Black people have been characterized as threatening to White people, Black neighborhoods have been characterized as threatening and treated as such—for example, by virtue of being disinvested from and discriminatorily policed.

Accordingly, at both the individual and institutional level, we should interrogate the assumptions behind how we describe, navigate, and portray different spaces. The clear disjunction between how people often understand their neighborhoods and what demographers measure (Wong et al. 2012), along with people's common reliance on heuristics when choosing where to live (Krysan and Crowder 2017), indicate that some scope exists for better information sharing and more positive, honest portrayals of neighborhoods. Rothstein (2017, ch. 12) further points out the scope to educate students about our sordid history of segregation, and about the complicity of both government and individual actors within it, in light of the number of history textbooks that promote the fiction that segregation happened on accident. And there is certainly scope for media institutions to address their reproduction of structural biases—an issue powerfully highlighted by both scholars and artists today.[3]

Of course, at the end of the day, the pictures in our heads are not completely detached from the world outside. We must disrupt both the assumption *and* the reality of characteristics often correlated with race. It is one step to tell people about the good things happening in communities that are often stigmatized based on racial makeup alone. It is another step to actively incentivize people to live in a neighborhood where theirs is not the majority race, while also working to ensure that the neighborhood is indeed a desirable place to live (see Krysan and Crowder 2017). In taking that step, we should remember that today's world was built largely through the agency of White actors and institutions, and through direct, aggressive policy. Forgetting this risks perpetuating myths like the one Rothstein (2017, 198) points out regarding segregation: that today's world "can only be reversed by accident, or, in some mysterious way, by changes in people's hearts"—rather than by "equally aggressive policies to desegregate."

For people and politics: Beyond colorblindness and complacency

A final area to consider is this book's implications for how people engage with each other and in our shared politics. Throughout much of the time I was researching this book, commentators were circling around the question of whether we were moving into a new era—in which the dominance of implicit racism and colorblind rhetoric was being cast aside for explicit racism, and for explicit appeals to White racial identity. It no longer seems too soon to tell. We know the presidency of Barack Obama unleashed a resurgence of racism and that these flames were fanned in unprecedented ways by the presidency of Donald Trump. At the same time, we undeniably have seen a shift in White awareness of racial injustice (e.g., Tesler 2020) along with increased attention to phenomena such as White racial sympathy or collective guilt (e.g., Chudy, Piston, and Shipper 2019).

These developments have challenged common understandings of "colorblindness" as a shield for racially hostile attitudes or racially harmful policy positions. In King and Smith's (2005) classic account, the "colorblind" racial policy alliance, as opposed to the "race conscious" alliance, offers an institutional home for many actors who oppose policies intended to help Black people (or who support policies that effectively harm Black people). Also relevant at the individual level, colorblindness often is said to function as a rhetorical strategy to allow White people to avoid sounding racist while still speaking negatively about Black people (Bonilla-Silva 2002).

There have been recent updates or challenges to both accounts. King and Smith (2021), for example, have recently commented on the embrace of White protectionism by Trump as an alternative to a colorblind logic (see also Jardina 2019). Similarly, Mueller's (2020) theory of racial ignorance, which I mentioned previously, directly challenges colorblindness as an explanation for racial cognition at the individual level, placing more emphasis on the intentionality with which White people pursue ignorance in order to protect White dominance.

Both of these recent arguments are consistent with many of the themes in this book. Indeed, during my time in Baton Rouge in 2016, I had noticed that colorblindness seemed more orthogonal to the racism/antiracism spectrum than existing accounts suggested. There were certainly elements of colorblindness in the arguments made for St. George, particularly in the public messaging around it. But in conversation with White supporters of the effort, I encountered willingness to talk about race, attentiveness to what they believed was the "right" way to do so, and occasional support for racially separatist ideas (e.g., in deferring responsibility to Black people for their own challenges). Their speech may have been power-blind, but not colorblind. I have discussed how my findings would have been shaped by key features of my research, such as the salience of race in the interview setting due to both my presence and Baton Rouge's demographics (accompanied by White Southerners' fluency in talking about or around race as needed). With increasing media and political attention given to race in the United States more generally, and the greater salience of race as a result, it seems consistent that increasing numbers of White people are abandoning habits of colorblind speech—whether to express explicit anti-Black animus or simply to "protect" Whiteness in a country so long dominated by it.

The issue weighing on this book somewhat more heavily is what it says about the White Americans who have abandoned colorblindness to express *affinity* for Black Americans or concerns about racism. Indeed, this book has identified the activation of racially tolerant attitudes among White Americans in a number of lights, both qualitatively among the White Baton Rougeans who fought the St. George movement, and quantitatively, particularly in Chapter 4's identification of the amplification of support for welfare spending among racially tolerant White people.

I have warned of the limitations to these findings. I also have been intentional throughout in calling White individuals with low levels of traditional prejudice or racial resentment racially "tolerant," rather than necessarily racially "progressive" or "liberal." These latter terms would imply more active criticism of racial injustice than simply the toleration of difference. To draw on political theorist Wendy Brown's (2008, 15) critique of tolerance: we often praise tolerance as a moral good, while ignoring the history and power relations that produced and sustain the very differences that need to be tolerated. Of course, tolerance is preferable to prejudice. And numerous White individuals in the samples I analyze would likely go beyond tolerance to express more assertive, positive views about Black people and direct criticism of racial injustice. Yet, as my qualitative analysis in Baton Rouge showed, and as my quantitative analysis of affirmative action views in Chapter 5 sought to corroborate, such views can easily coexist with ingroup-oriented feelings of prejudice—a sense of superiority, and a feeling of entitlement.

The wave of sentiments that emerged following George Floyd's murder, specifically the spike in White interest in antiracism, raised some new questions. Besides the question of how this interest might ebb over time, the fundamental question that remains is what will come of it. At one point in June 2020, every title in the top ten of the *New York Times* nonfiction bestseller list was about antiracism. How many were read? Or, as Lauren Michele Jackson (2020, par. 6) has asked, what were all the reading recommendations *for*? (Jackson suggests the recommendations were, of course, for the people asking for them—but also that "the person who has to ask can hardly be trusted in a self-directed course of study.")

Such questions should by no means discourage more White people from starting the work of educating themselves about their unearned privilege and its consequences for Black lives. We need White people—and their political, social, and economic capital—to have much hope of fundamentally reshaping the racial order. It is because we need them that it is important to question where this momentum might take us.

Thus, the last lessons this book might offer concern the possibilities and perils of White antiracism in the dismantling of the racial order. We can see one of the likely perils by returning, at last, back to where the book began: on a hot Wednesday afternoon at LSU in July 2016, when I was attending a vigil for Alton Sterling and the officers who had been killed.

Among the chorus calling for unity and healing at the vigil, one of the White student speakers boldly proclaimed that he had faith in his fellow students to take up this charge. As he put it: "Complacency is not in the LSU student's vocabulary."

To be complacent is to be uncritically or even smugly self-satisfied. I got the sense that the student speaker was using complacency as a synonym for passivity, rather than self-satisfaction—but my initial reaction was nonetheless skepticism. Is "complacent" not the perfect word to describe many White LSU students, as well as many White people in Baton Rouge and the United States more generally?

Complacency may not be the only word, but it points to the real danger of self-congratulation within declarations of antiracism, and the danger of confusing declarations of antiracism with antiracism itself. Ahmed (2004, par. 12) reminds us that "declaring whiteness, or even 'admitting' to one's own racism, when the declaration is assumed to be 'evidence' of an antiracist commitment, does not do what it says." In other words, declaring oneself antiracist is not the same thing as being antiracist. Ignoring this fact can easily lead to congratulating oneself on one's own enlightenment. Even more perniciously, it can fuel what Ahmed calls the "narcissism of a perpetual return" (par. 59)—a perpetual turn inward, to Whiteness, to the White subject, to the goodness of antiracism for White people—rather than outward, to the world, to others.

In light of this, what words *should* be in the LSU student's vocabulary? In White people's vocabulary? In everyone's? One clear word is "responsibility." I refer less to a sense of duty to address one's individual wrongs than to a sense of *political* responsibility, as Iris Marion Young (2003, 13) conceptualizes it: a more positive, forward-looking duty to "bring about results, [which] thus depends on the actions of everyone who is in a position to contribute to the results" (see also Young 2010). A sense of political responsibility should compel all of us to do the difficult work of stepping away from the places and behaviors that feel most comfortable to us, acknowledging how our perspectives and experiences have been socially constructed, and asking which results we are in a position to contribute to (see also Medina 2012).

In other words, it's not that one shouldn't turn to the self when declaring antiracism; it's that one shouldn't stop there. In Eddie Glaude's (2020, xxv) commentary on James Baldwin's works, he writes that Baldwin "insisted that we see the connection between the disaster of our interior lives and the mess of [our] country.... What we made of ourselves in our most private moments, we made of the country." This is why issues like schooling and residential segregation lay bare so much of what White Americans believe and are willing to do: what someone makes of their most private decisions, about where their children will be educated and where their family will live, they make of the country. Reckoning with one's own racism is necessarily self-focused, private work—but it cannot be separated from one's political responsibility to reckon with the historical and continued results of racism, in our schools, in our neighborhoods, and across our nation.

In these last reflections, I have started using a more collective third person—recognizing the responsibility "we" all have, White and non-White Americans included. Indeed, Young's definition of political responsibility captures the kind of responsibility Baldwin (1984, 8) himself invokes when he says, on the topic of the Negro problem, "[a]ppearances to the contrary, no one in America escapes its effects and everyone in America bears some responsibility for it." Young, Glaude, and Baldwin all recognize we have different kinds and degrees of responsibility depending on our structural positions. But, at the end of a book that has focused primarily on White people, it is worth ending with a recognition of the political, institutional, and social structures that also sustain the racial order. White actions and attitudes are symbiotic with a host of additional factors—from the complexities of American federalism (e.g., K. S. Johnson 2006) to the realities of path dependency (e.g., Pierson 1993) to the reproduction of prejudicial attitudes and behaviors by non-White people (e.g., Flores and Lobo 2013).[4] One consequence of this is that, while White Americans may have played the dominant role in constructing the Negro problem, more of us have a role to play in deconstructing it.

May more of us, then, turn beyond the self. Critical and collective reflection on our beliefs and actions is not the whole solution. But people talk before they vote (Elizabeth Anderson 2006). And, as Danielle Allen (2004, xxi) points out in the quote that opened this chapter, our relationships and interactions will be as much a part of our legacies as anything else we leave behind. Allen does not endorse a superficial, "interracial buddy movies" style of friendship. Rather, she refers to friendship, and interaction more generally, as a political practice: actions that constitute not only our relationships but also our institutions and society. This is friendship as a metaphor for citizenship—a political practice based on recognition. It involves recognition of the sacrifices made to be part of the body politic, including those sacrifices made in disproportionate, involuntary number by Black Americans past and present. It arguably also involves recognition of our differently situated perspectives, our unequal burdens of interpretive labor, and the different roles we have to play in the conversation. Thus, this is a call not for a "kumbaya" approach to friendship, but rather for commitment, self-consciousness, and attentiveness to the workings of power in all our relationships. At minimum, we should be conscious of the spaces we occupy and the people with whom we surround ourselves; the discourses we reproduce and the ideas we take for granted; and how often we cross our boundaries of comfort—to talk across the racial divide, to reflect on our own roles in the racial order, and to accept our responsibilities to play a part in whatever change is going to come.

APPENDICES

APPENDICES

Supplementary Materials for Chapters 2 and 3

Attributes of Interview Participants

Table A.1 offers an overview of the forty-eight residents of the Baton Rouge area who partic-ipated in interviews in July and August 2016. The "cipher" column includes the pseudonyms I use to refer to the respondents whose remarks feature most prominently in Chapter 3. Note that most respondents without ciphers are also cited at some point throughout the reporting of my results, although they are not given pseudonyms to avoid introducing more characters to the story than necessary.

Interview Protocol

This section summarizes the interview protocol used for the semi-structured interviews informing the insights of Chapters 2 and 3, as referenced early on in Chapter 3. The same protocol was used for all interviews, although the themes discussed in most detail varied con-siderably depending on the respondent. For example, with active supporters of and opponents to the St. George effort, I discussed the history and details of the movement at length; with respondents connected to the school system, I spent more time on East Baton Rouge schools; and so on. I always began with the research introduction and discussion of Baton Rouge's geography, and always ended with reflections on the future, but the order in which we discussed topics in between occasionally varied depending on where a respondent took the conversation.

Research Introduction

At the start of each interview, I provided respondents with an information sheet that detailed the research project, explained that all data would be anonymized, and made sure they would be able to contact me with any questions or concerns.

I explained that I was broadly interested in geography and politics, and that my research project was focused on public opinion among residents of U.S. metro areas. I shared that I had wanted to speak to some such residents firsthand, particularly given that I was living in England at the time. I further explained that I had chosen Baton Rouge for this purpose both because of my family connections to Louisiana and because there were multiple ongoing local issues there that I thought would be interesting to explore. When speaking to St. George advocates, opponents, or school district affiliates, I more specifically shared that I was interested in the incorporation effort. When speaking to observers, I mentioned my interest in St. George but emphasized that knowledge of the effort was not a prerequisite for the interview, and that I also was interested in residents' views on issues such as schooling in general and the upcoming election for a new mayor-president of Baton Rouge and East Baton Rouge Parish. When necessary, I also clarified that it was not the killing of Sterling or the officers that had brought me to Baton Rouge, and that my trip had been planned well before July 5th.

After this initial introduction, each respondent was asked to give oral consent to the interview process and to indicate whether they were happy for me to record our conversation.

Table A.1 Interviewee Attributes

Interviewee	Cipher	Gender	Race	Age Group	Party ID	Respondent category
1	Fred	M	White	40–49	Independent	St. George opponent
2	Larry	M	White	50–59	Democrat	Observer
3		M	White	60–69	Independent	Observer
4	Greg	M	White	40–49	Democrat	Observer
5	Isabel	F	White	20–29	Independent	Observer
6		M	White	20–29	Democrat	Observer
7	Nancy	F	White	60–69	N/A	School affiliate
8	Richard	M	Black	70+	Independent	Non-White respondent
9	Susan	F	White	60–69	Democrat	Observer
10		M	White	30–39	N/A	Observer
11	Kenneth	M	White	60–69	Republican	St. George supporter
12		F	White	30–39	Democrat	Observer
13		F	White	50–59	Republican	School affiliate
14	Elizabeth	F	White	50–59	Democrat	St. George opponent
15	Diane	F	Black	60–69	Democrat	Non-White respondent
16	Joanne	F	White	60–69	Republican	School affiliate
17	Kathy	F	White	60–69	Democrat	Observer
18		F	White	50–59	Republican	School affiliate
19	Randy	M	White	60–69	Republican	St. George supporter
20	Carol	F	Black	60–69	Democrat	Non-White respondent
21		M	Black	60–69	Democrat	Non-White respondent
22	Brian	M	White	50–59	Republican	Observer
23		M	White	30–39	Republican	Observer
24		F	White	50–59	Independent	Observer
25		M	White	60–69	Republican	St. George supporter
26	James	M	White	60–69	Independent	St. George opponent
27	Pamela	F	Black	60–69	Democrat	Non-White respondent
28		M	White	50–59	Republican	School affiliate
29	Tonya	F	Black	40–49	Democrat	Non-White respondent
30	Elise	F	White	50–59	Republican	St. George supporter
31	Michelle	F	Black	40–49	Democrat	Non-White respondent
32		M	Black	70+	Democrat	Non-White respondent
33	Wayne	M	White	30–39	Republican	St. George supporter
34		M	White	60–69	Democrat	Observer
35		M	White	50–59	Democrat	Observer
36	Deborah	F	White	50–59	Democrat	St. George opponent
37		M	White	30–39	Republican	St. George opponent
38	Lance	M	Black	40–49	Democrat	Non-White respondent
39	Joshua	M	Black	40–49	Democrat	Non-White respondent
40	Mark	M	White	20–29	Republican	Observer
41	Tammy	F	White	40–49	Democrat	St. George opponent
42		M	Black	70+	Democrat	Non-White respondent
43		M	White	60–69	Republican	St. George supporter
44	Chad	M	White	30–39	Republican	St. George supporter
45		M	White	70+	N/A	St. George opponent
46		M	Black	60–69	Democrat	Non-White respondent
47		M	White	50–59	N/A	St. George supporter
48		M	White	40–49	Independent	St. George opponent

Note that I did not frame my project as specifically about race or racism. I instead observed whether and how race came up in conversation about St. George or other local issues in order to see how my respondents more naturally approached the topic (recognizing that my presence subtly racialized the interview setting). If respondents asked further questions about my research interests, which most commonly happened after race had already come up in conversation, I would share that racial diversity was one of the elements of U.S. metro areas that interested me with regard to public opinion. But I did not, for example, ask about the racial makeup of particular neighborhoods or about racial motivations behind St. George. I instead let respondents characterize their local geography or the motivations of the St. George effort as they saw fit.

The geography of Baton Rouge

After introducing the research, I began by asking each respondent to reflect on the Baton Rouge area, providing a map as a visual aid if they wanted to use it. This was generally perceived as a natural question for me to ask as a visitor, and it also served to locate respondents within the parish, to introduce their perspective on the area, and to reveal patterns in respondents' understandings of their local geography. See Figure A.1 for an example of how one respondent annotated the map, as several did over the course of our conversations.

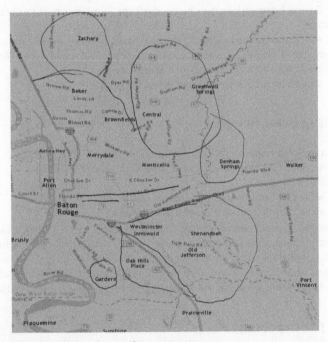

Figure A.1 Example Annotated Map of Baton Rouge

Annotations by a St. George opponent on the map I provided at the start of each interview. This respondent drew a line emphasizing Florida Boulevard as the "equator" dividing the city. She also circled the general St. George area as well as Gardere in the lower half of the map. In the upper half, she marked a line where the majority-Black areas of North Baton Rouge and Baker turned into the more integrated Zachary, and circled Zachary, Central, and Denham Springs as sites where many White Baton Rougeans had settled when moving out of the central city.

- What are the different neighborhoods of Baton Rouge?
- What are some of the characteristics of each of those areas?
  - If needed, I would prompt respondents by asking, does anything else come to mind? What kinds of places would you find in that area—residences, commercial establishments, amenities? Do you know what most of the people who live in that area do for a living? Do you ever go to that area? I also would ask respondents what they meant by certain words if they used adjectives that seemed racially coded, for example, "nice," "dangerous," or "middle-class."
- Where do you currently live?
- If you had to move elsewhere in the parish, where would you move?

The St. George incorporation effort

This section of interviews explored each respondent's knowledge of and position on the St. George initiative. In no case were respondents entirely ignorant of the incorporation effort, but the length of this section varied greatly according to a respondent's familiarity. For those proximate to the effort or its opposition, this section of the interviews offered insight on how the movement developed. For all respondents, this section offered insight on how St. George was perceived.

- What do you know or have you heard about the movement to incorporate a city of St. George?
- What was the motivation behind the effort? What were the goals of the movement?
- Let's imagine St. George incorporated as of next year. What would it look like?
- What would have been different about that area five years later?
- What would have been different about Baton Rouge?

Schooling in Baton Rouge

This section explored respondents' perceptions of the school system in Baton Rouge. These questions often naturally came up in relation to the discussion of St. George.

- What is the East Baton Rouge public school district like?
- What about the private/parochial schools in the area?
  - Example themes I would ask respondents to elaborate on if they arose included adjectives often used to describe schools such as "good," "bad," "safe," "dangerous," or "failing"; what they understood a community-based school or neighborhood school to be; and what they considered to be "best" for children or for children's needs.
- What do you think schools in an independent St. George district would be like?

City and parish politics

This section investigated what respondents saw as important local issues separate from schooling or St. George, including in light of the ongoing campaign for mayor-president.

- Have you had any thoughts about the upcoming election for mayor?
- Is there a candidate you are planning to support?
- Are there any particular issues you hope to see addressed?

Outlook on the future

This section explored respondents' evaluations of the trajectory of their area to understand where they identified problems or possibilities. This section of the interview was typically when respondents would bring up the killing of Sterling and the officers, if those events had not been referenced already.

- What do think the future looks like for the Baton Rouge area?
- Where would you hope to see the area going in the next few years?
- Do you plan to live in Baton Rouge for the next five, ten, twenty years?

Concluding the interview

I ended each discussion by gathering more details on respondents' demographics, thanking them for their time, and making sure they had the opportunity to raise any other issues on their minds.

- In what year were you born?
- How would you describe your occupation?
- How long have you lived in Baton Rouge?
- Do you have children? If so, where did or do they go to school?
- Generally speaking, do you think of yourself as a Republican, Democrat, Independent, or something else?
- Those are all my questions. Thank you for your time. Is there anything else you would like to ask me?

Technical Appendices to Chapters 4 and 5

Technical Appendix to Chapter 4

Extracting a Racial Resentment Factor

To operationalize a racial resentment variable for use in Chapter 4, I conducted exploratory factor analysis on five variables from the 2000 GSS, following the approach of Tarman and Sears (2005). These authors examined five GSS surveys administered between 1994 and 2000 in order to demonstrate consistency in the conceptual distinction between old-fashioned and symbolic racism over time. Following Tarman and Sears's approach adds valuable external validity to my measure, although I use the terminology of "racial resentment" rather than symbolic racism.

Note that I keep the racial resentment (RR) factor produced by the factor analysis but discard the old-fashioned racism (OFR) factor, instead focusing on the Black laziness stereotype to measure traditional prejudice. The laziness stereotype offers a simple measure whose relevance to White policy preferences has been well demonstrated (most notably by Gilens). Moreover, in light of this book's overarching focus on redistributive policies and public goods, a question about whether Black Americans work hard is arguably more pertinent to their "deservingness" of support in the contemporary era than the OFR measure's emphasis on Black Americans' lack of inborn ability or intelligence.

Factor loadings are reported in Table B.1, revealing that the racial resentment factor most strongly captures agreement with the following beliefs: that worse outcomes for Blacks are due to a lack of motivation to succeed; that Blacks no longer face discrimination; and that Blacks should "work their way up" as other minority groups have.

Distribution of racial attitudes across MSAs

In Chapter 4, I acknowledged the concern that my analysis could be influenced by racially hostile White individuals being clustered in the MSAs that have the largest Black population shares or poverty rates. If this were true, my findings might be highlighting these geographic patterns rather than systematic variation in how similarly minded White individuals respond across different contexts.

The graphs in Figure B.1 indicate this likely is not the case. In each graph, White GSS respondents are distributed along the y-axis according to either their endorsement of the Black laziness stereotype or their level of racial resentment, with more hostile attitudes on both scales being placed closer to the top. While there are slight upward trends in both variables, particularly in racial resentment in the highest-density Black metro areas, the sample nonetheless includes a range of White individuals located across different kinds of MSAs. Moreover, the laziness stereotype is correlated with both MSA percent Black and poverty rate at around 0.09; the correlation between racial resentment and poverty rate is 0.07, and that between racial resentment and percent Black is still only 0.17.

Thus, I conclude the aforementioned concern should not invalidate my results. As always, however, we should keep in mind the influence that factors such as local history and culture inevitably play in shaping local White opinion in different geographies.

Table B.1 Racial Attitude Factor Loadings: Chapter 4

	RR Factor	OFR Factor
Racial resentment (RR)		
Discrimination not responsible for racial disparities	**0.49**	−0.13
Lack of motivation is responsible for disparities	**0.47**	0.26
Black people should work their way up; no special favors	**0.51**	0.10
Old-fashioned racism (OFR)		
Lack of inborn ability is responsible for disparities	0.02	**0.48**
Black people lack intelligence (compared to White people)	0.11	**0.44**
Interfactor correlation = 0.36		

Table reports coefficients from exploratory factor analysis, oblique rotations, including all non-Black respondents. Factor loadings exceeding 0.40 are bolded. Note that only the racial resentment (RR) factor is used for the analysis presented in Chapter 4. *Source:* 2000 General Social Survey ($n = 2,213$).

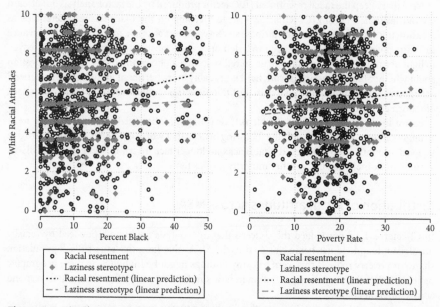

Figure B.1 Distribution of Racial Attitudes across Metropolitan Area Demographics

Figure illustrates distribution of White racial attitudes across MSAs with different Black population shares and poverty rates.

Are racial attitudes themselves predicted by context?

Some applications of the threat hypothesis argue that a greater minority presence increases the expression of prejudice among majority group members, posing animus itself rather than vote choice or policy preferences as the dependent variable (e.g., Quillian 1995). My analysis in Chapter 4 instead assumes that racial attitudes (e.g., traditional prejudice or racial resentment) are exogenous to the settings in which people live. This assumption is imperfect, but with policy preferences as the outcome variable, it would be futile to investigate the predictive power of

Table B.2 Effect of Racial Context on White Racial Attitudes

	(1) Dep. Var.: Laziness Stereotype	(2) Dep. Var.: Racial Resentment
Percent Black	0.00689 (0.005)	0.0286*** (0.010)
Poverty Rate	0.0118 (0.008)	0.00355 (0.022)
Age	0.0125*** (0.003)	0.0142** (0.005)
Gender	0.0948 (0.083)	0.356** (0.145)
Marital Status	0.0328 (0.090)	0.165 (0.195)
Education (years)	−0.0734*** (0.020)	−0.230*** (0.038)
Income (thous.)	0.000107 (0.001)	−0.00323 (0.002)
Independent	0.100 (0.114)	0.406* (0.238)
Republican	0.0876 (0.095)	1.077*** (0.226)
Constant	5.316*** (0.328)	7.193*** (0.794)
Observations	1051	728
MSAs	95	93
R-squared.	0.0678	0.151

Standard errors in parentheses; table reports results of OLS regression.

Source: 2000 General Social Survey; White respondents only; party base category is Democrat.

* $p < 0.10$, ** $p < 0.05$, *** $p < 0.01$.

context without controlling for individuals' orientations toward Blacks (see Branton and Jones 2005 for a similar approach).

To support my contention that it is appropriate to control for racial attitudes in the same models as contextual variables (e.g., Black population share and poverty rates), this brief appendix demonstrates that the effects of context on the racial attitude variables are minimal in the 2000 GSS sample, evidenced by the results of ordinary linear regression in Table B.2 (clustering standard errors by MSA). A unit increase in percent Black predicts an increase of 0.03 on the 0-10 racial resentment scale ($p < 0.01$). Beyond this small effect, Black population share is not significantly related to the Black laziness scale, and poverty rate is not significantly related to either of the two racial attitude variables.

I conclude that the predicted effect of Black population share on racial resentment is not large enough to bias my results when controlling for context and racial attitudes together. Furthermore, even if levels of racial resentment are slightly higher in more diverse contexts, the fact that economic rather than racial geography is predicted to amplify the effect of racial resentment on welfare preferences dampens concerns about endogeneity in my racial resentment models.

White opposition to "assistance to the poor"

Comparing White opposition to the more neutral "assistance to the poor" offers an opportunity to test the logic that the racialized image of "welfare" is what makes White opinion on the latter sensitive to racial and economic contexts. Both racial attitude variables are predictive of opinion regarding assistance to the poor in the first two models of Table B.3. Simply put, attitudes about Black people are implicated even when a less racialized term is used.

However, neither previously identified interaction between racial attitudes and context holds when assistance to the poor is the dependent variable. Racial geography does not make traditional racial prejudice more accessible in regard to a race-neutral reference to redistribution, and economic geography is similarly insignificant in determining the effect of racial resentment on views about assistance to the poor. In a similar vein, party identification was a significant predictor of welfare views—reflecting the Republican Party's embrace of the argument that welfare incentivizes dependency—but is not significant in predicting views on assisting the poor.

Table B.3 Null Effect of Context on White Opposition to Assisting the Poor

Assisting the Poor	(1)	(2)	(3)	(4)
	Laziness Stereotype		Racial Resentment	
Racial Attitudes				
Laziness Stereotype	1.418***	1.839***		
	(0.170)	(0.379)		
Racial Resentment			1.171**	1.238
			(0.077)	(0.200)
Contextual Variables				
Percent Black (log)		1.763		0.795*
		(0.944)		(0.097)
Poverty Rate		1.005		1.037
		(0.025)		(0.067)
Laziness Stereotype × Percent Black (log)		0.883		
		(0.078)		
Racial Resentment × Poverty Rate				0.997
				(0.009)
Constant	0.00680***	0.00212***	0.0360***	0.0301**
	(0.008)	(0.003)	(0.038)	(0.045)
Observations	505	505	347	347
p	0.247	0.0426	0.351	0.168
Log likelihood	−200.5	−199.1	−146.0	−144.6

Exponentiated coefficients; standard errors in parentheses.

Table reports odds ratios from logistic regression estimating probability of White respondents saying too much is spent on assisting the poor.

For concision, control variables are not displayed.

Source: 2000 General Social Survey.

* $p < 0.10$, ** $p < 0.05$, *** $p < 0.01$.

County-level predictors of welfare preferences

To conclude the technical appendix to Chapter 4, I report the results of analysis with county-level measures of Black population share and poverty rate to ensure that my results are not purely the product of how MSA boundaries are drawn. I have defended my focus on the MSA (or MD when applicable) on the grounds that urban residents are likely to cross county lines in their daily activities and also be aware of populations in neighboring counties. However, counties are similar to MSAs as midsize containers, and county-level data should produce similar results.

Table B.4 presents the results of this analysis. The interactions between both measures of racial geography (either Black population share or racial segregation) and the laziness stereotype hold when measuring context at the county level. The interaction between income segregation and racial resentment also remains significant. The interaction between racial resentment and county poverty rate, however, is no longer significant ($p = 0.107$). This result is consistent with the reasoning behind my incorporation of central city poverty rates in the main analysis. It is possible that sorting within an MSA produces variation in poverty rates among the counties that comprise the MSA. Despite this sorting, we would expect metropolitan area residents to have a general awareness of visible, central city poverty.

Technical Appendix to Chapter 5

Extracting a racial resentment factor

As in Chapter 4, I conduct factor analysis on five variables from the GSS to create a measure of racial resentment. The results of this analysis are reported in Table B.5. I again keep only the racial resentment factor, discarding the old-fashioned racism factor.

Measuring White perceptions of Black political influence on the ANES

Respondents to the ANES are given three options to evaluate Black and White Americans' influence in U.S. politics (1= "too much," 2 = "the right amount," or 3 = "too little"). We cannot know what standard a respondent is using to determine what "the right amount" of influence a group should have in politics. What matters for my analysis, however, is a respondent's *relative* placement of Black and White Americans. Whatever influence someone thinks each group deserves, we can still determine whether that person believes the balance of power is wrongly tilted in one direction.

In the GSS sample, White respondents are likely to think that their own group has the right amount of influence in politics (67%) or else too much (26%). White respondents also tend to think that Black people have the right amount of influence (52%) or else too little (38%). This outcome maps onto the pattern in economic status evaluations—White respondents generally believe that Black people are poorer than White people—indicating that both variables reflect an awareness of true racial disparities.

To gauge how a given White individual evaluates the racial groups in relation to one another, I construct a categorical variable reflecting whether the respondent perceives Black people as relatively disempowered, equal to White people in influence, or relatively influential. This produces five categories, depending on how strongly a respondent believes the balance of power is shifted in either White people's or Black people's direction: (1) White people are perceived to

Table B.4 White Welfare Preferences across Counties

Opposition to Welfare	(1)	(2)	(3)	(4)	(5)	(6)
	Laziness Stereotype			Racial Resentment		
Racial Attitudes						
Laziness Stereotype	1.257***	0.961	1.043			
	(0.101)	(0.139)	(0.125)			
Racial Resentment				1.219***	0.977	1.652***
				(0.066)	(0.141)	(0.234)
Contextual Variables						
County Percent Black (log)	1.005	0.503**		1.066	1.052	1.081
	(0.084)	(0.150)		(0.112)	(0.112)	(0.111)
County Poverty Rate	1.028	1.024	1.026	1.024	0.906	
	(0.023)	(0.023)	(0.021)	(0.030)	(0.072)	
Laziness Stereotype × County Percent Black (log)		1.140**				
		(0.065)				
Racial Segregation			0.866**			
			(0.051)			
Laziness Stereotype × Racial Segregation			1.025**			
			(0.011)			
Racial Resentment × County Poverty Rate					1.021	
					(0.013)	
Income Segregation						1.339*
						(0.207)
Racial Resentment × Income Segregation						0.943**
						(0.022)
Control Variables						
Age	0.992	0.992	0.992	0.993	0.991	0.994
	(0.006)	(0.006)	(0.006)	(0.007)	(0.007)	(0.007)
Gender	1.283	1.299	1.287	1.249	1.212	1.161
	(0.248)	(0.252)	(0.245)	(0.291)	(0.284)	(0.274)
Marital Status	1.138	1.142	1.134	1.105	1.109	1.102
	(0.221)	(0.221)	(0.215)	(0.261)	(0.269)	(0.270)
Education (years)	0.930**	0.932**	0.930**	0.953	0.953	0.952
	(0.034)	(0.033)	(0.034)	(0.043)	(0.045)	(0.044)
Income	1.000	1.000	1.000	1.000	1.000	1.000
	(0.000)	(0.000)	(0.000)	(0.000)	(0.000)	(0.000)
Independent	2.158***	2.125***	2.116***	2.255***	2.146**	2.411***
	(0.559)	(0.559)	(0.553)	(0.688)	(0.644)	(0.743)
Republican	2.379***	2.335***	2.420***	1.821**	1.810**	1.907**
	(0.530)	(0.520)	(0.541)	(0.491)	(0.488)	(0.526)

Table B.4 Continued

	(1)	(2)	(3)	(4)	(5)	(6)
Opposition to Welfare	Laziness Stereotype			Racial Resentment		
Constant	0.324	1.298	0.940	0.234	0.985	0.0644**
	(0.270)	(1.287)	(0.875)	(0.209)	(1.215)	(0.084)
Observations	512	512	512	361	361	361
p	0.0000106	0.00000817	0.000000344	0.000639	0.000910	0.0000889
Log likelihood	−323.3	−321.0	−321.2	−223.5	−222.1	−220.2

Exponentiated coefficients; standard errors in parentheses.

Table reports odds ratios from logistic regression estimating probability of White respondents saying too much is spent on welfare.

Source: 2000 General Social Survey; party base category is Democrat.

* $p < 0.10$, ** $p < 0.05$, *** $p < 0.01$.

Table B.5 Racial Attitude Factor Loadings: Chapter 5

	RR Factor	OFR Factor
Racial resentment (RR)		
Discrimination not responsible for racial disparities	**0.28**	−0.09
Lack of motivation is responsible for disparities	**0.29**	**0.25**
Black people should work their way up; no special favors	**0.38**	0.09
Old-fashioned racism (OFR)		
Lack of inborn ability is responsible for disparities	0.02	**0.33**
Black people lack intelligence (compared to White people)	0.05	**0.28**

Table reports coefficients from exploratory factor analysis, oblique rotations, including all non-Black respondents. Bolded values exceed 0.25. Note that only the racial resentment (RR) factor is used for the analysis presented in Chapter 5. *Source:* 2006-2010 General Social Survey ($n = 2,916$).

Table B.6 Perceptions of the Balance of Power between Black and White Americans

	Perceived relative influence of races	White respondents in category
1	Whites much greater influence	22%
2	Whites greater influence	16%
3	Equal influence	51%
4	Blacks greater influence	7%
5	Blacks much greater influence	4%

Table summarizes White evaluations of Black people's influence in U.S. politics, relative to the influence of White people. *Source:* 2016 ANES ($n = 2,581$).

have too much influence and Black people too little, (2) White people are perceived to have the right amount of influence and Black people too little, (3) White and Black people are perceived to have the same amount of influence (whether that is too much, the right amount, or too little), (4) Black people are perceived to have too much influence and White people the right amount, or (5) Black people are perceived to have too much influence and White people too little.

The distribution of White individuals among these categories in the sample is summarized in Table B.6. The categories with higher numbers indicate White people who perceive Black people to be closer to White people (or to even surpass White people) in political influence.

Notes

Chapter 1

1. Throughout this book, I capitalize "Black" and "White" unless quoting an author who chooses not to capitalize. There is a long debate behind the capitalization of race terms: W. E. B. Du Bois, who was pivotal in standardizing the capitalization of "Negro" in the late 1920s, famously called "the use of a small letter for the name of twelve million Americans and two hundred million human beings a personal insult" (qtd. in Tharps 2014). I capitalize "Black" in support of Du Bois's logic and to recognize the word as a proper noun: referencing a population that occupies a specific location in the American socio-political structure based on race, and that generally shares a racial identity. This view has recently and quickly become more commonplace, as numerous writers, commentators, and style guides adopted the capital "Black" in response to the wave of Black Lives Matter activism in the summer of 2020.

   I argue it also is important to capitalize "White." This is partly for a similar reason: White Americans share a structural position and racial identity, too, even if they are less likely to recognize it. But contrary to concern about the "personal insult" of using a lowercase letter to reference Black people, my concern about writing "white" in lowercase letters is that it only reifies the pernicious assumption that Whiteness is the norm—the one common noun—from which all other racial identities are a deviation.

2. Baton Rouge police officers Blane Salamoni and Howie Lake II, both White, responded to a 911 call about a man said to have a gun outside the Triple-S Food Mart in North Baton Rouge. Sterling, who was well known in the neighborhood for playing music and selling CDs outside the Triple-S, put his hands on the hood of the police car as instructed when the officers arrived. But when Sterling asked what he had done, the situation broke down, leading Salamoni to put his gun to Sterling's head and shout expletive-laden threats to kill him. When Sterling exclaimed that the officers were hurting him, Lake used his Taser on Sterling, after which both officers tackled him to the ground. Salamoni announced that Sterling was going for a gun and then fired several shots into Sterling's chest. When Sterling started struggling to get up, Salamoni fired three more shots into Sterling's back. Though investigations were conducted by the U.S. Department of Justice and the Louisiana Attorney General's office, neither federal nor state charges were brought against the officers. After spending two years on paid administrative leave up to this point, Salamoni was ultimately fired from the police force in 2018; Lake served a three-day suspension and then returned to work.

3. The sniper, Gavin Long, expressed his intention to avenge Sterling and other Black victims of police violence both in a YouTube video posted several days prior and in a note he left in his rental car. Long also had searched for the addresses and phone numbers of the officers responsible for Sterling's death on July 7th, the same day another military veteran, Micah Johnson, had killed five members of Dallas law enforcement during a peaceful march in response to Sterling's killing. Both Johnson and Long were Black and showed signs of

psychological trauma and mental instability upon returning from their military service. Their actions were inexcusable while also pointing to the complicated history of mental health, racism, and America's armed forces.

4. The Pew Research Center compared White opinion on Black Lives Matter (BLM) in June and September of 2020, in surveys conducted both shortly after and several months after the nation's attention was turned to the killing of George Floyd, the 46-year-old Black resident of Minneapolis who died after a police officer knelt on Floyd's neck for 9 minutes 29 seconds. The video of the incident also brought renewed attention to the deaths of Breonna Taylor, Ahmaud Arbery, Nina Pop, Rayshard Brooks, Tony McDade, Dominique "Rem'mie" Fells, Riah Milton, and other Black Americans who were killed by both state and non-state actors in the late spring and early summer of 2020.

   Whereas White support for BLM was 60% in June 2020, by September 2020 the percentage had fallen to 45%—closer to the 40% of White Americans who had expressed support in a 2016 Pew survey—suggesting the potentially fleeting nature of White support (Horowitz and Livingston 2016; Thomas and Horowitz 2020). Note, however, the stark partisan differences in these attitudes: a larger (and potentially more durable) increase in support has come from White Democrats. Disaggregating White support for BLM as of June 2020 reveals that only 37% of White Republicans supported the movement, versus 92% of White Democrats. This figure for Democrats remained at 88% in the September Pew poll, and represents a considerable increase from the 64% of White Democrats who supported BLM in 2016.

5. For example, Melissa Harris-Lacewell (2003) points out the absence of the modifier "White" in the title of Martin Gilens's classic *Why Americans Hate Welfare*, which focuses on White public opinion. Joe Soss and Vesla Weaver (2017) point out that theorizing on American democracy often ignores how race- and class-subjugated communities are extensively policed and surveilled, in contrast to typical portrayals of a distant or hands-off American state. More broadly, Hanes Walton Jr. (1995) points out that the historical popularity of the "race relations" approach to studying race in America—which prioritizes interracial harmony, even if Black people remain subjugated—exemplifies the dominance of the belief that, because racial harmony is good for White people, it is good in absolute terms.

6. A vestige of French, church-based rule, Louisiana is the only state to call its local governmental units parishes rather than counties.

7. Black, along with Indigenous and Latino Americans, were at least 2.6 times more likely to have been killed by COVID-19 in 2020 than White Americans when adjusting for age (see Pham and Mitra 2020; see also Millett et al. 2020).

8. Rogers Smith (1993) in particular highlights how scholars from Tocqueville to Myrdal to Hartz have easily dismissed racism as a peripheral issue.

9. Baldwin makes this comment in the unfinished manuscript that inspired Raoul Peck's documentary *I Am Not Your Negro*. One of the first formulations of this theme, however, comes from Du Bois's (1903, 4) famous articulation of the question he felt was on the tip of the tongue of any White who saw him: "How does it feel to be a problem?" Du Bois's explicit aim in *The Souls of Black Folk* was that his White readers understand that this problem, "the strange meaning of being Black," should be of interest to them, too. That, after all, was why "the problem of the Twentieth Century" for White and Black people alike would be "the problem of the color-line."

10. Inherent in this principle are two more fundamental ones: first, that race is a central axis of social relations, at both the individual and societal level (Omi and Winant 1986); and second, that race is a central axis of politics around which political institutions and actors have organized themselves throughout American political development (King and Smith 2005; see also Hutchings and Valentino 2004). Seeing race as a fundamental axis means that racism does not present an exception to the normal functioning of society, nor is race superseded by other social categories. The power associated with Whiteness stretches across the spectrum of White Americans' class identities, just as the stigma of Blackness stretches across the spectrum of Black Americans' class identities—as varied as the intersections between race and class might be.

11. In her history of the NAACP's fight against lynching and mob violence (and its influence on US political development in the process), Megan Ming Francis (2014) reminds us that the most basic right of citizenship—the right to live—was the foundation of later civil rights fights for access to education and voting.

12. It is striking, though not surprising, that this mortality gap persists even after a recent uptick in White mortality, largely due to "deaths of despair" such as suicide and drug and alcohol poisoning (Case and Deaton 2015). Also note that news of the reversal of direction in the trend of White mortality has tended to gloss over the persistent racial gap: that Black lives are shorter is the norm.

13. Diverse settings do not always lead to negative outcomes—something I consider in my application of the threat hypothesis, which identifies the possible amplification of racially tolerant attitudes. This book does not, however, evaluate the "racial contact" hypothesis, which, per Allport (1954), argues that interracial interaction brings benefits in situations where groups are of equal status, have common goals, and receive institutional support for cooperation. Assessing the contact hypothesis would require a different approach to that taken here, specifically requiring greater focus on interpersonal interaction than on the salience of racial and economic demographics in a given metropolitan area. For more on the benefits of contact in reducing prejudice, see Pettigrew and Tropp (2006)—but also see Paluck et al. (2021) on the limitations and weaknesses of research in this area.

14. Specifically, these authors point out that large Black populations historically powered Southern economies, meaning that White elites would not want to drive Black people away to reduce a racial threat; if anything, White people would desire a larger Black population whose labor to rely on (or exploit), and would then seek to control this population with measures such as segregation and Jim Crow laws. More broadly, this argument leads Acharya et al. to challenge scholars for focusing too much on contemporary demographics in trying to identify racial threat responses. I support this critique, even as I take a different approach to engaging with historical power dynamics in my applications of the threat hypothesis. That is, I focus on how a direct conceptualization of White people's empowered perspective—a function of our racial history—can enhance the typical focus on contemporary demographics alone. Additionally, when it comes to the fundamentally redistributive policies I examine in this book, there is more sense in expecting White people to perceive (on objective or subjective grounds) a threat from Black people in terms of competition for a social good or for a policy's benefits rather than responding to an economic incentive to exploit the labor of a large Black population.

15. One recent example is Ashley Jardina's (2019) *White Identity Politics*, which obviously and directly references White people—although it still paints a largely sympathetic,

power-blind picture of them. Jardina offers compelling evidence that her survey constructs measure White identity as distinct from anti-Black animus, at least in empirical terms. But in light of America's historical, social, and spatial realities, Jardina minimizes the extent to which Whiteness has been defined and violently defended in contrast to Blackness. Put differently, in theoretical terms, she minimizes the deeply relational nature of the Black–White color line, including as it has shaped other color lines.

16. Giles and Evans ultimately find that "actual" threat only leads to perceived threat (in political terms) among White people who feel less political efficacy, a finding that highlights White people's inclination to maintain their power in the racial hierarchy. The authors also discuss, as I noted Taylor (1998) similarly does, how their findings complicate assumptions about when Black populations will be seen as threatening; I will return to these findings in Chapter 5.

17. It is not impossible for someone who occupies a dominant identity to achieve insight into how power shapes knowledge—particularly given the many ways that marginalized and non-marginalized identities intersect. Nonetheless, standpoint is not an appropriate description of the common perspective that either Frankenberg's research subjects or mine reveal. If anything, Frankenberg reveals the limits of her own White perspective by falling into the same power-evasive rhetoric she identifies among her interviewees. She is at the very least passive in articulating her research question as how "white women are created as social actors primed to reproduce racism," which positions White women as victims of a racist system (Frankenberg 1993, 5).

18. GSS location files were obtained under special contractual arrangements designed to protect the anonymity of respondents. Those interested in obtaining GSS Sensitive Data Files should contact the GSS at GSS@NORC.org.

19. Note that Chapter 4 includes and expands upon findings I have previously reported (Yancy 2019), including by connecting my quantitative findings on White welfare preferences to the qualitative insights and discursive practices illuminated in Baton Rouge.

Chapter 2

1. Samuelson's comment in *The Washington Post* on June 25, 1986, is proudly cited by the Federal Highway Administration on its website (Federal Highway Administration 2017).

2. In an update to the 2009 report, the 2020 *Portrait of Louisiana* (K. Lewis 2020) uses parishes as the main unit of analysis, rather than parish "groups" as used in the 2009 analysis (see Table 2.1). The 2020 analysis identifies Ascension Parish (which neighbors the St. George area) as the area with the highest level of human development, and East Carroll Parish (a rural parish in the state's northeast corner) as the area with the lowest. While this update reflects trends associated with continued outmigration from EBR to Ascension Parish, it also shows how much inequality within EBR—specifically between NBR and the rest of the parish—is masked when looking only at parish boundaries.

3. Baton Rouge experienced a population shock of about 17,500 people after Hurricane Katrina in 2005, bringing new White and Black residents to the area. It has proved difficult to measure the population fluidity that followed, and to know whether households leaving the parish after 2005 were Katrina evacuees or existing residents. However, this

population shock did little to stem (and may have exacerbated) White flight (see Mitchell 2015).

4. The impact of the Interstate's construction in Baton Rouge deserves more attention than the scope of this book allows. The broader story of Black neighborhoods being destroyed by highways, however, is well documented. For example, see Avila (2014) on the toll that the building of the Interstate system had on Black communities across the country; Keating (2001) on the racial impacts of highway construction in Atlanta; and Caro (1974) on the experiences of Black communities in New York City under the reign of urban planner Robert Moses.

5. Louisiana's school districts are larger than other states' because they are more consolidated: in contrast to the degree of local control in places such as Cook County, IL, which has 150 different school districts, almost every parish in Louisiana belongs to a single district. St. George advocates cite the abnormality of EBR's size as an argument in favor of creating smaller districts within the parish, although many contemporary education advocates argue that consolidation is more efficient in providing resources across a district.

6. See 1980–1982 GSS data. White respondents in regions encompassing southern states expressed noticeably lower support for integrated schools (75%) and slightly more opposition to busing (84%).

7. Based on analysis of EBR student enrollment data as of fall 2016. Data available from the Louisiana Department of Education (www.louisianabelieves.com).

8. The next largest demographic at Baton Rouge Magnet High School is Asian Americans, making up about 15% of the population. For reference, 3.3% of the population of EBR was of Asian descent as of the 2010 census.

9. Although the Obama administration slowed the process by requiring districts to present desegregation plans before being released, the number of schools under federal oversight has continued to decline. Less than 180 schools of more than 13,500 nationwide remained under oversight as of 2017 (Felton 2017). These numbers are also increasingly difficult to track, as basic monitoring of desegregation orders has largely fallen into disarray at both the local and federal levels (Hannah-Jones 2014).

10. To form a school district in Louisiana requires the passage of a constitutional amendment in the state legislature. See LA Rev Stat §17:72–72.1 for legislation on the establishment of the City of Baker school system, LA Rev Stat §17:64–64.1 for Zachary Community Schools, and LA Rev Stat §17:66–66.1 for Central Community Schools. The fact that Baker and Zachary were already their own municipalities eased the process of lobbying for their own school districts in the legislature. Central, on the other hand, was twice denied its request to form an independent school district, leading it to pursue municipal incorporation as a means to establish the district. This is the process that served as inspiration for St. George—although the St. George effort is much larger in scale, as Central is home to less than one-third as many people as the area proposed in the initial St. George campaign.

11. One thing that stands out in Table 2.2 is the racial makeup of Zachary's school district, which holds across the district's seven schools (even if students of different races might be unevenly sorted within schools, e.g., into honors-level classes). With this level of integration, Zachary often is pointed to as evidence that the racial makeup of schools is irrelevant to outcomes, because "it's class, not race" that matters.

Zachary's strong performance is helped by the city's affluence: compared to the average White and Black household incomes in EBR of $71,000 and $48,000, respectively, the average is $95,000 for White Zachary residents and $67,503 for Black residents. Although there are wealthier White communities elsewhere in the parish, Zachary is home to the parish's largest high-income Black population. Zachary thus offers an example of the possible success and stability of integrated schools in settings where Black students are not disproportionately disadvantaged. The problem with holding up Zachary as a paradigm, however, is that it celebrates an end (educational success for Black and White students) without recognizing the means required to get there (e.g., reducing inequality between Black and White families—education being one way of doing so).

It is also worth noting that, while Zachary is usually referred to as an "integrated" area, Central is described as a "not rich" area. Table 2.2 shows that Central is similarly affluent to Zachary, although much less racially mixed. Central therefore receives the same treatment as St. George—which, as I show in the next chapter, was also often identified as "not rich." White respondents thus downplay an area's economic advantage when they are concerned it might easily be portrayed as a wealthy, White community—and invite criticism as "racist." Alternatively, when talking about a racially mixed community such as Zachary, it is permissible to talk more openly about economic advantage—in support of the "class, not race" argument, but also revealing an understanding that affluent White people living in integrated communities are less vulnerable to criticism for economic privilege.

12. In the next chapter, I discuss in more depth the St. George organizers' typical avoidance of reference to Baker. Baker began agitating for an independent school district as early as the 1980s, and voted to create a district in 1995, despite not seeing the district come into effect until after the desegregation litigation ended. During the long process of establishing the district, Baker's demographics changed drastically, from a city population that was 84% White on the 1980 census to only 20% White today. Its present student population is 94% Black, and 81% of students are poor enough to qualify for free or reduced lunch.

13. This comment was included in a press release posted on July 15, 2014, by St. George leadership on their website (Committee to Incorporate St. George 2014b). The statement has since been removed.

14. This quote came from the official website for the City of St. George (Committee to Incorporate St. George 2014a), which has since been revised.

15. See 2011 Louisiana Laws, Revised Statutes, TITLE 33—particularly, LA Rev Stat §33:1–3.

16. BRAF is a community foundation that works with philanthropists and local leaders to fund projects meant to serve the "civic good" (http://www.braf.org/). BRAC is, in effect, a chamber of commerce and works to attract jobs and promote economic development in the larger metropolitan area (http://www.brac.org/).

17. The Metro Council was a major force behind the annexations, helped by organizations such as BRAF and BRAC; it was in the interest of the city–parish to absorb as much of the unincorporated area as possible in order to keep more tax revenue within the official city limits of Baton Rouge. But the sites that were being annexed often had their own interest in joining the city, too. While some may have been opposed to St. George on principle, annexation let them avoid the uncertainty that a change of local government would bring, particularly in regard to taxes.

18. To be fair, incorporation has at times been a tool of self-determination for Black people (M. W. Anderson 2012). In one notable recent effort, members of a majority-Black

community in the Atlanta area successfully incorporated the city of Stonecrest, GA, in 2016, in a controversial use of the same strategy that primarily wealthy, Whiter unincorporated areas around Atlanta have pursued over the last two decades (i.e., like its neighbor cities, Stonecrest's departure has hurt the county's finances and left behind more disadvantaged, Blacker areas; see Rosen 2017). While this book lacks the scope to address the incorporation of majority-Black cities, stories like Stonecrest's are important to avoid simplifying municipal incorporation as a tool available only to White people. At the same time, the reality of racial inequality and power imbalances means that incorporation has much more often been used by White people withdrawing from redistributive burdens that tie them to Black communities than vice versa.

19. The final petition contained 17,788 legitimate signatures, but 17,859 were needed. Although the organizers collected an additional 4,600 names after the ruling in March that they were short by 2,700, scores of names were also removed in the final weeks of the effort by signatories who changed their minds—due to Better Together or OCOSD's efforts or otherwise.

20. St. George supporters have characterized the lawsuit against St. George as an attempt to overturn a democratic vote. However, the lawsuit does not contest the results of the vote but instead asks the court to block the incorporation because of the negative impact St. George's creation would have on EBR Parish's finances. Federal courts have upheld both Weston-Broome's and Metro Councilman LaMont Cole's (one of her coplaintiffs) rights to pursue this route as elected officials of the jurisdiction that stands to be adversely affected by St. George. See LA Rev Stat §33:4.

21. Based on 2019 American Community Survey data on state of residence by place of birth.

22. Notably, Herbert Hyman's et al. (1954) study of Black people in Memphis, TN, found drastic underreporting of even minor details, such as education or car ownership, when an interviewer was White (see also Schuman and Converse 1971).

23. The majority of exceptions come from non-White authors. Black feminist sociologist France Winddance Twine (2000, 6–14), for example, offers a critical discussion of the various reasons race matching does not necessarily produce "better" data, especially given the other identities that intersect with race. Twine also points to the critiques of Ann Phoenix and Penny Rhodes—the former Black and the latter White—that advocating for race-matching risks marginalizing Black researchers to study only Black subjects, making invisible the contributions of Black researchers on any other topics. It is also worth referencing examples such as Charles Gallagher (2008), a White sociologist who has discussed the possibility that White researchers endorse racist ideas among White interviewees by never challenging them (per the logic of Stuart Hall's 1981 critique of "inferential racism"). Further, in pointing out that other elements of his identity make him an outsider to the White individuals he studies, Gallagher valuably challenges the depiction of White-on-White interview settings as "pure." On the whole, however, Gallagher does more to advocate for reflectiveness among White researchers than to support the legitimacy of non-White researchers speaking to White subjects.

24. This tendency has been called the "Wilder effect," due to its origins in 1989 gubernatorial election in Virginia, when Black candidate Douglas Wilder won the race by a considerably smaller vote share than predicted. However, it seems likely that the Wilder effect is a product of specific political contexts rather than a general principle (Hopkins 2009).

25. Note that as a Black, middle-income researcher, Moss served as a direct contrast not only to his research subjects' race but also to the very issue he sought to study: lower-income White people's conceptions of Whiteness. This is different from my policy-oriented conversations: while my presence made race salient, and was brought into conversation at points, I was not directly asking respondents to reflect on my own identity in comparison to theirs.

26. Collins specifically cites Black women's particular legacy of playing the "stranger" as domestic workers within White households and argues that Black women play a similar role in the academy, a space long dominated by and centered on the White man.

27. I conducted three interviews by phone, when an in-person meeting was not possible. In at least two of these three interviews, the respondent nonetheless was aware that I was Black.

Chapter 3

1. To protect the anonymity of my respondents, all names have been changed. Pseudonyms were selected by referencing the Social Security Administration's lists of popular names in the year a respondent was born, and in Louisiana specifically for those born after 1960 (the year from which more granular data are available). Minor biographical details have also been changed in cases where mentioning a respondent's occupation, for example, could compromise anonymity. Quotes are presented here in minimally edited form, with the occasional removal of interjections or filler words for concision and clarity. Finally, the quotes reported throughout this chapter were selected by virtue of exemplifying the four discursive practices used by the White respondents, at times colorfully so, but are representative of patterns identified across the universe of data analyzed.

2. One interview was conducted by phone due to the respondent's scheduling constraints, and the other two due to flooding that immobilized Baton Rouge in August 2016.

3. The obvious reference to make here is to Foucault (1972), who called discourses the "common sense of a culture," thus reflecting the power interests that get to determine what is common sense.

4. The term "habitus" itself long predates Bourdieu. It was originally coined by Aristotle and then used sporadically by other thinkers, most notably Emile Durkheim and Marcel Mauss in the 20th century. But, Bourdieu is the one who translated habitus into an analytically useful, sociological concept.

5. Louisiana's private school enrollment primarily reflects the prevalence of Catholic schools. The New Orleans metro area holds the first place spot nationwide, with 25.1% private school enrollment.

6. This hypothetical headline was Wayne's formulation, but he was right that St. George had been portrayed as a potentially segregationist effort in news coverage that was critical of the effort. Example headlines include "Richer White People in Greater Baton Rouge Seek to Secede from Poorer Black Neighbors" (*Huffington Post*, January 2014) and "The St. George Movement in Baton Rouge: An Education Revolution, or White Flight?" (*The Guardian*, April 2015).

7. I thank one of the anonymous OUP reviewers for illuminating this point. For an example of the latter of the two "community school" discourses I reference, see the New York City Department of Education's overview of their community school philosophy

(i.e., partnering with nonprofits to provide social services) at https://infohub.nyced.org/
working-with-the-doe/community-school-partners/community-schools.

8. With over 40,000 students, EBR is four times larger than the average district in Louisiana,
which has large districts to begin with. It also, however, has the most economically
disadvantaged population of any district its size in the state, based on October 2016
Student Enrollment Statistics released by the Louisiana Department of Education.

9. As we saw in Chapter 2, many Black residents of Baton Rouge lamented the negative
impact of Parker's desegregation order on schools in Black communities, which lost many
of their best teachers and their tight-knit sense of community. Elsewhere in the country,
Black communities took assertive action inspired by similar concerns about local control.
One notable example comes from Brooklyn's Ocean Hill-Brownsville neighborhood,
which was allowed to form a community school board in 1968 as part of a pilot program
in New York City. When the community school board went on to fire a group of
nineteen predominately White teachers and administrators they deemed underperforming, it set off an explosive conflict between the teacher's union and the neighborhood
(see Disare 2018).

10. Louisiana's Industrial Tax Exemption Program (ITEP) has historically been controlled by
a central state body, the Board of Commerce and Industry. However, in 2016, Governor
John Bel Edwards issued an executive order stipulating that either local governing
bodies would have a say in granting corporate tax exemptions, companies applying for
exemptions would have to offer proof of job creation or retention, or both. The order's
signing largely reflected the activism efforts of Together Baton Rouge, and one of the first
signs of the order's impact came in 2019, when the EBR school board denied a routine
request from ExxonMobil for the first time, for about $3 million in tax breaks.

11. Regarding the equation of Black and White professionals, it helps to note that, based
on 2016 census estimates, 61% of White households in the parish earned over $50,000
annually, compared to 35% of Black households—and only 47% of Black households in
the parish owned their homes as opposed to 71% of White households.

12. For example, Valerie Johnson's (2002) study of Prince George County, MD, documents
similar efforts by Black suburbanites to limit the number of public basketball courts in
their community, explaining this as an effort to keep lower-status Black people away.

13. Another Tiger football team, of Clemson University, also calls its stadium Death Valley
and claims to have originated the nickname. There are a variety of origin myths explaining
how the two Tiger stadiums took on the same name, and which one is more deserving of
the ominous title, but LSU fans do not seem to care too much.

14. LSU football has a clear Confederate lineage, as the team's "Fighting Tigers" nickname
was taken from a Louisiana military regiment that fought in the Civil War. While there
have been small rumblings around whether LSU should change its tiger mascot, the LSU
version of the Confederate flag has been the subject of considerably greater controversy.
Most notably, in 2005 the LSU chapter of the NAACP organized large student protests
to call upon then-Chancellor Sean O'Keefe to ban the flag (Gibson 2005). O'Keefe
declined a ban, citing First Amendment concerns, although he did issue a statement
saying the university did not condone the flag or the sale of it (Associated Press 2005).
The flag remains a familiar sight for many, however, as evidenced by contemporary
op-eds and comments from LSU students in online forums, by the observations of my
Black respondents, and by my own sightings of the flag around Baton Rouge.

15. At the time of writing, the "Behind the Curtain" video has been viewed over 5,500 times.

16. Wayne's approach was to distinguish the wealthier homes around the Country Club of Louisiana from other parts of the proposed St. George incorporation—a fair point, as it would make sense for middle-income residents of the area to be more upset than upper-income residents about the cost of private school tuition. It is worth noting, however, that the mean household income in the proposed St. George area of about $90,000 per year is in the top 20% of the household income distribution in the United States, as well as in Louisiana. Moreover, the mean income for St. George is lowered by places such as Gardere, where the mean household income was just above $50,000 as of 2016; elsewhere in the southeast, the mean income is over $180,000.

17. The U.S. Department of Agriculture defines food deserts as low-income census tracts where 33% of the population lives a mile or more from a grocery store. A joint effort by Together Baton Rouge's Food Access Policy Commission and Baton Rouge's "Healthy BR" commission identified between 75,000 and 103,000 individuals living in these census tracts (R. Allen 2018).

18. The state closed NBR's Earl K. Long Medical Center in 2013 to cut costs; in 2015, Baton Rouge General Hospital followed suit in closing its Mid City emergency room on account of losing money on the amount of care provided to uninsured patients (Griggs 2017).

19. A demonstrative, though historical, example is the 1972 murder of two Black students, Leonard Brown and Denver Smith, at a peaceful protest at Southern University by state police. The shootings followed similar incidents at Kent State and Ohio State Universities. No officer was ever charged. Almost fifty years later, the decision was made to award Brown and Smith honorary degrees at Southern's 2017 commencement exercises (the first commencement after Sterling had been killed; see Sentell 2017). Another demonstrative example is more recent: reports of widespread mistreatment of Black people by Baton Rouge police officers as witnessed by state troopers from other states who were sent to help after Hurricane Katrina in 2005 (see, e.g., Associated Press 2010).

20. This trend reflects the dominance of the *Brown v. Board* paradigm, and related endorsements of Allport's racial contact hypothesis and the power of interracial interaction to improve race relations (see, e.g., Bowen and Bok 2000). While it is unsurprising that White respondents in Baton Rouge prioritized this way of thinking about racial "progress," we should nonetheless remember that this approach typically centers Whiteness by focusing on what White people themselves stand to learn or gain from interacting with Black people.

21. Carol's experience is not uncommon. See, for example, a 2016 feature by the *Chicago Tribune* on the practice of Black business owners hiding their racial identity or concealing their ownership position in order to better grow their businesses (C. V. Jackson 2016). Although support for Black-owned businesses spiked considerably in the summer of 2020 following George Floyd's murder, any longer-term trends in support for Black businesses remain to be seen; Black businesses also, notably, suffered far more than White-owned businesses as a result of COVID-19–related shutdowns.

22. Together Baton Rouge describes its goals as an organization as (1) "to build relationships across our community based on trust and a willingness to listen to each other," (2) "to equip our members and leadership with skills and practices to get results," and (3) "to achieve change on concrete issues, as part of our common call to justice" (see Together Baton Rouge, "What Are We Building," accessed February 15, 2021,

https://www.togetherbr.org/about). Joshua was, in effect, arguing that the third of these goals is most important, and that it should not be contingent on goals concerned with interracial relationship building and leadership development.

23. Similar criticism of White people's selective references to Black bodies occasionally came up in relation to the topic of abortion. I did not ask interviewees about reproductive rights. However, at least two Black residents shared frustration about White Baton Rougeans who would cite abortion rates among Black women as antithetical to support for Black Lives Matter. An example of the kinds of statements that provoked this sort of frustration came from one of my White respondents, who said of the Black Lives Matter movement: "What about the Black lives you kill in the womb?" Carol called this an example of White people only referencing Black lives when convenient to make an argument. "These babies are born in last place and end up murdered anyhow," she said bluntly.

Chapter 4

1. Note that portions of the analysis and discussion of White welfare preferences presented in this chapter have been previously published (Yancy 2019; see also Yancy 2016).
2. Here, I reference only those census tracts east of Interstate 1–110. The sliver of land in the ZIP code that lies west of the Interstate primarily encompasses ExxonMobil's giant refinery there.
3. Massey and Denton draw this insight based on the fact that, even at the height of European immigration, the isolation of no ethnic group approximated the isolation that Black Americans still experience today.
4. Both the history and lingering presence of racial covenants have been well documented in a number of American cities, including Chicago, Hartford, CT, Minneapolis, Seattle, St. Louis, and Washington, DC, among others. See, for example, the Seattle Civil Rights and Labor History Project (2021) at the University of Washington, whose investigatory work has helped pass recent laws allowing homeowners' associations and homeowners to modify racially restrictive language in their governing documents or land title records.
5. There is debate, however, over to what extent the outmigration of nonpoor Black people occurred; I discuss this topic further in Chapter 5.
6. Hancock offers another powerful example of the secondary marginalization (i.e., political isolation within an already marginalized community, per Cohen 1999) of poor Black women, based on Guida West's (1981) case study of the National Welfare Rights Organization (NWRO), a grassroots organization of low-income, single Black mothers that was active from 1966 to 1975. Specifically, Hancock points out the "utter lack of support" given to the NWRO during its existence, by either Black churches—the strongest independent organizations in the Black community at the time—or the Congressional Black Caucus—which largely refused to hear or advance the NWRO's concerns with Nixon's proposed Family Assistance Plan (Hancock 2003, 37).
7. I thank one of the anonymous OUP reviewers for this insight.
8. Oliver and Mendelberg do not examine welfare preferences, but their argument comports with evidence that welfare provision is less generous in more diverse states, given that welfare is administered at the state level (Wright 1977; Orr 1976; R. D. Brown 1995; Plotnick and Winters 1985; Hero and Tolbert 1996).

9. Welfare is among the policy areas Branton and Jones analyze: they identify greater welfare opposition in settings with a high representation of multiple racial/ethnic groups.

10. As Kendi (2016) notes of Black enslaved Southerners, "It had always been amazing to enslaved people how someone could lounge back, drink lemonade, and look out over their fields, and call the bent-over pickers lazy" (235–236). And as he describes the experiences of the Black Americans who, a generation later, made it North only to find the same racism: "They called these migrants, who had moved hundreds of miles seeking work and a better life, lazy" (309).

11. As discussed in Appendix B, I follow Tarman and Sears (2005) analysis of the GSS; the version of racial resentment Kinder and Sanders (1996) produce based on analysis of the ANES is slightly different, as the two surveys include different questions, but the core sentiment of the questions is similar.

12. "Nonrural" refers to all respondents living near an urban center with a population of at least 50,000. Where applicable, I use data for metropolitan divisions, the subcategories into which the eleven largest MSAs are divided.

13. I cluster errors rather than use a multilevel model. This is because hierarchical analysis of the data produces an intraclass correlation coefficient (ICC) of only 0.01 in a null model, short of the typical threshold of 0.10 that would call for multilevel modeling. The number of respondents per MSA is small (9.5 on average), which further reduces the need for a multilevel model. Thus, the results of a multilevel logistic analysis nesting individuals in MSAs are almost identical to those reported in Table 4.2.

    However, even a small intraclass correlation can increase the Type I error rate. To make my analysis more robust against identifying a relationship between geography and welfare preferences where none exists, I cluster standard errors by metropolitan area. This step allows for correlation between observations in the same MSA, which increases the size of the confidence intervals in the model and raises the bar for finding significant effects of the predictor variables on welfare preferences.

14. Two examples of newer measures in the debate over how to measure segregation and its effects include Logan and Parman's (2017) measure based on next-door neighbors, and Ananat and Washington's (2011) measure using railroads as an instrumental variable (based on the ease of segregation in cities that were crisscrossed by more railroad tracks).

15. Using a household-based measure of segregation brings the assumption that all members of a household are of the same race. While rates of interracial marriage have increased drastically in recent years, the overall rate was still only 10% as of 2015 (up from about 3% in 1970)—meaning mixed-race households would comprise no more than a small percentage in most settings. Moreover, both Black Americans and White Americans are less likely to intermarry than Asian Americans and Latinos (Livingston and Brown 2017).

16. Specifically, the exposure index is less commonly used to measure racial segregation than the dissimilarity index (D), which measures the evenness with which a racial group is spread across an area. The dissimilarity index is not sensitive to the size of a minority population, as the exposure index is. While this makes the dissimilarity index helpful for understanding how segregation affects Black outcomes, a measure based on underlying population size is in fact more appropriate for my effort to capture the visibility of certain populations. Moreover, the exposure index measures segregation both from the perspective of a majority group and from the perspective of a minority group, allowing

me to measure the exposure of White people to Black people as distinct from the exposure of Black people to White people.

17. Segregation measures are drawn from the American Communities Project, directed by John Logan at Brown University. White–Black interaction is calculated as $\Sigma[(w_i/W) * (b_i/t_i)]$, where w_i, b_i, and t_i represent the White, Black, and total population of a given census tract, and W represents the White population of the metropolitan area. The more commonly used component of the exposure index captures the isolation of Black households from White households in order to study the deleterious effects of segregation on Black people. However, White exposure to Black people is more appropriate for capturing how segregation shapes White people's experiences of their surroundings.

18. At the most extreme, congressional districts encompass a whole state. For greater comparability to the GSS, I remove ANES respondents who reside in rural areas (defined as living more than 50 miles from an urban center) as well as those who reside in "at large" districts, which represent entire states.

19. I use this variable for comparability to the GSS, given that the 2000 ANES does not contain the variables necessary to replicate my original factor analysis. The "work way up" question loaded strongly on the racial resentment factor extracted from the GSS data and captures the core sentiment of this racial attitude.

Chapter 5

1. Note that Smith and King (2021) use the concept of "protectionism" differently than does Lavelle (2014), whom I cited in Chapter 3. Whereas Lavelle's concept referenced White people's attempts to portray other White people as fundamentally good, particularly in recounting memories of the Jim Crow South, Smith and King reference the strategy demonstrated by President Trump, abandoning colorblind politics to instead promise to "protect" White Americans in a modern world they perceive to be turning against them.

2. An analysis of 2016 census data by the Federal Reserve Bank of St. Louis produced Gini coefficients of 0.48 for Black households, 0.47 for Latino households, 0.44 for White households, and 0.43 for Asian households. Note that the Gini ratio is only one way to measure inequality, focusing on inequality among the entirety of a population. Other metrics—most notably, the ratio of income between the 90th percentile of earners and the 10th percentile—capture trends such as the drastic divergence between the top 10% and bottom 10% of Asian households over the last several decades. Even on this metric, however, Black households are not far behind. The top Asian earners take in 10.7 times as much income as those in the bottom decile, whereas the top Black earners taking in 9.8 times as much as Black households in the bottom decile. The ratio for both Latinos and White Americans is 7.8.

3. Both Richard's and my parents' stories are introduced in Chapter 4.

4. As discussed in Chapter 4, this nuanced expression of prejudice was first introduced by Kinder and Sears (1981) as "symbolic racism"; it has since been reformulated as "modern racism" (McConahay 1986) or "racial resentment" (Kinder and Sanders 1996; Tesler 2016a). I follow previous scholars' extraction of a symbolic racism factor from the GSS, which helps ensure the external validity of my measure. However, throughout this book I use the term "racial resentment" to refer to this sort of prejudice.

5. Confirming *status perceptions hypothesis 1* offers one benefit beyond supporting my conceptualization of status perceptions as a descriptive, rather than normative, evaluation about the racial order. In line with findings that opposition to affirmative action is more closely tied to racial resentment than to traditional prejudice (Williams et al. 1999), I posit racial resentment as a predictor of affirmative action views in the models presented later in Chapter 5. Because these models also posit status perceptions as predictive of affirmative action preferences, confirming *status perceptions hypothesis 1* further demonstrates that status perceptions and racial resentment are not collinear or endogenous.

6. See Chapter 4, under "Segregation and the Visibility of Threat," for my discussion of segregation measured as exposure between households. This topic is also revisited later in Chapter 5.

7. As of 2000, residents of majority-Black neighborhoods were *five times* more likely to refinance in the subprime market than residents of White neighborhoods at the same income level (HUD-Treasury Joint Task Force 2000). As of 2010, Black families were 47% more likely to experience foreclosure than White families (Bocian, Li, and Ernst 2010).

8. To consider whether a more conventional racial threat response can be identified among my sample, and following the same logic discussed in relation to my analysis in Chapter 4 (see Appendix B), I also investigated whether either of the racial attitude measures registers greater hostility among White people in settings with larger Black populations. I find no significant effect of Black population share on either racial attitude variable. Black population share also is not a significant predictor of affirmative action views.

9. As in Chapter 4, where applicable, I use data for metropolitan divisions (MDs), the subcategories into which the eleven largest MSAs are divided. Over the course of the panel, 181 individuals move from one MSA to another. The starting number of MSAs (and MDs) in 2006 is 79.

10. Another way to operationalize the economic status of the races would be to focus on wealth, where the economic disparity between Black and White Americans is most severe. However, income is more easily measured across geographies; it also is more closely tied to employment than wealth is, since wealth accumulation is helped by intergenerational transfer.

11. The occasional instances where the Black–White income gap is negative (places in which Black median household income is higher than White median income) are almost exclusively those where Black residents make up very small percentages of the population and may be sensitive to measurement error.

12. I incorporate dynamic measures of context rather than fixed effects in my perceptions of BRS models for both theoretical and empirical reasons. Theoretically, I am interested in how perceptions of BRS vary between White people who live in different settings. I expect this variation to be predicted in part by longstanding characteristics of MSAs: neither the size of a Black population nor the median income is likely to register much change over the course of a few years. Empirically, support for allowing random effects comes from a Hausman test on the final contextual models of perceptions of BRS indicating that we cannot reject the null hypothesis that unique errors for each individual (u_i) are uncorrelated with the predictor variables.

13. On the potential effect of place-specific experiences, these are difficult to model, but note that the relationships I identify in Chapter 5 hold when controlling for the region in which an MSA is located.

14. It is not surprising that unemployment is the only significant contextual variable in Model 3 of Table 5.6, in light of considerable increases in unemployment at a time when Black population share and Black–White income differentials were steady in most MSAs. Also note that identifying as a Republican becomes significant in Model 3. This suggests that White Republicans' perceptions of BRS may be more sensitive to contexts of increasing unemployment than White Democrats' perceptions of BRS. See under "Considering Alternative Explanations" in Chapter 5 for further discussion of partisanship.

15. Note that repeating the analysis with unemployment rates disaggregated by race produces almost identical results. This is an expected finding, as the rates by race are almost perfectly correlated. Yet, it also confirms that White people perceived rising Black status as both White people and Black people were losing jobs.

16. Skrenty argues that, in addition to the fact affirmative action never received much public support, a second "irony" characterizes this policy area: that is, the broad unpopularity of race-based preferences despite the fact that American society is rife with preferences for particular groups. Skrenty is right to point out how many exceptions the United States has historically made for White people, men, heterosexual individuals, veterans, children, the elderly, and other group. However, it is hardly ironic that considerations for Black people have been less popular. It is arguably more ironic that opponents of federal action to reduce racial inequality ignore the role of the federal state in *creating* this inequality to begin with, as well as the centrality of the federal state in making the limited amends that have been achieved (King 1995).

17. In 2009, a group of White and Latino firefighters challenged the decision of the New Haven Fire Department to invalidate the results of a promotion test due to the fact that no Black candidates scored highly enough to be considered for promotion.

18. There is disagreement over the best way to conceptualize political sophistication: many studies use a measure of educational status, but others argue that political knowledge is a more appropriate predictor of engagement in politics and ideological constraint. For my purposes, it is sufficient to conceptualize sophistication as the product of either education or political knowledge, in either case giving elite members of a dominant group an advantage in justifying opposition to policies that would help the subordinate group.

19. Hochschild (1998) has argued that public opinion on affirmative action may not be as impassioned or polarized as the scholarly debate makes it seem. She cites examples such as Democratic opposition to affirmative action, broad support for reforming rather than ending affirmative action policies, and even the fact that a large number of White people have no associations with affirmative action at all (see also Steeh and Krysan 1996). While these insights are valuable for a deeper understanding of public opinion on affirmative action, a wealth of survey data nonetheless demonstrates that affirmative action is, on the whole, unpopular among White Americans. Even if they are sensitive to question wording that deemphasizes race, White people are more committed to their views on affirmative action than other racial policies, even when they are asked follow-up questions intended to change their minds (Sniderman, Brody, and Tetlock 1993, 145).

20. The word "respectable" brings to mind scholarship on the politics of respectability—or the policing of a marginalized group's actions and appearance by group members themselves. This chapter lacks the scope to fully explore this concept's roots in Black feminist work (see Higginbotham 1993) or its larger influence in the Black community (for a review, see Harris 2014). However, my reference to respectability intends to evoke a problematized

concept that has become part of White America's excessive governance, stigmatization, and judgment of Black Americans as a disproportionately disadvantaged population. For one of several examples of work on this topic, see Soss (2011).

21. Using linear models with binary outcomes is often avoided due to the inherent nonlinearity of the relationship between predictor variables and a binary outcome. There is also the possibility that, at the extreme, a linear model can produce probabilities above 1 or below 0. However, a linear model allows me to retain more observations, as opposed to losing a large portion of the sample when binary logistic regression is used to add fixed effects. Binary logit models also bring their own uncertainty depending on the location of a particular observation on the estimated logit curve. Finally, the evidence provided for the significance of perceptions of BRS in the random effects model supports my use of a linear fixed effects model to ensure that this significance holds when accounting for unobserved individual-level factors.

22. While there is some individual-level variation in racial resentment over the panel, this variation is not predictive of affirmative action views—furthermore, contextual measures of Black population share, unemployment rate, and White population change do not predict levels of racial resentment (as they predicted perceptions of BRS).

23. All statistics drawn from the 2010 ACS 5-Year Data.

Chapter 6

1. Ahmed (2004, par. 2) draws this connection between her argument and Lorde's, specifically regarding the project of Whiteness studies as undertaken by non-White scholars.

2. Examples of such works have been cited throughout the book—such as Pattillo's research on the tenuous status of the Black middle class, or works by Hancock, Threadcraft, Lorde, and hooks that explore the intersections of gender and race. Beyond the academy and particularly in the arts, there are abundant examples of works that illustrate Blackness in its many forms and on its own terms.

3. See, for example, Moon-Kie Jung's (2015) analysis of racially disparate *New York Times* coverage of unemployment rates, or Alexandra Bell's (2017) "Counternarratives," an artistic response to the same newspaper's coverage of racialized events and reproduction of stereotypes.

4. Flores has demonstrated the aversion non-Black racial minorities often exhibit to living near Black people. A much broader conversation that I lack scope to take up is how either Black people or other minority groups have participated in or supported the creation of racialized systems, or have internalized or reproduced negative racial stereotypes.

References

Abrajano, Marisa, and Zoltan L. Hajnal. 2017. *White Backlash: Immigration, Race, and American Politics.* Princeton: Princeton University Press.

Abramowitz, Alan, and Jennifer McCoy. 2019. "United States: Racial Resentment, Negative Partisanship, and Polarization in Trump's America." *The ANNALS of the American Academy of Political and Social Science* 681 (1): 137–156.

Acharya, Avidit, Matthew Blackwell, and Maya Sen. 2018. *Deep Roots: How Slavery Still Shapes Southern Politics.* Princeton: Princeton University Press.

Ackerman, Robert Argento, Gerhard Fries, and Richard A. Windle. 2012. "Changes in U.S. Family Finances from 2007 to 2010: Evidence from the Survey of Consumer Finances." *Federal Reserve Bulletin* 100: 1–80.

Ahmed, Sara. 2004. "Declarations of Whiteness: The Non-Performativity of Anti-Racism." *Borderlands* 3 (2).

Ahmed, Sara. 2009. "Embodying Diversity: Problems and Paradoxes for Black Feminists." *Race Ethnicity and Education* 12 (1): 41–52.

Alesina, Alberto, Reza Baqir, and William Easterly. 1999. "Public Goods and Ethnic Divisions." *The Quarterly Journal of Economics* 114 (4): 1243–1284.

Alesina, Alberto, and Edward Glaeser. 2004. *Fighting Poverty in the US and Europe: A World of Difference.* Oxford: Oxford University Press.

Allen, Danielle S. 2004. *Talking to Strangers: Anxieties of Citizenship since* Brown v. Board of Education. Chicago: University of Chicago Press.

Allen, Rebekah. 2018. "EBR Offcials Seek to Address 'Food Deserts' in Poor Neighborhoods." *The Advocate* (Baton Rouge) October 17. https://www.theadvocate.com/baton_rouge/news/article_64fe114d-8ceb-5afc-be4a-07c?bf0bfa0.html%7B%5C%25%7D0AEBR.

Allport, Gordon. 1954. *The Nature of Prejudice.* Cambridge, MA: Addison-Wesley.

Als, Hilton. 2003. "Ghosts in the House: How Toni Morrison Fostered a Generation of Black Writers." *The New Yorker* October 27. https://www.newyorker.com/magazine/2003/10/27/ghosts-in-the-house.

Ananat, Elizabeth Oltmans. 2011. "The Wrong Side(s) of the Tracks: The Causal Effects of Racial Segregation on Urban Poverty and Inequality." *American Economic Journal: Applied Economics* 3 (2): 34–66.

Anderson, Carol. 2016. *White Rage: The Unspoken Truth of Our Racial Divide.* New York: Bloomsbury Publishing USA.

Anderson, Elijah. 2012. "The Iconic Ghetto." *The ANNALS of the American Academy of Political and Social Science* 642 (1): 8–24.

Anderson, Elizabeth. 2006. "The Epistemology of Democracy." *Episteme: A Journal of Social Epistemology* 3 (1): 8–22.

Anderson, Michelle Wilde. 2012. "Dissolving Cities." *Yale Law Journal* 121: 1364–1446.

APSA Task Force. 2011. *Political Science in the 21st Century.* American Political Science Association. https://files.eric.ed.gov/fulltext/ED527000.pdf.

Associated Press. 2005. "Rebel Flag Flap at LSU." *Washington Times* April 4. https://www.washingtontimes.com/news/2005/apr/4/20050404-112519-8051r/washingtontimes.com/news/2005/apr/4/20050404-112519-8051r/.

Associated Press. 2010. "Reports Allege B.R. Police Misconduct Post-Katrina." *The Times-Picayune* (New Orleans) March 15. http://www.nola.com/news/index.ssf/2010/03/reports_allege_br_police_misco.html.

Avila, Eric. 2014. *The Folklore of the Freeway: Race and Revolt in the Modernist City.* Minneapolis: University of Minnesota Press.

Bader, Michael D. M., and Siri Warkentien. 2016. "The Fragmented Evolution of Racial Integration since the Civil Rights Movement." *Sociological Science* 3: 135–166.

Baldwin, James. 1961. "The Dangerous Road Before Martin Luther King." *Harper's Magazine* February.

Baldwin, James. 1964. *The Uses of the Blues.* New York: Pantheon Books.

Baldwin, James. 1984. *Notes of a Native Son.* Boston: Beacon Press.

Baldwin, James. 2017. *I Am Not Your Negro.* Edited by Raoul Peck. London: Penguin Classics.

Bamfield, Louise, and Tim Horton. 2009. *Understanding Attitudes to Tackling Economic Inequality.* Joseph Rowntree Foundation. https://www.jrf.org.uk/report/understanding-attitudes-tackling-economic-inequality.

Baurick, Tristan, Lylla Younes, and Joan Meiners. 2019. "Welcome to 'Cancer Alley': Where Toxic Air Is About to Get Worse." *ProPublica* October 30. https://www.propublica.org/article/welcome-to-cancer-alley-where-toxic-air-is-about-to-get-worse

Baybeck, Brady. 2006. "Sorting Out the Competing Effects of Racial Context." *Journal of Politics* 68 (2): 386–396.

Beckett, Katherine, and Megan Ming Francis. 2020. "The Origins of Mass Incarceration: The Racial Politics of Crime and Punishment in the Post–Civil Rights Era." *Annual Review of Law and Social Science* 16 (1): 433–452.

Behr, Roy L., and Shanto Iyengar. 1985. "Television News, Real-World Cues, and Changes in the Public Agenda." *The Public Opinion Quarterly* 49 (1): 38–57.

Bell, Alexandra. 2017. *Counternarratives.* New York. http://www.alexandrabell.com/public-work.

Bell, Jeannine. 2007. "Hate Thy Neighbor: Violent Racial Exclusions and the Persistence of Segregation." *Ohio State Journal of Criminal Law* 5 (1): 47–77.

Bellinger, Larry, and Amy J. Hillman. 2000. "Does Tolerance Lead to Better Partnering? The Relationship between Diversity Management and M&A Success." *Business & Society* 39 (3): 323–337.

Bethencourt, Daniel, and Charles Lussier. 2014. "Opponents Say St. George School District Would Force Construction of More Schools than Proponents Plan." *The Advocate* (Baton Rouge) November 3. http://www.theadvocate.com/baton_rouge/news/education/article_da1b06da-c9c1-5e39-8e79-b4df6e262ef6.html.

Bischoff, Kendra, and Sean F. Reardon. 2014. "Residential Segregation by Income, 1970–2009." In *Diversity and Disparities: America Enters a New Century,* 43. New York: The Russell Sage Foundation.

Blalock, Hubert M. 1967. *Toward a Theory of Minority-Group Relations.* New York; London: John Wiley & Sons, Inc.

Blumer, Herbert. 1958. "Race Prejudice as a Sense of Group Position." *The Pacific Sociological Review* 1 (1): 3–7.

Bobo, Lawrence. 1983. "Whites' Opposition to Busing: Symbolic Racism or Realistic Group Conflict?" *Journal of Personality and Social Psychology* 45 (6): 1196–1210.

Bobo, Lawrence. 1998a. "Mapping Racial Attitudes at the Century's End: Has the Color Line Vanished or Merely Reconfigured." *Aspen Roundtable Project on Race and Community Revitalization,* 1–46. https://www.aspeninstitute.org/wp-content/uploads/files/content/upload/16Bobo_0.pdf

Bobo, Lawrence. 1998b. "Race, Interests, and Beliefs about Affirmative Action: Unanswered Questions and New Directions." *American Behavioral Scientist* 41 (7): 985–1003.

Bobo, Lawrence, and Vincent L. Hutchings. 1996. "Perceptions of Racial Group Competition: Extending Blumer's Theory of Group Position to a Multiracial Social Context." *American Sociological Review* 61 (6): 951.

Bobo, Lawrence, and James R. Kluegel. 1993. "Opposition to Race-Targeting: Self-Interest, Stratification Ideology, or Racial Attitudes?" *American Sociological Review* 58 (4): 443.

Bobocel, D. Ramona, Leanne S. Son Hing, Liane M. Davey, David J. Stanley, and Mark P. Zanna. 1998. "Justice-Based Opposition to Social Policies: Is It Genuine?" *Journal of Personality and Social Psychology* 75 (3): 653.

Bocian, Debbie Gruenstein, Wei Li, and Keith S. Ernst. 2010. "Foreclosures by Race and Ethnicity." *Center for Responsible Lending:* 4–6.

Bonastia, Christopher. 2006. *Knocking on the Door: The Federal Government's Attempt to Desegregate the Suburbs.* Princeton: Princeton University Press.

Bonilla-Silva, Eduardo. 2002. "The Linguistics of Color Blind Racism: How to Talk Nasty about Blacks without Sounding 'Racist.'" *Critical Sociology* 28 (1–2): 41–64.

Bonilla-Silva, Eduardo. 2006. *Racism without Racists: Color-Blind Racism and the Persistence of Racial Inequality in the United States.* Lanham, MD: Rowman & Littlefield Publishers.

Books, John, and Charles Prysby. 1999. "Contextual Effects on Retrospective Economic Evaluations: The Impact of the State and Local Economy." *Political Behavior* 21 (1): 1–16.

Bourdieu, Pierre. 1990. *The Logic of Practice.* Stanford: Stanford University Press.

Bowen, William G., and Derek Bok. 2000. *The Shape of the River: Long-Term Consequences of Considering Race in College and University Admissions.* Princeton: Princeton University Press.

Boyce, Christopher J., Gordon D. A. Brown, and Simon C. Moore. 2010. "Money and Happiness: Rank of Income, Not Income, Affects Life Satisfaction." *Psychological Science* 21 (4): 471–475.

Branton, Regina P., and Bradford S. Jones. 2005. "Reexamining Racial Attitudes: The Conditional Relationship between Diversity and Socioeconomic Environment." *American Journal of Political Science* 49 (2): 359–372.

Braun, Virginia, and Victoria Clarke. 2006. "Using Thematic Analysis in Psychology." *Qualitative Research in Psychology* 3 (2): 77–101.

Brewer, Marilynn B. 1999. "The Psychology of Prejudice: Ingroup Love or Outgroup Hate?" *Journal of Social Issues* 55 (3): 429–444.

Briffault, Richard. 1993. "Who Rules at Home? One Person/One Vote and Local Governments." *The University of Chicago Law Review* 60 (2): 339–424.

Brodkin, Karen. 1998. *How Jews Became White Folks and What That Says about Race in America.* New Brunswick, NJ: Rutgers University Press.

Brooks, Richard R. W., and Carol M. Rose. 2013. *Saving the Neighborhood: Racially Restrictive Covenants, Law, and Social Norms.* Cambridge, MA: Harvard University Press.

Brown, Robert D. 1995. "Party Cleavages and Welfare Effort in the American States." *American Political Science Review* 89 (1): 23–33.

Brown, Wendy. 2008. *Regulating Aversion: Tolerance in the Age of Identity and Empire.* Princeton: Princeton University Press.

Burd-Sharps, Sarah, Kristen Lewis, and Eduardo Borges Martins. 2009. *A Portrait of Louisiana: Louisiana Human Development Report 2009.* American Human Development Project of the Social Science Research Council. https://measureofamerica.org/louisiana/.

Burd-Sharps, Sarah, and Rebecca Rasch. 2015. *Impact of the US Housing Crisis on the Racial Wealth Gap Across Generations.* Social Science Research Council. https://www.aclu.org/files/field_document/discrimlend_final.pdf

Burr, Vivien. 2003. *Social Constructionism*. New York; London: Routledge.

Butler, Judith. 1993. "Endangered/Endangering: Schematic Racism and White Paranoia." Chap. 1 in *Reading Rodney King/Reading Urban Uprising*, edited by Robert Gooding-Williams, 15–22. New York: Routledge.

Caldas, Stephen J., and Carl Bankston. 1997. "Effect of School Population Socioeconomic Status on Individual Academic Achievement." *The Journal of Educational Research* 90 (5): 269–277.

Campbell, Andrea Louise. 2007. "Universalism, Targeting, and Participation." In *Remaking America: Democracy and Public Policy in an Age of Inequality*, edited by Joe Soss, Jacob S. Hacker, and Suzanne Mettler, 121–140. New York: Russell Sage Foundation.

Carmines, Edward G., and Geoffrey C. Layman. 1998. "When Prejudice Matters: The Impact of Racial Stereotypes on the Racial Policy Preferences of Democrats and Republicans." Chap. 4 in *Perception and Prejudice: Race and Politics in the United States*, edited by Mark Peffley, 100–134. New Haven: Yale University Press.

Carmines, Edward G., and James A. Stimson. 1989. *Issue Evolution: Race and the Transformation of American Politics*. Princeton: Princeton University Press.

Caro, Robert A. 1974. *The Power Broker: Robert Moses and the Fall of New York*. New York: Alfred A. Knopf.

Carr Riggs & Ingram. 2015. *Estimated Operating Budget for the Proposed City of St. George, Louisiana*. Metarie, LA. Accessed September 15, 2016. http://www.stgeorgelouisiana.com/_photos/Final%20St%20George%20Report%202015%20(1).pdf.

Case, Anne, and Angus Deaton. 2015. "Rising Morbidity and Mortality in Midlife among White Non-Hispanic Americans in the 21st Century." *Proceedings of the National Academy of Sciences* 112 (49): 15078–15083.

Cavaillé, Charlotte, and Kris-Stella Trump. 2015. "The Two Facets of Social Policy Preferences." *Journal of Politics* 77 (1): 146–160.

Chetty, Raj, Nathaniel Hendren, Maggie R. Jones, and Sonya R. Porter. 2020. "Race and Economic Opportunity in the United States: An Intergenerational Perspective." *The Quarterly Journal of Economics* 135 (2): 711–783.

Chetty, Raj, Nathaniel Hendren, and Lawrence Katz. 2016. "The Effects of Exposure to Better Neighborhoods on Children: New Evidence from the Moving to Opportunity Project." *American Economic Review* 106 (4).

Chetty, Raj, Nathaniel Hendren, Patrick Kline, and Emmanuel Saez. 2014. "Where Is the Land of Opportunity? The Geography of Intergenerational Mobility in the United States." *The Quarterly Journal of Economics* 129 (4): 1553–1623.

Cho, Wendy K. Tam, and Charles F. Manski. 2008. "Cross Level/Ecological Inference." *Oxford Handbook of Political Methodology*, 547–569.

Choi, Ann, Keith Herbert, and Olivia Winslow. 2019. "Long Island Divided: Steering homebuyers is illegal. We found evidence of it." *Newsday* (Long Island, NY) November 1. https://projects.newsday.com/long-island/steering-real-estate-agents/

Chudy, Jennifer, Spencer Piston, and Joshua Shipper. 2019. "Guilt by Association: White Collective Guilt in American Politics." *Journal of Politics* 81 (3).

Clark, Jess. 2019. "In Diverse East Baton Rouge, an Affluent White Area Seeks Its Own City, School District." *New Orleans Public Radio* October 11. https://www.wwno.org/post/diverse-east-baton-rouge-affluent-white-area-seeks-its-own-city-school-district?fbclid=IwAR2sGm2R4ot0lX_qI-m2wqK-U918ornCeED3-Jffpzf16zfUrJgTM7LzWTY.

Clark, W. A. V. 1991. "Residential Preferences and Neighborhood Racial Segregation: A Test of the Schelling Segregation Model." *Demography* 28 (1): 1–19.

Climek, Michael, and Maxwell Means. 2013. "Support/Opposition for the Proposed City of St. George in East Baton Rouge Parish." LSU Public Policy Research Lab. https://pprllsu.com/

wp-content/uploads/2015/12/Support-Opposition-for-the-Proposed-City-of-St-George.
pdf.

Coates, Ta-Nehisi. 2017. "The First White President." *The Atlantic* October. https://www
.theatlantic.com/amp/article/537909/.

Cohen, Cathy J. 1999. *The Boundaries of Blackness: AIDS and the Breakdown of Black Politics.*
Chicago: University of Chicago Press.

Cohen, Cathy J. 2010. *Democracy Remixed: Black Youth and the Future of American Politics.*
New York: Oxford University Press.

Cole, Luke W., and Sheila R. Foster. 2001. *From the Ground Up: Environmental Racism and the
Rise of the Environmental Justice Movement.* New York: New York University Press.

Collins, Patricia Hill. 1986. "Learning from the Outsider Within." *Social Problems: Special
Theory Issue* 33 (6): S14–S32.

Collins, Patricia Hill. 1998. *Fighting Words: Black Women and the Search for Justice.* Minneapolis; London: University of Minnesota Press.

Collins, Patricia Hill. 1999. "Reflections on the Outsider Within." *Journal of Career Development* 26 (1): 85–88.

Committee to Incorporate St. George. 2014a. *About Us.* Accessed May 30, 2017. http://www
.stgeorgelouisiana.com/about.

Committee to Incorporate St. George. 2014b. *Response to PBS Frontline "Documentary."*
Accessed May 30, 2017. http://www.stgeorgelouisiana.com/latest-news/response-to-pbs
-frontline-documentary.

Converse, Philip E. 1962. "Information Flow and the Stability of Partisan Attitudes." *Public
Opinion Quarterly* 26 (4): 578–599.

Cowen Institute. 2010. *Louisiana Desegregation Case Studies: East Baton Rouge, West Carroll, and Tangipahoa.* Tulane University, New Orleans. http://www.coweninstitute.com/
wp-content/uploads/2010/08/Louisiana-Desegregation-Case-Studies.pdf.

Cramer, Katherine J. 2016. *The Politics of Resentment: Rural Consciousness in Wisconsin and the
Rise of Scott Walker.* Chicago: University of Chicago Press.

Crosby, Faye J., Aarti Iyer, and Sirinda Sincharoen. 2006. "Understanding Affirmative Action."
Annual Review of Psychology 57: 585–611.

Cutler, David M., Edward L. Glaeser, and Jacob L. Vigdor. 1999. "The Rise and Decline of the
American Ghetto." *Journal of Political Economy* 107 (3): 455.

Daniels, Jessie. 2013. "Race and Racism in Internet Studies: A Review and Critique." *New Media
& Society* 15 (5): 695–719.

Dawson, Michael C. 1994. *Behind the Mule: Race and Class in African American Politics.*
Princeton: Princeton University Press.

Dawson, Michael C. 2001. *Black Visions: The Roots of Contemporary African-American Political
Ideologies.* Chicago: University of Chicago Press.

Dawson, Michael C. 2013. *Blacks In and Out of the Left.* Cambridge, MA: Harvard University
Press.

Debord, Guy. 1967. *La Société du Spectacle (The Society of the Spectacle).* Paris: Buchet-Chastel.

Delmont, Matthew F. 2016. *Why Busing Failed: Race, Media, and the National Resistance to
School Desegregation.* Oakland: University of California Press.

DiAngelo, Robin. 2011. "White Fragility." *International Journal of Critical Pedagogy* 3 (3):
54–70.

Disare, Monica. 2018. "Fifty Years Ago, Teacher Oustings That Led to New York City's Massive
Teacher Strikes." *Chalkbeat* May 10.

DiTomaso, Nancy. 2013. *The American Non-Dilemma: Racial Inequality without Racism.*
New York: Russell Sage Foundation.

Dixon, Angela R., and Edward E. Telles. 2017. "Skin Color and Colorism: Global Research, Concepts, and Measurement." *Annual Review of Sociology* 43: 405–424.

Donohue III, John J., and James Heckman. 1991. "Continuous Versus Episodic Change: The Impact of Civil Rights Policy on the Economic Status of Blacks." NBER Working Paper 3894, Cambridge, MA. https://www.nber.org/papers/w3894.

Douglass, Frederick. 1881. "The Color Line." *The North American Review* 132 (295): 567–577.

Drake, St. Clair, and Horace Cayton. 1945. *Black Metropolis: A Study of Negro Life in a Northern City.* New York: Harper & Row.

Du Bois, W. E. B. 1899. *The Philadelphia Negro: A Social Study.* Philadelphia: University of Pennsylvania Press.

Du Bois, W. E. B. 1903. *The Souls of Black Folk.* Chicago: A.C. McClurg & Co.

Eberhardt, Jennifer L., Phillip Atiba Goff, Valerie J. Purdie, and Paul G. Davies. 2004. "Seeing Black: Race, Crime, and Visual Processing." *Journal of Personality and Social Psychology* 87 (6): 876–893.

Edelman, Murray. 1988. *Constructing the Political Spectacle.* Chicago: University of Chicago Press.

Edsall, Thomas Byrne, and Mary Edsall. 1991. *Chain Reaction: The Impact of Rights, Race and Taxes on American Politics.* New York: W.W. Norton & Company.

Ehrenhalt, Alan. 2012. *The Great Inversion and the Future of the American City.* New York: Knopf.

Ellison, Ralph. 1952. *Invisible Man.* New York: Vintage Books.

Ellison, Ralph. 1970. "What America Would Be Like without Blacks." *Going to the Territory,* 104–112. New York: Random House.

Enos, Ryan D. 2016. "What the Demolition of Public Housing Teaches Us about the Impact of Racial Threat on Political Behavior." *American Journal of Political Science* 60 (1): 123–142.

Enos, Ryan D. 2017. *The Space between Us: Social Geography and Politics.* Cambridge: Cambridge University Press.

Enos, Ryan D., and Christopher Celaya. 2018. "The Effect of Segregation on Intergroup Relations." *Journal of Experimental Political Science* 5 (1): 26–38.

Evans, Stephanie Y. 2007. "Women of Color in American Higher Education." *Thought & Action* 23: 131–138.

Fairlie, Robert W., and Alexandra M. Resch. 2002. "Is There 'White Flight' into Private Schools? Evidence from the National Educational Longitudinal Survey." *The Review of Economics and Statistics* 84 (1): 21–33.

Faulk & Winkler LLC. 2014. *A Review of Finances for the Proposed City of St. George.* Technical report December. Baton Rouge Area Foundation and Baton Rouge Area Chamber. http://www.braf.org/braf-research/2016/2/29/analysis-operating-st-george-may-require-tax-increases.

Feagin, Joe R. 2013. *The White Racial Frame: Centuries of Racial Framing and Counter-Framing.* New York; London: Routledge.

Feagin, Joe R., and Melvin P. Sikes. 1994. *Living with Racism: The Black Middle-Class Experience.* Boston: Beacon Press.

Federal Highway Administration. 2017. *Highway History Interstate Highway System—Quotables.* Accessed February 15, 2021. https://www.fhwa.dot.gov/interstate/quotable.cfm.

Federico, Christopher M., and Jim Sidanius. 2002. "Racism, Ideology, and Affirmative Action Revisited: The Antecedents and Consequences of 'Principled Objections' to Affirmative Action." *Journal of Personality and Social Psychology* 82 (4): 488.

Feinberg, William E., and Norris R. Johnson. 1988. "'Outside Agitators' and Crowds: Results from a Computer Simulation Model." *Social Forces* 67 (2): 398–423.

Felton, Emmanuel. 2017. "The Department of Justice Is Overseeing the Resegregation of American Schools." *The Nation* September. https://www.thenation.com/article/the-department-of-justice-is-overseeing-the-resegregation-of-american-schools/.

Few, April L., Dionne P. Stephens, and Marlo Rouse-Arnett. 2003. "Sister-to-Sister Talk: Transcending Boundaries and Challenges in Qualitative Research With Black Women." *Family Relations* 52 (3): 205–215.

Finkel, Steven E., Thomas M. Guterbock, and Marian J. Borg. 1991. "Race-of-Interviewer Effects in a Preelection Poll: Virginia 1989." *The Public Opinion Quarterly* 55 (3): 313–330.

Flores, Ronald J. O., and Arun Peter Lobo. 2013. "The Reassertion of a Black/Non-Black Color Line: The Rise in Integrated Neighborhoods Without Blacks in New York City, 1970–2010." *Journal of Urban Affairs* 35 (3): 255–282.

Fogelson, Robert M. 1971. *Violence as Protest: A Study of Riots and Ghettos.* Garden City, NY: Doubleday.

Ford, Richard Thompson. 1994. "The Boundaries of Race: Political Geography in Legal Analysis." *Harvard Law Review* 107 (8): 1841–1921.

Fortin, Jacey. 2020. "The Long History of the 'Outside Agitator.'" *New York Times* June 8. https://www.nytimes.com/2020/06/08/us/outside-agitators-history-civil-rights.html.

Fossett, Mark A., and K. Jill Kiecolt. 1989. "The Relative Size of Minority Populations and White Racial Attitudes." *Social Science Quarterly* 70 (4): 820–835.

Fotheringham, A. Stewart, and David W. S. Wong. 1991. "The Modifiable Areal Unit Problem in Multivariate Statistical Analysis." *Environment and Planning* 23 (7): 1025–1044.

Foucault, Michel. 1972. *The Archaelogy of Knowledge and the Discourse on Language.* New York: Pantheon Books.

Fox, Cybelle. 2012. *Three Worlds of Relief: Race, Immigration, and the American Welfare State from the Progressive Era to the New Deal.* Princeton: Princeton University Press.

Fox Piven, Frances, and Richard Cloward. 1971. *Regulating the Poor.* New York: Pantheon Books.

Francis, Megan Ming. 2014. *Civil Rights and the Making of the Modern American State.* Cambridge: Cambridge University Press.

Frankenberg, Ruth. 1993. *White Women, Race Matters: The Social Construction of Whiteness.* Minneapolis: University of Minnesota Press.

Frazier, E. Franklin. 1939. *The Negro Family in the United States.* Notre Dame, IN: University of Notre Dame Press.

Frazier, E. Franklin. 1957. *Black Bourgeoisie.* Oxford: Simon & Schuster.

Frydl, Kathleen. 2009. *The GI Bill.* Cambridge: Cambridge University Press.

Frymer, Paul. 2008. *Black and Blue: African Americans, the Labor Movement, and the Decline of the Democratic Party.* Princeton; Oxford; Princeton University Press.

Fullilove, Mindy Thompson. 2016. *Root Shock: How Tearing Up City Neighborhoods Hurts America, and What We Can Do About It.* New York: New Village Press.

Gallagher, Charles A. 2004. "Transforming Racial Identity Through Affirmative Action." In *Race and Ethnicity: Across Time, Space, and Discipline,* edited by Rodney D. Coates, 153–170. Leiden, NL: Brill Publishers.

Gallagher, Charles A. 2008. "'The End of Racism' as the New Doxa: New Strategies for Researching Race." Chap. 10 in *White Logic, White Methods: Racism and Methodology,* 163–178. Lanham, MD: Rowman & Littlefield Publishers.

Gasman, Marybeth. 2013. "The Changing Face of Historically Black Colleges and Universities The Changing Face of Historically Black Colleges and Universities." Penn Center for Minority Serving Institutions. https://repository.upenn.edu/gse_pubs/335/.

Gates Jr., Henry Louis. 1989. "TV's Black World Turns—But Stays Unreal." *New York Times* November 1. http://www.nytimes.com/1989/11/12/arts/tv-s-black-world-turns-but-stays-unreal.html.

Gay, Claudine. 2004. "Putting Race in Context: Identifying the Environmental Determinants of Black Racial Attitudes." *American Political Science Review* 98 (4): 547–562.

Gay, Claudine. 2006. "Seeing Difference: The Effect of Economic Disparity on Black Attitudes toward Latinos." *American Journal of Political Science* 50 (4): 982–997.

Geertz, Clifford. 1973. *The Interpretation of Cultures.* New York: Basic Books.

Gibson, Ginger. 2005. "Fans Continue To Fly Banned Flag at LSU." *New York Times* October 17. https://archive.nytimes.com/www.nytimes.com/uwire/uwire_KJB101720055296427.html.

Giddings, Paula J. 1996. *When and Where I Enter: The Impact of Black Women on Race and Sex in America.* New York: Bantam.

Gieryn, Thomas F. 2000. "A Space for Place in Sociology." *Annual Review of Sociology* 26 (1): 463–496.

Gilens, Martin. 1995. "Racial Attitudes and Opposition to Welfare." *Journal of Politics* 57 (4): 994–1014.

Gilens, Martin. 1996. "'Race Coding' and White Opposition to Welfare." *American Political Science Review* 90 (3): 593–604.

Gilens, Martin. 1999. *Why Americans Hate Welfare: Race, Media, and the Politics of Anti-Poverty Policy.* Chicago: University of Chicago Press.

Giles, Micheal W. 1977. "Percent Black and Racial Hostility: An Old Assumption Reexamined." *Social Science Quarterly* 58 (3): 412–417.

Giles, Micheal W., and Melanie A. Buckner. 1993. "David Duke and Black Threat: An Old Hypothesis Revisited." *Journal of Politics* 55 (3): 702.

Giles, Micheal W., and Arthur S. Evans. 1985. "External Threat, Perceived Threat and Group Identity." *Social Science Quarterly* 66 (1): 50.

Gingrich, J., and B. Ansell. 2012. "Preferences in Context: Micro Preferences, Macro Contexts, and the Demand for Social Policy." *Comparative Political Studies* 45 (12): 1624–1654.

Gingrich, Jane. 2014. "Visibility, Values, and Voters: The Informational Role of the Welfare State." *Journal of Politics* 76 (2): 565–580.

Glaeser, Edward, and Jacob Vigdor. 2012. *The End of the Segregated Century: Racial Separation in America's Neighborhoods, 1890–2010.* Civic Report No. 66, Center for State and Local Leadership, Manhattan Institute. https://www.manhattan-institute.org/html/end-segregated-century-racial-separation-americas-neighborhoods-1890-2010-5848.html.

Glaser, James M. 2001. "The Preference Puzzle: Educational Differences in Racial-Political Attitudes." *Political Behavior* 23 (4): 313–334.

Glaude, Eddie S. 2020. *Begin Again: James Baldwin's America and Its Urgent Lessons for Our Own.* New York: Crown.

Glick, Peter. 2005. "Choice of Scapegoats." In *On the Nature of Prejudice: Fifty Years after Allport,* edited by John F. Dovidio, Peter Glick, and Laurie A. Rudman, 244–261. Malden, MA: Blackwell Publishing.

Goffman, Erving. 1978. *The Presentation of Self in Everyday Life.* London: Harmondsworth.

Graeber, David. 2015. *The Utopia of Rules: On Technology, Stupidity, and the Secret Joys of Bureaucracy.* London: Melville House.

Gramsci, Antonio. 1995. *Further Selections from the Prison Notebooks.* Minneapolis: University of Minnesota Press.

Griggs, Ted. 2017. "Long-Awaited North Baton Rouge Emergency Room to Open Nov. 15, OLOL Says." *The Advocate* (Baton Rouge) October 25. http://www.theadvocate.com/baton_rouge/news/business/article_3669260c-b99f-11e7-8b54-078d2d22ee04.html.

Hall, Stuart. 1981. "The Whites of Their Eyes." In *Silver Linings,* edited by George Bridges and Rosalind Brunt, 23–38. London: Lawrence/Wishart.

Hancock, Ange-Marie. 2003. "Contemporary Welfare Reform and the Public Identity of the 'Welfare Queen.'" *Race, Gender & Class* 10 (1): 31–59.

Hancock, Ange-Marie. 2004. *The Politics of Disgust: The Public Identity of the Welfare Queen.* New York: NYU Press.

Hannah-Jones, Nikole. 2014. "Lack of Order: The Erosion of a Once-Great Force for Integration." *ProPublica* May 1. https://www.propublica.org/article/lack-of-order-the-erosion-of-a-once-great-force-for-integration.

Hannon, James T. 1984. "The Influence of Catholic Schools on the Desegregation of Public School Systems: A Case Study of White Flight in Boston." *Population Research and Policy Review* 3 (3): 219–237.

Hannon, Lance. 2015. "White Colorism." *Social Currents* 2 (1): 13–21.

Haraway, Donna. 1988. "Situated Knowledges: The Science Question in Feminism and the Privilege of Partial Perspective." *Feminist Studies* 14 (3): 575–599.

Harding, Sandra G. 2004. *The Feminist Standpoint Theory Reader: Intellectual and Political Controversies.* New York; London: Routledge.

Harris, Fredrick C. 2014. "The Rise of Respectability Politics." *Dissent* 61 (1): 33–37.

Harris-Lacewell, Melissa V. 2003. "The Heart of the Politics of Race: Centering Black People in the Study of White Racial Attitudes." *Journal of Black Studies* 34 (2): 222–249.

Hartigan, John. 1997. "Establishing the Fact of Whiteness." *American Anthropologist* 99 (3): 495–505.

Hartsock, Nancy C. M. 2004. "The Feminist Standpoint: Developing the Ground for a Specifically Feminist Historical Materialism." In *The Feminist Standpoint Theory Reader,* edited by Sandra Harding, 35–54. New York: Routledge.

Harvey, David. 1985. *The Urbanization of Capital: Studies in the History and Theory of Capitalist Urbanization.* Baltimore, MD: Johns Hopkins University Press.

Harvey, Richard D., and Debra L. Oswald. 2000. "Collective Guilt and Shame as Motivation for White Support of Black Programs." *Journal of Applied Social Psychology* 30 (9): 1790–1811.

Haynes, Bruce D. 2001. *Red Lines, Black Spaces: The Politics of Race and Space in a Middle-Class Black Suburb.* New Haven: Yale University Press.

Heckman, James J., and Brook S. Payner. 1989. "Determining the Impact of Federal Antidiscrimination Policy on the Economic Status of Blacks: A Study of South Carolina." *The American Economic Review* 79 (1): 138–177.

Hero, Rodney E., and Morris E. Levy. 2018. "The Racial Structure of Inequality: Consequences for Welfare Policy in the United States." *Social Science Quarterly* 99 (2): 459–472.

Hero, Rodney E., and Caroline J. Tolbert. 1996. "A Racial/Ethnic Diversity Interpretation of Politics and Policy in the States of the US." *American Journal of Political Science* 40 (3): 851–871.

Hersh, Eitan D., and Clayton Nall. 2015. "The Primacy of Race in the Geography of Income-Based Voting: New Evidence from Public Voting Records." *American Journal of Political Science* 60 (2): 289–303.

Hetherington, Marc J. 2009. "Review Article: Putting Polarization in Perspective." *British Journal of Political Science* 39 (2): 413–448.

Hewitt, Roger. 2005. *White Backlash and the Politics of Multiculturalism.* Cambridge: Cambridge University Press.

Higginbotham, Evelyn Brooks. 1993. *Righteous Discontent: The Women's Movement in the Black Baptist Church, 1880–1920.* Cambridge, MA: Harvard University Press.

Hirsch, Werner Z., and Joel G. Hirsch. 1979. "Exclusionary Zoning: Local Property Taxation and the Unique-Ubiquitous Resource Distinction." *Southern California Law Review* 52 (6): 1671–1726.

Hochschild, Jennifer L. 1995. *Facing Up to the American Dream: Race, Class, and the Soul of the Nation.* Princeton: Princeton University Press.

Hochschild, Jennifer L. 1998. "The Strange Career of Affirmative Action." *Ohio State Law Journal* 59 (3): 997–1037.

Hochschild, Jennifer L., Vesla M. Weaver, and Traci R. Burch. 2012. *Creating a New Racial Order: How Immigration, Multiracialism, Genomics, and the Young Can Remake Race in America.* Princeton: Princeton University Press.

hooks, bell. 1992. *Black Looks: Race and Representation.* Boston: South End Press.

hooks, bell. 2000. *Feminist Theory: From Margin to Center.* London: Pluto Press.

Hopkins, Daniel J. 2009. "No More Wilder Effect, Never a Whitman Effect: When and Why Polls Mislead about Black and Female Candidates." *Journal of Politics* 71 (3): 769.

Hopkins, Daniel J. 2010. "Politicized Places: Explaining Where and When Immigrants Provoke Local Opposition." *American Political Science Review* 104 (1): 40–60.

Hopkins, Daniel J. 2011. "The Limited Local Impacts of Ethnic and Racial Diversity." *American Politics Research* 39 (2): 344–379.

Hopkins, Daniel J. 2012. "Flooded Communities: Explaining Local Reactions to the Post-Katrina Migrants." *Political Research Quarterly* 65 (2): 443–459.

Horowitz, Juliana Menasce, and Gretchen Livingston. 2016. "How Americans View the Black Lives Matter Movement." *Pew Research Center: Fact Tank* July 8. http://pewrsr.ch/29B5xIE.

HUD-Treasury Joint Task Force. 2000. *Curbing Predatory Home Mortgage Lending.* U.S. Department of Housing and Urban Development. https://www.huduser.gov/portal/publications/hsgfin/curbing.html

Hughes, Langston. 1934. *The Ways of White Folks.* New York: Knopf.

Hughey, Matthew W. 2010. "The (Dis)similarities of White Racial Identities: The Conceptual Framework of 'Hegemonic Whiteness.'" *Ethnic and Racial Studies* 33 (8): 1289–1309.

Hughey, Matthew W. 2014. "White Backlash in the 'Post-Racial' United States." *Ethnic and Racial Studies* 37 (5): 721–730.

Hunt, Vivian, Dennis Layton, and Sara Prince. 2015. *Diversity Matters.* McKinsey & Company. https://www.mckinsey.com/business-functions/organization/our-insights/why-diversity-matters.

Hunter, Marcus Anthony, Mary Pattillo, Zandria F. Robinson, and Keeanga-Yamahtta Taylor. 2016. "Black Placemaking: Celebration, Play, and Poetry." *Theory, Culture and Society* 33 (7–8): 31–56.

Hunter, Margaret. 2007. "The Persistent Problem of Colorism: Skin Tone, Status, and Inequality." *Sociology Compass* 1 (1): 237–254.

Hussar, Bill, Jijun Zhang, Sarah Hein, Ke Wang, Ashley Roberts, Jiashan Cui, Mary Smith, Farrah Bullock Mann, Amy Barmer, and Rita Dilig. 2020. "The Condition of Education 2020." NCES 2020-144. National Center for Education Statistics. https://eric.ed.gov/?id=ED605216.

Hwang, Sean-Shong, and Steve H. Murdock. 1998. "Racial Attraction or Racial Avoidance in American Suburbs?" *Social Forces* 77 (2): 541–565.

Hutchings, Vincent L., and Nicholas A. Valentino. 2004. "The Centrality of Race in American Politics." *Annual Review of Political Science* 7 (1): 383–408.

Hyman, Herbert H., William J. Cobb, Jacob J. Feldman, Clyde W. Hart, and Charles H. Stember. 1954. *Interviewing in Social Research.* Chicago: University of Chicago Press.

Iceland, John, Daniel H. Weinberg, and Erika Steinmetz. 2002. *Racial and Ethnic Residential Segregation in the United States: 1980–2000.* U.S. Census Bureau. https://www.census.gov/prod/2002pubs/censr-3.pdf.

Jackman, Mary R. 1978. "General and Applied Tolerance: Does Education Increase Commitment to Racial Integration?" *American Journal of Political Science* 22 (2): 302–324.

Jackson, Cheryl V. 2016. "When Building Your Business Means Hiding That It's Black-Owned." *Chicago Tribune* April 14. https://www.chicagotribune.com/business/blue-sky/ct-black-entrepreneurs-downplay-ownership-bsi-20160414-story.html.

Jackson, John L. 2001. *Harlemworld: Doing Race and Class in Contemporary Black America.* Chicago: University of Chicago Press.

Jackson, Lauren Michele. 2020. "What Is an Anti-Racist Reading List For?" *New York Magazine* June 4. https://www.vulture.com/2020/06/anti-racist-reading-lists-what-are-they-for.html.

Jacobs, Jane. 1961. *The Death and Life of Great American Cities.* New York: Random House.

Jardina, Ashley. 2019. *White Identity Politics.* Cambridge: Cambridge University Press.

Jargowsky, Paul A. 1996. "Take the Money and Run: Economic Segregation in U.S. Metropolitan Areas." *American Sociological Review* 61 (6): 984–998.

Jhally, Sut, and Justin Lewis. 1992. *Enlightened Racism.* Boulder, CO: Westview.

Johnson, Kimberly S. 2006. *Governing the American State.* Princeton: Princeton University Press.

Johnson, Rucker C. 2014. "In Search of Integration: Beyond Black and White." *NYU Furman Center Blog* January. https://furmancenter.org/research/iri/essay/in-search-of-integration-beyond-black-white.

Johnson, Valerie C. 2002. *Black Power in the Suburbs: The Myth or Reality of African American Suburban Political Incorporation.* Albany: SUNY Press.

Jung, Moon-Kie. 2015. *Beneath the Surface of White Supremacy: Denaturalizing US Racisms Past and Present.* Stanford: Stanford University Press.

Kam, Cindy D., and Camille D. Burge. 2018. "Uncovering Reactions to the Racial Resentment Scale across the Racial Divide." *Journal of Politics* 80 (1).

Katz, Daniel. 1960. "The Functional Approach to the Study of Attitudes." *Public Opinion Quarterly* 24 (2): 163–204.

Katz, Michael B. 1989. *The Undeserving Poor.* New York: Pantheon New York.

Kaufmann, Eric, and Gareth Harris. 2015. "'White Flight' or Positive Contact? Local Diversity and Attitudes to Immigration in Britain." *Comparative Political Studies* 48 (12): 1563–1590.

Keating, Larry. 2001. *Atlanta: Race, Class and Urban Expansion.* Philadelphia: Temple University Press.

Kefalas, Maria. 2003. *Working-Class Heroes: Protecting Home, Community, and Nation in a Chicago Neighborhood.* Berkeley: University of California Press.

Kellstedt, Paul M. 2003. *The Mass Media and the Dynamics of American Racial Attitudes.* Cambridge: Cambridge University Press.

Kendi, Ibram X. 2016. *Stamped from the Beginning: The Definitive History of Racist Ideas in America.* New York: Nation Books.

Keum, Brian TaeHyuk, and Matthew J. Miller. 2018. "Racism on the Internet: Conceptualization and Recommendations for Research." *Psychology of Violence* 8 (6): 782.

Key, V. O. 1949. *Southern Politics in State and Nation.* New York: Vintage Books.

Khan, Shamus Rahman. 2011. *Privilege: The Making of an Adolescent Elite at St. Paul's School.* Princeton: Princeton University Press.

Kim, Mikyong Minsun, and Clifton F. Conrad. 2006. "The Impact of Historically Black Colleges and Universities on the Academic Success of African-American Students." *Research in Higher Education* 47 (4): 399–427.

Kinder, Donald R., and D. Roderick Kiewiet. 1981. "Sociotropic Politics: The American Case." *British Journal of Political Science* 11 (2): 129–161.

Kinder, Donald R., and Tali Mendelberg. 1995. "Cracks in American Apartheid: The Political Impact of Prejudice among Desegregated Whites." *Journal of Politics* 57 (2): 402.

Kinder, Donald R., and Lynn M. Sanders. 1990. "Mimicking Political Debate with Survey Questions: The Case of White Opinion on Affirmative Action for Blacks." *Social Cognition* 8 (1): 73.

Kinder, Donald R. 1996. *Divided by Color: Racial Politics and Democratic Ideals.* Chicago: University of Chicago Press.

Kinder, Donald R., and David O. Sears. 1981. "Prejudice and Politics: Symbolic Racism Versus Racial Threats to the Good Life." *Journal of Personality and Social Psychology* 40 (3): 414–431.

King Jr., Martin Luther. 1967. *Where Do We Go from Here: Chaos or Community?* Boston: Beacon Press.

King, Desmond S. 1995. *Separate and Unequal: Black Americans and the US Federal Government.* Oxford: Oxford University Press.

King, Desmond S. 2009. *Making Americans: Immigration, Race, and the Origins of the Diverse Democracy.* Cambridge, MA: Harvard University Press.

King, Desmond S., and Rogers M. Smith. 2005. "Racial Orders in American Political Development." *American Political Science Review* 99 (1): 75–92.

King, Desmond S. 2016. "The Last Stand? *Shelby County v. Holder* and White Political Power in Modern America." *Du Bois Review: Social Science Research on Race* 13 (1): 1–20.

Klor, Esteban F., and Moses Shayo. 2010. "Social Identity and Preferences over Redistribution." *Journal of Public Economics* 94 (3–4): 269–278.

Kruse, Kevin M. 2005. *White Flight: Atlanta and the Making of Modern Conservatism.* Princeton: Princeton University Press.

Krysan, Maria, and Michael Bader. 2007. "Perceiving the Metropolis: Seeing the City through a Prism of Race." *Social Forces* 86 (2): 699–733.

Krysan, Maria, and Kyle Crowder. 2017. "What Would It Take to Promote Residential Choices That Result in Greater Integration and More Equitable Neighborhood Outcomes?" Paper prepared for the Harvard Joint Center for Housing Studies conference, "A Shared Future: Fostering Communities of Inclusion in an Era of Inequality" Cambridge, MA, April 2017.

Krysan, Maria, and Reynolds Farley. 2002. "The Residential Preferences of Blacks: Do They Explain Persistent Segregation?" *Social Forces* 80 (3): 937–980.

Kuklinski, James H., Paul M. Sniderman, Kathleen Knight, Thomas Piazza, Philip E. Tetlock, Gordon R. Lawrence, and Barbara Mellers. 1997. "Racial Prejudice and Attitudes Toward Affirmative Action." *American Journal of Political Science* 41 (2): 402–419.

Kuziemko, Ilyana, Ryan W. Buell, Taly Reich, and Michael I. Norton. 2014. "'Last-Place Aversion': Evidence and Redistributive Implications." *The Quarterly Journal of Economics* 129 (1): 105–149.

Laurence, James. 2014. "Reconciling the Contact and Threat Hypotheses: Does Ethnic Diversity Strengthen or Weaken Community Inter-Ethnic Relations?" *Ethnic and Racial Studies* 37 (8): 1328–1349.

Lavelle, Kristen M. 2014. *Whitewashing the South: White Memories of Segregation and Civil Rights.* New York: Rowman & Littlefield.

Leach, Colin Wayne, Aarti Iyer, and Anne Pedersen. 2006. "Anger and Guilt about Ingroup Advantage Explain the Willingness for Political Action." *Personality and Social Psychology Bulletin* 32 (9): 1232–1245.

Lefebvre, Henri. 1991. *The Production of Space* [English translation]. Edited by Donald Nicholson-Smith. Oxford: Blackwell.

Lewis, John, and Sut Jhally. 1995. "Affirming Inaction: Television and the New Politics of Race." In *Marxism in the Postmodern Age: Confronting the New World Order,* edited by Stephen Cullenberg, Carole Biewener, and Antonio Callari, 133–141. New York: Guilford Press.

Lewis, Kristen. 2020. *A Portrait of Louisiana 2020: Human Development in an Age of Uncertainty.* Measure of America of the Social Science Research Council.http://measureofamerica.org/louisiana2020/.

Lewis, Oscar. 1966. *La Vida: A Puerto Rican Family in the Culture of Poverty—San Juan and New York.* Vol. 13. New York: Random House.

Linly, Zack. 2016. *Why It's Time Black People Simply Disengage with White People in Discussing Race.* Accessed October 15, 2017. https://thoughtforfood.live/2016/08/16/why-its-time-black-people-simply-disengage-with-white-people-in-discussing-race/.

Lippmann, Walter. 1922. *Public Opinion.* New York: Transaction Publishers.

Litvinov, Amanda. 2019. "Educators Look to End the Big Corporate Tax Giveaway." Education Votes: National Education Association March 21. https://educationvotes.nea.org/2019/03/21/educators-look-to-end-the-big-corporate-tax-giveaway/

Livingston, Gretchen, and Anna Brown. 2017. "Intermarriage in the U.S. 50 Years after *Loving v. Virginia.*" Pew Research Center: Social and Demographic Trends May 18. https://www.pewsocialtrends.org/2017/05/18/intermarriage-in-the-u-s-50-years-after-loving-v-virginia/.

Local Schools for Local Children. 2014. *Behind the Curtain: East Baton Rouge School System.* Accessed January 28, 2021. https://vimeo.com/67358394.

Logan, John R. 2011. *Separate and Unequal: The Neighborhood Gap for Blacks, Hispanics and Asians in Metropolitan America.* American Communities Project of Brown University. https://eric.ed.gov/?id=ED471515.

Logan, Trevon D., and John M. Parman. 2017. "The National Rise in Residential Segregation." *Journal of Economic History* 77 (1): 127–170.

Lorde, Audre. 1984a. "Poetry Is Not a Luxury." In *Sister Outsider: Essays and Speeches,* revised ed., 36–39. Berkeley: Ten Speed Press.

Lorde, Audre. 1984b. "The Uses of Anger." In *Sister Outsider: Essays and Speeches,* revised ed., 124–133. Berkeley: Ten Speed Press.

Ludwig, Jens, Greg J. Duncan, Lisa A. Gennetian, Lawrence F. Katz, Ronald C. Kessler, Jeffrey R. Kling, and Lisa Sanbonmatsu. 2012. "Neighborhood Effects on the Long-Term Well-Being of Low-Income Adults." *Science* 337 (6101): 1505–1510.

Lussier, Charles. 2019. "A St. George School District Could Start Out with Ample Funding, but Costs Will Grow If Popular." *The Advocate* (Baton Rouge) September. https://www.theadvocate.com/baton_rouge/news/education/article_c16b3896-dbab-11e9-9798-5f6d6b869334.html.

Luttmer, Erzo F. P. 2005. "Neighbors as Negatives: Relative Earnings and Well-Being." *The Quarterly Journal of Economics* 120 (3): 963–1002.

Marcus, Frances Frank. 1981. "As Busing Begins in Schools, Louisiana Clears Way for Teaching in Homes." *New York Times* (New Orleans) September http://www.nytimes.com/1981/09/25/us/as-busing-begins-in-schools-louisiana-clears-way-for-teaching-in-homes.html.

Massey, Douglas S., Len Albright, Rebecca Casciano, Elizabeth Derickson, and David N. Kinsey. 2013. *Climbing Mount Laurel: The Struggle for Affordable Housing and Social Mobility in an American Suburb.* Princeton: Princeton University Press.

Massey, Douglas S., and Nancy A. Denton. 1988. "The Dimensions of Residential Segregation." *Social Forces* 67 (2): 281–315.

Massey, Douglas S., and Nancy A. Denton. 1993. *American Apartheid.* Cambridge, MA: Harvard University Press.

Massey, Douglas S., and Jonathan Tannen. 2015. "A Research Note on Trends in Black Hypersegregation." *Demography* 52 (3): 1025–1034.

Matsubayashi, Tetsuya, and Renee R. Rocha. 2012. "Racial Diversity and Public Policy in the States." *Political Research Quarterly* 65 (3): 600–614.

Mazumder, Bhashkar. 2014. "Black–White Differences in Intergenerational Economic Mobility in the United States." *Economic Perspectives* 38.

McCarty, Therese A. 1993. "Demographic Diversity and the Size of the Public Sector." *Kyklos* 46 (2): 225–240.

McConahay, John B. 1986. "Modern Racism, Ambivalence, and the Modern Racism Scale." In *Prejudice, Discrimination, and Racism,* edited by John F. Dovidio and Samuel L. Gaertner, 91–126. New York: Academic Press.

McGhee, Heather. 2021. *The Sum of Us: What Racism Costs Everyone and How We Can Prosper Together.* New York: One World.

McGoey, Linsey. 2012. "Strategic Unknowns: Towards a Sociology of Ignorance." *Economy and Society* 41 (1): 1–16.

McIntosh, Peggy. 1988. "White Privilege: Unpacking the Invisible Knapsack." In *Race, Class, and Gender in the United States: An Integrated Study,* 6th ed., edited by Paula S. Rothenberg, 188–192. New York: Worth Publishers.

McPherson, Miller, Lynn Smith-Lovin, and James M. Cook. 2001. "Birds of a Feather: Homophily in Social Networks." *Annual Review of Sociology* 27 (1): 415–444.

Mead, Lawrence M. 1993. *The New Politics of Poverty: The Nonworking Poor in America.* New York: Basic Books.

Medina, José. 2012. *The Epistemology of Resistance: Gender and Racial Oppression, Epistemic Injustice, and the Social Imagination.* Oxford: Oxford University Press.

Mendelberg, Tali. 2001. *The Race Card: Campaign Strategy, Implicit Messages, and the Norm of Equality.* Princeton: Princeton University Press.

Mershon, Carol, and Denise Walsh. 2016. "Diversity in Political Science: Why It Matters and How to Get It." *Politics, Groups, and Identities* 4 (3): 462–466.

Miles, Matthew B., and A. Michael Huberman. 1994. *Qualitative Data Analysis: A Sourcebook.* Beverly Hills, CA: SAGE Publications.

Miller, Lisa L. 2015. "What's Violence Got to Do with It? Inequality, Punishment, and State Failure in US Politics." *Punishment & Society* 17 (2): 184–210.

Millett, Gregorio A., Austin T. Jones, David Benkeser, Stefan Baral, Laina Mercer, Chris Beyrer, Brian Honermann, et al. 2020. "Assessing Differential Impacts of COVID-19 on Black Communities." *Annals of Epidemiology* 47: 37–44.

Mills, Charles Wade. 1997. *The Racial Contract.* Ithaca: Cornell University Press.

Mitchell, David J. 2015. "Baton Rouge Grew After Katrina While Forging Closer Ties to Recovering New Orleans." *The Advocate* (Baton Rouge) August 29. http://www.theadvocate. com/baton_rouge/news/article_4871291f-0606-520b-a6b5-df73c446c750.html.

Moss, Kirby. 2003. *The Color of Class.* Philadelphia: University of Pennsylvania Press.

Moynihan, Daniel Patrick. 1965. *The Negro Family: The Case for National Action.* Washington, DC: United States Department of Labor.

Mueller, Dennis C., and Peter Murrell. 1986. "Interest Groups and the Size of Government." *Public Choice* 48 (2): 125–145.

Mueller, Jennifer C. 2020. "Racial Ideology or Racial Ignorance? An Alternative Theory of Racial Cognition." *Sociological Theory* 38 (2): 142–169.

Murray, Charles. 1984. *Losing Ground: American Social Policy, 1950–1980.* New York: Basic Books.

Myrdal, Gunnar. 1944. *An American Dilemma: The Negro Problem and Modern Democracy.* New York; London: Harper & Brothers.

Newman, Benjamin J., Yamil Velez, Todd K. Hartman, and Alexa Bankert. 2015. "Are Citizens 'Receiving the Treatment'? Assessing a Key Link in Contextual Theories of Public Opinion and Political Behavior." *Political Psychology* 36 (1): 123–131.

Norton, Michael I., Samuel R. Sommers, Evan P. Apfelbaum, Natassia Pura, and Dan Ariely. 2006. "Color Blindness and Interracial Interaction: Playing the Political Correctness Game." *Psychological Science* 17 (11): 949–953.

Nossiter, Adam. 2003. "Baton Rouge Desegregation Case Ends." *The Washington Post* August 17. https://www.washingtonpost.com/archive/politics/2003/08/17/baton-rouge-desegregation-case-ends/0b0cec5c-67dc-4464-b6ff-64a3d57b01b5/?utm_term=.c13e32101a0c.

O'Brien, Eileen. 2016. "The Transformation of the Role of 'Race' in the Qualitative Interview: Not If Race Matters, But How?" Chap. 5 in *Rethinking Race and Ethnicity in Research Methods,* edited by John H. Stanfield II. London; New York: Routledge.

Oliver, Eric. 2012. "Suburban Politics." In *The Oxford Handbook of Urban Politics,* edited by Peter John, Karen Mossberger, and Susan E. Clarke, 1–13. Oxford: Oxford University Press.

Oliver, J. Eric, and Tali Mendelberg. 2000. "Reconsidering the Environmental Determinants of White Racial Attitudes." *American Journal of Political Science* 44 (3): 574–589.

Omi, Michael, and Howard Winant. 1986. *Racial Formation in the United States: From the 1960s to the 1980s.* New York: Routledge & Kegan Paul.

One Baton Rouge. 2019. *Get the Facts About St. George.* Accessed January 28, 2021. http://www.onebtr.com.

Orr, Larry L. 1976. "Income Transfers as a Public Good: An Application to AFDC." *American Economic Review* 66 (3): 359–371.

Paluck, Elizabeth Levy, Roni Porat, Chelsey S Clark, and Donald P Green. 2021. "Prejudice Reduction: Progress and Challenges." *Annual Review of Psychology* 72 (1): 533–560.

Patterson, Orlando. 1997. *The Ordeal of Integration: Progress and Resentment in America's Racial Crisis.* Washington, DC: Civitas/Counterpoint.

Pattillo, Mary. 1999. *Black Picket Fences: Privilege and Peril among the Black Middle Class.* Chicago: University of Chicago Press.

Pattillo, Mary. 2005. "Black Middle-Class Neighborhoods." *Annual Review of Sociology* 31 (1): 305–329.

Pattillo, Mary. 2008. *Black on the Block: The Politics of Race and Class in the City.* Chicago: University of Chicago Press.

Pattillo, Mary. 2009. "Investing in Poor Black Neighborhoods 'As Is.'" In *Public Housing and the Legacy of Segregation,* edited by Margery Austin Turner, Susan J. Popkin, and Lynette Rawlings, 31–46. Washington, DC: The Urban Institute Press.

Pattillo, Mary. 2015. "Foreword." In *Black Metropolis: A Study of Negro Life in a Northern City,* edited by St. Clair Drake and Horace R. Cayton, 912. Chicago: University of Chicago Press.

Patton, Michael Quinn. 2002. *Qualitative Evaluation and Research Methods,* 3rd ed. Thousand Oaks, CA: SAGE Publications.

Peffley, Mark, and Jon Hurwitz. 1998. "Whites' Stereotypes of Blacks: Sources and Political Consequences." In *Perception and Prejudice: Race and Politics in the United States,* edited by Jon Hurwitz and Mark Peffley, 58–99. New Haven: Yale University Press.

Pettigrew, Thomas F., and Linda R. Tropp. 2006. "A Meta-Analytic Test of Intergroup Contact Theory." *Journal of Personality and Social Psychology* 90 (5): 751–783.

Pettigrew, Thomas F., Ulrich Wagner, and Oliver Christ. 2010. "Population Ratios and Prejudice: Modelling Both Contact and Threat Effects." *Journal of Ethnic and Migration Studies* 36 (4): 635–650.

Pham, Cong S, and Devashish Mitra. 2020. "The Color of Coronavirus." APM Research Lab December 3. https://ssrn.com/abstract=3757854.

Pierson, Paul. 1993. "When Effect Becomes Cause: Policy Feedback and Political Change." *World Politics* 45 (4): 595–628.

Plotnick, Robert D., and Richard F. Winters. 1985. "A Politico-Economic Theory of Income Redistribution." *American Political Science Review* 79 (2): 458–473.

Price, Janet R., and Jane R. Stern. 1987. "Magnet Schools as a Strategy for Integration and School Reform." *Yale Law & Policy Review* 5 (2): 291–321.

Quillian, Lincoln. 1995. "Prejudice as a Response to Perceived Group Threat: Population Composition and Anti-Immigrant and Racial Prejudice in Europe." *American Sociological Review* 60 (4): 586.

Quillian, Lincoln. 1996. "Group Threat and Regional Change in Attitudes Toward African-Americans." *American Journal of Sociology* 102 (3): 816.

Quillian, Lincoln. 2002. "Why Is Black-White Residential Segregation So Persistent? Evidence on Three Theories from Migration Data." *Social Science Research* 31 (2): 197–229.

Quillian, Lincoln. 2012. "Segregation and Poverty Concentration: The Role of Three Segregations." *American Sociological Review* 77 (3): 354–379.

Randle, Wilma. 1993. "Corporate Conscience Linked To Profitability." *Chicago Tribune* (Chicago) May 25. http://articles.chicagotribune.com/1993-05-25/business/9305250047_1_socially-financial-returns-mid-size-firms.

Rankine, Claudia. 2014. *Citizen: An American Lyric*. Minneapolis: Graywolf Press.

Reardon, Sean F., and Kendra Bischoff. 2011. "Income Inequality and Income Segregation." *American Journal of Sociology* 116 (4): 1092–1153.

Reardon, Sean F., Lindsay Fox, and Joseph Townsend. 2015. "Neighborhood Income Composition by Household Race and Income, 1990–2009." *The ANNALS of the American Academy of Political and Social Science* 660 (1): 78–97.

Reardon, Sean F., Elena Tej Grewal, Demetra Kalogrides, and Erica Greenberg. 2012. "Brown Fades: The End of Court-Ordered School Desegregation and the Resegregation of American Public Schools." *Journal of Policy Analysis and Management* 31 (4): 876–904.

Reardon, Sean F., and John T. Yun. 2006. *Private School Racial Enrollments and Segregation*. Technical report. The Civil Rights Project, Harvard University. https://www.civilrightsproject.ucla.edu/research/k-12-education/integration-and-diversity/private-school-racial-enrollments-and-segregation.

Reeves, Andrew, and James G. Gimpel. 2012. "Ecologies of Unease: Geographic Context and National Economic Evaluations." *Political Behavior* 34 (3): 507–534.

Reeves, Richard V., and Edward Rodrigue. 2015. *Five Bleak Facts on Black Opportunity*. Brookings Institution, Washington, DC http://www.brookings.edu/blogs/social-mobility-memos/posts/2015/01/15-mlk-black-opportunity-reeves.

Rehm, Philipp, Jacob S. Hacker, and Mark Schlesinger. 2012. "Insecure Alliances: Risk, Inequality, and Support for the Welfare State." *American Political Science Review* 106 (2): 386–406.

Richardson, James, Jared Llorens, and Roy Heidelberg. 2013. *On the Possibility of a New City in East Baton Rouge Parish*. Baton Rouge Area Chamber and Baton Rouge Area Foundation, Baton Rouge. Accessed September 15, 2016. http://brac.org/docs/pdf/BRAC_White_Paper_New_City_EBR.pdf.

Richardson, James A., and Jared J. Llorens. 2018. *An Examination of Revenues and Expenditures for the Proposed City of St. George*. Public Administration Institute, Louisiana State University, Baton Rouge. Accessed February 20, 2021.http://onebtr.com/docs/stg_finances_study.pdf.

Ritterhouse, Jennifer Lynn. 2006. *Growing up Jim Crow: How Black and White Southern Children Learned Race*. Chapel Hill, NC: University of North Carolina Press.

Robertson, Mary. 2014. "Separate and Unequal." *PBS Frontline*. https://www.pbs.org/wgbh/frontline/film/separate-and-unequal/

Rocha, Rene R., and Rodolfo Espino. 2009. "Racial Threat, Residential Segregation, and the Policy Attitudes of Anglos." *Political Research Quarterly* 62 (2): 415–426.

Roediger, David R. 1999. *The Wages of Whiteness: Race and the Making of the American Working Class*. London; New York: Verso.

Rosen, Sam. 2017. "Atlanta's Controversial 'Cityhood' Movement." *The Atlantic* April. https://www.theatlantic.com/business/archive/2017/04/the-border-battles-of-atlanta/523884/.

Rosenthal, Aaron. 2019. "Investment and Invisibility: The Racially Divergent Consequences of Political Trust." *Du Bois Review: Social Science Research on Race* 16 (2): 511–533.

Rossell, Christine. 2010. *The Carrot or the Stick for School Desegregation Policy: Magnet Schools or Forced Busing.* Philadelphia: Temple University Press.

Rothstein, Richard. 2017. *The Color of Law: A Forgotten History of How Our Government Segregated America.* New York: Liveright.

Ruch, John. 2019. "Sandy Springs To Bring Most Government Services In-house, Ending Much of Landmark Privatization." *Reporter Newspapers* May 14. https://www.reporternewspapers.net/2019/05/14/sandy-springs-to-bring-most-government-services-in-house-ending-much-of-landmark-privatization/.

Rugh, Jacob S., and Douglas S. Massey. 2010. "Racial Segregation and the American Foreclosure Crisis." *American Sociological Review* 75 (5): 629–651.

Rugh, Jacob S. 2014. "Segregation in Post-Civil Rights America." *Du Bois Review: Social Science Research on Race* 11 (2): 205–232.

Sampson, Robert. J. 2012. *Great American City: Chicago and the Enduring Neighborhood Effect,* Chicago: University of Chicago Press.

Sampson, Robert J., Jeffrey D. Morenoff, and Felton Earls. 1999. "Beyond Social Capital: Spatial Dynamics of Collective Efficacy for Children." *American Sociological Review* 64 (5): 633–660.

Savitch, Hank V., David Collins, Daniel Sanders, and John P. Markham. 1993. "Ties That Bind: Central Cities, Suburbs, and the New Metropolitan Region." *Economic Development Quarterly* 7 (4): 341–357.

Schelling, Thomas C. 1971. "Dynamic Models of Segregation." *Journal of Mathematical Sociology* 1: 143–186.

Schneider, Mark. 1989. *The Competitive City: The Political Economy of Suburbia.* Pittsburgh: University of Pittsburgh Press.

Schuman, Howard, and Jean M. Converse. 1971. "The Effects of Black and White Interviewers on Black Responses in 1968." *Public Opinion Quarterly* 35 (1): 44–68.

Schuman, Howard, Charlotte Steeh, Lawrence Bobo, and Maria Krysan. 1997. *Racial Attitudes in America: Trends and Interpretations.* Cambridge, MA: Harvard University Press.

Schwartz-Shea, Peregrine, and Dvora Yanow. 2012. *Interpretative Research Design.* New York: Routledge.

Sears, David O., and Donald R. Kinder. 1971. "Racial Tension and Voting in Los Angeles." In *Los Angeles: Viability and Prospects for Metropolitan Leadership*, edited by Werner Z. Hirsch, 51–88. New York: Praeger.

Sears, David O., Colette Van Laar, Mary Carrillo, and Rick Kosterman. 1997. "Is It Really Racism? The Origins of White Americans' Opposition to Race-Targeted Policies." *The Public Opinion Quarterly* 61 (1): 16–53.

Seattle Civil Rights & Labor History Project. 2021. *Racial Restrictive Covenants: Neighborhood by Neighborhood Restrictions across King County.* https://depts.washington.edu/civilr/covenants.htm.

Seligman, Amanda I. 2005. *Block by Block: Neighborhoods and Public Policy on Chicago's West Side.* Chicago: University of Chicago Press.

Sentell, Will. 2017. "Nearly Half a Century Later, Southern University to Award Degrees to Two Slain Students." *The Advocate* (Baton Rouge) March 31. http://www.theadvocate.com/baton_rouge/news/education/article_ede3aaa8-1654-11e7-9064-1bb7a09d9014.html.

Sharkey, Patrick. 2008. "The Intergenerational Transmission of Context." *American Journal of Sociology* 113 (4): 931–969.

Sharkey, Patrick. 2009. *Neighborhoods and the Black-White Mobility Gap.* Economic Mobility Project: An Initiative of The Pew Charitable Trusts. https://www.pewtrusts.org/en/research-and-analysis/reports/0001/01/01/neighborhoods-and-the-blackwhite-mobility-gap.

Sharkey, Patrick. 2014. "Spatial Segmentation and the Black Middle Class." *American Journal of Sociology* 119 (4): 903–954.

Sherman, Rachel. 2019. *Uneasy Street: The Anxieties of Affluence.* Princeton: Princeton University Press.

Shertzer, Allison, and Randall P. Walsh. 2016. "Racial Sorting and the Emergence of Segregation in American Cities." NBER Working Paper 22077, Cambridge, MA. http://www.nber.org/papers/w22077.

Sidanius, Jim, and Felicia Pratto. 2001. *Social Dominance: An Intergroup Theory of Social Hierarchy and Oppression.* Cambridge: Cambridge University Press.

Sidanius, Jim, Felicia Pratto, and Lawrence Bobo. 1996. "Racism, Conservatism, Affirmative Action, and Intellectual Sophistication: A Matter of Principled Conservatism or Group Dominance?" *Journal of Personality and Social Psychology* 70 (3): 476–490.

Sirin, Selcuk R. 2005. "Socioeconomic Status and Academic Achievement: A Meta-Analytic Review of Research." *Review of Educational Research* 75 (3): 417–453.

Skrentny, John David. 1996. *The Ironies of Affirmative Action: Politics, Culture, and Justice in America.* Chicago: University of Chicago Press.

Smith, Dorothy E. 1990. *The Conceptual Practices of Power: A Feminist Sociology of Knowledge.* Toronto: University of Toronto Press.

Smith, Rogers M. 1993. "Beyond Tocqueville, Myrdal, and Hartz: The Multiple Traditions in America." *American Political Science Review* 87 (3): 549–566.

Smith, Rogers M., and Desmond S. King. 2021. "White Protectionism in America." *Perspectives on Politics* 19 (2): 460–478.

Sniderman, Paul M., Richard A. Brody, and Phillip E. Tetlock. 1993. *Reasoning and Choice: Explorations in Political Psychology.* Cambridge: Cambridge University Press.

Sniderman, Paul M., and Thomas Piazza. 1993. *The Scar of Race.* Cambridge, MA: Harvard University Press.

Sniderman, Paul M., Philip E. Tetlock, and Thomas Piazza. 1991. *National Race and Politics Survey.* Survey Research Center, University of California, Berkeley.

Soja, Edward W. 1989. *Postmodern Geographies: The Reassertion of Space in Critical Social Theory.* New York: Verso.

Soss, Joe. 2005. "Making Clients and Citizens: Welfare Policy as a Source of Status, Belief, and Action." In Deserving and Entitled: Social Constructions and Public Policy, edited by Anne L. Schneider and Helen M. Ingram, 291–328. Albany: SUNY Press.

Soss, Joe, Richard C. Fording, and Sanford Schram. 2011. *Disciplining the Poor: Neoliberal Paternalism and the Persistent Power of Race.* Chicago: University of Chicago Press.

Soss, Joe, and Sanford F. Schram. 2007. "A Public Transformed? Welfare Reform as Policy Feedback." *American Political Science Review* 101 (1): 111–127.

Soss, Joe, and Vesla Weaver. 2017. "Police Are Our Government: Politics, Political Science, and the Policing of Race-Class Subjugated Communities." *Annual Review of Political Science* 20: 565–591.

Spitzer, Steven. 1975. "Toward a Marxian Theory of Deviance." *Social Problems* 22 (5): 638–651.

Steeh, Charlotte, and Maria Krysan. 1996. "Trends: Affirmative Action and the Public, 1970–1995." *The Public Opinion Quarterly* 60 (1): 128–158.

Stein, Robert M., Stephanie Shirley Post, and Allison L. Rinden. 2000. "Reconciling Context and Contact Effects on Racial Attitudes." *Political Research Quarterly* 53 (2): 285–303.

Stenner, Karen. 2005. *The Authoritarian Dynamic*. Cambridge: Cambridge University Press.

Stone, Clarence N. 1989. *Regime Politics: Governing Atlanta, 1946–1988*. Lawrence: University Press of Kansas.

Strolovitch, Dara Z. 1998. "Playing Favorites: Public Attitudes Toward Race- and Gender-Targeted Anti-Discrimination Policy." *NWSA Journal* 10 (3): 27–53.

Stults, Brian J., and Eric P. Baumer. 2007. "Racial Context and Police Force Size: Evaluating the Empirical Validity of the Minority Threat Perspective." *American Journal of Sociology* 113 (2): 507–546.

Taber, Charles S., and Milton Lodge. 2006. "Motivated Skepticism in the Evaluation of Political Beliefs." *American Journal of Political Science* 50 (3): 755–769.

Tajfel, Henri, and John C. Turner. 1979. "An Integrative Theory of Intergroup Conflict." *The Social Psychology of Intergroup Relations* 33 (47): 74.

Tarman, Christopher, and David O. Sears. 2005. "The Conceptualization and Measurement of Symbolic Racism." *Journal of Politics* 67 (3): 731–761.

Taylor, Keeanga-Yamahtta. 2012. "Back Story to the Neoliberal Moment: Race Taxes and the Political Economy of Black Urban Housing in the 1960s." *Souls: A Critical Journal of Black Politics, Culture, and Society* 14 (3–4): 185–206.

Taylor, Keeanga-Yamahtta. 2019. *Race for Profit: How Banks and the Real Estate Industry Undermined Black Homeownership*. Chapel Hill: University of North Carolina Press.

Taylor, Marylee C. 1998. "How White Attitudes Vary with the Racial Composition of Local Populations: Numbers Count." *American Sociological Review* 63 (4): 512.

Taylor, Monique M. 2002. *Harlem: Between Heaven and Hell*. Minneapolis: University of Minnesota Press.

Tesler, Michael. 2012. "The Return of Old-Fashioned Racism to White Americans' Partisan Preferences in the Early Obama Era." *Journal of Politics* 75 (1): 110–123.

Tesler, Michael. 2016a. *Post-Racial or Most-Racial? Race and Politics in the Obama Era*. Chicago: University of Chicago Press.

Tesler, Michael. 2016b. "Trump Is the First Modern Republican to Win the Nomination Based on Racial Prejudice." *Washington Post* August 1.https://www.washingtonpost.com/news/monkey-cage/wp/2016/08/01/trump-is-the-first-republican-in-modern-times-to-win-the-partys-nomination-on-anti-minority-sentiments/

Tesler, Michael. 2020. "The Floyd Protests Have Changed Public Opinion about Race and Policing—Here's the Data." *Washington Post* June 9. https://www.washingtonpost.com/politics/2020/06/09/floyd-protests-have-changed-public-opinion-about-race-policing-heres-data/.

Tharps, Lori L. 2014. "The Case for Black With a Capital B." *New York Times* November 1. https://www.nytimes.com/2014/11/19/opinion/the-case-for-black-with-a-capital-b.html.

Thernstrom, Abigail, and Stephan Thernstrom. 1998. "Black Progress: How Far We've Come—And How Far We Have to Go." *The Brookings Review* 16 (2): 12.

Thomas, Deja, and Juliana Menasce Horowitz. 2020. "Support for Black Lives Matter Has Decreased since June but Remains Strong among Black Americans." *Pew Research Center: Fact Tank* Sept 16. https://pewrsr.ch/3hD9RYv.

Threadcraft, Shatema. 2016. *Intimate Justice: The Black Female Body and the Body Politic*. Oxford: Oxford University Press.

Tobler, Waldo R. 1970. "A Computer Movie Simulating Urban Growth in the Detroit Region." *Economic Geography* 46: 234–240.

Together Baton Rouge. 2014. *St. George, Student Displacement, and School Capacity in Unincorporated East Baton Rouge Parish*. Accessed September 15, 2016. http://www.togetherbr.org/wp-content/%20uploads/2010/09/TBR_St.-George-Student-Displacement-and-School-%20Capacity_11-20146.pdf.

Trounstine, Jessica. 2009. "All Politics Is Local: The Reemergence of the Study of City Politics." *Perspectives on Politics* 7 (3): 611.

Trounstine, Jessica. 2018. *Segregation by Design: Local Politics and Inequality in American Cities.* Cambridge: Cambridge University Press.

Turner, Bobbie Green. 1993. *Federal/State Aid to Dependent Children Program and Its Benefits to Black Children in America, 1935–1985.* New York: Garland.

Twine, France Winddance. 2000. "Racial Ideologies and Racial Methodologies." In *Racing Research, Researching Race: Methodological Dilemmas in Critical Race Studies,* edited by France Winddance Twine and Jonathan Warren, 1–34. New York: New York University Press.

Tyson, Christopher J. 2014. "Municipal Identity as Property." *Pennsylvania State Law Review* 118: 647–696.

Valentino, Nicholas A., Vincent L. Hutchings, and Ismail K. White. 2002. "Cues That Matter: How Political Ads Prime Racial Attitudes during Campaigns." *American Political Science Review* 96 (1): 75–90.

Velez, Yamil Ricardo, and Howard Lavine. 2017. "Racial Diversity and the Dynamics of Authoritarianism." *Journal of Politics* 79 (2): 519–533.

Voss, D. Stephen. 1996. "Beyond Racial Threat: Failure of an Old Hypothesis in the New South." *Journal of Politics* 58 (4): 1156.

Wall, Howard J. 2009. "This Recession's Effect on Employment: How It Stacks Up for Blacks, Whites, Men and Women." *Bridges* Winter 200.

Walton Jr., Hanes, Cheryl M. Miller, and Joseph P. McCormick II. 1995. "Race and Political Science: The Dual Traditions of Race Relations Politics and African-American Politics." In *Political Science in History: Research Programs and Political Traditions,* edited by James Farr, John Dryzek, and Stephen T. Leonard, 145–174. Cambridge: Cambridge University Press.

Waters, Mary C. 1990. *Ethnic Options: Choosing Identities in America.* Berkeley: University of California Press.

Weber, Christopher R., Howard Lavine, Leonie Huddy, and Christopher M. Federico. 2014. "Placing Racial Stereotypes in Context: Desirability and the Politics of Racial Hostility." *American Journal of Political Science* 58 (1): 63–78.

Weiss, Robert S. 1994. *Learning from Strangers: The Art and Method of Qualitative Interview Studies.* New York: The Free Press.

Welch, Susan, and Lee Sigelman. 2011. "The 'Obama Effect' and White Racial Attitudes." *Annals of the American Academy of Political and Social Science* 634 (1): 207–220.

West, Guida. 1981. *The National Welfare Rights Movement: The Social Protest of Poor Women.* New York: Praeger.

West, Kimberly C. 1994. "A Desegregation Tool That Backfired: Magnet Schools and Classroom Segregation." *The Yale Law Journal* 103 (8): 2567–2592.

Wilcox, Jerry, and Wade Clark Roof. 1978. "Percent Black and Black-White Status Inequality: Southern versus Nonsouthern Patterns." *Social Science Quarterly* 59 (3): 421–434.

Wilkerson, Isabel. 2010. *The Warmth of Other Suns: The Epic Story of America's Great Migration.* New York: Random House.

Williams, David R., James S. Jackson, Tony N. Brown, Myriam Torres, Tyrone A. Forman, and Kendrick Brown. 1999. "Traditional and Contemporary Prejudice and Urban Whites' Support for Affirmative Action and Government Help." *Social Problems* 46 (4): 503–527.

Williams, Patricia. 2018. "Intimate Injustice." *The Times Literary Supplement* January 2. https://www.the-tls.co.uk/articles/public/intimate-injustice-black-girls-williams/.

Wilson, William Julius. 1978. *The Declining Significance of Race: Blacks and Changing American Institutions.* Chicago: University of Chicago Press.

Wilson, William Julius. 1987. *The Truly Disadvantaged: The Inner City, the Underclass, and Public Policy.* Chicago: University of Chicago Press.

Wodtke, Geoffrey T. 2016. "Are Smart People Less Racist? Verbal Ability, Anti-Black Prejudice, and the Principle-Policy Paradox." *Social Problems* 63 (1): 21–45.

Wong, Cara, Jake Bowers, Tarah Williams, and Katherine Drake Simmons. 2012. "Bringing the Person Back In: Boundaries, Perceptions, and the Measurement of Racial Context." *Journal of Politics* 74 (4): 1153–1170.

Wright, Gerald C. 1977. "Racism and Welfare Policy in America." *Social Science Quarterly* 57 (4): 718–730.

Yancy, Nina M. 2016. "The Spatial Logic of Racial Inequality." *Discover Society* 33. https://archive.discoversociety.org/2016/06/01/the-spatial-logic-of-racial-inequality/.

Yancy, Nina M. 2019. "Racialized Preferences in Context: The Geography of White Opposition to Welfare." *Journal of Race, Ethnicity, and Politics* 4: 81–116.

Young, Iris Marion. 2003. "Political Responsibility and Structural Injustice: The Lindley Lecture." University of Kansas, Department of Philosophy.

Young, Iris Marion. 2010. *Responsibility for Justice.* Oxford: Oxford University Press.

Zaller, John. 1992. *The Nature and Origins of Mass Opinion.* Cambridge: Cambridge University Press.

Zuberi, Tukufu, and Eduardo Bonilla-Silva. 2008. *White Logic, White Methods: Racism and Methodology.* Lanham, MD: Rowman & Littlefield Publishers.

Zubrinsky, Camille L., and Lawrence D. Bobo. 1996. "Prismatic Metropolis: Race and Residential Segregation in the City of the Angels." *Social Science Research* 25 (4): 335–374.

Index

Note: Page numbers followed by *f* indicate a figure on the corresponding page. Page numbers followed by *t* indicate a table on the corresponding page.